PAULA CO

SAHARA

BANTAM

SYDNEY AUCKLAND TORONTO NEW YORK LONDON

Some names and the location of certain events have been altered in order to protect the identity of individuals involved.

A Bantam book
Published by Random House Australia Pty Ltd
Level 3, 100 Pacific Highway, North Sydney NSW 2060
www.randomhouse.com.au

First published by Bantam in 2009

Addresses for companies within the Random House Group can be found at
www.randomhouse.com.au/offices

National Library of Australia
Cataloguing-in-Publication Entry

Constant, Paula.
Sahara.

ISBN 978 1 74166 929 9 (pbk).

Constant, Paula – Travel – Sahara.
Hiking – Sahara.
Sahara – Description and travel.

916.60433

Cover design by Two Associates
Internal design by Midland Typesetters
Typeset in 11/14 Sabon by Midland Typesetters, Australia
Printed and bound by Griffin Press, South Australia

Random House Australia uses papers that are natural, renewable and recyclable products and made from wood grown in sustainable forests. The logging and manufacturing processes are expected to conform to the environmental regulations of the country of origin.

10 9 8 7 6 5 4 3 2 1

For my family and friends –
when I thought I could walk no farther,
you carried me.

And if tonight my soul may find her peace
in sleep, and sink in good oblivion,
and in the morning wake like a new-opened flower
then I have been dipped again in God, and new-created.

And if, as weeks go round, in the dark of the moon
my spirit darkens and goes out, and soft strange gloom
pervades my movements and my thoughts and words,
then I shall know that I am walking still
with God, we are close together now the moon's in shadow.

And if, as autumn deepens and darkens
I feel the pain of falling leaves and stems that break in storms
and trouble and dissolution and distress
and then the softness of deep shadows folding, folding
around my soul and spirit, around my lips
so sweet, like a swoon, or more like the drowse of a low, sad song
singing darker than the nightingale, on, on to the solstice
and the silence of short days, the silence of the year, the shadow,
then I shall know that my life is moving still
with the dark earth, and drenched
with the deep oblivion of earth's lapse and renewal.

And if, in the changing phases of man's life,
I fall in sickness and in misery
my wrists seem broken and my heart seems dead
and strength is gone, and my life
is only the leavings of a life:

and still, among it all, snatches of lovely oblivion, and snatches of
        renewal,
odd, wintry flowers upon the withered stem, yet new, strange
        flowers
such as my life has not brought forth before, new blossoms of me –

then I must know that still
I am in the hands of the unknown God,
he is breaking me down to his own oblivion
to send me forth on a new morning, a new man.

                                        'Shadows', D. H. Lawrence

Chapter One

It's late at night and we are lying on a mattress in a southern Morocco prison yard. Beside me the guard is reclining, smoking an enormous spliff. Opposite me our contact, Kadar, lounges on the best cushions in the house, drinking whiskey. Limbs of a pomegranate tree hang dark and still over my head, its leaves limp after another fierce Saharan summer day. Above me the desert stars are crystal clear, and the shimmering heat has given way to a sweet, cool breeze.

It is the first of August, 2005, and today we arrived in M'Hamid after walking 5000 kilometres from Trafalgar Square.

'So, welcome to my prison!' Kadar cracks, laughing. 'I am sorry to be meeting you here, but there was a little accident with the police, and so here I am for three weeks. Ah, but it is good' – he smiles wickedly – 'because here there is no wife, no family and no work – just a little vacation for Kadar. And I have everything I need. No problems.'

Gary and I are exhausted, exhilarated, and in a weird state of suspended disbelief. We've just finished the first leg of our walk after a year on the road, jumped straight onto a bus and hurtled 100 kilometres back up the road we had just walked, to Zagora, to meet the man I had visited some three years before to talk about planning our desert crossing. We had an hour-long interview with the police in order to visit Kadar in prison and, having been served freshly cooked tajine, are now quaffing booze in the prison yard with a stoned guard. We may as well be back on a beach in Australia for all this feels like a prison. The strangely unsettling thing is that Kadar assumes as much control here as at the hotel he runs in M'Hamid, ordering the guard around like one of his lackeys. One could be forgiven for thinking he was the host of the place rather than an inmate.

'And now, after three years, you are back for your desert walk,' says Kadar, cigarette in hand. 'And where is my money?' His raucous laugh rings out again and he props himself up on one hand to look directly at me. 'Three years I've been waiting for my money! So now you are back, and we make the desert trek! I knew you would come back.'

I remember the force of his presence from the last time I met him, and lower my eyes. I feel strangely unsettled, lying here on the hard, packed earth in the desert night. Outside the prison walls I can hear the familiar sounds of Moroccan life: the discordant music of a celebration; women ululating and laughing, perhaps at a wedding; the sound of dirty water being thrown from a doorway onto the street; the hollow clop of a donkey being ridden past, its rider clicking to it. I'm intoxicated by the place, and excited by the man in desert robes looking at me. I realise that there is something very wrong, something dangerous here.

For two and a half months we have been walking through this country. In the heat and dust and exotic nature of the trek, in the heart of this dream that Gary and I conceived together, something between us is fading – and it's not until this moment that I know this. I wonder why I am lying here feeling more in tune with a Bedouin nomad in a prison yard than I do with the man I chose to marry. I feel a restlessness deep within.

'What is it that you want to do, exactly?' Kadar asks after a moment.

Gary is lying peacefully beside me, and I wait for him to answer the question. In a culture where gender roles are so firmly delineated, we agreed that Gary should establish himself as the driver of our plans. I know well, and deeply love and respect, Gary's strength and quiet courtesy. He is not a man who needs to announce his presence with fanfare. But right now I need him to answer the challenge, both personal and professional, that I see Kadar throwing out in his dramatic bearing.

For the longest moment, there is nothing but silence, and I keep my eyes lowered, willing Gary to speak, to be decisive and concise. I can feel Kadar eyeing us quizzically. Gary finally says, 'Well, we're really just looking at our options at the moment.'

Kadar looks bemused, waiting for something further, but as far as Gary is concerned he has said his piece. With my customary impatience – Gary calls it 'Paula-time' – I plunge in and take over.

'We're walking from London to Cape Town, South Africa,' I begin. 'For the last year we have walked 5000 kilometres through England, France, Spain, Portugal and Morocco. We finished in M'Hamid today – that was the end of our first stage.

'Now we'd like to continue but, as you know, there is a rather large desert we need to cross. We'd like to find out, first, if it's possible to organise a camel expedition into the Sahara; secondly, where it's possible to go; and finally how much it will cost. We don't want to travel like tourists, riding the camels, since the expedition is about walking the entire distance. We want to learn, and live as the nomads do, working with everything as we go: cooking, camels, the lot. My dream remains the same as the last time I saw you – we would like to cross the Sahara all the way from west to east. But I am not sure what's possible, or if it's within our reach financially. I hoped by talking to you that we could begin to research what our options are.'

Kadar nods at me, glances once at Gary, and reclines again, thinking.

'So. It is different from the last time. You are nomads already, ha!' He laughs, quietly this time, and then addresses me. 'I will have the figures for you by tomorrow. I think that it is best if we think about first just getting you to Dakhla, on the Mauritanian border. Since the frontier with Algeria has been closed, this is the only place you can cross into Mauritania. I think you will need at least five months, just so you can take the time, learn the culture, the language, about camels – all of these things. After Mauritania, I do not know – I will need to talk with some people. But from M'Hamid to Dakhla, I think this will be very good for you –

beautiful walking, safe country – and I can come to visit you. Yes, I think this is the best way to begin.

'So, tomorrow you will come to see me again, and we will eat some more good tajine, and I will tell you how much money you will give to me. In the meantime, Rahul' – he indicates the lithe young man who met us earlier in the day – 'will help you with everything you need. If you want to go anywhere, Rahul will go with you. Okay?' He fires directions at Rahul, who grins and nods. It's useless to insist we don't need a minder. As far as Kadar is concerned, we are in his domain now – prison or not – and we are his responsibility. His energy is all-encompassing.

We leave to walk back to the hotel and Rahul accompanies us. He is charming, speaks very good English and has perfect looks, which seem to be a requisite for Kadar's acolytes. He gives stern orders to the man on reception, leaving him in no doubt that we are now VIPs, before arranging to meet us the following morning and bidding us goodnight.

'Well, I thought that went really well, don't you?' says Gary as he sits down on the bed. 'I guess we'll wait until tomorrow, find out what it all costs and look at our options,' he says complacently, rolling over to go to sleep.

'Any thoughts on how we'll pay for it?' I venture timidly. Amid the strain of walking the last few months in the burning heat of summer, finances have become something of a taboo subject, resulting in harsh words and stony silences. It was easy to put the issue on the backburner. Now we don't have that luxury anymore. I'm not sure whether selling our house back in Australia is an option, or if perhaps Gary has some other idea. 'I'm sure we'll think of something. Kadar is obviously very capable; I know we can trust him,' he says before drifting off.

I lie on the hard bed, in an anonymous hotel, and beyond the torn fly screen I can hear the same distant wedding, now in full swing. I can smell roasting camel meat, and in the pale desert dark, young boys play soccer on the warm dust. I want to believe that I'm in the same place, the same adventure that I was when we walked here today. I want to feel the sense of the shared dream that has carried us so far, and the reassurance of the love I have relied upon for so many years. But instead I feel more enamoured by the world outside the window, and unreasonably impatient with Gary. I think of Kadar in prison: although he may be surrounded by guards and gates, I'm the one who feels trapped.

The next few days pass in manic organisation. Kadar comes up with the sum of €15,000 for the three-month expedition – this for four camels and two guides. Two because, as Kadar explains, 'The desert guide will speak only Hassaniya Arabic – you will need another person with French also, and to help with everything. Like this I think will be good for you.' Gary and I break down the figures and it all adds up. We are comfortable with what he's quoted, knowing that these three to six months will give us a chance to relax and learn what we need to in a safe environment.

I still don't understand exactly where the money is going to come from and feel rebuffed in my attempts to discuss it. I sense a reticence and reluctance in Gary's conversation, whether we are discussing how to raise the money, where we will stay back in England or the actual desert trek we are about to undertake. With every guarded exchange I feel more stung; I want to revel in our achievement with love and happiness, and instead my perception of being rejected by Gary leaves me feeling defensive and resentful. My response in turn is to be contemptuously critical and sarcastic.

Nothing like taking a mature approach when the chips are down.

In between all of this I am fighting to finish editing the book about the first leg of the walk to send to an agent in London who has expressed interest, before we arrive back there for our planned month-long break. But between the late nights at the prison, meeting with people during the day and catching up on all the correspondence on the internet, I am finding it difficult to concentrate.

We travel back up to Spain, long bus ride after long bus ride. The first part of it is country that we walked – the unforgiving, barren plains of the hamada.

'Remember that ditch?' Gary points out of the window at a barely noticeable depression in the hard earth, overhung by a scraggy, pathetic bush, gone in seconds as we race by. 'We were so glad to find that shade, remember? That day we thought our water would run out . . .'

We share a long look, the kind I imagine survivors of trench warfare may once have done. We are both thinking back to the days that, although so recent, already seem like a different time, a different life, now that we are here among other tourists in the comfort of a bus. I feel almost shaky at the abrupt change in perspective. I'm a little nervous about returning to the UK.

We take the boat across from Nador to the Spanish port of Almeria. It is an overnight trip, much longer than the last one from Algeciras across to Tangier. Gary falls asleep almost immediately. I sit up in the salon, drinking overpriced Heinekens at the bar. Returning Moroccans lounge everywhere, clustered in cheerful groups, equipped with their blankets and dinner.

I watch a European woman walk in with her Moroccan husband, their children and a large entourage of what I take to be his family. The Western woman stands out: she is tall, blonde and wears a headscarf in a typically European bohemian fashion, wound about her face but not covering the crest of her head. It is a nod to custom but a world away from the neatly pinned veils, marked with discreet Dior logos, the other women wear. She sits slightly apart from the rest of the group, trying to contain her overtired children. She herself looks exhausted and fed up. The Moroccan women with her huddle into a cosy circle laughing and joking, slapping hands and handling each other's children. The blonde woman is obviously excluded from the coterie. Although they offer her the food they are eating, and occasionally ask her if she is okay, there is no denying she is separate.

I see her look angrily over to the bar, where her husband drinks beer with his friends. They are at ease, laughing loudly. At some stage she rises and walks stiffly over to him. He glances at her in ill-feigned annoyance and embarrassment: *Why is she disturbing him when he is with the men? Why isn't she with all the other women?* She asks him for some money, and he takes out a purse and gives it to her. The other men greet her courteously but with obvious distance, despite her politeness and warm smiles.

There's a moment's silence as she turns to walk away, a pause when everybody is aware that something uncomfortable has just taken place. The women are watching her, the men looking studiously at the wall. She walks back across the salon, too tall and proud and blonde for this place, her children whining at the tension in the air. Crimson-faced, she buys her kids some crisps, and they sit down at a distance to the others. She looks across in exhaustion and frustration at her husband, but he has ostentatiously turned his back. The women carry on talking and do not offer her solace.

I imagine she has been to Morocco for a holiday with the family and is returning to Europe with those who also live there. I sense she probably lives a long way from the others – even perhaps in another country. She has probably spent ten days in the frantically social whirl of a Moroccan home, left to the company of the women while her husband revelled in being back with his friends and family. She must struggle with the language and culture and her children's obvious difference. I have deep sympathy for her and want to walk over and offer to take care of the kids, help in some way, but I sense she is probably so frustrated that I would just make the situation worse. No matter how strong the love is between two people, mixed-culture marriages – particularly when one is such a strong cultural identity – are hard and heartbreaking. It takes a hell of a lot of strength to deal with all this stuff.

And then I look across to where Gary is peacefully slumbering and feel a wave of incomprehensible loneliness sweep over me. Marriage is hard whether there are cultural differences or not.

Our return to 'reality' in London is a far cry from the triumph I'd once imagined.

I stay with friends, Gary with his father in Northamptonshire. Our conversations are coloured by misunderstanding and resentment. We'd discussed selling the house. I was fairly sure that this was where the money for the walk would come from – and it is – but it turns out that Gary has made an agreement with his mother, Jan, that she will take out a bridging loan to cover us until the house is sold.

I feel guilty – for putting his mother into such a position, because I have no more money to put into the walk, and because Gary has to sell the house that he bought in Melbourne before we were together. Even after eight years of marriage, I still see the house as his. So does he, I think, and that hurts too. I wonder why, if this walk really is a shared dream, that I should feel all this guilt. Gary is shouldering the financial burden, but I am carrying the emotional and logistical weight of the walk itself. We seem to be victims of the issues that are dividing us rather than bound by the strength and romance of the journey.

I apply for every grant I can find on the internet and continue to pitch for sponsorship. I sit up late at night and talk to friends about every option I can think of but, despite their optimism, I still feel that we have little to offer a sponsor at this point. The competition for sponsorship dollars and grant money is huge – every bloke who wants to climb Everest in his underpants is chasing a dollar. By comparison, our walk through Europe looks like nothing more than a light-hearted backpacking trip.

My confidence is further eroded by a visit to my father, who tells me in no uncertain terms that he feels I should get off my backside and take a real job in order to fund my 'holiday'. His words are like a dentist's drill hitting a nerve at high speed. Every one of them slams into me with brute force, revisiting every painful late-night doubt that has haunted me. I leave his house the next day – my confidence is too fragile to withstand parental scrutiny.

Back home in Australia, my mother has been diagnosed with breast cancer. She is in the depths of chemotherapy and suffering badly. She won't hear of me coming home to look after her. Gary's mum is caring for her at the moment, which deepens my feelings of guilt. Mum tells me repeatedly that our walk is a source of excitement and energy for her, and that she wants nothing more than for us to continue. I feel helpless and worried.

The one highlight is having my book picked up by an agent. Over lunch in central London, he tells me the words I am dying to hear: 'I think this is a very, very good book.'

Despite all my hopes, and Gary's encouragement, I'd lived in abject fear that my writing was simply not up to scratch. To have someone who really knows the industry actually tell me that it is okay brings a rush of emotion up through my chest, an exhilaration I've rarely felt in my life. I nearly burst into tears on the spot and can barely listen to the rest of the conversation.

I finish my glass of very good wine and float out into the bustle of central London, thinking: *I have an agent. I am a writer. I am going to have a book.* Despite everything, I am thrilled and triumphant, and beam happily at startled passers-by.

Our departure date hurtles toward us, and I feel little has been resolved. Gary has organised the loan, and Kadar has already chosen our camels and the local equipment we will need. I have spent much of the time in London writing articles for a friend's magazine and talking with friends. Gary and I have barely spent any time together.

Gary is flying to Spain and travelling down to Marrakech. I'm flying directly into the city a couple of days later, due to a visa issue, and meeting him there. I leave London in a fitful state – excited to be back on our walk at last, but dreading the inevitable eruption of the simmering volcano.

Chapter Two

Gary and I are in the hotel in Marrakech. The room is dark and cool, with pretty mosaic tiling in the bathroom and a window that opens onto the internal courtyard. A fountain bubbles in the garden, a quiet alleyway behind thick wooden doors. It's cheap and beautiful in Morocco's elegant way.

I'm so familiar with this city now that it no longer feels like a place I travel to, but more like a part-time residence. We know the guy on the hotel desk. We know where to find a good restaurant or shop for what we need. We are comfortable here.

Tomorrow we will meet Kadar before we travel down to M'Hamid. This will be our last night in peace for a while, and I want to sort some things out before we are consumed by the walk.

'I really think we need to talk,' I start.

We lie on the bed and Gary holds my hand. It seems like I talk for hours. I tell him I felt hurt and frustrated back in the UK, and I name my fears. I apologise for the things I feel I have done wrong. I talk as honestly as I ever have in our marriage.

I get to the end and say, 'Thank you so much for listening. What do you think? How do you feel about it all?'

Gary kisses my cheek, gives me a little smile, and answers, 'I think we'll be fine. Thank you for talking to me. We'll work it out.'

The dusk gathers around us, and I listen to the Moroccan sounds from beyond the window: the warning cries of men driving their donkeys and carts; the distant wail of the pipes the snake-charmers use in the central market, the Djemaa el Fna; the bird-like, warm chirruping of women speaking Arabic. I smell the heady scent of mint as a seller cycles past with the bundle strapped to his bicycle.

I wonder why I notice these things when I feel so desolate. I wonder if I asked the wrong questions, or said the wrong thing. And most of all, I wonder how well this bodes for the coming expedition. If we can't sort out our emotional issues here, in the privacy of a hotel room when we've no pressure, then how on earth will we cope in the desert isolation, among people not of our own culture?

We are sitting in a tea salon with Kadar; his wife, Selkha; and Ramzi, their little boy. Selkha is six-months pregnant. It's the first time I've seen her out of traditional Saharawi dress. Today, she wears loose pantaloons and a long blouse that covers her backside, a common city Moroccan outfit not unlike the Indian *salwar kameez*, with a conservative headscarf rather than *melekhva*, the long material wrap I usually see her in.

She looks totally different, more modern, from when I have met her in M'Hamid. I get a glimpse of the girl I know she must have been, the one who studied geography at university in Agadir. I comment on the difference, and she smiles.

'Yes, but here in Marrakech, there are no Saharawi,' she points out. I realise she's right. While I see plenty of women dressed in *djellaba* or *salwar kameez*, I've seen barely any dressed in *melekhva*. Those who do, look out of place and somewhat over-dressed. Marrakech is modern and vibrant, and there are more girls in jeans and T-shirts than in *melekhva*.

'When I come to the city, I wear modern clothes. I like to come up here and go shopping, and see what everyone else is wearing,' Selkha tells me. It's not so different from people at home in Australia who live way up north or in the outback, coming into one of the cities and putting on a skirt and sandals instead of the usual jeans and boots.

If Selkha looks comfortable and sophisticated in her modern outfit, by comparison Kadar looks startling to me. He is in jeans and shoes, and without the arrogant twitch of robes as he stands, his feet in traditional slippers, a turban slung about his neck, he appears diminished. Waiting to meet an American with whom he is hoping to do business, he looks tired, stressed, and ordinary. I think that he is a duck out of water – a man from the desert who does not suit the city.

The conversation feels strained and uneasy. Kadar barely speaks to me but focuses on Gary. While I believe this is exactly as it should be, I feel excluded by them. Then I ask myself what exactly I expect and try to immerse myself in conversation with Selkha. But that is strained too. She likes me, I'm sure, but I get the feeling that she doesn't want to have to communicate more than necessary.

Kadar will be away for the next few days on business, so we'll be collected the following day by his acolytes and driven down to the hotel, where he'll meet us when he is finished.

He shakes my hand and kisses me on both cheeks when he leaves, but he looks tense and distracted. After the many hassles of the past few weeks, I'd gone to the meeting hoping to find a renewed feeling of security and purpose. I leave it feeling lonely and uneasy.

We travel down to M'Hamid in a Land Rover crowded with people who work for Kadar, various friends and hangers-on picked up on the way who need a lift.

Some I know, like Rahul, the young bloke who met us in Zagora. Others have familiar faces, either from Zagora or from the first time I visited M'Hamid with my friend Sarah. A couple actually remember me and greet me with big smiles and warm handshakes. They're all, to a man, hospitable and friendly, and I feel absorbed immediately into their world.

Gary and I watch as the country outside whizzes past. Rahul says, 'Tell me the places where you stayed when you walked this way.'

I point them out as we pass: *There*, we stayed with a Berber family in their village; *there*, we camped on the roadside; *there*, we were thrilled to find a cheap pension.

I'm amazed, as we labour up the winding road into the Atlas Mountains, to think we actually *walked* all of this. I remember every bend in the road, every changing view of the landscape. I remember where our camps were before we even drive past them. Every inch walked has a memory attached.

We stop at Taddert, the same mountain hamlet where Gary and I once found a cheap hotel. This time is different again, as we are ushered to a table at the back. Our companions know everyone in the place; we get the best food – fast – and a gaggle of locals huddle around and listen eagerly as Rahul explains what we are doing.

They exclaim in amazement. Some remember us from when we walked through a few months earlier, laughing as they recount with their hands how big our packs were – *'like this!'* with their arms spread wide, and we chuckle.

It's so strange to think that these people watched us, wondered who we were and what we were doing. Back then, I was so tired and fed up with being the object of attention that I'd stopped noticing the stares. We were here in the middle of summer. By the time we got to this hotel, we'd staggered thirty kilometres with packs on, uphill. No wonder I don't remember much.

We trundle on through the mountains and down the other side, over the pass and into the hard, rocky country. It's cooler now, the furious heat is gone. Gary and I can't help but talk about the last time we were here, and the others in the car shake their heads, incredulous. I love being bound to Gary by the memory of our adventure.

Not long after Agdz, but before Zagora, the Draa Valley opens up into a beautiful, lush palmeraie. There are rocky cliffs to one side, and, startling after the long kilometres of barren hammada, the river itself.

The four-wheel drive swings to a stop by a roadside stall selling dates. We disembark with the others. The men murmur *'Hamdullah'*, 'Praise God', as they gaze on the water, stretch their legs and buy boxes of dates. Rahul winks at me, 'You must forgive us. For nomads, water like this . . . it is very good, very good to see . . .'

The men get their turbans and robes out of plastic bags and change out of their city dress. Some of them pray in the dusk. The haunting beauty of the rocky valley and lush palmeraie envelop us in a deep, still calm. After the bustle of Marrakech and the drone of our vehicle, it is bliss to feel the city tension dropping away. In the familiar rhythm of the mens' prayer, sung to the warm red sky in the East and echoing deep in the tall rocky cliffs, I feel the desert coming closer again.

In the last kilometres before we reach M'Hamid, the men put on a cassette that has them all clapping, beating the dashboard and singing.

'*Tumbaramazaina, layla* . . .'

Their singing grips me, and I wonder what the song means.

'These are M'Hamid men, singing now,' Rahul tells me, indicating the cassette. 'This is Saharawi music. *Our* music.'

They wind their turbans around their heads and sing in beautiful harmony. The desert air steals into the vehicle, beckoning me onwards and inwards, to the wild places on this earth and within myself that I have always wanted to go.

I walk into the hotel. It's hot, but not like before. The nights are cool now and the days not painful.

The hotel is, as always, full of an array of gorgeous young men, turbaned and robed to suit the tourists' picture of desert nomads. I often wonder if Kadar chooses his hustlers for their looks. There is certainly not an ugly face among them, although they all display mouthfuls of yellowed, rotting teeth.

Although most of them have been raised in town and have gone no further into the desert than the tourist-circuit routes, they play their romantic roles to the hilt.

They lounge lazily on the low floral couches lining the walls and smoke furiously, eyeing me and every other female from beneath sooty black curls. Despite their studied interest, they also serve Gary's and my every need with a deeply ingrained courtesy. I now know a lot of the men by name and simply feel excited and relieved to be back here, at the real start of our next adventure, out of England and the horrible depression that dogged me in the grey surrounds of London.

The hotel is somehow empty without Kadar, despite being littered with all manner of his family and friends. After spending so much time in Morocco during the last walk, its easier for me to make sense of the hotel now – to see what is real and what is for show. I notice the manual workers, the young boys like Madani, who are dressed in casual old Western clothes, and who are always in the kitchen or scrubbing floors. It's these guys who sleep on roll-out mats on the tiled floor, long after everyone else has either left or retired to their rooms. They leap to the bidding of the older men, and all seem to be accomplished cooks, attentive waiters and obedient servants to their elders.

Then there are the hustlers, the tourist guides. They live outside the hotel and arrive every day in the midmorning to 'work'. For the most part, this constitutes barking orders at the young boys to bring them tea or food. It's these guys who speak various languages and meet the tourists as they pull up in the centre of town, charming and cajoling them into taking their tour rather than one from the various competitors who also operate out of M'Hamid. The market for the tourist dollar is fiercely contested, and at the first sound of a four-wheel drive entering town, there is a rush of movement as a dozen authentic-looking hustlers converge on the central parking area.

On Kadar's return, I learn that it is Madani, the smiling young man I have noticed cleaning diligently, who will be walking with us in addition to our main guide.

'I have selected a good guide for you, *lalla*,' Kadar tells me, using the Moroccan word for 'honoured lady' or intimate friend. He is lounging on the cushions in the front salon, robed and turbaned once more, the king of the castle back in his domain. Gary and I are drinking yet more tea; it is already becoming an addiction. 'His name is M'Barak. He is a friend of my father's brother and knows the desert very, very well. All of my family has agreed that this man is the right one for you.

'But he doesn't speak any French, only Arabic and Tamazight (the Berber language), and so you will need another one – someone to translate, to cook, to help with the camels. So this is why Madani will go with you. He is my cousin; he works hard. You can trust him.'

I feel a sense of losing control, that the autonomy of our trip will be taken away. After so many months of being entirely independent, making all our decisions ourselves, it is disconcerting to hand over the reins, no matter how temporarily.

I want to make it clear that the cooking and camel handling – these are *our* jobs to learn, not to pay someone else to take care of. But I suppress my natural indignation. I know deep down that Kadar understands this. The best way to really learn how to do all of those things is to have the best support that we can.

'I have found you four good camels. You will meet them when M'Barak arrives in a couple of days. I will take you out to the camp and you can see your tent and the equipment, and learn how to use everything, with Madani, until then. Like this, you will be ready when M'Barak comes. Madani!'

He beckons the young, lithe Saharawi over. Madani is wearing bright purple pantaloons, tight around the ankle and full around his skinny flanks, in the traditional style. And a lurid shirt of tropical flowers. Anywhere else he would look ridiculous, but I rather think he fancies himself on the sharp side. His grin is as wide as his face, and he greets us both shyly.

'The boys, they all argue about who will walk with you,' Kadar tells us confidentially. 'Everyone wants this job. But Madani, I think for you he is the best – he is hard worker and not talk too much, you know?'

'What about our clothes?' Gary asks. 'We still need to buy proper clothes – we don't want to wear tourist gear.'

'Of course,' Kadar says. 'We will do that now.'

We walk up to the tiny local store, and Gary buys pantaloons. Kadar has already bought him robes; they are the billowing, decorative type favoured by Saharawi as dress robes, rather than the hard-wearing *djellaba*-style shift worn by working nomads. At the time, I think little of it, but later I'll wonder if this was a direct attempt on Kadar's part to undermine Gary and make him uncomfortable. The robes are impractical and difficult to manage.

I go with Selkha to buy the women's wear undergarments: a pair of light cotton trousers, a long-sleeved cotton shirt, and a long sleeveless dress that covers both. Over this I am to wrap *melekhva*, the long swathe of colourful cotton that will cover my body and head.

I spend a hugely amusing afternoon in Selkha's home as she patiently teaches me how to tie and fold my *melekhva*. I struggle with the process – I have never been good at anything involving my hands, like folding or arranging things. Selkha giggles frequently at my poor attempts.

'No – not like that,' she says, trying not to laugh as I trip over the long material. 'First, you keep the majority of it in front of you – like this,' she says as she places the top edge of the material in my hands to hold. I am standing still like a fashion mannequin, feeling absurd and clumsy. 'Then you take some of the material around your back, so it is like a sack with no ends, and you make it so there is plenty of room.' Much of what she says is in Arabic, with just a little French, so I'm left largely to watch and deduce. My Arabic is virtually zero at this point. She demonstrates tying the back and front of the material together at the shoulder top, forming a crude shift so that my left arm is poking through a type of sleeve. On the right, the excess fabric trails away in an formless mass.

'Right, I get it to this stage,' I say, and then try the Hassaniya word for 'understand': *fhempt*.

Selkha's eyes light up and she laughs. '*Fhempti?*' she asks, using the correct tense when addressing a female.

'*Ayyeh,*' I reply in the affirmative, and we both laugh at my efforts.

'*Le mushkil,*' I begin in my clumsy mélange of French and Arabic – *mushkil* means 'problem', and it's one of the first words I learned. 'The problem is what I do with the rest of this stuff.' I indicate the fabric lying on the floor.

'Like this,' Selkha says, also in French, and efficiently picks up the length and sits it over my head so it hangs down my back. She draws the remainder around my front and again lifts it over my head, this time tucking in the last of the material tightly around my face. I look in the mirror and see my little white face poking out incongruously from the tightly wrapped cocoon, a bit like a Russian doll. By comparison Selkha's *melekhva* falls around her face in elegant, loose folds. Like a teenage girl looking at her far more stylish older sister, I say, 'But I want to look like you!'

She laughs heartily and indicates that I should unwrap the *melekhva* and do it up myself. 'With practice, you will do it like mine, and it will be easy,' she says.

I roll my eyes questioningly and obediently attempt to emulate her, but I end up turning circles on the spot and falling over the seemingly endless piles of cloth. Not once do I manage to do it correctly.

'*Macayn Mushkil*,' Selkha laughs in sympathy – *no problem*. 'All with time.'

I'd like to believe her. Frankly, all I want is to take the sodding thing off. It is hot and annoying – and how on earth am I going to walk in it?

She gives me a small pot of heavily scented ointment, to rub in my hair when it starts to smell, and some perfumed crystals to throw on the fire. They scent one's robes – and self – she tells me. All these fascinating rituals, lotions and potions feel like an indoctrination into secret women's business.

We discuss washing. I say that I'm used to having a splash wash every night when I walk, and she nods in agreement. 'There is also the desert *hammam*,' she explains. 'Madani will show you how to make this but, because you are moving, you will make it with tarp and sticks, not a proper desert *hammam* with rugs and hot stones like the nomads have who camped for a long time.'

I doubt I will bother making a proper bathhouse each day when we stop – a bush has always sufficed for my ablutions. Even so, I wish Selkha could come with us and show me the desert traditions. But she is pregnant now, and a part of me suspects also that she is not used to long desert travel. She was raised in town, in Zagora, rather than in the desert. Unlike most Saharawi wives, Kadar has told me that Selkha does not get on with his mother

and sisters, and so they now live separately from the family. I'm
learning that Selkha is of a more modern, educated generation of
Saharawi women and has less time for traditional ways. As the
young wife of their son and brother, her mother and sisters-in-law
had demanded subservient obedience. I like her a lot and completely understand her desire to live away from the cloistered,
pressured environment of a traditional family home.

Finally, we go and buy our nomad's sandals.

I wonder just how smart buying these is. Made from truck tyres
on the bottom, they've minimal padding in the sole, just a few thin
layers of leather nailed in with basic tacks. With a crisscrossed
leather upper and no arch support, they're as basic as a shoe comes.
After much thought, Gary and I decided to wear what the nomads
themselves do, under the happy theory that a style of sandal that
has worked for hundreds of years should work okay for us.

We will discover soon enough if the theory stands up.

The following day we drive out to the camp, only a few kilometres from town.

Madani walks out of the tent, smiling. He must have walked
out here from town earlier that morning.

'So,' Kadar says, 'this is your camp. These are your things. Let
me show you.'

We enter the tent. It is unlike the nomad tents I see scattered
around the dunes. Those are permanent tents, *hayma*, not to be
packed up and moved daily. Ours is a *guiton*, a modern tent made
of white canvas and heavy cord. It is a classic square block on
which any side can be rolled up. It has one centre supporting pole
and heavy steel pegs tying the cord down on the corners, and no
floor. It's tough and durable and reminds me of army bivouacs.

It's also unbearably hot.

The tent has been erected near a few of the traditional hessian-
and-wood affairs. These are open on all sides and much cooler to
rest in, so we sit in there as Kadar goes through the equipment
with us.

There is a carton full of basic camp cutlery, far more than Gary
and I are used to after carrying all of our belongings in packs. The
stove is a gas bottle with an attachment that screws onto the top,

on which a pot can sit. I am surprised and a little disappointed, thinking we would rely more on fires. There are four large wicker panniers, which have two deep spaces with a support that stretches over the camel. The camel saddles sit beneath them. There are four thirty-litre jerry cans, several five-litre ones and several thin mattresses with good quality camel-hair blankets, which will sit between the camel and the panniers.

Kadar, it seems, has thought of everything. I feel irrelevant, caught up in his operation rather than running my own. But once again, I suppress those concerns in the knowledge that this is the whole idea of paying someone to set it up. This next walk is our training walk, the time when we will learn what we need to in order to navigate the west-to-east crossing of the Sahara. I have never done this before – I cannot be expected to have the skills – but it feels tiring to be back at the start again.

Kadar bids us farewell and skids out of the camp in a cloud of sand. The huge quietness of the desert settles over us, and suddenly we are alone – at least for a few days. It is time to start learning, before M'Barak turns up.

I turn to Madani and wave my *melekhva* at him.

'Any chance you can help me organise this thing?' I say, and his face cracks into a huge smile.

'Of course, *lalla*,' he says. 'I have three sisters.'

Two days later, I'm watching eagerly, waiting for the first glimpse of the man who will guide us 3000 kilometres through the desert to Dakhla. My eyes scour the dull horizon for movement, waiting for my camels, waiting for M'Barak. The small, dirty dunes where we are camped are low enough to see some distance, but in the heat of midday the sky and sand blur into a hazy, dull cloud that blinds with light refraction. It's difficult to discern movement. My eyes dart back and forth, searching for a flicker, something out of the ordinary. I wonder if I will ever truly become accustomed to this landscape, if there will ever come a time when I feel that I really understand this huge, wild place.

'There he is!' Madani shouts in French, gesturing excitedly as he runs off across the sand to meet the little procession coming our way. When he points, it is suddenly obvious; but my eyes had slid past that exact spot barely a moment ago and I had perceived nothing.

Gary remains propped up on a mattress in the shade of the hessian tent. I pop up like a jack-in-the-box, *melekhva* hanging awkwardly. I don't know what I should do. I watch as the figures come into view – a wiry man wearing tough, durable robes and a long black turban leads four brown camels. His robes are a different colour and style to those worn by Kadar and his glamorous clique. This man wears a long *djellaba*, like the Berber goat herders I used to see when we were walking through the Atlas Mountains. It's belted with a wide, solid brown leather girth. Rather than the cornflower blue, billowing robes worn by the Saharawi hustlers in the hotel, which constantly require adjustment and swirl in the wind like the ones Kadar bought for Gary, this man is clad in a practical shift that is cut sparingly and hangs neatly about his form, over the loose voluminous trousers and Western-style shirt I am accustomed to seeing. The material is thick and coarse, but of obviously good quality. His turban is weathered and long, wrapped about head, face and neck. His sandals are plain and practical. His one small bag is strapped to the top of the camel he leads.

But as he draws close to us, eyeing us curiously, we realise that his clothes are the least striking thing about him.

'Look at his face!' Gary mutters.

As if I can look at anything else.

It's like gazing into a photograph from the classic era of exploration, a face from a history book. Walnut brown, wizened and lined, his skin is dark and polished like a stone worn smooth by years of exposure. His eyes are deep and brown and sparkling, and when he smiles his teeth are even and white.

'*Salaam aleikum.*' After shaking Gary's hand he reaches for mine, to my surprise. Subconsciously, I have formed an expectation, possibly based on reading the British explorer Wilfred Thesiger so long ago, of how I or any woman would be treated by nomadic Muslim men. Those expectations did not include being touched – even casually – or being in any way considered an equal. Despite my interactions with Kadar, I'd seen him as somewhat Westernised and accustomed to European traditions and behaviour. I'd made no such assumptions about M'Barak, and in fact had imagined he would be a somewhat stern and uncompromising figure, adhering rigidly to a strict strain of Islam and contemptuous of me as a Western, non-Islamic woman. But his eyes meet mine with warmth and friendliness, and his handshake is firm. I don't sense anything untoward in his manner, nor in the way he examines me. I find this heartening.

It also jolts me into a realisation of my own prejudices. Hastily, I think that I had better identify what else I have made assumptions about and discard them before they get me into trouble. Sometimes the only way we realise what our prejudices are is when reality contradicts them.

I immediately excuse myself and go to the kitchen tent to prepare lunch. In my naïve attempts to conform to my own somewhat odd perceptions of what a 'proper' Saharawi woman should be, I'm desperate to make a good impression. I squat and chop the vegetables for salad, sweating in the sweltering midday heat, flies crawling over my face. I long to be outside in the breeze. I'm trying to hold the *melekhva* out of my face with one hand and cursing whichever stupid nomad thought that either tents or *melekhva* were a good idea.

M'Barak appears at the entrance of the tent, Madani hovering anxiously in the background. The older man nods in approval and says something in Arabic.

'He says it is good – traditional,' Madani tells me, smiling broadly in relief. I hope that the 'traditional' comment is also an accolade, as I bend dutifully over my preparations in the blistering heat. I personally think the tent is hell on earth at this time of day; I fancy myself rather the martyr.

Then M'Barak steps inside the tent, and his face falls. He shakes his head decisively, steps out and is gone. I look enquiringly at Madani, who shrugs and grins apologetically.

'He says it is too hot in here at this time. He's going to make tea in the other tent.'

Thank God, I think. *At least he's got a brain.*

But, unsure what is expected of me, I continue to prepare the meal, worried that perhaps this is time for only the men to meet and that my place is here.

After a further five minutes Madani's face appears in the doorway again. This time he looks anxious and apologetic once more.

'Umm, *lalla*, you need to come with me. We are having tea now and you need to be here to welcome him – it is respect, tradition . . .' His voice trails off and he looks at me pleadingly, as if apologising for custom. I curse myself. Of course I know this – tea first. Always tea first. I'm quite cast down at my inability to remember even this simple rule.

I walk over and sit carefully in the circle but away from the men, my *melekhva* wrapped as best I can manage to ensure I'm showing no expanse of flesh. I know from watching Selkha in her home that it should be my job to make tea, but I'm not yet confident that I actually can manage the complicated ritual of pouring from great heights, despite having practised with Madani incessantly over the past couple of days.

Gary is wonderfully relaxed and self-assured in any company. I envy his carefree pose, lying relaxed on a cushion. I admire, too, his calm acceptance of his role in this first meeting, his noticeable lack of concern in comparison to my own self-conscious worry. I notice that M'Barak has already adjusted the hessian tent, having rolled up a corner exactly at the angle of the breeze so that a cool draught blows through the shade. It is like air conditioning after the hot white canvas.

I am seated closest to the door of the tent. M'Barak hands me a short glass of tea so dense and black that I assume it is the first brew, the rinse, which is customarily tossed out as it is so bitter. Proud of my knowledge, I empty it peremptorily with a practised flick of my wrist into the sand and hand the glass back nonchalantly, as I have seen Madani do so many times.

There is a moment's stunned silence. Madani is purple with embarrassment. M'Barak is shocked, and Gary is pissing himself laughing, albeit internally.

I just threw out the all-important first glass of tea.

In a split second I realise that I've cocked up. And suddenly I can only see the funny side of all my careful preparations and efforts to conform, and how precious I am being. I relax into laughter, shaking my head in self-mockery.

'I'm so stupid – he makes such strong tea I thought it must be the one you throw out!' I tell Madani. 'Please explain that I am new to all this and make stupid mistakes – still a tourist – and this is why I need him so much, to teach me everything so that I don't embarrass myself like this again.'

Even before Madani has begun to translate, M'Barak's face has relaxed into a merry grin. He watched me closely as I spoke and, without understanding the words, has already perceived the motivation behind them and responded immediately in kind. When his eyes meet mine they reflect a willingness to understand, and he hands me another glass of tea immediately.

'M'Barak says it's his fault; he made the first one too strong anyway – he's been out in the desert for too long,' Madani says. I'm touched by M'Barak's courteous and kind response, and I can also tell that Madani is relieved by the exchange. I feel for the earnest, cheerful translator. At such a young age, only twenty-one, he is carrying an enormous burden by having to handle the undercurrents of all communication, and suffer the agonies and embarrassments of miscommunication along with us.

Gary is still cackling to himself at my faux pas, but his smile is sympathetic, despite him shaking his head in pretend bemusement.

We drink tea and talk about the trip to come. I get the maps out, trying to ascertain the route we will take, but M'Barak eyes them with nothing more than contempt and bewilderment, and beckons me to the sand at the edge of the tent.

'He will show you where we go,' Madani tells me.

M'Barak lies on his side and begins to draw in the sand. His fingers are bony and long, expressive and curiously elegant. I'm struck by how illustrative his gestures are, as if his hands themselves are telling the story.

'We're here,' Madani begins, translating as M'Barak draws a dot in the sand and speaks in Arabic. 'From here, we'll walk like this' – the line in the sand indicates a south-west line – 'to Foum

Zguid, Tissinnt and Tata.' Each town is delineated by a small dot and a precise amount of line between them. 'Then, down here' – this time the line turns more sharply south – 'to Assa.' The line turns almost due west. 'Then to Tan-Tan.' At this M'Barak stops and looks up at us, his expression more serious.

Madani speaks. 'Here, M'Barak says it gets hard. From here is Western Sahara – Laayoune, Boujdour, Dakhla. Very hard. Landmines, Polisario. Very dangerous. We are lucky if we get there, he says.'

'Really?' I ask curiously. 'Does he think it's really a security risk? Can we actually walk through there?'

Madani translates. They both look at me, smile and shrug. Simultaneously, they raise their hands and say, '*Inshallah*.'

Of course. The Arabic answer to all unknown things: *Inshallah*. If God wills.

It's the first real taste I have of what lies ahead – of the strange, complex nomadic culture, the wonderland down the rabbit hole, where I will never know what is coming around the next corner, or get a straight answer to any question worth asking. I look at Gary. His brow is furrowed and he looks concerned. I know he has questions, the same ones in my head, like, 'What happens if we can't get through? Why didn't Kadar mention we may be stopped?' But I don't have the answers. And anyway, I had always known from my research that there would be uncertainties in that area. I'm prepared to take what comes.

Under normal circumstances Gary and I would talk about it all – and probably end up laughing over the whole thing. But it is symptomatic of things between us just now that I somehow can't bring myself to reach out towards him. Instead of wanting to communicate, I find myself feeling defensive, even though I am sure our concerns are the same. I know that my impatience and refusal to engage is unfair and dangerous, but somehow I just can't seem to feel empathy. It is as if a wall is being built inside me, higher and higher, and Gary is being bricked out from my view. I keep trying to peep over the wall; but the higher it gets, the harder it seems. When I do get a glimpse, I feel as if he has built an even higher wall. I don't only have to find the will to climb my own, but also the perseverance and strength to climb his too. And for the first time I can ever remember, I just can't find the will to do either. Instead, I feel despair and hurt, and that comes across as impatience and anger. Perhaps he feels the same way. I really don't know how to find out.

Another part of me feels restless and wired and teetering on some kind of precipice, fuelled in part by the constant tension of Kadar's watchful, provocative presence in the camp and at the hotel.

I don't want to find him attractive.

It's the worst of clichés, to my mind, that a woman should begin having trouble in her marriage and suddenly find someone else deadly irresistible. I despise myself for even thinking of him, and in the back of my mind I wonder how much he is trying to make Gary feel uncomfortable and me at home – he strikes me as someone who has the Machiavellian ability to subtly intimidate if he chooses. But some other side of me is unfairly impatient with Gary for not somehow sensing the power play and addressing the issue head-on.

Of course, it never occurs to me to do so, either. But I don't feel angry at myself or at Kadar – just at Gary. It is horribly unfair, to the point of real cruelty, but I don't see it at all. It's incredible how easily we can choose to be blind to our own part in catastrophe.

Most of all, I'm driven by this walk. I'm almost obsessed with it: the desert, adventure, culture. And if there are holes in the plan, I don't want to have them pointed out to me, because I'm doing this walk – landmines or not – and I'm not really interested in hearing about what may or may not get in my way. Even from Gary.

Especially from Gary.

We leave M'Barak out at the camp and go for our last excursion into Zagora, to meet with Kadar and the chief of police to discuss getting an extended visa.

We're early, so we wait in a café and drink tea, watching townspeople as they pass. Groups of women in *melekhva* shuffle past in their ponderous gait, large backsides rolling beneath the voluminous folds of material. They link arms and chatter happily, their children scampering about. Children as young as six wander between the tables of the cafés, selling cigarettes. Robed men lounge in shady areas, smoking and talking desultorily. Occasionally a nomad walks past, driving his goats in front of him. The cars range from new, expensive four-wheel drives to clapped-out bangers that belch smoke and threaten to fall apart on every corner. Old two-stroke motorbikes pass frequently, engines squealing.

As one in particular buzzes by, somehow carrying an entire family of two adults and two small children, Gary and I grin at each other. He loves this too, the wonderful eccentricity of this place; and in our momentary understanding, I miss him, miss *us*, with a sudden, hard pang.

We leave the café and go to the police station for our appointment.

Morocco issues tourists with a ninety-day visa. Our problem is that we're likely to need double that time to make it to the border, and we don't want to have to leave the country in order to get new visas, or possibly encounter problems on re-entry. Kadar has assured us that he has already spoken to the chief involved, who will issue us with an extension before we leave.

But – in my first real encounter with Moroccan inefficiency and red tape – we are stonewalled.

We're shown into a spare, concrete room, furnished with a shabby desk, ancient typewriter, plastic chairs with cigarette burns, and overflowing ashtrays on every surface. The air is fuggy with smoke. The fat, shabbily dressed public servant leans back in his chair and eyes us with calculating contempt. Kadar stands off to the side, looking slightly nervous and decidedly deferential, offering the man cigarettes and staying quiet unless spoken to.

I am aware that Kadar has already paid a substantial amount of *baksheesh*, the customary but underhanded monetary 'donation' that aids most official transactions in Morocco. But it doesn't seem to be going quite as planned.

Under his interrogative stare, Gary and I answer question after question. What are our professions? Our home addresses? Our purpose here? How much money do we earn? How have we organised our trek? What are we doing about security? Do we know about the military situation in the Western Sahara? What will we do when we get there? Where's the letter of permission from our own government?

Our responses are, inevitably, largely fiction. We've no address. I list teaching as my profession. We lie about our income; we say the walk is for our own interest and as research for my teaching. We've a letter that I requested long ago from the Australian Embassy in London for just this eventuality – it says nothing more than that the Australian government is aware of our journey and requests that we pass unencumbered, but it has an official seal and is in English. I figure – rightly – that it will look impressive. We lie about insurance and say we'll deal with the Western Sahara when we get there. I mention that Kadar is our expedition supervisor.

The policeman puffs on his cigarette and opens our passports from the back, Arabic style. He barely glances at them. After a long, tense silence he ignores us and addresses Kadar.

I watch Kadar's face and see that, although he tries to hide it, he's worried. He jokes and smiles and cajoles, and in the end he shakes the man's hand and we're abruptly dismissed. There are no stamps in our passports.

'He says that he cannot do it,' Kadar explains. 'But he says it is not a problem – when the ninety days are up, you come up here, to Zagora, and he will stamp your passports for you then. There are new laws now and he cannot do it here, today.'

'But we'll be 1500 kilometres away by then,' I say, aghast. 'I don't want to have to come all the way back here – and besides, we might not be anywhere near a bus! This is a nightmare.'

'Ah, so what,' Kadar says dismissively, laughing at my consternation. 'So you take a couple of weeks off. Come back to M'Hamid. It will be Christmas! We make a party! You take a little holiday. This is not a big deal.'

I walk away, steaming. I resent the feeling of being *managed*, and I especially resent having paid good money for a result I didn't get. The last thing I want to be worried about when I'm out there on our beautiful trip is walking out of our way to find some bus to come back up and deal with bureaucratic red tape. I'm annoyed by Kadar's casual indifference and critical of myself for delegating such an important task. I may have resolved to approach all bureaucratic dealings with equilibrium, but here, at the first hurdle, I could stamp my feet in frustration with the fat policeman and his contemptuous superiority. Gary voices his own discontent, and I feel somehow responsible for that, which exacerbates my own.

On the way back to M'Hamid we buy alcohol at the tiny roadhouse in Tagounite, the last booze before M'Hamid. This will be our last night at the hotel before we walk. The grand farewell.

We sit outside, under the clear night sky, and all the boys turn up – every hotel hanger-on who has gathered in the preceding days to ogle us, the mad tourists embarking on a ridiculously ambitious desert trek.

We drink whiskey and talk politics and religion, the conversation shifting from English to French to Arabic and back again. The mosque is in sight of the hotel. I cannot help but note that all of the men drinking with us also attend the mosque. It is my first taste of Moroccan hypocrisy in relation to alcohol.

There is a group of us and after a time the boys start singing. I shiver in delight as the deep voices and clapping stretches up into the night. Tossing my head back and looking at the brilliant stars, I thank every god in heaven that I'm here and not back in the dense city fug.

Gary goes to bed early. I watch him rise with a mixture of resentment and guilt. I should go too, and I don't like myself very much for not showing solidarity. But not enough to make me get up and leave such an exciting night.

Kadar is sitting to my left, and when they start singing he is eyeing me – I can feel it. Suddenly he leans back and begins to sing, and the others immediately fall into respectful background harmony. His voice soars authoritatively, holding the long and deep notes. And I can't look at him because I feel every note somewhere deep in my soul, and I know he is singing for me. I glance up, once, and he is watching me.

He finishes the song and says he must go, but soon returns, mumbling some excuse about Selkha being ill. I suddenly see the sordid nature of the game that I'm allowing to unfold here. Disgusted with myself, I make my excuses and retreat to the hotel room.

Gary is sleeping. I lie in bed beside him and feel the gulf that is growing. I feel again the sudden sense of attraction and danger with Kadar. I wonder what the hell I am playing at, and why. I roll over suddenly, wanting to be close to Gary, to reassure myself that I have not yet broken our covenant. But he groans and pushes me away and huddles into his side of the narrow bed, and I wish I had stayed drinking with Kadar.

The next morning the hotel is quiet. I walk to the toilet block and Kadar is perched on the wall, watching the men working on the new part of the hotel. He turns to pull me up beside him. We sit there in the early morning sun for while, in silence, close but not touching. He's not looking at me.

'I'm glad we're going out to the camp today,' I say finally. I have to say something; his nearness unnerves me. He turns and eyes me quizzically. His gaze never allows me an out clause, and I feel the familiar twist in my guts, as if he sees straight inside me. I jump down off the wall.

'I think it's dangerous for me here,' I say softly. I don't know where the words come from. They just fall out.

He holds my eyes and jumps down so he is standing right in front of me, way too close. His eyes are intensely serious.

'Is not just dangerous for you,' he says quietly. 'Is dangerous for everyone around you.' He moves even closer, his face inches from my own. When he speaks again his voice has a hard edge: 'Once I start with you I can't stop. I know this. I *feel* it.' And for a long moment we stand like that, both of us barely breathing. Suddenly, with a rush of robes and decisive turn, he is gone.

I stand for a moment in the hard morning sun, and I think, *So now it is real.*

And I want to cry, because I don't want this. I don't want this as much as I do.

※

It is dusk and we are driving out to the camp, the four-wheel drive loaded with the last of our supplies for the first few weeks. I'm sitting in the front with Kadar; Gary is in the back. My *melekhva* is slipping and I can't make it stay fast; it gets caught in everything and whips into my face. Kadar drives recklessly, and I light him a cigarette from my own. The warm desert wind blows in my face. The moon rises high and bright. I am excited and wired, anxious to get to bed and sleep before we set out tomorrow. Anxious to be alone with my thoughts.

I know we'll be walking the next morning. I want it to change everything. I want things to be like before, between Gary and me: a team against the world, walking together. Our expedition. Our dream.

But I know it's not the same. It feels as if we are having separate walks now, and separate experiences. I want with all my heart for our walk to come to the rescue, to reunite us.

I want to look at Kadar and not find him attractive.

I want our dream back.

We are late leaving. It takes forever to pack up. Gary and I stand around uselessly, watching everything being put together. Despite the fact that I'm desperate to be learning and packing, I know that this morning, with an audience and under pressure to leave, is not the time. There is nothing worse than people who know nothing trying to help. There will be days for that out there in the emptiness. I just stand and watch the men loading our camels with our bags, and fiddle with my awkward *melekhva* in the growing morning. M'Barak is stressed and impatient, ordering Madani around. Gary and I have been through all of this before, the first-day blues.

Finally, everything is packed. The sun is high. A group of tourists is leaving beside us, on the same route for a day. They sit up on their camels, cameras in hand and trekking trousers on. They find us immensely amusing.

'So. You go now. Be good. Be safe. I pray for you. *Bismillah*!' Kadar shouts, using the phrase that means 'In God's name' and is traditionally always spoken before eating or commencing any other activity. He raises his clasped hands in a salute as we walk off in a clumsy procession. His acolytes dance about us, singing and clapping Madani on the shoulder. I can't bear to look back; I feel as awkward as I did at the beginning of the first walk, clumsy in my desert clothes, flat-footed in my nomad's sandals, inadequate to the task. I watch M'Barak leading the caravan from the front and I think, *Will this be my desert walk? Stumbling uselessly along in the wake of my own camels, fundamentally extraneous to the entire expedition, just some paying tourist to be coddled?*

And for a moment I feel the old despair crush down again. I look over at Gary, plump and equally awkward in his desert dress, and remember how I felt when I saw him overloaded for our European walk. I see in my shadow the weight I have regained in London, and looking down I see my white, fat feet, so out of place on this sand. I feel like a dreaming idiot and wonder what on earth I'm doing here, why I ever thought in my arrogance that I could make this work.

'The first day is always difficult, *lalla*, yes?' Madani has walked up beside me, and he beams, white teeth gleaming out of his lean, cheerful face. I laugh.

'Always, always difficult,' I say, so incredibly grateful to him for smoothing the path that I will do anything to keep the conversation going. 'It will get easier after this.'

'Of course, much easier,' he says.

'And I want to learn everything,' I say. I feel as if I tell Madani this at least five times a day, about everything from cooking to Arabic to hobbling the camels. He always nods and gives the same response he gives now: '*Inshallah*, *lalla*, you are Saharawi by the end of this walk. And me, I learn English!'

I laugh with him and reiterate that, yes, we must do more language exchange. Then I glance across at Gary. My mood has lifted; I want to grin at him conspiratorially, share this moment with him, acknowledge that we're here. We made it. We are still a team.

But Gary has his head down and the MP3 player plugged in under his turban. He's frowning and deep in thought.

Chastened, my smile fades, and I turn back to talk to Madani.

We stumble along clumsily that first day, and it bears more than one resemblance to the last time I set out on a walk. Within only several kilometres, my feet are blistered, sore and aching in the hot nomad sandals; my *melekhva* is awkward and annoying, and constantly in need of tying up and readjusting. I feel sweaty, tired and despondent. The earth beneath our feet is uneven and sandy, and I lose my footing and stagger about. Gary is walking well and seems far more at home. Even though his feet are covered in blisters as quickly as mine, I am reminded of the old stoicism I love about him – he just keeps on plodding. I fall further and further behind and am pathetically grateful when I see M'Barak draw to a halt beneath a clump of thorny acacia trees and begin to unpack the camels.

The tourists from this morning have stopped at the same place. There are two Texan women in the group. They are both wearing shorts, from which poke large, pale, mottled legs. They wear singlet tops, their bra straps on show, and have teamed their outfits with turbans and sunglasses. As they dismount from their camels they throw themselves down in the shade, groaning about their exhaustion and the heat and how hard it all is.

I don't think they have done much camping before. Earlier, one of them asked me how to go to the toilet on a sand dune. Their guide is Kadar's brother, Hamid, whom I'm familiar with from the past week. Hamid's jokes are notoriously crude and politically incorrect. Currently, he's telling the group one about Osama bin Laden. Unfortunately, both of the Texans are looking bemused. Hamid speaks with a thick accent, and when he pronounces bin Laden's name, it is with an Arabic inflection. I'm sure the two girls have no idea who he is talking about. I see an expression of comprehension dawn on the face of one, and she leans forward excitedly. 'Oh!' she says in sudden revelation, 'you mean *bin*

Laaarden!' I hold my breath and seriously hope she will stop there – but she doesn't. 'You see, you're not saying it properly! You gotta say, *bin Laaarden . . .*' And she goes on to give her Saharawi, Arabic-speaking guide a language lesson.

Gary looks at me, and suddenly we are grinning surreptitiously at each other, and I feel less alone in my discomfort. 'How are your feet?' he asks quietly.

'Bloody struggling a bit, actually,' I admit. 'Not such a fan of these sandals, thus far.'

'Me either,' he says. 'I can't believe we've only come ten kilometres or so. It feels like the first day out of Trafalgar Square all over again.'

'I feel really useless, too,' I tell him. 'When we stopped, I wanted to help M'Barak unpack, but he waved me away. I hope they don't keep on treating us like paying guests.'

'I know how you feel,' Gary says. 'I don't want to get in the way, but we do need to learn all this stuff. I am trying to take it easy today – it's only day one – and I'm sure there will be time to work it all out as we go.'

I feel calmed and reassured by the conversation, and by the knowledge that it isn't only me feeling out of step. More than anything, I am cheered by having some kind of exchange with Gary himself at last. I wonder cautiously if we may actually be okay.

We eat some lunch, prepared by Madani and the other young guy walking with Hamid – of course, it would be totally beneath Hamid's dignity to do any menial work. After a couple of hours where all of us pass out beneath the shade, M'Barak wanders off and ropes the camels, who have been grazing, hobbled at the feet. We go through the long packing-up process again, and I suspect it's much like Gary and I and our backpacks in the European leg: over time, the baggage will become streamlined and the task much quicker. For now, it is a tedious procedure, taking well over an hour – even with Gary and me fetching and carrying for the other two.

As we stand to lead the camels away, Hamid comes running up behind one of the animals and lewdly raises his robes, making sexual thrusts in the direction of the camel.

'This one, hey, M'Barak!' he yells in English, to the slightly bemused chuckles of his tourist audience.

'When you get lonely in the desert after long time, you fuck this one, young and sweet, hey?' M'Barak, oblivious to the English words but wise to the gestures, nods in reasonably good humour. Everyone else giggles awkwardly, unsure how to respond to the outright crudity. Hamid likes unsettling his culturally conscious group.

'What do you actually call a baby camel?' one of the Texan tourists asks Hamid earnestly.

'Camel like this? Young camel? You know the French for camel – *chamel*?' Hamid replies, suddenly slipping into serious mode.

'Yes, yes,' the girls nod, looking at him eagerly.

'Well, when the *chamel* is a baby, we call this, '*chamlette*',' says Hamid, perfectly straight-faced.

'Oooohh,' the girls sigh admiringly. '*Chamlette*! How cute!'

'Yes, is very cute. So that what I nickname this camel – now he is called *Chamlette*,' says Hamid decisively. Madani, Gary and I walk on with our faces averted, trying desperately not to howl with laughter.

Even funnier, the name sticks.

We walk for a further ten kilometres, and at last we are away from the others and into what feels like less-inhabited terrain. I know that the entire area from M'Hamid out to Erg Chigaga – the big dunes I visited last trip, about sixty kilometres from the town – is used by both nomads and tourist operators alike, and is a relatively populated locale. But even here, only thirty kilometres away from the town, it's already beginning to feel like 'real' desert to me, not like the scrubby dunes on the edge of town.

We've been walking through a mixture of sandy tracks and hard-packed, gravel-covered terrain. Our first camp is beneath another acacia tree, its acacia branches spreading out in that queer, almost ethereal, sparse cloud evocative of so many photographs of African plains. Surrounding us are low shrubs of various types and, when I ask, M'Barak begins to tell me the names that will become so familiar over time: *atil*, *listrif*, *sabay*. He points out the ones the camels eat, and those they do not.

Madani gasps in horror when I take my sandals off and he looks at the shredded remains of my feet. He and M'Barak consult intently for a moment. M'Barak leans over, picks up my foot and turns it around, tut-tutting. 'Henna,' he says to Madani.

Madani rummages around in the baggage and comes back with a small packet of green powder, which he mixes with water to form a paste. 'I will put this all over the soles of your feet,' he tells me. 'It will help with the pain and protect them.'

'What about Gary's?' I ask. He is also suffering.

'No! No! Not Gary,' says Madani, killing himself laughing as he repeats my comments to M'Barak. M'Barak duly rolls about on the ground where he is lying, fit to bust, and then sits up and shakes his finger at Gary. 'No henna! No!' he says, shaking his head for emphasis.

Gary and I look quizzically at Madani for the explanation. 'Henna is for women only,' he tells us. 'Even for me –' he looks somewhat abashed – 'after I finish doing this for you, *lalla*, I will have henna on my hands for days, and this is not usual for a man, so I will be very embarrassed if anyone sees me. Women make henna on their hands and feet in patterns for weddings – or just for decoration. But for men: *never*. And the way I make it for you now, just a black layer, it is only nomadic women who make it like this, with no pattern. Like this is only for protection. But it will help you.'

I translate his response into English for Gary. M'Barak continues to chuckle, watching Gary's face as he gets the joke, then roars again and slaps the ground as he sees Gary understand. The level of hilarity the whole exchange has induced seems slightly over the top, a bit like adolescent boys sniggering at having to wear a pink sports bib.

The naïve level of sophistication in all gender matters is something that will take time to become accustomed to, and never cease to be annoying. Despite appreciating the cultural gulf, Gary and I are only mildly amused.

As Madani finishes the henna, we hear the sound of animals approaching and look up to see a young nomad wearing a *djellaba* and turban much like M'Barak, driving a herd of about fifty camels, all females with offspring. Many of the camels wear a protective covering over their udders, fastened by a rope around the belly. This is explained when the nomad walks over, unties the covering and works the udder to produce a steady stream of frothy milk straight into a saucepan. He brings it up to where we're sitting and offers it around.

M'Barak drinks deeply, as does Madani, and they pass it to Gary. He takes a good swig and raises an eyebrow at me in an 'it's not so bad' indication. I go to take the bowl, but M'Barak immediately grabs another cup and pours some into it for me. I see the warning in his expression and do not comment, just take it and drink.

The milk is thick and quite sweet. It's not at all offensive, but tastes rich and quite fatty. I have been allergic to cows' milk since infancy, and after a brief swallow I am pretty sure this contains the same animal fats. I feel it curdling in my stomach. But I know I won't be sick, just uncomfortable, so I drink the cup and make appreciative noises.

The nomad makes his camp by ours and joins us for food. Madani makes a separate meal for Gary and me, and we feel alienated as we watch the three men squatting about their plate and eating companionably, talking in Arabic. We eat our prepared dinner in silent discomfort.

As the dusk falls, M'Barak walks out to collect the camels from where they have been grazing and brings them in close to camp. He settles them on their knees with a tug on the rope and a verbal instruction, a 'woosh' sound that I'm already familiar with. On each, he ties a rope around one of their knees, so that they cannot rise onto all fours, and leaves them. They are still able to hop around a little, eating here and there; but they can't stray far from camp.

Madani's already laid out our beds. There has been no need for the tent today, and our mattresses are laid side by side, complete with sheets and camel blankets, slightly set apart from the camp. Again, I feel awkward and uneasy about the servile role he has taken. Equally, I can see Madani's eagerness to be perceived as hard working and would be ungrateful to do anything other than thank him.

Gary and I lie down on our individual mattresses. Something I hadn't thought of a great deal before setting out is just how much the presence of the two guides would inhibit our physical relationship. During the day, it is totally inappropriate for us to touch in any affectionate manner. At night, the deep silence of the desert means that every sound will carry. While this is the one time of day when we can talk freely, unwatched by the others, we still need to be aware of our tone and the fact that voices carry.

I feel the sand beneath my mattress. Looking up, I can see the brilliant, crystalline starscape that hangs over me like a divine kaleidoscope. Behind me I hear the camels snorting and shuffling, munching contentedly. Beyond them, though, there is nothing – no sound of the town, no distant voices carried on the wind – just a deep, profound quietness. I feel the enormous peace of that expanse envelop me, and for the first time I think of the term that will become my own name for the Sahara.

'It's the Big Empty,' I whisper softly, to no one in particular. Beside me, Gary stirs in his sleep; above me, the sky shines down in ancient patterns that I wonder if I will ever understand. Deep within, I feel my adventure begin.

Chapter Three

It's midmorning and we've stopped for our customary break. Already, only a couple of days into the walk, a routine has emerged. After a few hours – three at the most – we pause; *woosh* the camels down; eat some dates, nuts and biscuits; and share a bottle of water that Gary flavours with a sachet of orange powder. I was sceptical when he put it in the supplies, but it's a huge hit with Madani and M'Barak, and I love the sugar hit in the heat as much as anyone. It's become a staple.

When the bottle comes to me, I pour the drink into a cup that is left handy for the purpose, as I've done for the last couple of days. But M'Barak brushes me away this time, says something to Madani in Arabic, then looks at me and smiles.

'*Kulshi nomads!*' he says, nodding happily. I understand his comment: '*kulshi*' is the Arabic word for 'all' or 'everyone'. He is saying that we're all nomads together, and there is no need for me to drink separately. But I am confused.

'But he put the milk in a different cup when the nomad was with us the other night,' I say to Madani. 'I thought that because I was a woman it was not okay for me to drink from the same cup as you.'

Madani translates, and M'Barak kicks his legs in the air, as he always does when he finds something particularly funny, and laughs.

'M'Barak and I thought it was *you* who didn't want to share with us,' Madani explains. 'With a nomad who we don't know, or a stranger to our camp – yes – we will always give you a separate cup because that man may be a very strict Muslim. But also, within our camp, we are family – and so there is no need for you to drink separately. For other men, you are *our* family, so we cannot let their lips touch the same cup as yours – that would be disrespectful. But here, in our camp, it is fine for us all to share, as long as you don't mind. And to eat together. While we are "*fee Sahara*" [in the desert], then we are family. All right?'

M'Barak nods earnestly throughout this speech and looks anxiously at me. I smile and nod my agreement, and he nods back in satisfaction. Gary is confused, since he doesn't understand most of the exchange, so I translate for him.

I'm rapidly tiring of the endless process of translation. From M'Barak to Madani in Arabic, Madani to me in French, and me to Gary in English; it's exhausting and frustrating to have a conversation. While it is often possible to communicate more quickly with sign language, facial expression and a little willingness to understand, there is a lot of room for confusion. Obviously, it is Madani and I who talk the most, as we form the link between Gary and M'Barak as well as ourselves. At times I find myself simply chatting to Madani in a queer mélange of French, Arabic and English that the two of us have nicknamed 'Padani' and not bothering to translate.

With every conversation I feel as if I am learning more and more about the language and culture. I feel almost guilty; it is more knowledge that I have that Gary doesn't. Gary is undoubtedly trying his hardest to follow everything. I watch him laughing and talking in hand signs with both Madani and M'Barak, particularly with the latter. He has a good rapport and is characteristically patient with M'Barak's endless attention.

But, perhaps exacerbated by the long months of walking before, I'm tired of the role of translator. It's just another area where I begin to feel and express frustration rather than understanding, as if I'm actually trying to drive Gary away. Gary, of course, is increasingly withdrawn, and his withdrawal fuels my unwillingness to have sympathy with his language difficulties. It's a rotten cycle, and I somehow feel helpless in it.

That night we camp among small dunes, just west of the bigger dunes, at Erg Chigaga. As I did three years ago, I climb as high as I can and look out over the endless sea of sand.

'How long will it take us to cross it?' I ask M'Barak, via Madani. He shrugs. 'A day,' Madani answers.

'*What*?' I ask, thinking I must have misheard. 'I mean, how long will it take to cross all of those dunes?' I indicate beyond us, to where the golden dunes stretch out, seemingly into infinity.

'Yes – a day, like this. We walk around, over there' – Madani indicates a route into the smaller dunes to our west – 'and at the end we will come out onto Lake Iriki, an old dried lake. Now, *that* will be hard walking.' And he and M'Barak get into a discussion about crossing the barren expanse of the lake.

But I'm barely listening.

Three years ago, I sat up on the top of those dunes and looked out into what I believed was the real heart of the Sahara, an awe-inspiring expanse that I somehow imagined must stretch clear across Northern Africa, interspersed regularly by tiny oases, like the one we had passed only a day ago – a small palmeraie surrounding a well, with good grazing for the animals. As I examine this thought, I realise how utterly ridiculous it is; I've seen photos of diverse landscapes and already know from where we have walked that sand is only a small part of it. I read the book by Marq de Villiers, *Sahara: the Life of the Great Desert*, in which he carefully describes the many geographical vagaries encapsulated under the one generic term, Sahara, which is in effect simply the Arabic word for 'desert'.

But somehow in my mind, my only real memory of this place, my only deep association, is that day in 2002 when I sat on top of the dunes at Erg Chigaga and dreamed of my walk. How impassable these dunes had seemed then – how incomprehensible! And yet here I am, with my own camels and camp, about to cross the expanse – in one day. I sit with my knees up and shake my head in wonder at the strangeness of it all, and at the bizarre assumptions I had made while my logical side slept.

Later that afternoon I head off into the dunes with a kettle of water and my toiletries for a wash. Hidden in a deep bowl, far from view, I strip down and wash myself in the late-afternoon sun from top to toe. Around me the world is silent and still, and the sand lies in perfect ripples everywhere but where my tracks enter the natural chamber, and where I'm standing. There's something perfectly delicious about standing in that wild, beautiful place, bathed in warmth and light, feeling clean and healthy and so alive. I pull my cotton shift on over myself and wrap back up in *melekhva*, calm and content inside. I feel as if that bath washed away the grime of London and tension in M'Hamid. As I dress, I feel as if I am pulling the cloak of the Big Empty around me.

We sit up on a dune swapping stories and taking photos. M'Barak has just discovered the immediacy of digital photography and is posing in a variety of increasingly bizarre positions – inside the camel panniers, spread-eagled in the sand – imploring Gary to take his picture over and over. Gary obliges, and M'Barak cackles with delight when he looks at the pictures on the tiny screen and is spurred onto even crazier antics.

He has a clown's sense of humour, happily descending into slapstick at the slightest opportunity. Endlessly inquisitive, he will prod and poke at our equipment, or lie barely inches from my face as I write in my journal. He watches the process intently and then begs for a chance to use the pen himself, demonstrating the limited Arabic he can write. He's not happy unless he's involved somehow in an interaction or actually doing something. If he needs solitude, he'll wander far away from the camp to find it, on the pretext perhaps of looking for the camels.

Perhaps most ironic of all, although M'Barak has an ingenious knack of being able to fix virtually anything with only a piece of wire or a rubber band, he possesses an equal propensity to break almost everything merely by looking at it, like the radio or my knife. One cannot help but wonder if his magical abilities in the realm of repair stem from a case of sheer necessity. In the case of the knife, my pride and joy which I bought after long deliberation in Spain, I take one look at the ragged edge where he has attempted to sharpen it on a stray rock, and simply hand the useless blade over in its sheath as a gift. Crowing with delight, the knife becomes M'Barak's most treasured possession, and I will never see it off his waist belt for the walk's duration.

But as yet all of these issues are only minor irritants, lost in the greater picture of our adventure into the desert. They are glitches that will be ironed out with time, and I don't dwell on them. Today of all days, I am too excited to worry – tomorrow we'll walk through the dunes.

Gary is tremendously patient with M'Barak's endless tinkering and curiosity, even though it must drive him nuts. It's the times when I watch him, softly smiling and gently removing something from M'Barak's grasp to show him the correct way to use it, that I feel lost in love for him. His wry chuckles of amusement at the antics of the older man; the way he quietly keeps himself busy, often producing something surprising – like a lovely new way of cooking chicken, when I am struggling with the one-pot cooking process. All of these things touch me unbearably, make me want to lean over and throw myself into his arms and never leave.

But there are always two other people about, and the moment always passes. Worst of all, occasionally Gary looks up to see me watching him, and it seems that his face closes over guardedly when he does. And back up go both of our stupid, calloused walls.

That night, we all talk about our camels. After a few days, their separate personalities have begun to emerge.

Chamlette is the teenage boy of the pack. Loud, feisty and always keen to lead, he carries a heavy load, doesn't like being tied behind any of the other camels and is game for anything. Oddly enough, though, for an uncut male, he seems to show no interest in any of the female camels – *nagas*, in Arabic – which sometimes pass. We joke that maybe he bats for the other side.

Mimi is so called in Arabic because of his white nose, which looks like it has been dipped in milk. He's a big, strong, solid camel – but reluctant to take the lead and easily shaken off balance by loud noises or sudden movement. We usually tie him behind Chamlette.

Strong yet gentle-natured, Zarwel is my personal favourite. He's named for his colour, a grey-brown tone, and carries the heaviest loads every day, rarely complaining as he struggles to his feet. Zarwel plods steadily by my side, never missing a step. I usually lead him with the fourth camel, Habil, tied on behind.

'*Habil*' means 'crazy' in Arabic. We joke that this camel smokes the peace pipe when we're not looking. The poorest performer of the camels, Habil literally falls over his own feet, refuses to get up if the load looks at all heavy, and behaves in an unpredictable and somewhat eccentric fashion – suddenly deciding to try to eat turban, for example, or dropping to his knees in the middle of a walk for no reason at all.

The first time he does this, I'm rather startled: '*Fuck.*'

M'Barak looks at me questioningly, quite possibly relating the expletive back to Hamid's prolific use.

Soon after, Habil goes down again. M'Barak looks at me. 'Fuck?' he says.

I crack up, along with Gary and Madani. Delighted with this reaction, M'Barak says it again with great feeling. 'Fuck!'

Within seconds, highly chuffed with the impact he's making, M'Barak goes on merrily: 'Fuck! Fucken Fuck! Fucken! Fucken Fucken!'

By the time we can draw our breath, he has fallen in love with the word. Even after Madani explains that it is the most profane of profanities, nothing halts M'Barak. I just hope like hell that he will remember, when he meets an English-speaking tourist, that it isn't meant to be used with total abandon.

I'm leading two of the camels, Zarwel and Habil, through the sand behind Madani, who is with Chamlette and Mimi. Gary and I are side by side and at various times swap over the lead. Sometimes Madani hands his rope to Gary.

M'Barak is running ahead of us, up and down dunes, in and out of sight. He will mount a dune and then come running back towards us, waving his stick excitedly, yelling directions to

Madani and, to a lesser extent, us. His stick shows exactly where to lead the camels, and if we deviate by even a small amount, he yells furiously and comes back to hound us, grabbing the camels and leading them back onto the route he has mentally marked.

We weave our way in between the dunes, rarely needing to mount them. M'Barak's path inevitably takes that of least resistance, through firm sand. Even when we are climbing a tall dune, we are on the face that is packed tightly and on less of an angle for the camels to climb. Whenever we crest a dune and need to descend, M'Barak's demeanour becomes even more excitable and tense. I learn very quickly that we must descend slowly and with great care. I'm used to horses, which can usually be left to find their own footing. But camels, and especially heavily loaded camels, need to be nursed on the downhills, never left to gain speed, and gently guided to more even ground. M'Barak runs beside me on these descents, occasionally grabbing the rope from me when he feels the camels are starting to quicken their pace, correcting their line when he sees them taking a course that may be difficult.

In and out, over and through the dunes he weaves, never stopping, always running, looking, yelling, correcting. Our path negotiates dune after dune, as we scramble up, almost needing to run to stay in front of the camels. They gamely stride upwards, maintaining their momentum to balance their loads. Then we wade down the deep, soft sand on the other side, making sure we're following the exact path Madani took.

I want to pause and take photographs of this extraordinary place, surrounded on every side by tall, imposing walls of sand. But the pace never slows, and the concentration etched on M'Barak's face warns me not to halt. I'm tired and puffing, and the camels are breathing heavily. Gary stops sometimes to pull the camera out and photograph our progress. He seems much more collected, and I'm impressed by the way he manages to take great photos in quick moments, then runs to catch up. I'm frustrated with the clumsy swathe of *melekhva* and tie it up around my waist. I sling the top part lazily over my head, almost turban-like, and fix it anywhere to keep it out of my face and from wrapping about my legs. I couldn't care less how I look.

We halt for a drink and something quick to eat; but M'Barak is tense, and we don't stop for long.

'Will we camp in these dunes tonight?' I ask Madani dreamily, my mind drifting off into images of a romantic night lying under the stars.

M'Barak throws me the type of glance one reserves for total idiots when Madani repeats my question. His retort is quick and dismissive, as he gestures to the surrounding terrain.

'Um, no, *lalla*,' says Madani, smiling apologetically. 'You see, here there's no shelter for us, and nothing for the camels to eat. We must get out of these dunes before tonight.'

I look around. There is nothing within eyesight but sand. No tree for shade, no hint of foliage for the camels to nibble. I suddenly realise that every day when we've stopped, the camels have eaten incessantly. Feeling stupid that I had not really noticed this before, I ask Madani, 'How long can the camels go without eating?'

Madani shakes his head and laughs, obviously ready to answer but deciding to refer it on to M'Barak, who is listening carefully.

'Every day, the camels need to eat. Drinking, no. For water, the camels can last many days, particularly if the feed is good and full of moisture. But eating? Your camels must eat every day – and eat well. They are walking a long way and carrying a heavy load. They need to eat well or they will be skinny and weak. You want fat, healthy camels, and so always you need to make sure they are eating properly. This is the most important thing. You are walking long distances, and every day. If your camels are weak, you will stop. First is camels. Always, the camels come first.'

He stresses every point, jabbing the sand. I sit back and once again feel the weight of my ignorance pressing in on me. I don't even understand what kind of plants the camels actually eat. I think that if Madani and M'Barak disappeared right at this moment, not only would I have absolutely no idea where I am or where I should go, but I also wouldn't know what to do with the camels when I got there – how to hobble them, even how to unpack them. I would have no idea what they could and couldn't eat, nor how to catch them when they were finished eating.

Tracking them, putting the ropes through their mouths, saddling them . . . I can't even imagine where to begin.

I stand up from where I have been resting and feel the strain in my leg muscles, tired after only a few hours of stumbling through the dunes. I look around me at the dull sky and magnificently empty landscape, my camels resting peacefully on the ground, and I think: *This is it, Paula. No more practice runs. You are here. This is the walk. The time for being a tourist is over now; you have to learn all of this stuff. What happens if things go wrong? How would you survive? You need to learn – and fast.*

'Shall we go?' I say to M'Barak. He leaps to his feet and I follow in his footsteps, in a direction I do not know and along a path I do not have the skill to see.

It's well after midday when I notice the landscape suddenly changing. Instead of the golden-yellow, almost orange hues of the deep dunes, the sand has become bright white. It seems somehow uneven and rough. There are some scrubby, sticklike foliage poking through the sand. The dunes have become smaller. Increasingly, we walk an easy path through them, rather than needing to scale their sides. The earth is now hard-packed beneath my feet.

For the first time in hours I take my concentration away from where we are walking and turn to look behind us. In our immediate wake, the dunes loom, tall and steep. We are through them; we are actually out the other side.

We walk out onto a hard dusty plain. M'Barak points off to the right, and I can see the trampled earth and concrete trough of a well. There are several nomadic women clustered about the trough. In the immediate vicinity I can see two makeshift tents, and there are goats and some camels wandering about.

'We will camp over there,' M'Barak indicates, pointing towards a verdant acacia tree surrounded by clusters of foliage. It's perhaps 500 metres from the well, and slightly further from the other tents.

'You must never camp close to a well,' Madani explains as we walk. 'Unless you are very isolated. Wells are for everybody to use; often there are many people camped nearby, and they all need to use the water. Everybody washes their clothes and waters their animals. It's not a place for one person, one family, to own, so always camp at a respectful distance.'

Until today, we've had no need to pitch the tent. The weather has been calm and slightly overcast, the nights still. But today M'Barak looks at the sky, the sun almost red behind a dusty film, and shakes his head. 'We need to put the tent up,' he directs Madani.

We work together to secure the tent. Gary and I grow frustrated as Madani and M'Barak operate a little like a Laurel and Hardy production, getting caught up in the tent folds, laughing hysterically at their confusion. Gary attempts to impose a workable system, but Madani and M'Barak simply laugh and carry on. The tent is set up eventually – but it's lopsided and not at all stable.

M'Barak simply shrugs and wanders off to commune with the camels. Madani and I laugh about it and start preparing lunch. Gary shakes his head in weary resignation and tries to fix the tent. I sympathise with his frustration – last year, walking through Europe, we had the tent construction down to a fine, three-minute art, and it is impossibly annoying to deal with two people who not only aren't interested in working as a team, but who simply don't seem to care. At the end of a long day walking, small things like these can be wearing. However, I am reluctant to push the issue. It's another thing I put on the list of irritants to be dealt with at another time.

The day is a long way from done. Sitting in the tent on the sandy floor, preparing the lunch with Madani, the heat is intense and the air thick with flies. Outside the wind is beginning to pick up, so it's necessary to stay inside to prepare the food. The tent air is deathly still and sweat crawls down my face as the flies buzz about my head incessantly. I am wearing only my cotton trousers and top, as Madani and M'Barak have told me that once inside the tent I must dress comfortably – they don't expect me to wear *melekhva* here. So I'm totally unprepared when a little brown face surrounded by with wild, tousled hair, pokes curiously around the tent opening.

Madani greets our visitor – a girl, no more than six or seven, with a big smile, and she sidles inside and squats a few metres away, staring at me intensely and firing questions at Madani. After a short time she pokes her head out of the opening and yells something. Seconds later, another head appears in the doorway, then another. Within minutes, the tent is packed to the gills with children from the neighbouring tents, all squatting, watching with intense curiosity as I chop and prepare the food.

The girls wear layers of cast-off clothes: dirty dresses over long cotton leggings, mismatched jumpers over the top. They all wear a form of head covering, which even the youngest – perhaps four – deftly rearranges and knots. On seeing me about to reach for the water canteen to rinse my hands and knife, one of the younger girls, about five years old, quickly lifts the canteen. Indicating for me to hold my hands out, she pours just enough from the heavy container, carefully replaces the lid and puts it away. There's something about her actions that I find incredibly fascinating; I wonder how many five-year-old children I know who would've been able to anticipate my need in the first place, let alone have the motor skills and confidence to act so efficiently.

We smile and laugh together. I pause occasionally to take their photograph, showing them the results in the digital window. This causes much hilarity, covering of faces and giggling. The older boys – perhaps aged up to nine – squat by Madani and talk seriously, as adults would, about grazing, water and rainfall. From them we learn that all the children in this tent belong to only two families.

There must be at least eleven children here!

'No TV,' says Madani to me in English, and we both giggle.

After lunch I am exhausted, ready to just curl up and sleep. But M'Barak is talking animatedly to Madani, who then turns to me.

'You should do your washing while we are here, *lalla*,' Madani says. M'Barak is nodding furiously in the background. 'Also, if you want to make a proper *hammam*' – and here he blushes a little – 'you do it here, where there is water.'

'Of course.' I scramble to my feet, shaking off my exhaustion. Not for a second do I want to appear either lazy or unwilling to contribute. 'Um, Madani,' I begin, 'how do you wash clothes out here?'

My question is not as stupid as it may sound. The only container I can see that could possibly do for washing is a metal cooking pot, and I'm guessing that it's not exactly appropriate to wash my dirty knickers in the same pot I cook dinner in. We've only a small, cut-off container to fill the trough with for the camels to drink.

But M'Barak pulls down a heavy container made from tractor tyre. I've been helping to pack this onto the back of the camels every day since we left, without actually asking what it's for. I saw M'Barak feed the camels grain out of it one day when we were still camped back near M'Hamid, and so in my mind it was a makeshift feeder should we need it. More than once I wondered why we bothered.

Now I see that it doubles not only as a washing trough for clothes but also, as Madani explains, as a temporary water store should we find a water source with no concrete trough for the camels to drink from.

Madani and I walk over to the well, carrying the black rubber thing between us, the clothes and detergent inside. There are several women at the well, all squatting, fiercely scrubbing and pounding their washing inside similar containers. They stand and greet Madani and M'Barak, who has brought the camels over to drink.

M'Barak immediately lapses into friendly, familiar conversation. Madani explains that these nomads are Berber, and they have family in common with M'Barak. Their conversation is easy and open – far from what I had expected between men and women in this remote place. They laugh a lot, making direct eye contact, obviously finding immense enjoyment and good humour in their conversation.

One of the women squats down beside me and indicates that I should watch her. M'Barak hauls up a bucket of water from the well and tips it into her wash bucket. She immerses an armful of clothes – I inwardly smile to see her separate the lights from the darks – adds washing powder, sits back on her haunches and starts rubbing the clothes together.

I follow her example. M'Barak alternates between hauling up

buckets of water to put into the trough for the camels and pouring them into our wash basins. I am amazed at how many times the woman beside me tips her dirty water onto the ground and replaces it with clean. Accustomed to strictly rationing my water, her actions seem incredibly wasteful. I mention something of this to Madani, and he chuckles and shakes his head.

'No, there was good rain this year, plenty of water, use as much as you like.' He waves off my concerns. But it's something I am uncomfortable with; pouring out contaminated water onto the ground right next to a water source seems to me irresponsible. Using such copious amounts of it goes directly against the grain. I try to be as sparing as possible, but the woman beside me clucks at my efforts, and I realise she thinks I am unhygienic. I then copy her style of over three wash-and-rinse cycles, and my clothes come out cleaner than ever before. I couldn't say the same for my conscience.

While I am washing, M'Barak has taken the ropes out of the camels' mouths and threaded them instead through their nostrils. Madani explains that they cannot drink properly with the rope looped under their tongues. I notice that he is always careful to hobble the camels before moving the rope from mouth to nose.

'Otherwise the camel can run away, *lalla*,' Madani explains. 'And to catch a camel that is not hobbled, and has no rope on – this is very, very difficult.'

Finally, the washing and watering is done, and we wander back to the tent, again carrying the now heavy container of washing between us. I am not convinced of the efficacy of the wash container. It seemed to leak an enormous amount of water. I rather think a bucket would be far more productive, but I don't say anything.

I begin to tie the washing to the ropes on the tent, proud of my ingenuity. But M'Barak clucks at me reprovingly and grabs a couple items of clothing. Despite my desire to learn everything, it's exhausting to always be corrected, particularly when it's my knickers under dispute. I feel a momentary rush of irritation and want to grab my clothing back and hang it where I fancy. But I push it down and follow him to the acacia tree.

He stakes my clothing carefully over the long, sharp thorns poking out from the tree. His idea is brilliant. My clothes are spiked fast. They flap merrily in the breeze, but are not likely to fly anywhere. The only downside, as I discover when I go to remove them, is that picking them off the tree can be a painstaking process. Regardless, they dry in record time, and it's bliss to have nice-smelling, clean clothes.

I fall into bed that night shattered. Each day feels like a marathon. Unlike when I was in Europe and the actual walking was the trial to be endured, here it's as if every task, every communication, is a chore and a challenge. There's no downtime, no moment like in Europe when I could just throw my pack down and sink into oblivion. When we stop here, there are camels to unpack, tea to be make and ritual to observe. There's endless translation and incessant company. I feel I must always be 'on': friendly, open, willing to learn and patient. I can't simply decide not to do dinner tonight, or to do my washing tomorrow. There are four of us – a team – and there's no room to think about the individual. Gary and my relationship is part of a broader dynamic, and we rarely have the time or space to discuss anything other than issues pertaining to the walk.

The only time it seems that I can have peace is here, in the precious moments before sleep, lying under the camel blankets on the thin mattress that goes beneath the pack saddles. I lie beside Gary and look up at the stars blazing fiercely, feeling the tension drain from my body.

We head out onto Lake Iriki early. M'Barak was up and racing before dawn, the tension in his voice palpable. I know he's worried about this walk. Madani has already explained to me that it's a long, barren stretch, with no shade or feed. In the high sun the heat refracts from the ancient waterbed, causing baking conditions and dehydration.

We're on our way by sunrise. The day is overcast with a light breeze blowing, and M'Barak relaxes slightly. We move quickly out into the wide, flat expanse. For the first time since we left M'Hamid, I find a rhythm, my sandals steadily tramping across the earth. The camels plod calmly behind, and I walk hypnotically, falling into that wonderful meditative space that I remember so well from Europe. I revel in the pure joy of those first few hours when the cool morning sits easily and the pain has yet to sink in. I inhale the empty stillness of the desert morning and notice its gentle awakening: the rosy pink on the horizon, the slow creep of golden sunlight across the flat, dry lake bed. A few drops of moisture hang on the last pieces of foliage. As the day grows and the heat arrives the moisture quickly evaporates. The foliage disappears not long after.

We walk for miles without rest. I notice how free I feel without the burden of the pack. Now that I'm actually walking, rather than scrambling to find my feet or worrying about the camels and dunes, I can appreciate how truly liberating it is to stride along upright. My feet are certainly less comfortable in the flat, unforgiving nomad's sandals than they were in boots, but my body feels light. My legs feel strong beneath me and I'm thrilled to be walking, really walking, once again.

We trace the edge of the dry lake, and into uneven, rocky country where there is endless feed for the camels but the terrain is hard and uncomfortable under foot. It's real Berber country, M'Barak tells me.

The uneven rocks topple me off balance, even as I try to find my rhythm. Ahead of me M'Barak scrambles nimbly about like a mountain goat.

'*Labas, Toula?*' he calls to me. '*Labas*' is the ubiquitous greeting or inquiry after the wellbeing of another in Hassaniya Arabic – similar to asking, 'okay?' All the nomads I've met use it liberally, so there is nothing unusual in the exchange for me. The really amusing thing about it is the fact that M'Barak can't quite wrap his head around my name.

'*Paula,*' I correct him, smiling. I don't really care what he calls me, but I think it worthwhile to let him know he has it wrong.

'*Toula? Howla?*' M'Barak persists, shaking his head in confusion.

'Don't worry,' I say, 'you can just call me "Goddess" if you like.' Obviously I am joking, and in English, but M'Barak picks up on the word and smiles broadly.

'Goddess!' he says triumphantly. It comes out, in his heavy accent, sounding exactly like 'Good Arse'.

'Good Arse!' he repeats, delighted with the sensation he has caused. '*Labas*, Good Arse!'

We walk on, laughing so hard we can barely hold our balance. Every time we begin to subside, M'Barak, without turning around, will yell out: 'Good Arse!' And we laugh again.

That night, after we've eaten the plate of delicious tajine that Madani miraculously produces every night, we do our customary swapping of a few phrases.

'M'Barak wants to know how to say "Good night" in English,' Madani asks me in French. I tell him. M'Barak retreats, muttering the phrase over and over.

Shortly after this exchange, Gary and I crawl into our bedrolls to sleep. From the general direction of M'Barak's skinny lump under blankets, we hear a clear salute: 'Goodnight, Good Arse!'

Gary and I chuckle together. I love these moments with him, love hearing his quiet laughter.

The following morning, I hear M'Barak rousing Madani. He uses the young guy's last name, so the morning refrain is usually: '*Hannana! HANNANA!*' with increasing urgency, until Madani – not a morning person by any stretch – emerges bleary-eyed from his blankets. But this morning the chorus is slightly different:

'*Hannana! HANNANA!*' – pause – '*Fucken Hannana!*'

Gary and I stifle our giggles under the blankets.

M'Barak comes back from attending to the camels – he has taken the rope off their knee, and hock-hobbled them so they can graze – and we sit down to eat breakfast. He beams at us.

'Good morning, Good Arse! Fucken!' he declares.

Gary and I are laughing so much we can barely breathe.

'I think we'd better explain,' I say between gasps.

I quickly explain the play on words to Madani, who also begins to howl with laughter. He turns and explains to M'Barak, whose face immediately clouds over in distressed comprehension. He turns to us in dismay, horrified that he may have offended both Gary and me by referring to my butt.

'He says he is very, very sorry,' Madani translates. I can understand anyway; M'Barak is saying *'smelhiya, smelhiya'* over and over again, which, having made endless faux pas since arriving in Morocco, I know all too well – it means 'excuse me'.

'Tell him it's absolutely fine, no worries,' I say to Madani. Then, looking at M'Barak, I say, *'Macayn mushkil*, M'Barak. *Macayn mushkil.'* His face brightens. *'Macayn mushkil?'* He asks. Gary and I nod, smiling. *'Hamdullah, Hamdullah,'* he says. Praise God.

I think it a rather delicious irony that the first real phrase I master in Arabic is *'Macayn mushkil'*. It literally means 'there is no problem', and is used exactly like 'no worries' in Australia. I find it tremendously useful. As we all make continual mistakes, misunderstand each other and laugh it off, *macayn mushkil* is like the diplomatic glue that holds us together. I find there is very little I cannot apply it to.

That afternoon M'Barak makes bread in a sand oven. For days now, I've been helping to load and unload the huge sacks of flour onto the camels, and wondering what was the point in carrying them. Now I watch, fascinated, as M'Barak carefully mixes up the two different types of flour with some salt, sugar and yeast into spongy dough. He covers the saucepan and lets it rise in the sun, and we gather wood to make a fire in the soft sand in the dried creek bed.

'The trick is in the sand,' Madani tells me. 'You need good sand to make a good oven.' They build the fire into a blazing roar and feed it for about twenty minutes. Then they let it die down to a pile of glowing coals and minimal flame. M'Barak lays the dough out on a plastic sheet and pummels it into a round, inch-thick loaf – just like the damper my mum used to make when we camped as kids. Madani scrapes a hole in the centre of the coals, so that the hot sand beneath is exposed, and M'Barak deftly drops the loaf flat onto the sand. They push the coals and sand quickly back over the loaf, taking care not to leave any holes where the air may hiss through. After about ten minutes, M'Barak scrapes back the coals and taps the loaf, listening for the hollow sound that indicates it is cooked through. Then he lifts the loaf out with two sticks, turns it over and drops it back in, scraping the coals over once more.

Just as we have gathered round the mat, salivating, and said '*Bismillah*', another nomad comes past with his goats. The men pull back from eating, looking shamefaced.

'What? What is it?' I ask Madani.

'You remember it is Ramadan, *lalla*?' Madani mumbles, looking at me in embarrassment.

'I'd forgotten,' I say, bewildered. It was the first day of Ramadan, the traditional month-long fast on the Muslim calendar, the day we began walking from M'Hamid.

'But you and M'Barak have been eating the same as Gary and me – that's why I forgot,' I say. 'I thought it was forbidden for you to eat during daylight hours?'

'The Qur'an says there is an exception for some people – like, for example, people who are making long voyages,' Madani explains. M'Barak is nodding furiously. But the passing nomad, when it is translated for him, shakes his head and walks away. It's obvious that he is rather more strict in his adherence to Islamic custom.

Sniggering like naughty schoolboys, Madani and M'Barak wait until the nomad is out of sight; then they fall upon the bread and dips with unseemly appetite.

'Fucken nomads,' says M'Barak.

The most profound changes come about in the smallest, most innocuous ways. Eating is one – without even realising it, the dinner ritual becomes commonplace. The water bottle is passed around, and a small amount is put into a cup. Each of us turns away from the dinner circle while our neighbour pours the water over our hands, wrists and fingers. This is a ritual washing performed in a delicate, yet functional manner. There is no cloth, so we all shake dry. We then utter '*Bismillah*' as one and scoop the food up with our right hands. I know nothing more comforting and communal than the ritual of eating together in this fashion, of sharing every morsel on the plate with grace and mutual consideration. Interestingly, I never eat to total fullness – it seems right and just to leave the excess behind, even if I am hungry.

After only days, I am baffled when I think about our Western practice of individual plates, knives and forks. I find it difficult to imagine being back in the land of tables and cutlery – it seems slightly ridiculous, almost pretentious. I want to go home and encourage everyone I know to sit on the floor and eat out of a communal plate; I want them to feel how this process connects them with their family and friends – even strangers. I cannot help but wonder, if we all ate from the same plate more often, would we have more empathy and humour for each other?

Eating becomes another example of the way in which I am drawn into life here, swallowed down the rabbit hole, adapting my own behaviour to what is around me. And with every small change that takes hold, I lose something of myself; another tiny piece of self falls away. Sometimes, as I walk, I wonder what I will find beneath, after all of these pieces have gone, or if there will be anything left of the person I once thought I knew.

Chapter Four

A week or so into our walk, we camp several kilometres from a small town. We plan to walk in to buy supplies, water the camels and fill our jerry cans. We're also looking forward to having a proper wash in the town *hammam*. We've covered a couple of hundred kilometres, and for me the time has been a frenzy of learning and adjustment. It already feels as if we have been out here for weeks.

We all wander in, leaving our belongings under a tree, wrapped in a blanket and tied with a cord. 'Nobody will touch anything, *lalla*,' Madani reassures me. It's a strange feeling to walk away and leave everything we own secured with no more than a camel blanket.

The town is reminiscent of many that Gary and I walked through the previous year on our way to M'Hamid, but after only this short time out in the desert quietude, I feel overwhelmed by the frantic activity. It's market day. The centre of town is a knot of stallholders with their produce lying on the ground, women haggling and men lounging around, smoking and talking in their best robes, in from the desert for a day to buy or trade.

The houses are low mud brick, inset with iron doors, and all sport satellite dishes on their roofs. This far north, the towns actually have electricity; Morocco is in the middle of a development boom that is revolutionising life in these small towns. The first 1500 kilometres of our walk, from M'Hamid to Tan-Tan, is in the northern part of the Moroccan Sahara and thus passes small towns such as these every few weeks. There is a school, gendarme office and, of course, a mosque. There are several wells, from which most of the town-dwellers take their water. Only a few homes have their own supply.

We go with M'Barak to the well in the centre of the village and leave him there, chatting to the gaggle of gawking locals who are intrigued by our little band. I am suddenly uncomfortable. If I used to find it a little daunting walking through small villages wearing a pack, in local dress and with four camels in tow, now Gary and I present a more bizarre spectacle than ever before. It's already afternoon, and we have supplies to buy and errands to run, not to mention having a wash. I begin to feel flustered and tense, an experience I will come to associate with hectic stops in desert towns. After the huge, empty peace, it seems abrasive and confronting.

Gary goes to hunt some things down. Madani and I wander through the market, buying the fresh fruit and vegetables that continue to be widely available this close to arable land. I am surprised by the variety of fresh produce – it's difficult to think we are in the desert when it's still possible to buy fresh pomegranates. We also replenish our bread supplies. 'Soon we will run out of regular towns,' Madani says. 'Then we will need to make our own bread every day.' To be honest, I am looking forward to it.

Far more important than the supplies, I am in town to go to the *hammam*. I am dying to wash the sand out of my hair. My scalp is dry and itchy, and every night when I brush my hair out it seems to smell a little worse. We are just about to find the bathhouse when an old, battered police vehicle pulls up beside us. The police eye Madani and me suspiciously from the window, and order us closer.

They start a conversation with Madani in Arabic so that I am excluded. Their eyes examine me with frank interest as they question Madani, who begins to sweat slightly, his tone increasingly pleading. I decide I've had enough of standing on the sidelines and interrupt.

'What is this about, please?' I ask abruptly in French.

'We need to see his identity card,' the gendarme replies.

'He works for me. He is my cook and cameleer,' I say. 'Why do you need to see his card?'

'Because he needs to be qualified to work in that capacity,' says the gendarme.

I am not even prepared to go down this route. In Morocco, every citizen at the age of fifteen applies for and is given an identity card. Much more than a simple ID, this card describes the profession of its bearer – and limits the bearer to exactly that profession, particularly in the area of tourism. In order to work with tourists, the individual's ID card must bear the title of 'guide'; otherwise they are open to immediate arrest.

I had discussed all of this with Kadar before I left. The way we got around it was by virtue of the fact that both Madani and M'Barak are technically employees of Kadar, who *is* a licensed operator – a title which involved no qualification other than a hefty donation to the local authorities. I've a letter stating that our expedition is being run by Kadar and that Madani and M'Barak are working for him, under our supervision.

I explain all of this to the gendarme, being polite yet firm. He is becoming increasingly agitated, and for a moment I realise that this could end badly for us, since my letter is back at camp in a secure folder, along with my passport and Madani's ID card. The gendarme is blustery and belligerent, and I rather suspect that he is looking for a bribe.

I look him straight in the eye and try to bluff it out.

'My presence here is entirely legal. I've the correct visa; I've paid a *substantial* sum to the agency in M'Hamid in order to complete this expedition; and I'm also a journalist who writes for' – I drop the name of a well-known guidebook. 'I would hate to mention the fact that in the first town in Morocco that I reached, after a long stretch in the desert, I was unlawfully detained – or threatened in any way.'

I hold my stance and don't back down. One thing I learned in Morocco the last time I was here is that there are two phrases in English that every Moroccan who has any dealings with tourists understands: 'guidebook' and 'journalist'.

The first means tourist influx and good profits. The second can mean either big success or big trouble. Morocco has been on the receiving end of both good and bad reports, and it is a brave man who would willingly risk making his actions vulnerable to either.

My ploy is successful and the gendarme backs off, muttering that he will be out to see us later on that day to check our ID, before gunning his car and disappearing to harass some other hapless wanderer.

I feel slightly light-headed by our success; Madani is cavorting about in triumph at having outsmarted the uniforms. It's my first real encounter with what will become a depressingly familiar process.

The *hammam* is marked by a stamped picture of a woman over an innocuous doorway. I would not have found it without Madani. I head into the damp warmth and pay the lady behind the window.

I became used to *hammams* the last time I was in Morocco, although I didn't have many and went more as a novelty. But today I am in desperate need of a good scrub. I head into the changing room and strip down to my knickers. The woman behind the counter gives me two buckets. I already have a cup to use as a dipper, and my toiletries are in a plastic bag.

I walk into the wet room, which is nothing more than a large concrete chamber. Taps running hot and cold water are set into the wall. I fill both of my buckets, mixing the hot and cold so that I've two full buckets of warm water. I sit down on the piece of plastic matting I brought with me for just this purpose, dip my cup into the bucket and pour the water over my head.

The water runs over me like a waterfall. I pour and pour, until I am drenched, and begin washing my hair with sweet-smelling shampoo.

The room is full of women, all stripped to their knickers. Their young children run around and try to avoid being scrubbed down, playing and frolicking in the water buckets.

I take forever over my bath. I use a black olive paste that I bought in the market. The women here use it as an exfoliant. I slather it on and then scrub it off with a rough mitt. After a cursory glance, the other women leave me to my bathing, immersed in their own rituals. They are a sociable lot, gossiping happily and scrubbing each other's backs, washing their children and laughing. When I try to reach around to use the hand mitt on my own back, a woman next to me takes my arm and, smiling, turns me around and scrubs my back with long, relaxing strokes. After only a few days in solely male company, it's bliss to be touched with such gentleness and affection. When she kisses me on the cheek at the end, I grip her hand gratefully. I realise how much I miss the reassurance and comfort of a gentle touch and, in turn, how absent it has become in my marriage.

I rinse away the last of the soap, and, as is customary, remove my knickers only right at the end, washing myself thoroughly. In Marrakech the women may take a *hammam* in total nudity, but in the small towns nobody ever takes their knickers off until the very end.

In the changing area I lather myself with moisturiser and share my products with the other women. Nobody speaks French, but I understand some Arabic now, so we have hybrid conversations, interspersed with much gesturing and a lot of laughter. They all press their mobile numbers upon me when I leave, and clamour with their dinner invitations.

I emerge to find Gary and Madani waiting. They have also been for a *hammam*. I am feeling at peace with the world; I smile at Gary. 'How was yours?' I ask.

'Sheer bliss,' he says, smiling widely. 'I love that place. What a brilliant idea. I don't think I will ever enjoy a bath again after that – it is so much better, and cleaner. Mind you, the state some of the men were in before they washed . . .' We laugh, united in our joy in new discovery.

I've been longing for a cold drink – a sugary Coke or something similar. But nearly everything is shut. I suddenly remember that it is Ramadan. We eventually find a tiny café where they agree to serve us; but I am dressed in *melekhva*, so it is highly inappropriate for me to behave like a tourist and quaff down a cold Coke which, after the heat of the *hammam*, is what I am longing to do. In addition, poor Madani is also gasping for a drink, and he can't possibly indulge in front of his devout compatriots adhering to

Ramadan. After a few tense moments of watchful hostility, when greed gets the better of us, Gary and I hesitantly crack the Coke. The café owner bursts out with indignation – we are obviously Muslims! How can we possibly break Ramadan so blatantly?

Cowed and embarrassed, feeling like guilty schoolkids, we buy a couple of takeaway bottles of drink and escape from the town as quickly as we can on foot, giggling.

'Do you want something to drink?' I ask Madani.

'*Allahi!*', he says – by God! 'And *un garo!*' – a cigarette.

We hurry away from any residual dwellings and people, nudging each other and laughing at the memory of the deep disapproval on the café owner's face. As soon as we are on the outskirts, we raise the bottles to each other in a toast and light a couple of the American Legend contraband ciggies that Madani bought for about a dollar a packet. Madani catches my eye, and before he opens his mouth I know exactly what he is going to say, so we say it together: 'Fucken villages!'

We escape the town and make our way along rocky tracks and through mountainous, craggy terrain. These first few weeks are through relatively populated areas, interspersed at weekly intervals by villages. We had discussed all of this before we left, and quite deliberately taken a reasonably well-trodden route in order to be close to towns should we need things and to help us ease into the walk. But I find myself unenthusiastic about entering towns, even though they are very handy for bread and other fresh produce.

Despite the fact that we are not yet right out into the big, wild desert, I am unabashedly in love with everything. I feel endlessly intrigued; whether it is by learning, with Madani, how to make the one-pot tajine; practising making tea or by the seemingly endless procession of nomads who pass us by, or arrive when we stop walking, to share our tea, or food, or just to gossip and stare in fascination at the two white people walking in the desert. I love walking through the Big Empty and seeing, in the distance, a nomad with his stick over his shoulders, driving a herd of goats, and then hearing the courteous exchanges as he greets M'Barak and Madani. I try to discern the individual phrases and feast on every detail of clothing, curious about what may have meaning or not – the twist of a turban, the type of *djellaba*.

Soon I can tell the difference between the Saharawi nomads and the Berber, although there are more of the latter in this first phase of the walk. In the case of the women, it is particularly plain: the Saharawi wear an easily identifiable style of *melekhva* – brightly coloured and tie-dyed – in a unique fold around their faces. The Berber women tend to be clad in darker, plainer garb, and their clothing is multi-layered. They usually wear headscarves rather than *melekhva* and often have tattoos on their chins or foreheads, vestiges of the animist beliefs that prevailed before Islam became the ruling religion in the eleventh century – beliefs which exist now in stubborn concert with current doctrine.

If I had luxuriated in the initial sense of freedom on the European walk, here I am intoxicated by the thought that I am finally entering the part of our adventure that drove me from the start. The desert, the place that has haunted my dreams for so long, is all around me now. It is in the stillness of dawn, when the world awakens with a soft majesty unlike anything I've ever seen. It is in the fierce sun of midday, when I draw my *melekhva* overhead and try to shade myself and walk in the shadow of the camels, looking longingly at the shade thrown by the spare trees we pass. It is in the unceasing scree that we pick our way through, rocks that push up under our thin sandals and bruise our feet, and the tall gravelly mountains that rear up around us.

But most of all, I find my desert in the nights. In the quiet moments after I have crawled under my blankets, my body still at last and no need to talk to anyone, I begin to know where to look to find one constellation in relation to another. After only a short time, the sky is becoming more familiar.

I watch the moon and see it changing; I feel soothed knowing what phase it is in, knowing whether it will rise before the sun falls or after. I stare at the sky until my eyes are heavy, listening to the camels snort and shuffle close by. I wake in the night and inhale the desert, roll over and instantly fall back to sleep, indescribably happy to be exactly where I am. I feel safe and intoxicated at the same time; I sleep better than I ever did when rough camping in Europe. If I had felt an inherent rightness in the walking back then, now I feel the deep excitement of a new chapter taking hold. I am thrilled by every face the desert shows me.

I have a sense of walking in suspense, as if I am awaiting some major catalyst. While every day brings a new experience, on another level our band moves forward without the logistics altering: Madani and M'Barak still effectively run the show; Gary and I are passengers. I know that at some point the routine will need to change, but I am not sure at what point we need to step in to make that happen.

Meanwhile, in some ways I am flat out just absorbing the myriad of new experiences, without trying to learn anything practical. We acquire a donkey, which M'Barak nicknames 'Ali Baba'. Gary and I are slightly appalled at the way the animal is handled – M'Barak keeps it hobbled from front leg to back, even while he rides it all day, and constantly whacks it with a stick. Our objections are shrugged off.

One day when we make camp, we can see a shabby, low-lying tent only a few hundred metres away. As we unpack the camels, Madani says, 'So we will have good, fresh bread tonight, huh?'

I look at him, puzzled. 'Why? Is M'Barak making some?'

'No,' he says. 'The woman in the tent over there will bake it for us, *Inshallah*. We will take her the dough.'

When we have finished unpacking and made some tea, M'Barak mixes up the dough. Madani and I wrap it up and walk across to the tent. It is made from hessian, plastic and wooden poles and is roughly two metres across at its widest point and three long. In the immediate vicinity I can see a smouldering fire, over which a kettle sits, and water drums.

As we approach, I can make out a woman sitting cross-legged, nursing an infant in the dim confines of the tent. Woven matting covers the floor of the shelter, and there are stacked chests and blankets, obviously the family's possessions. As we draw nearer, I see that, in addition to the baby, there are five children, ranging from a toddler up to about eight, lying listlessly in the shade away from the midday heat.

We stand several metres away from the tent and Madani and the woman exchange greetings. In typical Saharawi fashion they don't look at each other as they go through the ritual exchange, but rather off to the side, so it seems almost absentminded. Greetings finished, the woman shouts orders to her children. They run off to put water on for tea and fetch cushions. I begin to protest that this is unnecessary, but her gestures suggest it would be rude of me to persist.

'Her husband is away with their herd of goats, looking for a better camp,' Madani translates. 'The two eldest children have gone with him. She just gave birth ten days ago, so she needs to stay here and rest until he returns.'

I look at the woman in amazement as she calmly sits there, in the middle of absolute nowhere, suckling her newborn.

'She gave birth here?' I ask, slightly incredulous. 'Was her husband with her?'

Madani shakes his head. 'No – just her eldest daughter.' He indicates the incredibly capable girl working at the fire, the one I had put at around eight years old.

The child brings over some hot coals, which she places in a metal holder. The woman opens the teapot and pours in a sparing amount of tea, closing the packet carefully so that not a shred is wasted. Her sugar, the same cone-shaped block all nomads here use, is also hoarded cautiously – there are no stray pieces falling to the ground, as often happens when we knock a piece off.

Madani and the woman chat for a while. He holds up the dough. Once again the eldest daughter comes running and Madani explains that they have a good clay oven already set up. They will prepare our bread and, in return, we will leave them with some loaves.

As we drink our tea, the woman says something and shrugs in what appears to be an apology. I turn enquiringly to Madani.

'She says she is sorry that she cannot welcome us properly,' he explains. 'She has no meat as her husband took all the animals with him. She says to please excuse her poor hospitality.'

I am aghast. 'Please tell her she has made us a wonderful welcome,' I say. 'Is there anything we can get her? Anything she needs? Does she want some food for the children or medical supplies?'

Madani translates what I've said, but the woman waves us away. She smiles at me, a sincere smile of such genuine warmth and intelligence that I feel touched, and somehow humbled.

'She says she has everything she needs,' Madani tells me.

We walk away, the woman smiling and waving after us. I look back at her tiny, flimsy tent that already houses seven – ten when everyone is home. It is frail on the harsh desert landscape; I think of that woman, no older than me I suspect, giving birth out here all on her own, as her young children stand by and watch. I look ahead at our camp and baggage. By comparison, it seems excessive for only four people. We are here simply as dilettantes, wanting an adventure. That woman has no choice. I feel saddened and ashamed.

Later that afternoon the young daughter runs over to greet us and gives us our bread. It is the best bread I've ever seen in the desert: fine layers of a fresh, moist texture, and at least four loaves. They must have added some supplies of their own to it. Madani tells me the family has kept two for themselves; I wish they would keep the lot. I feel guilty and reach into my pack to take out a packet of the lollies I bought in town to give away to children if I needed to. The child's eyes light up and she gives me a smile wider than Texas. Grasping the packet, she fairly flies back to her camp, calling to her brothers and sisters as she goes.

It is my first encounter with the serene dignity of the Saharawi women. The woman's face, both tired but proud, beautiful yet worn, will stay in my memory. Her kindness and generosity is an echo of stories I've read, times and people I've only imagined. The meeting draws me further into this place, humbles and impassions me. I only wish that I could speak enough Arabic to know her story and enter her life, rather than forever being on the periphery.

But I've only been here a couple of weeks. Maybe I need to chill out a little.

We are heading towards a tiny town that we expect to reach in our third week of walking. Kadar will drive out to meet us there, according to a phone conversation I had with him from the last town. I am determined to learn as much as I can by then.

But it is not easy to break the patterns set up around us by Madani and M'Barak. Although Madani involves me in all the food preparation, I am most definitely the kitchen hand rather than the chef. We have little to do with the camels. M'Barak has conniptions if we go anywhere near them. One day, after they are unpacked, I lean down to hobble one, and he runs over, red-faced and yelling at me to step away. I get such a shock I do exactly as he says; but I wonder afterwards when, exactly, he is planning to teach us how to handle them.

Gary is taking photos but still not as many as he would like. I stay out of conversations about them – on occasion, I see him set up his medium-format camera, but I don't want to enter into a discussion that may end in an argument about how many photos he is or isn't taking. We seem to have so very little to say that doesn't result in tension. We are both retreating into ourselves. Sometimes I watch him from a distance when he is working with the camera, love washing through me in a painful wave. I feel nostalgic for something I've not yet lost.

Perhaps as an escape mechanism, I spend most of my time talking with Madani. We are increasingly friends and confidants, fascinated by the intricacies of each other's worlds. I am intrigued by the many complications and nuances inherent in Moroccan life. Madani is fascinated by everything about Western life, from taxes to cinema, not to mention the freedom in sexual relations. We talk endlessly and in great depth about topics ranging from traditional marriage to flying in an aeroplane.

The sad truth is that Gary's and my increasing estrangement is obvious to both M'Barak and Madani. On more than one occasion I find myself needing to make excuses for our flat demeanour. I feel stressed by my defensiveness. This, in turn, makes me angry with Gary. It seems that he is increasingly isolated. Although he enjoys good relationships with both M'Barak and Madani, his lack of ability to communicate removes him from decision-making at the minor, day-to-day level. Whether this is actually the case or not is open to debate. But his withdrawal is apparent, a downward spiral that we cannot address without it flaring into open hostility.

It is with this tense emotional backdrop that we make camp in a gorge and prepare for Kadar's first visit to check on our progress.

We make a camp in a beautiful oasis by a palmeraie, cliffs sheer and high on either side, crystal water running at the base.

I go for a wash. We are close to the village, so we are able to get mobile phone reception and stay in touch with Kadar. The downside of this is that the children of the village are drawn irresistibly to peek at us. I am no sooner semi-undressed than I spy dark faces giggling and darting about on the other side of the water, gawking shamelessly at the odd white woman washing in their river. I give up, dress and beckon them over. The eldest girl carries her two baby brothers across; a few other toddlers come splashing after. We sit in companionable silence on the riverbank and they carefully examine all of my toiletries, picking each one up and looking at me questioningly. They cover their mouths and giggle when I mimic their functions – shampoo, deodorant, face wash. I cuddle the babies. After a while, I wave them all goodbye and wander back up to the camp.

Evening falls and Kadar phones to say that he and his cousin are still out on the *hammada*, having a terrible drive. They will be late.

Madani comes tumbling down the slope, back from the village, and gabbles out that the police in town just told him that bad weather is coming – we should move since the river is swollen upstream and will flood here.

I eye the river. I grew up in the Australian mountains; I know how fast rivers can swell with heavy rains. But we are a good ten metres above the water level, and the high-water mark is way below us. I don't see any danger. Besides, above us there is no shelter whatsoever. I don't like our chances of being caught in a violent storm on the exposed plains either side of the gorge. Gary and I are in agreement on this.

A brief argument ensues, but Gary and I prevail. We stay camped in the gorge. I look upwards at the darkening sky, though, and suggest tentatively that we should carefully pack away anything of value. I am largely ignored, except by M'Barak, whom I notice makes sure his belongings are tucked away and securely fastened.

The dusk is humid and still. Madani and I begin to make dinner when I hear a strange droning noise, much like a light aircraft.

We cannot make out where the sound is coming from and look around us, puzzled. Suddenly Madani cries out and slaps at his face.

'Quick, *lalla!* Cover up! Get inside the tent! Mosquitoes everywhere!' he yells, and we both run headlong into the tent.

Within seconds, the air around us is virtually black. I've never seen anything like it. Gary and M'Barak come stumbling into the tent and we all sit there, miserable, covering our heads and any exposed skin as the malicious suckers scream about in a vicious swarm. Madani and I were in such a hurry that we knocked the dinner pot over; the beginnings of tajine are strewn all over the ground.

As quickly as they arrived, the mosquitoes are gone, and we emerge timidly from our coverings and look around. 'That was totally bizarre,' I say to Gary, who nods. He seems annoyed by the disturbance.

'If it is anything like Australia, that means we're going to have one hell of a storm,' I say. Gary just looks at me as if I'm being a drama queen.

'I think everybody is overreacting,' he says. 'There are hardly any clouds.' I look at him in disbelief. The sky is purple-tinged. There is not a breath of wind; on the horizon, a darkness like night is approaching.

'Well, I think it looks really bad,' I say, trying to be tactful. 'Let's at least put everything away so we don't need to worry.'

For some reason Gary is infuriated. The solar equipment – which hasn't worked effectively since we left, and which I go nowhere near – is spread out all over the ground. Pointedly, Gary leaves it where it is and stalks away. I look at the sky and the equipment, weighing up what would be worse: Gary's fury at the equipment being lost or destroyed in the storm, or his anger at me for tidying it away without asking. I decide that even if it doesn't work, I would rather have the equipment than not. I pack it away in the rubber tyre container and cover it in plastic, tied down securely.

Not long after, the clouds become thick and heavy, and the wind starts. At first it's just a breeze, then it picks up. Suddenly the night is thick and visibility is gone as sand swirls through the air. The wind is howling, roaring down the tunnel of the gorge with a terrifying intensity. The tent rips up the heavy iron stakes pinning it to the ground, flapping wildly. The four of us hold the corners, frantically trying to pin it back down. The tent is holding us captive, and suddenly I realise not only the futility of the task, but also that nobody is in control here. All four of us are standing uselessly, trying to perform an impossible task in four different ways. We are not communicating. There is equipment to store, the camels to secure and dinner to salvage – for the second time. In that split second I do something that, although I don't know it at the time, will have far-reaching implications: I take control.

'Drop the tent!' I shout, indicating we should cover the exposed equipment. We do, and I yell to the others to use the camel saddles to pin it down so that it forms a barrier over the vulnerable food, flour and clothing. 'You go and get the camels,' I shout at M'Barak, who disappears immediately. I've just spoken to him in Arabic – only three words, basically 'you, look, camels', but somehow I knew what to say – and he understood me. I direct Madani to put the dinner pot under the cliff – it hasn't yet fallen in the storm and at some point we are going to want to eat.

Gary flaps about madly. He's yelling at me about the electrical equipment – he didn't want to drop the tent because he didn't know where it was. Knowing that I've already packed it into the tyre, I ignore him and focus on getting everything else sorted out. He is snappy and I feel annoyed with his childish behaviour.

Within minutes, M'Barak has returned with the camels and positions them down in a square, hobbled. Madani has the dinner safely stored. Suddenly the wind drops, and it is possible to start resurrecting the tent. I told Kadar we would wait up on the road so that he can phone when he is close and we can flash the torch to guide them in. In this weather, I think this is even more important, so I send Madani up onto the cliff.

Gary is furious with me, muttering and stomping about, searching through the equipment to see if everything is still there. Stupidly, I feel as if it is somehow my fault that the storm turned up. I already know where everything is. I've told him several times it is all safe, but he glares at me and continues to search. Gradually my anxiety to placate him turns into a slow, burning anger. Just then, as if by divine provocation, Kadar rings again. Madani calls down for me to stand up on the road and watch for his headlights.

With unseemly eagerness I leave Gary and M'Barak sorting out the tent and run up to the road where the storm is blowing madly and rain is hurtling down. The clouds scud across the sky, the brilliant moon poking through occasionally. The wind howls and whips up the dirt from the road, thrusting it into crazy spirals.

We wait for nearly an hour, damp and shivering even after the rain ceases and the wind drops, and finally we see the headlights roaring up the road below. I am trembling within as much as without. I am churned up by my irritation with Gary, by the storm and the intensity of the last three weeks. Kadar's arrival seems almost fatalistic in light of what happened in the camp tonight. But some part of me cannot quite bear to think about it. I want to laugh and have a drink, get out of the dark places in my head and somehow shake off the sick feeling.

Madani and I walk forward to greet the vehicle as it roars to a halt in a spray of gravel.

Madani and Kadar embrace and exchange greetings while I shake his cousin's hand, remembering him from M'Hamid. I feel suddenly, uncharacteristically shy and hang back as Kadar turns to me.

He wears white robes, a darker turban slung around his neck – he looks wild, arrogant and completely at home. I feel intimidated and nervous.

'It is good to see you,' he says.

'It's good to see you, too,' I reply. The others are going down the hill with bags of different things, and we're alone on the cliff top.

'Thank you so much for coming all the way out here,' I say. 'I know you are busy at the moment.'

'Very busy. But what can I do? Is Paula. Of course I must come.'

I laugh uneasily. His words are light, but he is not smiling. I move to walk down the cliff path, but he stops me.

'It is good to see you,' he says again. My skin prickles.

'We had a crazy night – *lejej*, big wind. The tent went, everything,' I say in an attempt to lighten the atmosphere.

'Ah yes! Us too.' He suddenly laughs, turning away. I'm not sure whether I am relieved or disappointed.

'Is still a crazy night,' he says to me quietly as we go down. 'I am here.' I glance at him, gauging his expression. He chuckles again and waves the whiskey bottle at me.

'But this is just for you – me, I don't drink tonight, because is Ramadan. But I know you want this.'

Oh God, do I ever.

The camp is calm when we return. Gary and M'Barak have erected the tent again, and Gary seems at peace with me and the world. I still feel shaken and unsettled.

We crowd into the tent and eat the long-ready tajine, me drinking the whiskey in great gulps, barely touching the food. Kadar eyes me knowingly across the dish, watching me drink and drawing his own conclusions.

I am seriously unhinged.

Gary seems unaware of the tension, yawning, nodding off and only occasionally entering the conversation. Not long after dinner, he rises and bids us all goodnight. He tells me to enjoy myself, without a hint of irony, smiling. Within minutes I can hear him snoring.

I don't understand if he is truly oblivious to the electricity between Kadar and me. I think with terror that perhaps he simply doesn't care. I'm unable to objectively view his actions. Madani, Kadar and I sit out on the mattresses. In the aftermath of the storm the air is fresh, the moon high and bright. Occasional wind eddies catch the sand from the cliffs and sweep it across the gorge in spiralling drifts. I drink frantically as we swap stories, and I try to describe to Kadar how deeply and contentedly I've fallen into this place, become part of it. He smiles and nods. He understands me.

Madani and I sing. It is a song that he has been teaching me in Arabic. Kadar tells me the song is one that a woman sings to her lover. I feign innocence. I know what the song is.

Sometime late that night Madani goes to sleep, and Kadar and I are left looking at each other.

'I love you,' he says quietly. 'I loved you the moment I ever saw you. I see your face, everywhere, I see your face . . .'

He kisses me.

I don't want this. I don't want it to happen, don't want to be here, be this person.

And somewhere between the storm and the whiskey, a part of me hovers outside, looking at myself from a distance. I watch who I am being, what I am doing, and know that I am lost somehow.

My stomach twists and turns, and I leave. I lie in bed, churning with exhilaration and shame, and I promise myself that this is nothing more than a stupid, superficial mistake. But the damage is done.

I cannot quite grasp the extent of my betrayal. It seems that Kadar and the desert are intertwined in my mind, a confusing, potent combination that won't fade. I am grateful for the time when we walk, when I can be alone with my thoughts. I look up at the glory of the stars, the night sky that I love so much, and see his wild face again. A whispering voice inside asks me what it is I truly want, but I cannot answer, I cannot see.

I went into marriage with a commitment to Gary. I've never broken that commitment, and I don't want to now. The deeper implications of the encounter with Kadar frighten the hell out of me. Whether superficial or significant, it should never have happened, and it leaves me feeling tarnished and torn. An impulsive accident, maybe – but definitely not one I wish to repeat.

My clear resolve is not to allow the situation to develop any further. Things might be rough with Gary but, more than anything, I want to find a solution. I don't want to lose our marriage.

But I cannot reach for Gary. I can only freeze at his touch and feel remote. I want to feel the terror of what is happening here – want to somehow grasp it and tackle it – but the more I panic, the more something in me retreats. I wonder why I can't reach out to him, when I so desperately want to. This is the man I've chosen to spend the rest of my life with and, right now, I can't even bear to look at him.

I notice animal tracks and changes in the wind and the way a date palm curves, but the intricacies of my own heart and soul are hidden from me.

One evening we camp on a rocky hillside; the desert sun is settling around us. The looming gravel mountains turn grey and then blue in the dusk. In the distance, the camels graze on the acacias. The horizon suddenly blazes into vivid tones, cumulus clouds smudge the brilliant backdrop. I look up from my journal and gasp, nudging Madani and Gary. 'Look at that!' I breathe.

Atop the mountain range ahead of us, a cloud has formed into the shape of a majestic, soaring bird. It rises over the mountains as if in full flight, so clear it should be real.

Gary is photographing it. Madani and M'Barak make awed noises. I sit, wrapped in a blanket, still and silent. It seems to me like an enormous bird of freedom. I rarely look for signs or portents; but here, in this wild, sacred place, that cloud seems sent as a picture of my future. I feel a strange bead of life flicker inside, a potent seed of strength. It feels as strong and sure as the bird on the mountain, beckoning me onward. I draw a deep shuddering breath and, for the first time since this surreal nightmare of the collapse of my world began, I feel hope. Strangely, it is not until that moment that I realise I had been so desperately *without* hope. Seeing that cloud, I know that somehow I will survive.

We are walking. We are walking as we have for so many kilometres, and we are talking. And then Gary says he wants to leave.

I knew things weren't good. God knows, I knew that if I was finding Kadar attractive then there must be something seriously amiss. But deep down, and despite my revelation only nights ago with the bird in the sky, I never really thought that we were in danger of splitting up. Lost in my own unhappiness, in my own discontent and frustration, I've failed to understand that Gary is equally miserable – although perhaps for different reasons.

His explanations make little sense. I barely hear him. Perhaps that's because the shock and humiliation of realising that he actually wants to leave, not only the walk but me as well, throws me into instant numbness. Despite my own fleeting infidelity, after nearly nine years together – and walking all this way – I cannot see his decision as anything but the most brutal of finalities.

I can't see through his words to the hurt that must lie beneath. I only hear what sounds like either excuses or criticism. Instead of giving in to the terror and devastation I feel, I come out sounding defensive and uncaring.

Injustice. In most break-ups it is the sense of injustice, of being misunderstood, that begins to layer over the wound in a horrible mass of ugly scar tissue. Injustice prevents the wound from really healing, because only our own injury is real. Like a child, we scream, 'It's not fair!'

Despite everything I've felt, all the defences I've built and the resolutions I have made, all I can see is the unfairness of his words and the stark, awful truth that he wants to leave me.

I have no idea what Gary sees, and perhaps I never will. All I know is in that conversation I lost every bit of faith I ever had in the pillars on which I've built my life. That the conversation itself ripped my heart out from its foundations and threw it into the hot desert wind. And I turn to look at this man, whom I loved the first moment I laid eyes on him, whose smile has warmed my heart every day for nine years, whose love has been my rock, and I think that I must never really have known him at all.

And it is this that hurts the most.

In horribly prosaic language we discuss the particulars of the break-up. Gary says that, although he definitely wants to leave and knows the walk is not for him, he would still like to walk through to the coast, to Tan-Tan. This is out of the question. The stretch after Assa to Tan-Tan is a twenty-five day trek through difficult, isolated terrain. I cannot bear the thought of going through it with someone who has already made it plain that he no longer loves me.

We agree that he will leave at Assa.

But before we reach Assa, we come to another small settlement, and Kadar drives out to celebrate the end of Ramadan with us.

Chapter Five

Oblivious to the mess Gary and I are in, Madani is so over-excited about Kadar's impending arrival that he can barely contain himself.

'Tonight we make a big party, *lalla*, yes?' he says.

Gary and I are drifting in a weird limbo. We are polite and civil, even talking about the new experiences that we're still sharing on the walk. We talk little about the impending separation. I remain lost in hurt confusion. Every conversation bewilders me. I'm not sure what I'm supposed to feel anymore and find it difficult to know how, or who, to be with him. I watch him surreptitiously sometimes, and try to see who the man is inside, try to understand. But I can't see beyond the banal. All I can feel is my own injustice.

Earlier on we were camped close to a small town. We spent a couple of days celebrating the end of Ramadan with a family we met there, eating at their house for the Eid celebration, the day of feasting that marks the breaking of the fast. Last night we sat outside in the courtyard and were showered with kindness and gifts, the women making me up, thrusting a new *melekhva* on me and painting henna designs on my feet and hands.

Madani has taken a particular shine to the sixteen-year-old daughter. She is, as he so delicately puts it, open to a bit of a '*zig-zag*' – she is Berber, not Saharawi, and so for Madani this means that he can happily 'zigzag' out of normal propriety.

Tonight Kadar will arrive, complete with endless amounts of alcohol and a mission to take Madani to the town and make sure he has a 'good time'. The outing has been sold to me as a boys' night. I imagine all of us sitting around the fire in the camp, then me staying behind while they all go out to some kind of Moroccan brothel in the town, which is about twenty kilometres away.

I am tired. The emotional strain has taken its toll. I don't really want to see Kadar at all; I feel sad and bewildered. But I ramp myself up into a shaky anticipation nonetheless.

Kadar arrives with several hangers-on, and the drinking begins immediately. I keep my distance from him and sit by Gary. Despite what has happened between Gary and me – or perhaps because of it – I am conscious of not wanting to shame or embarrass him.

I feel that I may as well not have bothered; Gary appears totally relaxed, talking freely. He seems friendly and unconcerned towards Kadar. *Does he honestly not care?* I wonder. *Or does he simply not see?* Kadar's suggestive looks, conversation and actions are so blatantly obvious that I find it embarrassing.

The night picks up pace, and the men announce they are all going into town. I don't even rise as I tell Gary to have fun.

'I'm not going,' he says. 'I'm tired.'

I'm actually disappointed; a part of me would have loved a night in the camp with a bottle and my own company. But I shrug in agreement.

'You may as well go, if you want,' Gary says, looking at me.

I am totally shocked. I examine his face for guile or sarcasm, but I find none.

'You don't mind me going into town, with Kadar, and all these guys? You do realise that they're basically going in on a pick-up mission,' I tell him bluntly.

Gary laughs. 'Have fun.'

I can't believe it. Not only has he told me that the marriage is finished and he's leaving, but he is now openly encouraging me to go out and get drunk with another man. One I have told Gary I feel attracted to.

There are degrees of hurt. This one slams into me with the added potency of humiliation and rejection. *Not only*, I think, *does Gary not want me – but he's not even concerned about some-one else possibly having me.*

Jesus.

I've never been one to take the quiet path. I put the shades on so I can't possibly look at where I am leaping; race my way through wine, whiskey and conscience; and proceed straight to hell – into Kadar's camel blankets.

For hell, it feels pretty damn good.

Gary's jump-off point is only days away. I've no desire to be alone with my thoughts or my now ex-husband in the interim, so I bury myself in the leftover booze and stupid conversations with Madani. Kadar has gone and nobody, it seems, is any the wiser to my rather substantial zigzag. All I want now is for Gary to go, leave me here in my desert peace so I can order some kind of sanity out of the whirlwind of craziness I feel enveloped in.

But the whirlwind is not done with me yet; it has not really even begun.

One day Gary is folding things into his backpack, separating our possessions, taking back what is his. I can't bear to watch the process, nor do I have any desire to engage in flippant conver-sation about it.

We begin talking about what may or may not happen after we split up. For the first time, Gary says he's worried that we are moving apart too fast. Perhaps, he feels, we should rethink the situation.

I look at him in total disbelief. I feel yanked about in a thou-sand different directions. I don't know what I think.

But I do know that marriage is marriage. Maybe we can put it back together, maybe not. But if we're seriously going to have a go at reconciling, then there is no room for the Kadar episode to stay buried. No matter how painful the truth is going to be, I love Gary far too much to do him the dishonour of concealing.

Kadar is involved in the expedition, and we'll have to keep deal-ing with him. If Gary wants to stay in the marriage and on the walk, then he needs to know what happened and have the choice to walk away from me or change the way we are running the expedition.

'I need to talk to you about something . . .' I begin.

The next few hours are the stuff of nightmares. They will haunt me, I think, for the rest of my life and leave me with a lasting, painful sense of guilt.

We both feel betrayed. Lost in our individual experiences of that betrayal, it seems that both of us become stuck in a position where we cannot forgive the other.

I no longer know how I feel about Gary, how I feel about Kadar or how I feel about myself. All I know is that we've committed to this walk down to Dakhla – we've paid for it – and I want to see it through. The walk is the only thing I really have left. I cannot, I *will* not, allow this stupid, sordid mess ruin something we have worked so hard for.

The next few days are hell. The nights are worse. Through incessant conversation, we move from Gary telling me that he is leaving, to the bizarre position whereby he wants to stay – and I am *insisting* that he must leave. I can't bear to think about walking for a month through the tough country to Tan-Tan with this dilemma swirling between us. Beyond personal consideration, in Gary's initial conversation about leaving he revealed that the walk was no longer interesting to him. In some elemental way, I feel there is no point him being here.

But deeper than that, no matter what is said, there is an angry part of me that still can't believe he thinks it's perfectly okay to get on a bus and leave me in the desert with two men I barely know. Not once does he say that he is worried, and it is not in my nature to admit I am scared. I am too proud to confess how frightened I feel at the prospect of being alone out here.

I also find myself feeling resentful that now, when we're out here in the middle of the desert, I am being asked to drop everything and put the marriage first, when I feel that I tried so hard to fix it before we ever left – and along the way. In the roiling blackness, I feel that the only thing left in my life that I can control or even understand is the walk, and whether I like it or not my mind is dragged headlong into thoughts of how to make a success of it.

I think of what I will need to do, how I will need to be, with Madani and M'Barak. We've told them that Gary is returning to the UK for family reasons. I am sure that they see it differently, but I'm not going to give away more than I need to. I'm determined to hold myself together in front of them; Madani is easier, but M'Barak needs to be watched. Married, I'm to be cared for and honoured. Single or divorced, he may well decide that I'm fair game, honourable though he may be. All the rules are going to change, and I know that I will need to adjust to the new reality.

And so I find myself in Assa, watching my husband board a bus, scared shitless of how I will cope out here on my own – but even more scared of the looming insanity if he should stay.

For a week I walk in a dull, mindless stupor.

I sink into the walk, and into learning, in an effort to block out the shame I feel about my own behaviour; the confusion I feel about Gary; and the dreadful, aching wound his absence has left. I study tracks on the ground or the scrub around me, trying my hardest not to think about my agony. It will be a long time until I recognise that these are classic symptoms of the mind's ability to cope under pressure – it simply shuts down the emotionally dangerous area, knowing instinctively that one must do so in order to keep one's sanity.

On some deep level I know that to think about Gary and my failing marriage will be to lose my mind. Kadar is an irrelevance, a wild fantasy that doesn't matter to me. Gary is my *everything*, the centre of a life I thought was mine. To contemplate what my life will be without him is too dreadful to even approach; when I do so, I become physically ill, my brain clouds over, and I simply stop being able to function. My solution is not to think about it at all, and when it comes unbidden into my mind, as it does, inevitably as I am walking, I begin to sing out loud or talk in rapid-fire to Madani to shut it out.

One of the main reasons is because with every step I take, I am increasingly certain that this walk is where I want to be. And perhaps one of the reasons that I was so frustrated with Gary while he was here is that I felt he wanted me to make a choice between him and the walk. Many months later, I will see that he probably simply needed to know that I wanted him as much as the walk, just as I wanted to be reassured that he still wanted me. But at the time I don't see this and feel as if I have to make a choice between the two. A part of me – a big part – is horrified that I have chosen to continue alone and thinks that I should simply run to the nearest village and beg him to take me back, reassure him that nothing is more important than us.

But the walk seduces me further every day, and the enforced contemplation brought on by the desert is a welcome relief from the last months of emotional tension.

On this long, isolated walk to Tan-Tan, we pass through deep, fertile valleys, surrounded on either side by soaring gravel mountains. The foliage in the valleys is green and lush, and the camels have an abundance to eat, needing no water for weeks on end. We walk for days, weeks even, without seeing anyone at all. Occasionally we come across a lone nomad or a tent, but often we don't pass a soul. We walk immersed in the deep silence of the open desert, camping every night in lush country, cooking our sand-oven bread and catching lizards to put in the tajine.

At a time when I cannot imagine where my life is going, I sometimes wonder if it should simply remain here. I could just put my tent up, buy a few goats and stay here, roaming as the nomads do. How simple it would be to do this: I could pay M'Barak and Madani off and sell a camel to buy other livestock. There is no reason I could not become a nomad myself. I fantasise about writing a book out here, becoming an expert on nomadic cultures and living here all year round.

But a part of me knows that my love of this place is the love of one who passes through it. I am my walk, and my walk is me. I do not want to *be* one of the nomads with whom I sit and drink tea, bearing up under their endlessly curious gaze. I want to be *among* them, passing through, seeing the desert in all its guises and formations, drinking tea with every tribe I come across – not just one. I crave M'Barak's praise and approval as I become more confident –

in choosing a good campsite, making the dough for the sand bread or cooking the tajine. My *melekhva* becomes easy to manage and part of my attire, and my feet move elegant among the uneven, rocky surfaces and across the hard-packed, pale-brown earth.

I love every step in this magnificent place. But my internal universe is a seething mass of fear, hurt, fiery anger and deathly insecurity. I cannot eat any more than a few mouthfuls per day, and I lose so much weight on the Assa–Tan-Tan stretch that not one pair of the cotton trousers I wear under *melekhva* fit me any longer. M'Barak has to unpick all the stitching and resew them.

On any walk, it is the first hour of the day that I love. The desert is a place of intimate, silent beauty when it wakes. We pass tall, imposing granite and sand mountains, the twisted trunks of acacia trees and juicy *listrif* shrubs peeking out among the boulders. The winds of the late afternoon and night have wiped any evidence of the previous day away, leaving a smooth, bland surface where the sand lies between the gravel covering. The tiny tracks of the dung beetle or the mouse-like jerboa pattern the newly formed ripples, leaving pristine traces of nocturnal activity on a pure, blank canvas. These tracks have become my friends. I don't need to ask M'Barak which ones belong to which animal anymore or the story behind their wanderings, if I care to look closely enough. I like this thought. It makes me feel better about my lack of knowledge, mindful that perhaps I am absorbing more than I know as I walk in my emotional stupor.

For that first hour I trip along, the camels bright and energetic behind me, turning my head every now and then to check that the baggage is balanced and nothing is falling off. The sun rises to my left and ahead of me, and I pull my *melekhva* down over the exposed part of my face and tuck into the last fresh breath of morning that lies in its shade.

By midmorning we have been walking for three hours and the heat has become tiresome once more, although nothing like it was earlier in the walk – we are into the cold season now. At the same time, M'Barak and I spot a likely looking tree, and we couch the camels and open our containers of nuts and dates. I mix up a packet of orange drink.

Within ten minutes M'Barak is fidgeting and anxious to move. It is tough on the camels being couched for long, fully laden. We stumble to our feet and I feel the beginning of the sullen, throbbing ache my feet get in these woefully inadequate nomad's sandals. I curse the loss of my lovely hiking boots I wore through Europe. I wish that I had been more intelligent in my choice of footwear, less idealistic. I wrap my *melekhva* up once more.

The camels groan as they heave themselves onto their hind legs, rocking up onto all fours. They open their mouths and roar at the audacity of our request that they move from their comfortable rest.

I know how they feel.

We walk into the heat of the day over rough gravel: incessant rocks that range from small pebbles through to basketball-sized, sharp-edged uglies. The camels pick their way carefully. As my feet curl around and over the uneven surface, heat radiates up through the thin sandals.

The mountains on either side of this seemingly endless gorge stretch high and far. In the distance, M'Barak points out a small indentation, a seeming break in the left-hand side wall.

'We cross there,' he tells me. I nod dully. I just follow the general direction the mountains delineate; my expertise is limited to picking the best path on a small scale, the path that offers the least resistance for the camels, who are surprisingly easy to unbalance. I pride myself on walking with dexterity in this smallest of roles; a few days ago I realised that I now go through most days without M'Barak ever correcting my choice or pointing out a better path, even when we walk down through steep gorges or into narrow channels. It's from small things like this that I gain my moments of pride and achievement, humble though they may be.

In the late morning we see a nomad come toward us, driving a herd of goats. He and M'Barak pause as they draw even. The nomad casts a shy eye at us and then looks away into the distance, and the exchange of ritual courtesies begins:

'Peace be upon you.'

'And on you.'

'How's it going?'

'Fine, praise God.'

'You are fine?'

'Praise God.'

'Your family is fine?'

'Fine, praise God.'

'All in your tent are fine?

'Praise God.'

'Your camels are fine?'

'Praise God.'

'Where have you come from?'

'Assa, praise God.'

'Where are you going?'

'Tan-Tan, God willing.'

'God willing. Have you seen anything strange on the way?'

'Praise God, no.'

'Praise God.

'Everything is good, thanks be to God.'

At this point the tables are turned, and M'Barak asks the same questions. The only ones designed to actually provide information are the final three – perhaps something strange has been spied, like a military camp or water. But in general the exchange is no more than a rote question-and-answer session, shot out with rapid-fire speed, the responder simply inserting '*Hamdullah*' – praise God – at the appropriate times and with varying degrees of fervour. I'm intrigued by the manner in which the Saharawi go through the whole greeting – not looking at the person with whom they are communicating, even if their hands are still clasped. It is almost a measure of how cool they are that they don't need to look.

Exchange complete, both M'Barak and the nomad squat down and pick up sticks with which they draw patterns in the sand as they talk or raise to illustrate a point. Madani whispers that they are talking about where I've come from and what I'm doing here, and about where there is good water or grazing. I'm struck by the elegant, expressive way they use their hands as they talk. When pointing out the direction of grazing, the nomad raises his hand to face height, fingers loosely held but strangely firm. Without looking at his hand, he indicates a general direction with a neat shake and then uses minute finger movements to indicate small distances and geographical features.

I've watched Aboriginal Australians do the same thing out in the desert back home, using their hand to indicate 'little bit long way' with almost exact precision. I wonder if it is a characteristic of desert dwellers, those who live in wide, isolated spaces. I'm entranced by their mutual courtesy and the way they lift their chins and purse their lips to indicate direction. I long to be able to participate in the discussion, rather than be an object of amusement and curiosity.

But I don't feel totally excluded. As M'Barak rises and we go to leave, the nomad moves close to me. He looks at me with frank interest and smiles broadly, then turns and calls something to Madani. He waits for him to translate, his eyes still on my face.

'He says you must be tired of always being with men – and also very brave to walk so far by yourself,' Madani translates. 'He says his tent is not far from here – maybe half a day's walk – and his family would love to welcome you. They will slaughter a goat for you, *lalla* – a huge honour.' Madani says this last line in a low tone, impressing upon me the significance of the offer. All the while Madani speaks, the nomad nods in emphatic agreement, his warm smile unwavering. I see nothing but kindness and concern in his eyes, and I smile back.

'Please thank him for me,' I tell Madani, and then do so myself in Arabic. His smile suddenly grows even wider, and he says to me, 'But you speak Arabic!' I shake my head and laugh.

'*Schwia*,' I say, indicating with my hand – a little bit. But he is delighted, and his insistence that we return with him to his family's tent increases.

Madani and M'Barak look at me longingly. We have been walking for over two weeks since Assa, and the only meat we have tasted has been the occasional scrap of lizard. We are making good time, and besides, I have never yet really been into a nomad's tent. *Why am I here, if not for this type of experience?* I am sick of dwelling inside my miserable head. I've been avoiding anything remotely confronting because I simply can't handle putting on any more of a face than I already have to with Madani and M'Barak. But this is the Sahara, after all; this is the world I have longed for. If not now, when?

I nod decisively, and we follow in the nomad's path.

From the outside, it seems a run-down, haphazard arrangement. A filthy white canvas exterior is pegged into the ground by heavy steel stakes, to which solid ropes are attached. The entire front of the tent is open to the elements, but facing away from the wind. Once inside, it is easy to see that any side of the tent can be rolled up to form the front on a given day. There are two slightly smaller tents either side of the main one.

I will become familiar with this set-up in the relatively wealthy Moroccan/Western Saharan camps. The main tent is the reception area – chiefly the men's domain but often shared with the women – where the finest rugs, cushions and mats lie. It's the place where guests are welcomed. Then there is a smaller tent, where the women eat and rest in privacy – where men venture with extreme caution. A further tent functions as the kitchen. Some twenty metres away is the site where the cooking fire is maintained and bread is made several times a day. Another small enclosure holds some chooks and other animals.

As we approach, it seems to hold little character or attraction – a desperate sort of primitive existence. But when I enter the tent, I draw my breath and begin my love affair with Saharawi elegance and style.

The floor is made up of colourful woven mats. On top of them lie lush, fluffy animal skins, some of which look like they come from a long-haired sheep. On these are cushions covered with beautiful materials, intricately patterned and stitched. They are firm and plump to rest on. The walls and roof are also covered by a riot of rich cloth, hand-stitched into complex and striking designs. Around the walls of the tent, ornate goatskin camel saddles are propped on hand-carved wooden stands. Thick camel-hair blankets are neatly folded and stacked in piles, and heavy steel chests holding the family's goods are lined up. The tea set is battered, beautiful silver, and the tray is engraved in a delicate filigree pattern. Everything is made from extremely high quality materials, and the entire scene is reminiscent of faded English aristocracy – I could be taking tea with Miss Havisham.

The matriarch of the family sits to the right of the doorway. As I slip off my sandals and bend down to enter the main tent, she stretches her hand out and greets me in cheerful, robust tones, making comments that have all the other characters of the tent guffawing in appreciation. She orders the more junior members of the tent to get me the best cushions, clear a proper space and sit me down.

On the other side of the tent several men are reclining on cushions. One particularly old man mumbles as he passes prayer beads between his fingers. There are two more middle-aged men, both of whom are smoking. Some other women cluster toward the back of the tent. One is notably darker, more typical of black African than the lighter-coloured, Arabic-featured Saharawi.

The wife of the nomad who brought us to the tent fusses over me as she sits down at the apex of the semicircle; I am to her immediate left. The other women arrange themselves to my left, sitting slightly back, so that I have a clear line of vision to the matriarch, who is still keeping up an incessant array of humorous remarks. Madani and M'Barak are seated to the right of the central woman and are already involved in greeting the men around them – in the Sahara, this is done individually between men with a handshake and verbally between members of the opposite sex. It would be extremely bad mannered to greet the tent at large.

Madani is laughing at the old woman, and I look at him quizzically. 'She says you must have walked a long way – you are skinny and tired! She says, "What on earth do you think you are doing, walking around like this – why aren't you riding the camels?" And she is telling M'Barak and me off for not looking after you better. She says it will have to be up to her to make sure you are fed properly and looked after. She has sent one of her daughters off to heat water so you can have a *hammam*; the men are slaughtering a goat for us to eat. She says that tonight we must rest here, as part of her family, and stay for as long as we need to.'

I look with enormous gratitude over at the old woman. I begin to thank her, but she waves me away and carries on talking. Madani shakes his head surreptitiously; I know enough of desert custom to know that thanks are irrelevant and unwanted, and I subside.

She is sitting behind a strange tripod made of long wooden poles. Suspended from its centre is a goatskin bag, upside down and tied at the feet. She is shaking it back and forth with a rhythmic, brisk motion.

'What is she making?' I ask.

'*Jeera*,' Madani tells me. 'It is goat's milk. She is shaking it into yoghurt. We will drink it when it is finished.'

I am entranced by the way she uses her whole rotund body to push the skin forwards and backwards, over and over, punctuating her speech with the movement. She sees me watching her and stops, calling to Madani and beckoning to me at the same time. I know she is asking if I would like to try.

The rest of the tent cackles and whoops as I rise, go over and sit in the place of the old woman. Madani pulls out the digital camera, which I have been teaching him to use, and asks if it is okay to take some photos. The nomads are more than pleased, jostling each other to pose.

I take hold of the goatskin and try to emulate the woman, but it is difficult to get the rhythm right while not upsetting the tripod. Never very spatially aware, I nearly toss the whole thing over more than once. Still, I am intrigued by the process and persevere, noting as I do the care and artisanship put into even the construction of the tripod and the stitching of the goatskin.

When the yoghurt is done, she pours it into a heavy wooden bowl and beats in a large lump of sugar. The bowl is passed around between us and I drink deeply. I have always liked goat's milk, but this – thick, heavy and sweet – is really something else.

Behind me the wife of the nomad we met is making tea. Out here in the desert I often miss the sweet, wild taste of the mint that is used in towns. But the woman has actually gathered a different plant, one Madani has pointed out to me before, a form of wild desert mint. She combines these leaves with the sap from a different tree and a thread of saffron. I have never seen such frothy, foaming tea; and it has a rich, creamy taste unlike any I have known before. As she makes it, using a battered silver filigreed tray standing about half a foot high on three legs, she passes the short, two-inch-high glasses along. As visitors, Madani, M'Barak and I are served first. I follow the example of the others and gulp my tea quickly, then pass the glass back to the woman with the tray. There are only four glasses, but she hastily wipes and refills them and passes them along until everyone has a glass. Then it is time to rinse the glasses and tray – and begin the whole process again.

For once, I have nothing to do. There is no dinner to prepare, no tea to make, no tent to put up or repair job to perform. I lie down on the cushions in the tent and the conversation buzzes around me. Outside the men have slaughtered a fat goat and are busily skinning and butchering it. After a short while they come into the tent with a large tin tray of hot coals covered by a wire rack. Directly from the carcass, they place the liver, kidneys and heart on the grill. As the sweetmeats cook, the rest of the family wrap pieces of meat in the lung tissue and skewer it to grill later. The intestines are cleaned in a tub of water and then cooked with the stomach lining in a rich stew. I sit up eagerly as the sweetmeats are taken off the coals and cut up on a plate. The others laugh at my obvious enthusiasm; I am salivating over the smell. They offer it to me first and I try not to look greedy, taking just a small piece.

'No, no! You must eat!' urges the small child holding the plate under my nose. I take a couple more pieces and sit back. There are at least ten people in the tent other than our party. I am sure that slaughtering an animal is not an everyday occurrence. I can see the children looking ravenously at the meat.

The feasting goes on all day and into the evening. I've never eaten so much meat, nor appreciated it more. Our diet over the last couple of weeks, after the meat from Assa ran out two or three days in, has been primarily vegetarian and carbohydrate – lots of bread, nuts and pasta. Apart from tins of sardines, meat of any kind has been sorely lacking. Those first few mouthfuls of succulent liver, although I've never really eaten it much before now, are glorious.

After lunch, the women take me a short distance down the hill. They have erected a *hammam* of the type Selkha described to me. Over a rounded shelter of twigs woven into a dome they have secured camel blankets so the interior is enclosed and lets in little air. Inside they have built a fire beneath rocks, and for some time now a large pot of water has been steaming away.

The women bring me my bag and close the blanket over, indicating that I should have a wash. I'm aware again that it is the darker-skinned woman who seems to be doing most of the work; I'm not sure where she fits into the family.

I luxuriate in the little *hammam* for nearly an hour, washing my hair and scrubbing my body. It is a far more effective steam room than the plastic affair we occasionally set up. I sweat, and grime runs out of my pores. By the time I finish, I've never felt so clean. I open the blanket and step outside into the cool, soothing dusk air. It is in moments like these when I look up at the deep dreaminess of the Big Empty and feel the hollow desert wind cocoon me in silence, that I feel the thrill of my adventure race through me like lightning.

In the evening I retire with the women to their tent and eat stew. They serve the men separately in the other tent. We eat after the men have finished with the dish, but I notice the meat has barely been touched.

'Oh, no,' explains the matriarch, shaking her finger at me. 'You are the guest, and we also have a pregnant woman with us. The men will make sure we get most of the meat.' Once again, I am taken aback by the obvious contradiction: I had assumed that the women, since they ate second, would essentially be given the men's leftovers. In fact, the men have quite deliberately ensured that the best cuts of meat and largest portion are left for the women.

The women of the tent fuss over me in the manner I am familiar with from Selkha's house. They slather me in their precious supply of creams, drawn from a tin chest, which is obviously the repository of their few important treasures. I'm sprayed liberally with perfume, and then I stand over the incense crystals that will air my *melekhva*. They brush and braid my hair, rubbing it with the ointment Selkha gave me. It's all I can do to persuade them not to henna my hands and feet – I know what a laborious process this can be and don't want to be incapacitated for the next six hours.

They rummage around deep in the chest and chatter among themselves, and then they come up holding a beautiful *melekhva* of thick, creamy material – far better quality than the thin fabric I wear now. I protest at their generosity, but they insist, pushing it on me with happy determination, dressing me and tucking the *melekhva* about my face. I rummage in my own bag and hand out my reserve pot of face cream and a lip balm. These are clucked over, descended on with fascination and carefully stowed away in the treasure chest.

When night falls I curl up in the corner of their tent, a couple of children tucked in by my side. There are several of us in the women's tent – the matriarch, small children and a couple of unmarried daughters. I roll over on the cushions and draw the blankets up over me, cuddling the children to my side and, for the first time since Gary left, I do not dread the silent moments before sleep.

In the morning, the family press gifts of bread and meat upon us, and gather to wave us off.

'Who was the black girl?' I ask Madani as soon as we are out of sight.

'Their slave,' he replies nonchalantly.

'Their *what?*' I ask. 'They have *slaves* here?'

'Oh, yes, *lalla*,' Madani says. 'Even my family – we have slaves, too.'

Until very recent times, slavery was not illegal in Mauritania. In fact, slave markets were held quite widely. Since the second Arabic incursion into Western Africa in the eleventh century, wealthy nomadic families have often taken slaves from the black African countries of the Sahel region, including Senegal and Mali. Over the centuries, many of the black tribes have been absorbed into the Arab–Berber mix that forms the modern Saharawi, and the darker-skinned tribes are now known as Haratin Saharawi. But in the more traditional desert families, or the more wealthy of Saharawi anywhere, it is still customary to have a worker – or indeed a family of workers – who are slaves in as traditional a sense as can be imagined. It is fascinating and shocking to me, and one of the many weird, exotic facets of the Saharawi that I never become accustomed to.

As we walk out of mountainous Berber country and further into the Western Sahara district near Tan-Tan, the land and people begin to change. The tents become more elaborate, less poverty stricken. The nomads seem taller and more beautiful. They are more Saharawi and less Berber, Madani tells me proudly.

The tribe here is known as Ait Tusa. In myriad complex conversations, Madani explains to me that the tribes with 'Ait' in their name are in fact a blend of the Saharawi Bedouin and the original Berber inhabitants, a blend that dates right back to the first days of the Mauritanian and Moroccan conquest by the Yemeni Beni Hassan tribe. Any tribe with 'Ait' is thus considered somewhat low on the tribal hierarchy, being by definition of mixed (rather than pure) Arab–Bedouin blood. Although Madani assures me that race is no longer so important in tribal relations and that people marry across the barriers, his own inherent superiority in being Areib Saharawi is obvious.

M'Barak, by implication, as a pure Berber man rather than Saharawi, is inferior. I have an interesting discussion about this when I ask him about how he learned to speak Hassaniya Arabic.

'I grew up in the desert helping my father with his goats,' M'Barak says. 'But one day when I was twelve, I was at the well with my animals and two Saharawi boys turned up. They tried to talk to me, but I couldn't understand them, as my whole family speaks Tamazight, a Berber language. The boys thought I was stupid and they started to laugh at me. We ended up having a fight and they beat me up. I decided then that I had to learn Hassaniya, since most of the people in the desert are Saharawi and don't speak Tamazight. So I did. By sixteen I was fluent,' he concludes proudly. 'And look at me – I can pass for Saharawi now! Nobody ever guesses I am only Berber!'

It is a telling comment – and a true one. In the *hammams*, the smallest, hottest room is known as the Berber room. The indigenous Berber culture – which spreads through all North African countries and has resulted in diverse and colourful tribes, such as the Malian Tuareg – was historically considered by the conquering Arabs to be little better than bestial. While attitudes may have softened over the intervening centuries, there is no doubting the superiority Saharawi Arabs still feel in relation to their Berber counterparts. Interestingly, the word 'Saharawi' actually refers to the mélange that is the reality of Mauritania and the Maghreb after the interbreeding of tribes over a long period. In this way, Saharawi will often distinguish themselves from 'the Arabs' quite proudly – they are Bedouin, not just Arabs. It is an odd distinction since their claim of superiority over the Berber comes from exactly this separation: it is their Arabic purity that is prized.

The desert is defined by tribal boundaries, separations and interwoven histories of warfare and marriage. When two nomads meet, discovering these links form the bulk of conversation.

On this leg of the walk, the isolated piste between Assa and Tan-Tan, as we walk further towards the Western Sahara and true Saharawi territory, I really begin to get a sense of the complex forms of desert communication.

'I feel so cut off,' I say to Madani as we walk along. 'I can say all the greetings, more or less, but most of the time the nomads we meet never address me. And I know it isn't a male–female thing, because the women we pass will happily talk to you and M'Barak. So why won't many of them exchange greetings with me? Or even look at me?'

Madani laughs at my consternation. 'Most of them think you are a ghost – or maybe one of our wives. When we say you're a tourist, paying to walk in the desert, they think we're joking. Then they ask why you don't ride the camels, where your husband is, why you're out here alone. They want to know why you do all of this. And they think you are very rich.'

M'Barak joins in at this point.

'Me, I get so sick of answering the same questions every time –' and he launches into a repetition of the dialogue I have heard so often, but this time he adds in the ones I frequently hear but had never understood: *Who is she? Where is her husband? Why is she walking? How much is she paying you? Does she own the camels? Where is she walking to? Why is she doing this? Where does she sleep? Where do you sleep? Does she cook?*

M'Barak recites them as we walk along, pitching his voice to perfection, just as in the question-and-answer sessions, until we are all laughing at his antics. He winds his turban around like the Saharawi nomads and mimics them brilliantly. But at the end, with great satisfaction, he says, 'Yes, nobody now can ever tell I am Berber. They all think I am Saharawi! I even know enough about their tribes to pretend to be Saharawi if I want to.' He nods, delighted with his cleverness. Madani – a boy thirty years his junior and infinitely inferior in wisdom and desert knowledge – smiles and patronisingly pats him on the shoulder: 'Yes, you are almost as good as Saharawi!'

M'Barak nods with delight, like a puppy being stroked. I look away, mildly disgusted by such an obvious display of racial superiority.

Although we share many laughs, their conversation is difficult for me to appreciate sometimes; and there are occasions when I worry that I have allowed an excess of familiarity into our relations. Not for the first time since Gary left, I'm conscious that I am, to a degree, a victim of changing circumstances. For example, I'm no longer entirely comfortable with the same jokes and bawdiness that seemed okay when Gary was in the camp. And even though M'Barak has always touched my leg for emphasis when he speaks, is it my imagination now or does his hand linger just a fraction too long? Does he find excuses to touch me? And does he make one too many comments about sex and women?

Sometimes I feel as if Madani and M'Barak talk about these two things incessantly. They ask me questions constantly about the habits of Western women, about what are normal freedoms and what aren't. If I object now, it could lead to me being misread as paranoid or insulting. But equally, I feel that if I do not, I leave myself open to accusations of improper conduct. Then I feel despairing because, let's face it, they know that I drink, smoke and swear. What is the point in me now pretending to be something I am not? It's too late to alter the codes of behaviour. I made those mistakes when I was shored up by Gary's presence, by the safety net of my marriage. I was just playing at propriety back then, for all of my efforts to conform to nomadic custom. Now I'm alone and I find myself in a bind.

I'm wearied by these concerns. Even worse, I'm dreading coming to the end of this stretch and having to deal with communicating with Gary. It has almost been a relief not having a phone or any kind of contact out here. I know that in Tan-Tan I will have to travel back up to Zagora to deal with the visa issue before I get into the really remote territory of Western Sahara. I can't bear to think about facing Kadar either.

I don't even want to think about any difficulties arising between M'Barak, Madani and me. My relationship with them both no longer seems as simple as it did. As the nights have descended into the true chill of desert winter, we've begun to sleep – all three of us – in the tent. Some nights I lay there frozen still until I'm sure I hear both of them breathing regularly.

I cannot confide in either of them about my marriage, but I am sure Madani knows the reality. M'Barak, I think, guesses at it. When I mention Gary coming back, which I frequently do, he shakes his head sorrowfully and says nothing.

At times I find Madani overbearingly protective, almost possessive. I get sick of him telling me how things are or what I must do. I sometimes feel that, in my ignorance of local custom, he is manipulating me to his own advantage. Despite the fact that he is obviously the local expert, he is also only twenty-one, and has never travelled further than his own village. While I am keen to learn about desert and custom, there is much that he himself has to learn about life in general. He can sulk with the best of them.

As we near Tan-Tan, I feel increasingly alone. I've been walking this stretch for nearly a month. In addition to my concerns about Kadar and Gary, I'm also now worried about money and equipment. Gary left with the GPS, solar equipment and laptop, all of which he has a right to claim ownership of, but which I'd assumed would be with us for the duration of the walk. I've very little money left and no idea where more is coming from. I still feel that I have learned little, and, despite walking well over 1500 kilometres now, achieved nothing. It's been a month since I spoke in English to anyone: all of my conversation is with nomads or the two men in my camp. I have no one to whom I can confide my worry and despair over the state of my marriage. I feel that if I crack up, on any level, I will give the men a chance to take over. The issue of who is actually running things out here has lain dormant for this stretch, but I am aware it is a thorny one that I will need to tackle.

And inside, I am so horribly, bitterly sad that I sometimes wonder why I am bothering at all, on any level, to worry about this bloody walk when I should probably just pack the whole thing in and run back to England in an attempt to save the tattered remains of my marriage.

It's a strange irony that the very time Gary left the walk, telling me he was bored by it, is the exact point at which the walk itself becomes fascinating. With every new experience I think sadly that Gary left before he could have any real glimpse into the true desert, that he is missing these beautiful places and people. Rather than dwelling on my own affairs, it's a relief to immerse myself in the intriguing otherness of life here. Once again, I often find my prejudices exposed and contradicted, and catch fascinating glimpses of life through another lens.

For example, I remain astonished at how open and often quite assertive the women are. Prior to the desert, my time with Moroccan women had been minimal – Kadar's family in M'Hamid, a few nights staying with families on the way through Morocco. In both cases, the majority of my interactions had been with the men – the women stayed largely out of sight.

But the women in the tents are far from reticent. In the beginning, I am almost slightly shocked by the bawdy outspokenness of the women I meet. They frequently interrupt male conversation to contradict the information one of them may have given regarding grazing or water sources. They have no hesitation in telling an anecdote or giving M'Barak advice.

I speak to Madani and M'Barak about the women and learn more every day.

'They seem so confident,' I say to Madani. 'How does it work for them when they marry? Do they get a say in the man they marry?'

He looks at me in astonishment. 'Of course they do! They are Saharawi! No man would ever marry his daughter to someone she really didn't want – this is not Islam to do this. Maybe first time, yes, the parents choose the husband – but only if the daughter is willing. And only the first time.'

I look at him, confused. 'What do you mean, "the first time"?' Is it customary to have more than one marriage?'

'Absolutely. Oh, yes,' Madani replies emphatically. 'Most women, they marry two or three times. Often more. Women are more highly prized after they have been married once – because they know what it is all about, you know?' He looks somewhat embarrassed and relaxes when he sees me grinning.

'Wife is much better after thirty,' M'Barak chips in. 'Nobody wants silly eighteen-year-old – for what? Doesn't know how to behave, how to cook well, how to make love. You need a woman who has been married and run a tent, about your age' – he gestures at me – 'but with a bigger bottom!' The Arabic word for 'bottom' is 'zefarl'; the word 'big' is 'kabeer'. M'Barak points gleefully at my dumbfounded expression and says, 'Zefarl kabeer!' He thinks this is immensely funny.

M'Barak talks frequently about the need for a woman to have a huge backside. He has pointed out more than once that my own considerably ample rear would improve by being even bigger, something I could never in my wildest dreams have imagined someone suggesting. I am not so sure how much I like him checking my butt out, but, apart from being sidetracked by the discussion, I remain intrigued by the marriage conversation.

'How do women in the desert divorce then?' I ask, curious.

'My mother,' begins Madani, 'was married first to an old man, a relative of her father's cousin. She was happy about the marriage, and they all thought he was a good man. But when she was taken back to his tent, she found that he was not good at all. He beat her a lot. His mother and sisters also were very mean.'

This is not an unfamiliar story to me after reading many accounts of Arabic women trapped in abusive and oppressive marriages. The bookshelves in recent years have been loaded with such 'behind the veil' tales of misery and confinement. I thought that perhaps it would be normal, and I mention this to Madani.

He looks at me curiously. 'This is not normal. Not at all. A man, a good Muslim – it is his duty to look after the women in his tent, to treat them well, with respect. The woman is the mother of his children. She is as his mother. How is it normal to beat her? No, this is not good.

'So, my mother, after one week, she decides to leave the man. In the night, she left his tent with just a small water bottle and set out to walk back to her family tent. But when she found the place, after two days walking, her family had moved on – they had gone to a new place. So she walked through the desert until she found a different family, who knew where her own had gone. They gave her a donkey to ride and some more water and food. It took her three days, but she found her family tent.'

'What happened when she got there?' I ask, fascinated. 'Did she get into trouble?'

'My grandfather told her to go back,' said Madani. But then his face lightens and he leans forward, and I know that this is the bit of the story he loves.

'But my mother – she took her knife, and she slit her *melekhva* from here' – he indicates his throat – 'to here' – he points to his navel. 'And she held the knife like this' – he points his knife so the tip almost pierces the skin on his heart, both hands around the knife handle. 'And she says to her father, "If you make me go back, I will push this knife in my heart, for with that man, I may as well be dead."' Madani sits back and smiles triumphantly, waiting for my admiration.

'But what happened?' I ask.

He looks at me as if I'm a complete imbecile. 'She stayed, of course. What father would risk losing his daughter like that? And then she made a good marriage, a good man, after that. And that was my father.'

'How old was she when the first marriage happened?'

'My mother was fourteen.'

'And her second?'

'Sixteen.'

'How old was your father when they married?' I ask.

'He was seventy,' Madani tells me. 'It was a very good marriage. My mother loved him for twenty years, until he died. It was love at first sight.'

There is so much in this story for me that it takes days to digest. I learn over time that due to recent changes in Moroccan law, divorce now needs to be actually sanctioned by civil authorities. But Saharawi women, unlike their less independent Moroccan counterparts, quite resent this intrusion into their freedoms. They have never felt the need to apologise for walking away from marriage, nor seen any shame in marrying multiple times. The only condition is that they wait three months after leaving one man before marrying another, thus ensuring there is no confusion regarding offspring.

In the depths of my own particular crisis, I find this attitude of the women – the self-confidence – strangely comforting.

Here, I am considered beautiful. My failed marriage, if that is what it will be, is seen as an asset, as nothing to be ashamed of. My age, now thirty-two, is considered a good one for marriage and not at all too late to have children. Far from all of my concerns and fears, I am not seen as damaged goods, as somehow a failure. The men and women alike are totally unconcerned with my husband having left me and instead are usually offering either to marry me or to find me a husband if I want one. They assure me that with four camels to my name I'm a good proposition.

Strange and totally removed from my life as it might be, I find this alternative reality a comforting one. At a time when my life feels as if it's falling down about my ears, there is no better place I could be than among these nomads who shrug pragmatically and look toward the future.

I watch the tall nomadic women stride across the desert plains with their herd of goats – calm, competent and proud – and I know that there is more to this walk for me than just making it through the desert. Through this experience I am peeling back the layers and seeing who I really am, and what I am capable of.

Over three weeks have passed since I watched my husband board a bus. We walk out of another valley and across a steep, viciously cold mountain pass, where we see a dead cobra coiled on the freezing earth, and come down the other side into the dusty, dilapidated streets of Tilemzoun.

The difference between the seemingly poor desert towns I have been in and this one is already apparent. I can feel the more deprived vicinity of the Western Sahara coming closer. There is a market day, but we are reliably informed that there is no real point in waiting around for it unless we are desperate. It is better to hitch into Tan-Tan, where one can buy everything. There's no electricity and the houses are part mud, part tent. The streets are quiet with few shops. We stop at one and are met with slack-jawed astonishment, slimy smirks and not even the offer of a cold drink. We walk through the deserted streets with growing weariness, eyes following our progress. They are the greedy, lazy eyes of town dwellers. I remember why I hate towns, especially here, after the open desert. While I desperately want the communications and luxuries they offer, I can't bear the endless attention and hassle.

We make a camp far away from the town. That night the wind and rain howl with a vengeance, and we finally pull the tent down rather than continually repegging it. We put the camels in a square, pull blankets over our heads and lie beneath the shelter of the camels and bushes. I drift off again immediately, not even waking during the night.

In the morning I think how easy all this seems to me now. I don't feel even remotely scared anymore when things like this happen. I find my way easily to the right place to shelter, lie down and peacefully drift off – my concerns are to make sure the camels and equipment are okay or that we are not likely to be in the way of a dried creek bed that is flooding.

A part of me thinks I should feel really proud; in some way I have fulfilled a vague childhood goal of becoming a tough 'bushie'. Instead, I feel a strange kind of fragmentation, a fading, as I become more of this place. I could wander forever, just fade into the desert and die out here. I feel so separate from any other life that I wonder if anyone would even notice or care.

We are close to the road when we look for a good camp on the second day, closer than I would like, as the way through to Tan-Tan is difficult, mountainous terrain. This is where we turn south. There is no point walking all the way to Tan-Tan, to the coast – we would only have to cut in again. So we are planning to navigate a large loop around the town, essentially walking in a semicircle and keeping about fifty kilometres between us and it. We need a camp that is reasonably close to the road and to town, with good feed. Madani and I will hitchhike into Tan-Tan and get ourselves organised with supplies and communications. We are then planning to go back to M'Hamid to sort out my visa, so M'Barak needs a camp where he and the camels are comfortable.

I am looking around, wondering if this place could serve the purpose, when something drops from my hand. With no warning, the ring I've worn since leaving England – the cheap wooden wedding rings Gary and I bought to replace our originals when we started our walk – suddenly cracks and falls into the sand. I look at the remains in horror.

I want to be sick or run away; or perhaps get drunk and scream, all at once. The blatant metaphor of my cracked wedding ring beats me around the head like a taunting nightmare. It drags me out of the desert and back into the hell that my life has become.

My husband is gone and my visa is about to run out. I am going to hitchhike into a strange town to read emails discussing the state of my marriage. I have to try to find out where I can get enough money to keep this whole walk going. I've barely enough money to buy supplies. I've no idea if Gary could care less whether I am alive or dead. I don't know if Kadar will live up to his promise to sort out this visa issue and have no idea what to do if he can't.

And above all of this, I feel desperately alone, my sanity hanging by a thread. There is nobody for me to fall into and ask for help. I need to be strong, focused and sure of the next step. Madani and M'Barak deserve to be secure that they will be paid and confident in my ability to continue. I want to see Kadar, but I dread it with equal measure. I am proud of myself and loathe myself in equal parts. I love Gary just as much as I resent him

So I look at my substitute wedding ring lying cracked in the sand, pick it up, dust it off and put it quietly in my bag.

I can't think about that now. I just can't.

The police come to see us that night and are, to my surprise, truly nice. They make a brief visit then leave, promising to call back in later. I have no idea why until they arrive in the afternoon with a steaming dish of homemade couscous and meat. We've seen nothing this calibre of food in weeks and fall upon it hungrily. They bring us nuts, dates and much-needed cigarettes, and assure us they will take us to a great spot tomorrow where M'Barak can stay with the camels. They also offer to give Madani and me a lift into Tan-Tan and show us a good, cheap place to stay.

I am thoroughly touched by their care, and enormously reassured. I know from bitter experience how ugly it can be to arrive in a strange town and attempt to get everything done.

The following day, Madani and I wrap up and bounce into town in the trayback of the police car. We are planning to head back to M'Hamid that evening for a week to sort out the visa issues. Unknown to me, I am about to enter the darkest, murkiest depths of cultural awakening – and the crucial turning point in my walk.

Chapter Six

The hotel in M'Hamid is a nightmare.

After travelling up from Tan-Tan in a mixture of excitement and trepidation, it takes only a day in the hotel for my illusions to be shattered and the unpleasant reality to sink in.

I am no longer part of a couple bound for an admirable adventure. Instead, I am Kadar's concubine, an object of tawdry fascination for the men of the town. They arrive at the hotel to gawk at me, and Kadar revels in the men's open admiration of his conquest. All I want is to be out of there.

But I cannot move into the house of Madani's family, because I need telephone, internet and some space to myself. I also need to abide by cultural norms in a family home – after weeks in the desert, I am craving some time to relax in a Western environment. The hotel is not quite that, but at least the conversation is in French, and I can occasionally see other travellers. Despite my best intentions to cut my relationship with Kadar back to a platonic level, my need for comfort and reassurance combine with the same electricity there has always been between us. Our relationship continues.

This same place that I had considered a refuge – my home in Morocco – has been tainted by my rash decision to sleep with Kadar. I no longer feel either safe or protected here, but rather caught in a dark labyrinth of conflicting cultures, of past and future. I arrived here married, proud and enthusiastic. I've returned single, caught in the worst of adulterous liaisons, my confidence and self-esteem in tatters. I can't bear even to walk down the street.

I'm too embarrassed to take up the warm invitations of Madani's family, who I'm sure know about my fall from grace but are too polite to ostracise me.

Selkha is in Zagora with her family, awaiting the birth of her baby. I'm glad she is nowhere nearby, grateful to be spared a direct confrontation with the victim of my decisions, particularly one who has been so kind to me. Although I was longing to get here, now that I actually am, I simply want to get my visa organised and get away. Kadar has lived in my mind over the past weeks as a mad desert fantasy, a living embodiment of everything I love about this place. What I hadn't expected is that I do not actually want a relationship with the man himself.

Gary and I speak by telephone and on the internet. The conversations are circular, emotionally charged and traumatic. Often, I am watched during these exchanges by the ever-present gaggle of idle males who scrutinise my every move. I feel claustrophobic and debased by their leering glances. Caught up as I am in my ongoing emotional saga, I am no longer the proud and independent woman Kadar met. I am sad and flat, searching for comfort and solace. I am searching in the wrong place. Kadar becomes increasingly detached and sometimes downright cruel.

I once heard a saying that, in Morocco, the country has two institutions: the bar and the mosque. The inference is that men often leave one to go the other. I see it all here, first hand, and the hypocrisy is staggering. Men who are pillars of the community stroll the street with their wives and children, then meet at night to drink beer and shag their girlfriends. There is barely any subtlety and no discernible concern over living a double life.

Close to the hotel, the old tourist gimmick sign to Tomboctou mocks me: M'Hamid–Tomboctou, 51 days. The sign relates to the ancient days of trading camel caravans who took an entirely different route – more direct than mine – through the now-closed border of Algeria. Over a thousand kilometres have been added to the route as a result of the border closure. But, despite the fact that this way is not open for me and I'm taking the most direct route possible, I can only feel a suffocating sense of despair. I feel no closer to Tomboctou. I wonder if I will ever make it there at all.

The third day that I'm in the hotel, a situation arises with Ali, casual acquaintance of Kadar's. He drives a taxi and often delivers Kadar's alcohol from the small roadhouse thirty kilometres away. Over a few drinks at the home of a friend of Kadar's, Ali takes a shine to me, unaware that I'm essentially spoken for. Kadar encourages him. He and the other men think it is immensely funny, a joke at Ali's expense.

I feel cornered and uncomfortable. I attempt to laugh it off, but I just want to leave. The game increases as the alcohol flows, and Ali tries to clumsily dance a traditional courtship dance with me, egged on by the various bystanders. I turn to one of the men, an educated man who holds a position of respect in the town.

'I don't like this,' I say to him quietly.

He looks at me with a pitying expression. 'Yes – this now, this is getting serious,' he says, confirming my fears that Ali takes the events as more than a game.

I look in horror at Kadar. 'You must tell him that I'm spoken for. I don't want to play along with this – it's stupid and cruel. I don't speak enough Arabic to explain. Tell him I'm your girlfriend, please, or whatever you need to tell him to make him stop this.'

Kadar looks at me in a slightly amused way.

'Don't be crazy,' he says lazily. 'Just play along. It is very good joke. This man, he is so stupid and arrogant – is good for him to be embarrassed. Is just a joke. Don't be silly, little girl.'

I'm fed up and furious. I have no emotional room for all of this crap – *none* – but I'm determined to keep a sweet face until I've my visa and can get away. And part of me suspects that this is all part of Kadar's own game: he likes seeing me, the 'rich' Western tourist, somewhat out of my depth, humbled and degraded. I know that deep down he bitterly resents the inequity of life that cast him in the role of begging for scraps from Europe's table, often from people he considers ill-educated and culturally inferior. I've had sympathy with him in this, but I am unwilling to be the one to assuage his resentment.

On a personal level, I refuse to let Kadar see that I'm upset. I don't want to give him the satisfaction. So I hold my head up and laugh it off, trying to make it clear to Ali that I'm not interested, without being rude. Kadar watches me from a distance with a grin. I sense that he knows exactly how uncomfortable I am.

The following day Ali turns up at the hotel bearing the first of traditional marriage gifts. He is nicely dressed and out to impress. He hands me the telephone to talk with his brother, who lives in France, speaks English and proceeds to tell me all about Ali's attributes. Ali looks at me pleadingly and goes so far as to begin to explain what the terms of the marriage will be.

I can't believe it. Kadar and his mates are laughing raucously in the salon at my discomfort. When I excuse myself and confront Kadar, he pleads with me, between laughs, to go along with it, just for fun, because Ali is such an arrogant idiot. I've lost any sense of humour I may have had in the farce.

I try to explain the situation to Ali, but like a dark parody of Mr Collins's proposal to Lizzie in *Pride and Prejudice*, he refuses to believe I am serious, smiling and waving off my explanations. When he leaves, it is with the promise that he will return to finalise things with my father over the phone. My sincere protestations fall on deaf ears. When I turn furiously on Kadar, he waves me away dismissively and leaves the hotel.

Things are getting darker.

While I can see how I got here, I can't believe it has gone so bad, so fast. I feel caught in a vortex of my own making; I have no idea how to get out.

We go into Zagora, supposedly to meet the police chief. Instead, I get dropped at the home of Selkha's family while Kadar goes carousing in the bar. It's bad enough that I must sit and look Selkha in the eye in her family home. Even worse is that she goes into labour that night and delivers a baby girl around midnight. Not only am I one of the first to hold the baby, I spend that night sleeping with other family on the floor of the salon, Kadar cuddling his other son barely two feet away.

Before I can say anything the following day, Kadar is gone. I'm desperate to get out of the house. In my newly single state, I have been semi-adopted by the family and treated with the same protective concern as one of their own would be. I feel like the proverbial snake in the nest and want only to be far away from the solicitous care I so definitely do not deserve.

I invent a plethora of lies to get out of the house with Madani for a cigarette.

Aware that it is fundamentally useless, I confide in Madani about my relationship with Kadar and my discomfort.

'I see this, *lalla*. I know,' he tells me sorrowfully. 'I know what is between you and Kadar the first time I see you together. But he will hurt you, *lalla*. He will not treat you well. He is going to try to cheat you out of your camels and the walk.'

My head begins to spin, even worse than before. Madani goes into a vicious dialogue about the many evils of Kadar and how it was always going to end in disaster. I feel tarnished by the endless flow of vitriol and gossip.

That night Kadar pulls up to the house in a blistering skid and virtually hauls me into the car. I'm wearing traditional *melekhva*, having been at home with the family. He drives straight to a five-star hotel in town that is for Western tourists – or wealthy Moroccan businessmen and their girlfriends. I hang back.

'I can't go in there dressed like this,' I say.

'Don't be stupid. You think anyone cares what a stupid tourist wears? You come in now, so you see this police chief. We get this business done, and you can go back to your camp and I can go back to my family and my baby daughter.'

His contempt could not be more blatant. For a piercing second I actually consider walking away, right there and then. I have enough money in my pocket to get to Marrakech; I could phone my family from there and ask for help to fly me out. I am an intelligent, capable, competent woman. *He has no right*, I think in blind fury.

But unfortunately, that is not entirely true. I am the idiot who slept with him. I am not in my own country and culture, playing by rules that everyone understands. I am in the zigzag country, where the rules are entirely different, and I chose to get involved in games I don't understand. Now, if I really want to make this walk work, I am going to have to outsmart these bastards on their own turf and find a way out of this swamp I've put myself in.

So I grit my teeth and go in to meet the police chief.

The fat, unpleasant imbecile I remember from the last time is sprawled on a couch, his arm around a local woman. There are several empty whiskey glasses on the table in front of them. He looks at me through bleary eyes, and his interest increases as Kadar tells him about my changed circumstances – that I'm now alone.

He jolts forward, talking voraciously, and asks me a dozen questions in a muddle of French and Arabic. He tries to tell me that I have been safe thus far purely because he called ahead to all the military posts to tell them I was coming. He proudly claims that he has looked out for me on this whole trip. I smile sweetly and pretend that I believe every foul lie spewed forth from his plump, pink mouth and am unutterably grateful.

Kadar steers the conversation around to the question of the visa. The chief guffaws, then nods knowingly. 'How about you and I get a room upstairs now, for the night, and then I will stamp your visa for all the time you want,' he says, putting his hand on my knee. He is totally sure I will acquiesce.

Kadar looks at me in horror. He may have done his own share of humiliating me in the past week, but even he is incapable of this kind of blatant outrage. I just smile.

I stand up and give the chief my hand to shake. 'It's a pity, in Morocco, that such a wonderful tourist trade should be ruined by such idiots,' I say, smiling politely. 'You just made a very big mistake, Mr' – and I say his name, slowly and correctly, so it's clear that I know exactly who he is. 'I'm sure the tourist board will be intrigued to hear how charming you are to international journalists,' I end, with one last smile.

And then I walk out. No visa in the world is worth this kind of filth.

Kadar follows me; one look at my face is enough to silence him.

'Take me back to M'Hamid,' I say.

To complete the nightmare, the chauffeur of the taxi in which I ride back to the hotel is the ever-hopeful Ali. He gets drunk and rants angrily at me for the duration. I just hope we don't crash.

I sit up that night and look at the facts. I am so done in that I can only look at them with complete detachment.

I've nearly a month left on my visa. I have walked about 1500 kilometres, and there is well over 1000 to go until I reach Dakhla. I can walk at least half of that in a month and then do a quick dash up to Spain to renew my visa.

I've no money. While Kadar is still paying Madani and M'Barak's wages from the initial sum we outlaid, and will also resupply us here in M'Hamid, I need ongoing cost money for communications, transport in and out of towns, and incidentals.

With only three of us, I can sell one of the camels. That will give me nearly 1000 euros to walk with; I can certainly get down to Dakhla on that.

I have submitted my final application to the Royal Geographical Society for a grant I've been shortlisted for. They haven't said no, yet. If I can make it to Dakhla and then the money comes through, there is no reason why I cannot carry on into Mauritania.

I speak with my mother. I have to break the news of Gary and me splitting up. She is wonderfully supportive. She is also very, very ill, suffering terribly in the aftermath of chemotherapy. She insists that she does not want me to come home for her sake.

I think, for a moment, of cutting my losses and going back. But – God knows why – I never seriously consider it. I may have to leave this walk. I may have to leave this place. But I will not do it on these terms – when I am down and out and beaten. If I leave, then it will be because I choose to, because I have done all I can. Not before.

I sit up all night and, in the dawn, I go to get Kadar.

'Organise me a car – I'm going back to Tan-Tan,' I say curtly.

He smirks. 'You cannot go back to the camp,' he says. 'You have no money. Your visa is nearly finished. Where are you going to go? What are you going to do? You have had good walk, *lalla*. Now is time for you to go back to your husband.'

But I cannot be hurt by words anymore; somehow, I have gone too far for that. So I just return his smile.

'Ah yes, maybe I have some problems. But this is easy for me: first, I will sell one of the camels. Then I will go back up to Spain and get a new visa. While I am there, I will organise more money from home. My family is wealthy, you know.'

I have never pulled this line out before; it's also entirely untrue. But I'm shameless now, and I also understand the Moroccan respect for wealth.

'I have paid you to organise things to this point. What I require you to do now is get me a car and get me back to Tan-Tan. I have a lot to do.'

Kadar is a master of the poker face; but I can tell that the comments about selling a camel, and my family, have shaken him.

'How are you going to sell a camel?' he asks, trying to be casual. 'You don't know what to do.'

'Actually,' I say, 'I do. I'm camped near a town in which there are three major camel dealers – M'Barak knows all of them. I can get an excellent price for one of the camels within a day. I'm not remotely concerned about selling them. Really, I'd prefer to keep them; but if I have to sell to continue, then I will.

'Also,' I continue, enjoying the bemused look on his face, 'since I've been here I've contacted some of my media associates in the UK. They're prepared to pay me to write some articles about my experiences; I'm sure you have heard of –', and I mention the name of a well- known newspaper. This is all complete rubbish. But he doesn't know that. He has seen me spend a large amount of time on the phone and internet, and has no idea who I may have been talking to. He cannot be sure that I am bluffing.

'Anyway,' I say, getting up, 'none of this is your problem. I need to get packed and get my supplies. You need to sort out my car. I will see you when we are ready to go.'

'Of course, *lalla*,' he says quietly. 'I will organise all of this for you – I still want for you to have your walk.'

I look at him and can barely stifle a hysterical laugh. In some strange way, I think he actually believes his own words. I put my head down and pack.

The last night in M'Hamid, Madani and I come to a crossroads. I have been essentially hiding in my room, avoiding everybody, Madani included. One of the local hotel boys, a good friend of Madani's, searches me out and silently helps me pack my things. Finally, he blurts out what has obviously been on his mind: it seems that Madani has made out to the other boys in the hotel that he is sleeping with me out in the desert.

I stare at him, numb. I don't know that I can take anything else in. 'That is simply not true,' I say to him quietly. 'I am very disappointed in Madani.'

I turn around; Madani is standing in the doorway.

He begins to cry and yell and plead his innocence. Behind him, from the courtyard, Kadar is watching the whole exchange, grinning like a Cheshire cat. I wonder just how much of the scenario he orchestrated. It suits him to have the camp divided; he is relishing the chaos.

'Call me when the car is ready,' I say and close the door on both of them.

We have one last exchange, just as I get in the car.

Kadar turns around, and suddenly he flashes that irrepressible, arrogant grin that has always made me laugh.

'Hasta la vista, baby,' he says and, despite myself, I start to laugh. It's all such a dire mess.

'*Allahi*,' I say. 'Fuck you, Kadar.'

'Fuck you, too, *lalla*.' For a second, we actually grin at each other, united somehow in the weird way we always have been.

Then I drive away.

The drive back to Tan-Tan is subdued. Madani slumps in the back and doesn't speak, just smokes incessantly. What was to be a triumphant return to his hometown, the conquering hero returning from the long voyage, has turned into a humiliating spectacle. He has been exposed to his friends as a liar. In addition, I suspect Kadar has deliberately taunted and excluded Madani all week. He did not like the obvious closeness of our friendship, despite the fact that it is entirely platonic.

In turn, I no longer know who to trust. The reality is I can't trust anyone. In addition, I'd thought that in the time I was out of the desert and in contact with Gary, we would somehow come to resolve our problems. In fact, I only feel more bemused and hurt than I did when he left. I'm exhausted by the machinations of the past week. I look like hell.

My emotional life has never really impacted on my appearance before. My appetite had always survived any emotional upset; if anything, I put weight *on*. Now, I'm the thinnest I've ever been. I will later discover that I've dropped over twenty kilos. My hair is actually falling out. My skin is sallow, my face lined and drawn. A deep furrow appeared between my brows overnight in M'Hamid, and another runs across my forehead – lines that will mark my face forever. I shake and, no matter how many clothes I wear, I'm always cold. I cannot eat more than a few mouthfuls on any given day. If I force more, I simply throw it up. I am perpetually exhausted. Most of all, I feel as if I'm holding onto my sanity by the weakest of threads – one false slip will send me over into the abyss.

I've barely communicated with friends or family. I can't begin to describe the bizarre reality of life here. Besides, I know they would, to a man, tell me to get the hell out of here. I'm already bombarded by concerned emails, wanting to know where Gary is, what I'm doing out here on my own. I've been smoothing it all over on the website, focusing on the grandeur of the desert, the incredible adventure I'm having on the walk; there is no place on light-hearted blogs for my complications.

We return to M'Barak. It's a miserable duo that exits the vehicle to his exuberant greetings. He stops, plainly horrified by my appearance. He races around getting water warm, virtually pushing me away to go and have a wash. I've done little but glance sideways in a mirror for weeks. I actually can't bear to look at myself.

The news in camp is not good. Mimi, one of my bigger camels, the one I was considering selling, has an injured foot. We don't know the cause, but he is unable to walk any distance. We'll be stuck for a few more days. It's also been raining incessantly, a somewhat bizarre occurrence but not exactly weather that camels are happy walking in.

We sit up that night and I begin to lay out some of the facts of our situation. I explain that I need to go back up to Spain to renew my visa. I say I no longer trust Kadar and want to move our camp further out into the desert, where he can't find it should he choose to come looking.

M'Barak and Madani launch into a sea of vicious complaints. Kadar has not paid them what he promised; Kadar told them I would never make it further than Tan-Tan; Kadar has always been planning that I would fail and he would take the camels back. The camels, Madani tells me, sickeningly eager to ingratiate himself after the debacle of M'Hamid, actually belong to Kadar's father. That's why Kadar was so nervous about me selling them on – the camels are not actually mine to sell.

I realise in dismay that I never got certificates of sale. I guess, if he chose to, Kadar could totally screw me over.

The night wears on and around us the rain falls in drenching sheets. I am tired and cold and totally confused, and I want to simply switch off the voices of Madani and M'Barak with their endless griping and gossip. All I want is to walk, to get the hell out of here, and finally I order everyone to sleep.

We stumble on for a couple of weeks. It feels like the walking wounded. I've abandoned any pretence at conviviality; I pack up, walk, unpack, lie down away from the camp, prepare dinner and go to bed. I don't attempt humour or explanation.

Madani is sullen and withdrawn, sitting by himself and smoking endless joints from the block of hash he brought back from M'Hamid. I won't allow myself to join him – I may fall apart in towns, but I will not fall apart in my own camp. We are walking a wide loop around Tan-Tan. For 300 kilometres we will be within a 100-kilometre radius of the town. This means there are incessant night-time convoys of contraband vehicles passing us, smuggling gasoline, booze, cigarettes and – somewhat incongruously – baby formula. Madani wants me to flag the vehicles down and buy booze; I don't want anything of the kind adding to the tension in the camp.

On occasion we hitch back into Tan-Tan to buy supplies – or, more accurately, for me to check the internet and talk with Gary. He and I agree to meet in Spain in January, when I go back up to renew my visa. Gary tells me, via email, that he has decided to come back on the walk. I don't know how I feel about this but, after everything that has happened, I want to give us every chance of fixing things. I cannot pretend I will not be glad to have some support back. But a lot has happened and I have learned so much – is there any chance for Gary to catch up? I put those thoughts out of my mind, and we continue our slow progress around the periphery of Tan-Tan.

It's Christmas Day, and I'm sitting in yet another nomad's tent as the wind hurls sand with unrelenting fury just beyond the entrance. I'm with the women. Madani and M'Barak are in the men's tent. There's no point trying to walk; this sandstorm has been blowing for three days now, and we can barely see a metre in front of our faces. We've been staying with this family for the last couple of days, gratefully taking refuge in their far more comfortable tents.

I've given up trying to explain the significance of the day. The women have never heard of Jesus Christ. I explain that he also was a prophet, like Mohammed. They shake their heads in consternation; there is only one prophet. There is only one way they know here: the way of the desert, of Islam, of their home. It's becoming my reality also.

For all that I am intrigued by the rituals of the women's tent, the hours pass slowly. I can hear Madani and M'Barak laughing, and I know they're lying down and Madani is smoking incessantly. It's totally unacceptable for me to smoke in the women's tent, so I don't; but I've never smoked as heavily as I do at the moment. I find the enforced break difficult. I also find the strain of trying to communicate, with so very little of the language available, extraordinarily hard. We don't even have the commonality of culture to aid us, and there are frequent moments when the conversation simply subsides out of mutual confusion and embarrassment.

Despite the difficulties, I manage two exchanges which are both revealing and thought-provoking. The first is with the matriarch of the tent, a mother of seven with three adult daughters still at home.

She sits cross-legged and mimics the act of putting small stones in her mouth. She opens her hands in supplication, the universal gesture for asking for something. It's clear that there is something she wants from me, but I've no idea what. The girls keep saying the same word over and over, looking at me intently – it's clear that whatever they're asking for is important, and somehow forbidden. The mother points to her belly, then points around the room and gestures at the girls I know to be her daughters. She appeals with raised hands again, now in frustration.

I begin to distinguish some of the individual words from the lines the girls are repeating: Children. Many. Sick. Dangerous. Father. Forbidden. Medicine. No children. No more. Mother. Sick. Please. Medicine. Doctor. Children. Dangerous. *Haram* – forbidden – *haram*, *haram*. Father. Sick. Dangerous . . .

And then the penny drops. I look at their mother picking up tiny stones from a pile and mimicking swallowing them, and then how she puts a cross over her belly, and I suddenly realise that the girls are asking for packets of contraceptive pills.

I go out to one of my bags and bring back a packet. They crowd around and laugh with glee that I've understood. They hold their hands out – do I have any more? How many can I spare?

In the end I give them nearly my whole supply – the pill is easily bought over the counter in Morocco. This woman has got to have far more need of it than I, especially if her husband forbids it.

The second exchange that affects me deeply comes some time afterwards. We are talking with our hands, about what men find attractive in my country and theirs. I'm telling them that their hair is to die for, their faces stunning – they would be greatly admired in my country. One of the girls pulls out an old, tattered picture, obviously cut long ago from some Moroccan pop-culture magazine. The girl featured is heavily made up in a garish imitation of

Western models. Her hair is dyed a lurid shade of orange, and she pouts in a manner meant to be seductive but which is laughable and grotesque. The girl waves her picture at me and asks anxiously: '*Is she beautiful?*'

I look at the faces turned to mine, anticipating my response with dread, and I throw my head back and howl with laughter. They slap my hands in relief, rolling about with mirth at my response. I look them straight in the eye and use the Hassaniya word for 'ugly' – *shaina* – over and over. '*Shaina BEZZEF!*' I giggle – VERY ugly! And one of the girls leans forward and lets her *melekhva* slip off, revealing reams of black, curly hair and a full, voluptuous body covered by her slip.

'I am beautiful,' she says, smiling at me openly with pride. 'And I am Saharawi, from a good tribe. Many men will want me.' She tosses her hair back and laughs.

One of the women points at me. 'You also, very beautiful,' she says in Hassaniya. 'But' – she gestures with hands close together – 'Too skinny! You need to eat more!'

Now it is my turn to laugh. Of all the things I may have been accused of over the years, being too thin is definitely *not* one of them.

The two exchanges echo within as I walk away from the tent and wave at the women, leading my camels out through the beautiful remains of an acacia forest and into yet another dramatic, winding gorge between ancient cliffs.

The conversation about the birth control pills shocked me because, until now, the women – indeed, all the nomads I met – while becoming a familiar sight had remained as remote and alien as martians. It had never occurred to me to think that they would even *know* about the pill, let alone defy their autocratic father or husband by taking it. They had appeared to me as curious oddities somehow apart from my own life. While fascinating to look at, the experience was akin to appreciating a *National Geographic* photo. I had entered their tent with an eye to getting a similarly good photograph. In that way, I'd never stopped to consider the human element – the universal – beneath the *melekhva* or behind the filigree tea set. I was simply blinded by the superficial cultural differences, the feeling that their life was 'nomadic', 'primitive' and so totally *other*, that I hadn't seen the reality.

And in a similar fashion, the exchange about ideal beauty had been revealing because I had a glimpse at how difficult it must be, in an age where images are so readily available, for these women to be out in the desert for months on end. They meet up with other nomads only rarely and virtually never go to town. It must be difficult to know that there is a life out there of make-up and hair dye and things they don't understand and will likely never experience. They must wonder if somehow they are missing out, imagining what that life is like and how they would stack up.

The comments about my weight fascinated me on a whole different level. Every one of the women I met had been completely at home in her own plump, feminine form. Everyone had been anxious to show off her good looks, openly stating their belief in their own beauty without shame or prevarication. There was none of the simpering coyness that can taint female conversation in Western culture: 'But I think I look so *ugly*! And my butt is so big! You think my hair looks nice like this? Because I don't, I hate my hair so much – it's so thin and straggly. And I'm so fat! I hate it and I keep meaning to go on a diet but . . .'

It's a process I have always struggled with, despite feeling at times totally insecure about my own appearance. I have never enjoyed playing the 'begging for reassurance' female game.

So it was wonderfully refreshing to come across such open self-assurance and an uninhibited celebration of beauty. I had unconsciously assumed that women clad in the veil were demure and insecure, waiting for some man to come along. These were bawdy, funny, sexy, loving, warm and smart women – and despite living a life of hardship, striding out with their goats through the desert every day, they had a seemingly endless store of good humour and smiles, and no limit to the warmth they offered me. I'm intrigued by them.

※

Tan-Tan continues to be the focal point in our journey, and it becomes as familiar to me as M'Hamid. I'm in talks with Kadar about him buying the camels back, so I haven't sold any. I have a little money left in a bank account in England, which Dad forwards out to me. I travel in and out from different points in the desert, in a variety of contraband vehicles, to pick up cash, use the internet or telephone home. These ventures are rarely simple, and often involve adventures with authorities – not to mention drunk or stoned drivers and long, late-night treks to find the camp again.

Strangely, at times I feel invigorated by the steady stream of challenges, as if they're a legitimate distraction from my life, somewhere to focus the negative energy. But at other times I feel tired and overwhelmed, as if there is no room for me to be soft anymore.

On one occasion, I hitchhike into town to do another internet check. I'm desperately hanging out for news on the Royal Geographical Society grant, among other things. I have gone in with a lovely bloke who has passed our camp more than once. He smuggles gasoline, backwards and forwards from Es Smara to Tan-Tan, and takes a route that often passes near the places we camp. We have begun leaving markers for him, and so when he passes he drives in from the piste track and brings fresh bread or fruit, often staying for a meal. If one of us needs a lift into town, we sling him a few extra *dirham* and he runs us wherever we need to go.

The only glitch in this system is that it's illegal for anyone to take money from tourists to drive them around unless they are legally licensed to do so. In the case of our contraband guy, he is doubly at risk, as he is carrying illegal product in the rear of his truck. But generally I just put *melekhva* on and cover my face, keeping my head down if we pass any police stops. Even more amusing, the guy who runs this particular contraband operation has paid a reasonable bribe in advance for his vehicles to pass unnoticed. Our man usually takes a well-worn path around the police checkpoints. He actually toots and waves to the men in uniform as he trundles by, who in turn look up from the tourist vehicles they are merrily extorting and wave as we pass. Bizarre.

But on this particular day, things do not quite go as planned.

I have struck up a conversation with a French guy in Tan-Tan. Jean is a photographer who is also involved in film production. Fascinated by what I'm doing, he is eager to come out and spend a couple of days walking with me and take some pictures. Since Gary has left I've found it hard to get many images of myself, despite Madani's best efforts, and so I am very keen to take Jean up on his offer. Madani is also thrilled, hoping to learn some new tricks from an expert.

Our contraband man pulls up, and we quickly heft our shopping and Jean's pack into the back of the truck. The driver is anxious to leave town as quickly as possible – he's worried about being too conspicuous with a second tourist on board.

Unfortunately, just as we go to pull out, Jean spots a child running off into the crowd – carrying the backpack he just deposited. The kid has lifted it and taken off at speed.

Jean is furious and determined to get the pack back. Our problem is that, as soon as he begins to yell, a crowd forms and our contraband man, sweating, takes off at high speed, calling to us that he will do everything he can to track the kid down. Madani explains to us, hands shaking, that if the driver is caught with the gasoline on board, plus tourists, he will face a crippling fine and up to three years in prison. He begs us not to contact the police. Jean says that unless his pack is returned he is going straight to the police – to hell with the driver. I feel rather differently, but decide to keep my opinions quiet and just see if we can track down the thief.

An undercover manhunt ensues. Half the town gets involved, all sympathetic to us not wanting police attention. Suspicious of the unusual activity, the police stop more than one roaming group involved in the search. Each time, we are quickly thrust out of sight and the problem is described as a local one of no consequence.

After knocking on a sea of doors and travelling the length of Tan-Tan's labyrinthine back alleys, the snivelling kid is triumphantly hauled in front of us by a yelling, excited mob. The pack, and most of its contents, has been recovered. But the mob is calling for justice. They are out for blood and looking to Jean and me to administer it. (Primarily me, as I am now known by many in town and thus seen as the injured one.)

'Hit him!' the crowd yells. 'He is yours! You can throw a stone at him, beat him!' They are surging forward, insisting I punish this miserable, skinny kid.

He kneels in front of me, pushed down by two older men. He is scared, already roughed-up by the crowd, his old clothes tattered and torn. I recognise him as one of the street rats I've seen before, sniffing petrol from a handkerchief; I doubt he has much home or family to speak of. I can feel little else but pity for him, and yet I am conscious that after the work the crowd has done in finding him, I am expected to act.

I put my hand under his chin and tilt his face up.

'Do you understand what you did?' I ask him sternly in Arabic. He looks at me and his face crumples into tears. 'You should be ashamed. We are visitors to Morocco, and everything my friend owns is in that pack. Where would he have slept tonight? How would he have gotten home? You took his passport, his money, everything. Would you do this to someone in your home? Morocco is your home. You should be ashamed.'

The crowd yells in approval, but they want more. Madani looks at me nervously. 'They want you to hit him, *lalla*,' he says.

I feel trapped and uneasy. I do not want to hit the kid, but I can feel myself gearing up to do it, incited by the rage and pack mentality of the crowd. My desire to behave with decency wars with my desire to escape this place, this situation.

At the last minute I am saved. The contraband driver, blisteringly furious at the trouble he has been caused, pushes his way through the crowd to where we are standing. He cuffs the kid on the side of the face and then punches him. Released by his captors, the kid sprints up the hill and away from the mob. He is taunted by catcalls and whistles as he goes, and the crowd throws stones in his wake. Some clip him.

Jean looks at me, his face a picture of incredulity. '*Mon Dieu*,' he says. 'This place is crazy.'

'Quickly,' I say, 'we need to get out of here before the police come.'

But we don't quite make it. As I finish speaking, the police van pulls in, siren blaring. Madani and the driver melt into the crowd. We agreed long ago that, when possible, it is better for Madani to leg it than go through all the explanations with police. Like this, I can pass myself off as a normal tourist just passing through. It's easier.

This time Jean and I are held for several hours. We are questioned over and over about what we're doing here and what happened. I tell them Jean is my husband – in Morocco it's not customary for man and wife to have the same surname, as the wife keeps her father's name, so they have no reason to doubt me. We are merely a tourist couple visiting Tan-Tan; we lost a bag, but the locals helped us find it. Everything is okay.

It still takes several hours. I'm rarely particularly nice or smiling to police anymore – I've had too many encounters with slimy officials who are interested in more than conversation to give them any kind of encouragement. This time it is complicated because I'm wearing *melekhva* and have local henna on my hands. They also heard me speak a little Arabic, so now they want to know exactly what I've been doing and where. Jean looks on in amazement as I answer question after question.

'Does this happen often?' he asks as they finally let me go.

'All the time. So often I've stopped noticing it. Every small town, every settlement – if we have to pass it, then we have to go through that process. It drives me crazy.'

He shakes his head. 'Is terrible. Is crazy. I couldn't do this, I think.'

We fall back to the place I knew Madani would be waiting, in a quiet square on the edge of town. Our driver, bless him, comes by soon after to check for us. We hightail it out of town. The only problem is he has waited so long for us that he has to drop us on the side of the four-wheel-drive track – fifty kilometres in from the road, but still five kilometres or so from our camp. Normally this is nothing; but in the dark, and carrying supplies, it's not much fun.

Jean watches in disbelief as Madani and I scout about to find the depressions and markers on the ground that tell us which direction to go. We walk off across the plateau, and I can tell that until we reach the actual tent, Jean is highly suspicious of our ability to find it.

'This whole day is just bizarre,' he says as we sit around the fire. 'How the hell do you deal with all this stuff? And how on earth do you know how to find the camp? I would have been totally, utterly lost – and I have done a lot of camping and orienteering.'

For a second I feel proud. Then I suddenly choke up over the fact that this kind of stuff has actually become normal. I can never explain the trauma I have gone through to get to here; the nights, so many nights, of hunting for a contraband vehicle in dusty desert holes, to drop us somewhere on the *hammada*, then walking back into camp. I can't explain the nights when I've worried we would never find the tent, or the times in towns when I thought the police wouldn't let us leave. I can't explain that this whole crazy world of contraband vehicles and corrupt police and midnight runs from towns has become normal – and that somehow I find that both thrilling and terrifying. I want to tell him that I honestly fear for my sanity sometimes, but that in the middle of it I feel a weird calm and a certainty that somehow everything will be all right.

I also want to tell him that I am not so tough, that I fear every day I'm getting so much wrong and that the constant mayhem of the life I have created here does not feel exciting all the time at all. Rather, I often feel as if I've mismanaged my relationships and the walk itself so much that it is a poor facsimile of what a true expedition should be – in this sense, I've failed already. I don't feel tough and competent. Most of the time, I'm just hanging on, hoping to God that I don't stuff up too much, but unsure how to even recognise the scenarios that lead to problems. I don't realise at the time how much I am learning by simply going through all this, how being thrown in at the deep end emotionally and culturally will prepare me so well for future stages. All I can see is that I'm getting it wrong now, and I find it difficult to be proud of the walk, and even harder to be proud of myself.

But in the end I say none of this, just smile and shrug. I'm so lacking in confidence that I can't bear to admit my fears and expose myself with humour as I once could. I am hanging on too tightly, living in too much fear to confess that I feel utterly inadequate to this place – and indeed, to life. I am intense and contained. I feel as if I don't really know myself anymore. And what I do know, I don't like very much at all.

Jean stays for a couple of days, then hitches back when we get near a road. He tells me that he couldn't last more than a week doing what I am – he says it would drive him crazy.

It's a slow and miserable couple of weeks. Mimi is still limping; the weather is still vile. But I've made a few decisions and, as we make camp by a decent well where there is good feed for the camels, I call a council.

'This last month has been bad,' I begin. M'Barak nods emphatically. Madani just looks sullen. 'You both know that I need to go back to Spain, but I think we all need a holiday.' The two men look up.

'It is Eid al-Fitr, the big festival, next week,' I continue. 'What I would like to do is stop the camp here. I will stay with the camels while you both go back to your families for the festival. Then, Madani, you can come back here and stay with them while M'Barak takes a break for another week and I go up to Spain. We can all meet back here in two weeks, after we have had a rest and some time-out. Mimi will have a chance to recover, the worst of the rainy weather should have passed, and we will all feel better for the break.'

They are both watching me closely.

'I need to sort out money and some other details,' I say strongly. I feel, somehow, that a lot rests on this conversation. I need to take control. 'From this point on, I will be paying you – not Kadar. These are my camels, and this is my camp. I am in charge of it, and there are some things that are going to need to change – like, for example, I need to actually learn how to run it, instead of you two doing everything for me.

'It has been a hard couple of months for me. When I come back, I need for us all to work together to make it down the last

1200 kilometres. I will pay you well, and I will be fair. But I am not interested in all this talk – about Kadar and M'Hamid and who is trying to cheat whom. This is not my business. What I want is to get to Dakhla. That's the only thing that matters to me. Do you understand?'

They both nod eagerly. I take a deep breath and look around. A part of me is terrified to leave my camels and camp, fearing that somehow I will be unable to return. But I know, more than anything, that the best way to get all of this back on track is for us to take a break.

And besides – when I come back, Gary will be with me.

I hire a local nomad to watch the camels for the last couple of days before Madani is due back, so that I can cross paths with him in Agadir. I leant him my camera to take pictures of the festival, and I need it back before I go to Spain. I travel up out of the desert and we meet in a tourist hotel, where we sit out the back and drink quietly – and legally. It feels like a haven of sophistication after the Western Sahara.

We talk and sort out our differences. I apologise for being hard on him; Madani apologises for being an idiot. He has been a good friend, on the whole. I don't want to alienate him.

I still have a few days before I am due in Spain. I am sitting in a café in Agadir when Kadar rings.

'I want to see you, *lalla*,' he says. 'I want to see you before you go.'

'I don't want to see you,' I say quietly. And then, childishly: 'I hate you.'

'I hate you, too,' he says, 'but you are going to come to Ouarzazate, and we are going to sort you out with this money and camels and all these fucking things, and so we finish our business good.'

'Ouarzazate! I am miles from Ouarzazate.'

'Yes, but you come anyway; like this we make a little party. I know many people in Ouarzazate and we can have little crazy time, talk good, have fun, and I can make things good for you. Please come, *lalla*, I feel bad for leaving things like this.'

'But *Allahi*, fuck you, and your Hasta la vistas,' I say. He is laughing – and so am I.

'So you will come?'

'One false move and I'm gone.'

'No false moves, *lalla*. I promise.'

In Ouarzazate we meet at a hotel I know, and Kadar says we will talk business tomorrow.

'Tonight we have some fun, yes, *lalla*?' he says. I can't help but laugh. He really is incorrigible.

We head out into the night, to the house of a friend of his. '*A house?*' I say. 'Kadar, I am in no mood for family dinners and *melekhva*. Why the fuck are we going to someone's *house?*'

He chuckles. 'This is not like house you know – this is friend of mine, good friend. Tonight you see other Morocco.'

We walk up quiet dirt streets and, oddly, after all of the chaos I still feel excited by all of this: the darkness and strange back streets, the characterless tin door he knocks at.

Why do I always find myself in the back streets?

The door opens and it is a normal Moroccan home, only not normal. There are candles instead of lights. The host, Mustapha, is one very chilled out bloke, and his girlfriend is cooking brochettes over a brazier. We sit down on the mats on the floor and start drinking whiskey, and he rolls a spliff. His girlfriend asks for a cigarette. This is zigzag Morocco. It is as familiar to me now as 'legitimate' society.

We eat, then Kadar says it's time to go. We walk out into the night and take a *petit taxi* to a bar he knows. As we walk in, the doormen greet him with respect. Everyone knows who he is. I laugh: he wanted me in Ouarzazate so he could show off to his friends. Here, he is a big man. I know him well enough by now.

The bar is hysterical. In any European country, it could only be an extremely unfashionable gay bar. The clientele is strictly male, although Kadar tells me the girls will come later. An atrocious cover band plays. The lead singer is as camp as Christmas, and the outfit is the kind of thing more usually seen in bad RSL clubs in rural Australia than in an inner-city bar. It's like revisiting the early 80s. Men gyrate on the floor, grinding suggestively towards each other – well, hell, there ain't no women to be seen. The music is bad Moroccan pop covers. We sit at a small table and drink beer.

The place is so ridiculous I have to do something. I just can't take it seriously, and Kadar is eyeing me quizzically, wondering what I find so funny. It's impossible to explain to a Saharawi nomad, who has never left Morocco, how dismal this place is. I get up and hit the dance floor to the enthusiastic applause of all the men present. I dance and dance, and gradually some other women arrive – prostitutes, of course – and I dance with them, too. I guess I also look like a prostitute; although I don't care what they think I am.

We leave and go to another place, another disco, this one even seedier than the first, though with more people, more women. I dance a lot, losing myself in the music from home, closing my eyes and imagining myself in London or Australia, opening them to see a dance floor filled with Moroccans intrigued by the Western woman dancing crazily. Kadar joins me, his robes swirling as he moves. I laugh: the song is REM's 'Losing My Religion'.

I sit down and roar with laughter, my feet in sequinned sandals resting across the arms of the chair. For the first time in months, I'm having *fun*; I'm laughing and dancing and for one mad night, before I go back up to Spain and try to repair the train wreck of my marriage, I can just be crazy and love it, here where I'm an out-sider – and yet not. I revel in the madness.

I go back to my room and sit so that I can see myself in the mirror. For the first time, I really look at the girl I saw earlier. I begin to talk, as if I'm talking to my best mate. I look right at myself and I talk it all out – my impressions of Morocco and what I've gone through. How I've changed and what I see. I talk about the women in *hammams* and the nomadic women and how tough they are. I talk about feminism and how in Morocco the women understand truly what it is to be feminist, because they simply don't look to men for their emotional happiness. I talk about how in our culture, women have fought so hard for freedom, and yet they are trapped now, in a place where they still look to a man to define them, to make their lives complete. Moroccan women don't do this, I say into the mirror. They know and accept that men will never be like them, never give them what they need. They look to their friends and family, the other women, for their emotional solace. And they use their men for money, children and sex. And somehow, it seems to me that they are happier.

I speak to the mirror for hours. I talk through how I have changed and what is coming next. When I go to bed I'm exhausted and wrung out and strangely at peace. I never knew it was possible to talk to myself and feel as though I've had a conversation.

Maybe I really am going mad.

I talk with Kadar about the money and the camels. No matter whether Gary comes back or not, I want to be financially independent. I want to make sure I can run this by myself. I get a written agreement from Kadar, witnessed at the local police station, to the effect that I own the camels and that Kadar is going to buy them back from me – one at a time – for the full price we paid for them. The payments are structured over time, and he will forward money via Western Union at each town I stop in. The first payment is due upon my return.

We agree that I will now take on the payment of Madani and M'Barak; in addition, I get a signed note from him to them both, with the balance of what he owes. Suddenly we are back on our old footing, as if nothing untoward had ever happened. He is polite and respectful. We joke and laugh and talk business without any problems. I don't really know what has changed; I'm just grateful that we are sorting this stuff out at last.

We have a final round of tea and I get on the bus to begin the long trek up to Spain to see Gary. I should be in Marrakech in a few hours, where I will get the train up to Tangiers and catch the ferry across the Strait of Gibraltar.

But of course, nothing ever goes to plan.

⋙

The bus is trundling up from Ouarzazate into the Atlas Mountains, and the weather is getting colder and colder. Although I have a poncho and a reasonably warm jumper, the bus isn't heated and we are headed into serious alpine terrain. Stupidly, having only passed this way in the summer, I'd forgotten that in winter this is snow country. My feet are already numb and I am shivering.

We roll to a halt at the end of a long line of vehicles. There is a barrier at the base of the Tizi n Tichka pass. The police have closed it after snow began falling an hour ago. The rumour up and down the line of vehicles is that there are snowploughs on the way. If they can clear the worst of it in the next hour, we will be allowed to pass. Otherwise, we will be waiting until the following morning. Some vehicles are circumventing the wait by paying the gendarmerie on the barrier a decent bribe. But, looking outside the windows of the bus onto the snow falling in a thick white curtain, I don't fancy the chances of the rickety old bus up that windy mountain road anyway.

The few cafés at the base of the mountain sold out of food long ago and have closed. Local women begin to appear on the roadside, selling bowls of soup for three *dirham*. The men ensure that the women are fed first, before the pots run out. I was befriended in the bus station by a lovely girl and her brother. They take me under their wing and offer me part of the bread they had packed for the journey.

The bus remains stationary for three hours. Eventually the driver boards and a conversation ensues involving all the passengers: the barrier will not open tonight. There are two alternatives. The bus can return to Ouarzazate, and we can all choose alternate routes, or the driver can chance the other mountain pass, which will mean a long and potentially risky detour, but the bus will still reach Marrakech by morning. In order to do this, he will need us all to pay a bit extra.

A heated debate breaks out, and everyone has their say. Eventually we all agree to carry on to Marrakech, and a couple of volunteers collect the extra money. I notice that there are a couple of women with small children who are unable to pay. The driver shrugs, and nobody comments.

The bus trundles off into the cold night. I am struck by the cheerful acceptance of all on board. Rather than expressing discontent at the delay, everybody is busily sharing out their blankets, passing food to their neighbours and simply ignoring the sub-zero temperatures. Across the aisle from me, two crusty old blokes are travelling together. After my time in the desert, I would place them as true nomads, making an out-of-the-ordinary trip to family in the big city Their baggage is minimal and they are clearly dressed in their best. Behind them is a woman with a newborn baby, struggling to cope with her two toddlers. Without a word, the men take control of the children, playing with them, cuddling them to sleep, keeping them warm. When we stop at the bitterly cold mountain settlements, where the cafés have again run out of food, due to the unexpected influx of detouring vehicles, the men take the children to the toilet and find scraps of food for them to eat.

Not once, through the entirety of the freezing, interminable night, do I hear anyone complain. The bus slides all over the road, often caught in traffic jams and heavy snow as bus after truck attempts to negotiate the treacherous mountain roads. We pass vehicles that have rolled, whole buses that have just fallen into ditches, their passengers inside huddled into blankets. I huddle down into my poncho and lean forward, my forehead against the seat in front, trying to squeeze my freezing body deep inside the woollen covering, attempting to drift off to sleep. The seats are crammed so close that I cannot move without seriously disturbing my neighbour, so I don't.

I'm struck by the fact that not once do I hear anyone mention the conditions they're in. They say only that they have been delayed but will be there soon, there is no need to worry – and then quickly enquire after the wellbeing of the other person on the line.

I'm heartened and inspired by the humble endurance of those around me, their calm acceptance of the night's trials. I feel touched by their kindness and good-humoured care of each other. Far from being a dark experience, that bus ride comes to epitomise, for me, all that I love about Morocco and its people, and serves to remind me, somehow, of why I'm here.

It's twenty-four hours later that we pull into Marrakech, after a trip that I expected to take eight hours. I feel as if there is so much I haven't had time to process.

I travel up to Tangier by train, to make my transition from one world to another.

After the ferry from Tangiers and a bus, I walk off into Malaga, Spain, and into another universe. All around me there are women – on their own! Dressed in skirts! Having a drink by themselves!

I've become so accustomed to the restrictive, oppressive nature of life in Morocco that I can barely hide my shock and amazement. I stare just as much as the Moroccan men who got off the same boat as me. All that temptation, all that *freedom*! I almost feel sorry for the bewildered men, gazing around them in disbelief.

Almost.

It's good to see Gary, despite everything. It's hard to communicate openly; our discussions are circular, sometimes hurtful. But on some other level we still enjoy each other's company. We wander along the beachfront and eat good food. I still love being with him as much as I ever have. We talk endlessly.

On some levels the conversations are healing and constructive; but on others, I think we both let ourselves down by remaining defensive, and, perhaps, less than emotionally honest.

Finally, Gary tells me that he has decided not to come back on the walk. The reasons are confusing. I'm left feeling that he doesn't want to come back to *me*, and I think that, from his perspective, he feels I don't want him there. On the last night, somehow all of our communication becomes twisted and ugly, and I feel like neither of us is saying what we really mean. The biggest killer of marriage is defensiveness – when both sides feel too vulnerable to be truly open, there is little real chance to mend things.

I feel as if this whole week has been some kind of charade, a test in a game I didn't realise I was playing. I feel bemused and battered by the whole process, and I just want to run back to my desert peace.

The next day I stand at the station with Gary, waiting for the bus that will take me back to Algeciras, and the boat back to Morocco. I can't bear to look at him. I don't want to say goodbye again; want desperately to beg him to come back with me; want to say that I don't feel brave, or strong, or independent – just sad, lonely and scared, reluctant to plunge back into the sinking sands of Morocco. I want to hold onto him and never let go. But in the back of my mind something stops me. A part of me is cautious, remembering just how devastated I've felt every time he has rejected me. And the proud, indignant – and perhaps insecure – part screams that he didn't want to come back anyway. Before coming to Spain he had already booked a return ticket to England, and then another one to Australia. I accept my own part in the whole thing, but I still feel that he doesn't really want me or the walk.

I hug him goodbye tentatively, not looking at him. I board the bus and look at his lonely figure standing there, forlorn and dejected, the pained, half-smile on his face, trying to be brave for me. In that moment, all I want to do is run from the bus and into his arms. But even as I rise, the bus begins to move, taking me away from him, taking me back to my craziness. All I can do is weep silent, choking tears, and wave at his face until it is taken from my sight, wondering somewhere inside whether or not I have just made the biggest, most horrible mistake of my life.

I cry for most of the trip back to Algeciras. I go through the usual hassle of carting baggage around the different agencies to find the cheapest boat ride back, and go to the port to catch my ferry.

For some reason we're delayed, and the boat rests in port for three hours before we leave. It's the most horrendous few hours of my life. I sit there, frozen to my seat, willing myself to get up and move, to take a bus out of here and back to Gary, telling myself it's still not too late. I can't believe I'm here again, in the same place I was in Assa, questioning my choices. I want more than anything to run off the boat; the longer it stays in port, I wonder if that is what I'm supposed to do. But I cannot move, and this scares me most of all, because I know that if I truly wanted to go back, I would already have done so. *God*, I think, *who am I? What have I become?*

And the reality is that I have no idea. There is only the walk now, and the walk *is* me. I have nothing else.

Two days and a lot of kilometres later, I'm back in camp with my camels. My days of madness and self-indulgence have passed. I can't afford to sink into that stuff. The only person who can make this work now, I know, is me. I have 1200 kilometres of one of the most barren and dangerous stretches of the Moroccan desert in front of me, full of landmines, bandits, low water supplies and hostile military posts. I have barely walked anywhere for the past month; I have very nearly lost my mind. But I look around me, at my camels grazing in the soft haze of sunfall and the tattered, dirty canvas of my once pristine tent. I look at my feet with old henna still marking them and the calluses on my hands from handling baggage and ropes. I look ahead to the distance, where the desert stretches away from me, calling me as it ever has, as deep and exotic as I've ever found it, and I think to myself: *This is not over.*

I have never felt more determined.

Chapter Seven

We're standing on the top of a rise and a new kind of country stretches away before us. The tall gravel mountains and verdant valleys are finished. Here begins the scrubby, sandy wastes of the Western Sahara, one of the most monotonous, barren parts of the desert I will walk through. M'Barak, Madani and I stand still on the rise for a moment and look out at the plateau below us. It's a washed-out blur of yellow and dull green. The terrain is broken up by numerous small dunes, as if someone has simply poured piles of sand on an outback house block, ready to build something. They are strangely out of place.

'Polisario! Hee!' M'Barak looks out at the horizon and shakes his head. I look at Madani for enlightenment.

'We are in Polisario country now,' Madani tells me. 'Not that we need to worry.' And he and M'Barak look at each other and laugh. They begin to compete, in an almost childlike manner, in whooping war cries as we head down on to the plateau.

The Polisario is a rebel front working for the independence of the Western Sahara from Morocco. It emerged in opposition to the Spanish rulers of the Western Sahara. When the Spanish withdrew in 1975, war erupted between Mauritania and Morocco over who should control the rights to the territory. In the middle of the dispute were thousands of Saharawi, a people who have roamed the area for centuries. Caught in a pincer movement between the two armies, thousands of Saharawi fled to neighbouring Algeria, where they regrouped in Tindouf and formed a government in exile – the Saharawi Arab Democratic Republic.

Mauritania withdrew its claim to the territory and struck a peace accord with the Polisario in 1979. Mauritania is the only country in the world to have a Saharawi government, and many of its citizens sympathised with the Polisario cause – and still do. The Moroccans immediately laid claim to the entire territory and fought on into the mid 80s. They eventually constructed a wall – known as the Moroccan Wall – which they staffed with an entire army of Moroccans, whose sole purpose was to keep the Saharawi out of the more lucrative areas of the Western Sahara – towns such as Es Smara and El Aaiun (Laayoune).

In 1991 the Moroccans and Polisario entered into a United Nations monitored peace accord centred on a referendum on independence. Unfortunately, in the intervening years, and despite repeated rounds of negotiations and discussion, the referendum has not materialised.

What this means on the ground is that two whole generations of Saharawi have now grown up either in the refugee camps in Tindouf or as second-class citizens in their own land. The population of the Western Sahara is no longer strictly Saharawi, since the notorious 'Green March' of 1975 in which the Moroccan government marched 350,000 of its citizens into the territory to reclaim it from the Spanish. Backed by the Moroccan military, the territory is now considered by Morocco to be a part of that nation; the mixed backgrounds of the populous reflect that.

Resentment simmers, and the threat of military engagement is real and ongoing. For the Saharawi, the dispute is met with passion, the wound deep. Thousands of lives have been lost. The Western Sahara is littered with landmines and the remains of live ammunition. Political activists are still jailed with monotonous regularity, and international human rights organisations report a distressing amount of abuse and repression by the Moroccan government in relation to the Saharawi.

Already on my journey I have been made fully aware of the deep contempt much of Moroccan authority displays towards the Saharawi. More than once, police officers have asked me, right in front of Madani, how I could 'lower myself' by travelling with a Saharawi guide. They've all warned me about being attacked by rogue Polisario fighters in the 'wilds' of the Western Sahara.

But from the start of this walk I've spoken to M'Barak and Madani about all of the issues involved. From the inside, as such, their views are rather different to the dark warnings espoused by the military I encounter. We talk about it again now.

'Do you think we will run into Polisario groups out here?' I ask.

'EEEEE! I hope so,' says Madani. M'Barak punches the air again and lets out another war cry in agreement.

Madani continues: '*Lalla*, I am Saharawi. Every nomad in this area is Saharawi. If you are Saharawi, you are Polisario. This is our land. Maybe we don't all fight; maybe we are not all in Tindouf or in the rebel forces – but every one of us, in our hearts, we are Polisario. Of course we are. So don't worry about coming across Polisario, *lalla*. For us, the Polisario are who we drink tea with. No, they are no problem. Our problem? Out here, we worry about the military. *That* is who we run from. Them, and the bandits only out to steal camels. They are who we worry about. But the Polisario? No, they are family, friends. No threat to us.'

In fact, I find myself more and more drawn to the Saharawi cause. Every night at dusk, the radio crackles to life – the rebel radio station broadcasts from Tindouf. It starts with the haunting, deep-soul groove of steel blues guitar, then comes the hand clapping and finally the chanting voices, singing evocative songs of freedom and defiance. The music is brilliant. Much later I will hear the acclaimed Malian desert band, Tinariwen, and think that they have nothing on the musicians of the Western Sahara.

At the first bluesy chord, all three of us leap from that sound like it's an electric prod, jumping to our feet, stamping the rhythmic dance that marries the music so well. Madani and I dance with our arms up and out to our sides; he stamps his feet and cocks his hand over his head, moving in short, abrupt punctuation marks. I hold my arms out and turn my hands; my hips roll and twitch beneath my *melekhva*. Every time the music gains momentum and pace, I throw my head back and feel as if they are singing in celebration of my life, too, of this nomadic wandering out here with my camels in the wild silence. Their music is mine – and so are their stories.

The songs are of pain, suffering, love and war. For all that they sing of loss, the nomads of the Sahara sing of the highest ideal of romantic love. I am seduced by their passion and strange naïvety. Even today, it is not unusual for a Saharawi man to spot a woman in the distance, to like the way she fills a *melekhva*, and by the end of the day to have declared his undying love and taken his marriage proposal to her parents. The music reflects this; there are plenty of moving poems set to the haunting strains of Saharan steel guitar, telling of the terrible wonder of loving with passion.

Gradually I begin to recognise some of the songs and, with Madani's help, to make out the words. One night I hear a song on the radio that Madani taught me at the start of the walk.

It is sung from a woman to her lover. She sings of seeing his beautiful face once and knowing she must have him; and when she does, she will tie him to her like the camel is tied, so he can never leave.

There is something unbearably poignant for me in being able to sing along to this song in another tongue. I rock back and forth and sing the chorus with the wailing voices. Their sound seeps into my bones as if I have always known it. I make Madani sing it to me over and over. I crouch close to the radio, trying to pick up the individual words in Arabic.

I also love the irrepressible cheek inherent in their culture. I hear 'Tumbaramazaina' on the radio one night. It's a song I associate with M'Hamid, a song I have heard the M'Hamid nomads sing many times. I have always assumed it was a ballad of love and loss, but when I ask Madani what it means, he tells me, 'It is about drinking Coca Cola with milk, and how good it makes you feel.'

So, of deep historical and emotional significance then.

We spot increasingly fewer tents now, but the nomads we pass are more hospitable, more open than any we have met before. One day, walking through a wide-open plain, an ancient, wizened man comes scurrying over to greet us.

'Salaaaaaaam aleikum!' he calls with enormous vigour. Then, without waiting for a response, he launches into a torrent of Arabic at high volume. As he draws nearer, I am astonished at the character in his face. He is as lined and wrinkled as a desiccated prune, his silver hair mere wisps on his head. He has barely a tooth left in his mouth and his hands are a constellation of spots and lines. But his body is wiry and tough. His eyes, set deep in the papery, sun-dried folds, are as bright as blue marbles.

Madani and M'Barak are chuckling at the antics of the old man, and I look at Madani quizzically, not understanding much of the Arabic.

'He says that we must take care of you,' Madani says. 'He came running over here to say, "You two reprobates look after this woman! You hear me! She is our honoured guest! You give everything to her – anything happens to this woman, you will be explaining to me!"' I look up and the old man is grinning wildly at me, his eyes full of good humour. I laugh and say in halting Arabic, 'I am so glad you are here, father! These two are not men! I am so pleased to know there are real men in the desert who know how to look after a woman!'

He cackles in delight, and for a good ten minutes we do nothing but exchange jokes and banter. When it's time to walk on, he presses a small bag on me – it contains a handful of juicy dates. I decline with a smile, not wanting to take what I am sure is his food for the day. But he insists and waves away my efforts to reciprocate. He wanders off, hands hanging down from the wooden staff slung over his shoulders, singing loudly to his herd of camels grazing down the plain. He turns once and yells again to my companions to look after me, then wanders on.

'You see,' says Madani as we walk, '*That* is the Polisario the military keep warning you about.'

At first it seems the Polisario, or indeed anything to do with bandits or the military, is the least of our problems. After months of relatively easy walking, the terrain has suddenly become hard, the conditions forbidding. Far from the peaceful, rambling days between Assa and Tan-Tan – rocky massifs rearing up on either side, stony watercourses and pretty palmeraies – this stretch is a long, flat, windswept bit of desolation.

The weather so close to the coast was always going to be a little inclement, but I find the problem is not that it changes constantly, rather it does exactly the same highly unpleasant thing every day.

The *lejej* (wind) starts off as a dull roar early in the morning, just enough to flap the tent about as we pack it up. The tent itself is heavy from the night's dense humidity and is difficult to fold and carry. By about 10 am, the dull roar becomes a whipping gale, making conversation impossible and the camels uncomfortable. Sand gets into every orifice. Despite the sun being pretty strong, the wind lowers the temperature so that one rarely gets out of heavy clothing and feels reluctant to stop for long. By early after-noon, when we stop, the *lejej* is blowing hard enough that erecting the tent is an almighty battle. Finding a place where there is either sand to weigh down the tent, stones to hold it or ground actually soft enough to drive the pickets into is nothing short of a miracle.

Once inside the tent, we are sheltered from the *lejej*; but we are also perhaps the only source of shelter for miles around, not to mention a rich source of food for the tiny black flies that call the desert home.

We make our tea and eat our lunch with the crawling black multitude and settle in to regard the fascinating sight of gravel hamada being stirred into dust balls by the ever-increasing wind.

And then, suddenly, it drops. Usually just after we have cooked and eaten dinner, and are preparing to get into bed, the tent stops shaking, the chill drops from the air and we find ourselves strip-ping off our layers and taking off blankets. The atmosphere has changed from raging winds to dense, suffocating humidity. Along with the lovely sound of *drip, drip, drip* as the condensation runs off everything, we are treated to the sultry symphony of that most delightful of insects – the mosquito.

They are called '*namoos*' in Arabic. Our long night is then punc-tuated by less than sophisticated utterances of pure frustration as, one by one, we are savaged by the little bastards. M'Barak, having long ago adopted the F-word as his own personal curse, thrashes about in his sleeping bag saying, 'Fucking *namoos*. *Allahi* fucking.'

As we walk further into the emptiness, though, the discomfort is overshadowed by the increasingly common evidence of the Polisario conflict. Accustomed to finding the odd bit of ammunition or remnants of exploded devices lying all through the desert, I've become a little blasé when sighting anything of the type. But now we begin to come across twisted car wrecks, blown to pieces by the dormant mines. As we follow an old Spanish road, covered over by sand drifts, there is endless detritus from violent encounters.

Not far after Tan-Tan, we are walking through an area bounded on both sides by a mountain range. Unusually, there is a four-wheel-drive track running in the direction we are walking.

M'Barak gestures at the track and says in Arabic, 'Today, you walk here only.' I look at Madani for elaboration; we rarely walk along tracks.

'He says there are many, many landmines along this part – it is a military area,' Madani explains. 'He says that here we must stick to the track, even if it takes us the long way, because if we go off it he cannot tell where the mines are. Here is very dangerous, *lalla*. Even if you want to go to the toilet, you ask M'Barak first; he will show you where it is safe. Please be careful.'

I can see little difference in the terrain, only that it looks slightly swampy, a bit like a dried watercourse. It is still and sheltered in the valley, and the track is deep and well travelled. It is obvious that nobody deviates from it; in places, the ruts are worn deep.

M'Barak will not stop, even for a drink of water. He hustles us through the valley, often racing ahead, scouting about, jumping off the donkey and back on, looking up, across, around. It's only when we climb the rocky path at the far end that I see him relax.

'Was it just landmines he was worried about?' I ask, watching M'Barak as Madani translates the question. M'Barak looks at me, then his eyes dart about as he searches for an answer.

'Tell him I want to know what's going on, please,' I say. Then I look at M'Barak and ask in Arabic, 'What is it, truly? A problem here?'

M'Barak squats down. Madani and I follow suit so we are in a little circle. I have become used to talking in this way.

'After Tan-Tan we made a group decision to walk deep into the desert, yes?' M'Barak begins. Madani is translating, but I understand much of what he says. We both nod in agreement.

'I think this is the right decision, because already before and around Tan-Tan we have come across many police posts and military checkpoints. They ask too many questions; they want *baksheesh*; they give us trouble. So I agree with walking this way – I think it is better.

'But out here we are nowhere – there is nothing, you understand? Not even the contraband vehicles go through here. Because out here is where the bandits live – the people who are not Polisario, not military, not nomads – just criminals. They steal goats and camels, and they will slit your throat for no reason. They do not care for getting caught, only for what you have. In certain places they are worse than others. If you are walking in this part of the desert, this is the only place to cross these mountains – through this valley. And there are landmines everywhere. But the bandits know where the mines are, and they know where to hide in the cliffs. They can find you – hijack you – easily.

'From here on, it is going to be like this a lot. Landmines, bandits. At night we need to have the camels close. Sometimes we will need to take turns watching them. Around here the nomads are not necessarily friends – especially if they are on their own. In the tents, yes, sure, Polisario and no worries. But one nomad on his own – be careful, he is probably a bandit or working for them. Yes? Do you understand?'

We walk on and I ask some more questions, but I get the picture.

Weirdly, though, it seems as if his warnings just don't penetrate – or at least don't cause me any actual fear. Perhaps it is the aftermath of the emotional trauma. Perhaps I don't care too much for my own life at the moment. But I take his warnings, shrug and agree to be careful. Then I go back into my walking stupor, and I feel as safe and calm here as I always have. Despite the fact that on occasion I go to pee and discover that I was about to squat on a mine. That will generally rouse me out of complacency for a whole five minutes. It happens more often than I care to think.

On the stretch between Tan-Tan and Laayoune, we're deep in the desert, walking a wide loop, almost doubling the distance we would travel if we were close to the road, which runs directly north–south along the coastline.

The problem for us is that the road into Laayoune and the surrounding areas is one of the most heavily patrolled in the whole country. Laayoune is the centre of the Saharawi independence movement and the town where the United Nations Mission for the Referendum in Western Sahara delegation (MINURSO) is based. Foreign journalists are not welcomed, and tourists are closely monitored. We are all aware that an expedition of my type could be closed down on sight, just out of misunderstanding or suspicion. We have all decided, after the various encounters with uncomprehending police and military, that avoidance and keeping an extremely low profile is by far the best policy.

I'm facing the kind of choice that will become increasingly familiar: walk the 'safe' route and risk military encounters or walk the 'bandit' route, or illegal one, and take my chances with the unsavoury elements.

I've taken the same decision I will tend toward throughout my desert trek – chance the bandit route. Thus far, the very worst type of bandits have been the ones who extort and harass in national uniform.

We have found a greater harmony in the camp since we all had a break. I am getting on top of the things that were concerning me. Although it terrifies the hell out of M'Barak, and despite his conviction that I am fundamentally incapable, I've begun to insist on working more closely with the camels. I have actually learned a lot from close observation. When I start handling them, I find I'm quite confident and encounter few difficulties. Of course, by this stage, having been in the hands of such an experienced cameleer, my animals are calm and well trained.

But, nonetheless, M'Barak can step out and allow me to do the jobs I'd previously watched.

I'm confident packing the camels now, but the one task M'Barak will not teach me is strapping the equipment down and making the final rope adjustments. I get angry and insist; I even go right ahead and do the job. He simply undoes my knots and refashions the ropes his way. Madani is equally frustrated. Despite my many explanations that after the Western Sahara I will be on my own and need to do these things myself, M'Barak simply shrugs, laughs and carries on.

On the positive side, I learn a vast amount from watching the way he adjusts and balances the baggage for different animals and differing conditions – mountain passes, dunes. M'Barak is a true camel man, and many of his lessons will stay with me for thousands of kilometres to come.

One afternoon, we are camped on an isolated hilltop. The camels are grazing on the plateau far below. We have camped up where there is a tree for shade and we have a good view of who is coming. M'Barak has gone for a ramble over onto the neighbouring hilltop. Madani has gone for a wash.

I'm watching the camels when I suddenly spy something out of the ordinary. I see a fifth body move. And suddenly, with dawning horror, I scream out to M'Barak. I'm already running down; I know he will not get there in time. Down on the plateau, I can see Mimi engaged in a fight with Chamlette but, far worse, in between them is a third camel. It is a *naga* – a female.

There are plenty of herds of them in the desert, groups made up solely of mothers and babies. They're usually closely watched by their nomadic guardians; any bulls are quickly chased off.

But we are not in customary grazing country, and undoubtedly the guardian of this group is sleeping behind a bush.

Whenever *nagas* are close, we guard our bulls with an iron fist. I've seen close up the performance they put on in the presence of females, the puffing up of the mouth bladder so it hangs out the side in a huge pink bubble, oozing froth. They prance and shy and become increasingly agitated and difficult to control. When we are walking, I will have both camels on the shortest possible lead, sometimes actually stopping until the females are out of the way. With another bull around, the situation is even more dangerous – in Australia, travellers are advised to simply shoot wild bull camels. They are nasty, dangerous and extremely aggressive. In Australia – and other Arabic countries – I will find it is not the custom to travel with bulls, only bullocks or cows. But in Morocco it is normal and, thus, the dangers are ever-present.

There are no stray bulls down there, but Mimi is attempting to mount the *naga*, and Chamlette has suddenly turned into a raging fighting machine, determined to drag Mimi off. It is a clear breach of protocol for one of my camels to impregnate the camel of another nomad without an agreement, but right now I'm worried that one of my bulls will end up severely wounded by the other.

I have seen M'Barak break up scraps between the camels before. I go racing down the hill, and pick up M'Barak's camel stick, his *dhabuz,* on the way. Screaming like a banshee, I launch myself headlong in the midst of the snarling, snapping camels, beating at all three of them like hell. I crack Mimi over the skull, and he jumps down off the *naga,* whom I belt on the rump. She runs away in the face of my vicious assault, and I turn to wield the stick on Chamlette and Mimi, who are still trying to lock on each other's necks, their teeth bared, spitting and foaming. I crack the stick in every direction until I'm standing right in the middle of the two and whacking indiscriminately.

Finally, I get Mimi to back off. He is panting and groaning. It takes a while longer for Chamlette's anger to subside.

I turn around and M'Barak has a rope in Mimi's mouth and the camel's knee-hobbled in lightning speed. Spitting furiously, M'Barak comes over, roughly shoves me aside and ropes Chamlette. I am shaking.

'*Nagas,*' I say weakly, indicating where the two females are heading over the hill. M'Barak ignores me and runs his hands over the camels' legs, checking for wounds or bruising. As the adrenalin subsides, I can feel myself starting to get angry. M'Barak appears to be cross at my interference. *What was I supposed to have done?*

Madani appears, having sprinted back from his wash when he heard the shouting. I gesture at M'Barak.

'Why is he angry at me?' I demand.

Madani speaks to M'Barak for a moment. I can see the older man's distress; he is gesticulating wildly and speaking in agitated tones, but his Arabic is too fast and complex for me to pick up more than phrases here and there.

'He says you could have been killed. He says you are his responsibility, in his care. Nobody should ever get between two fighting bulls – they will kill you. They are crazy when they are like this. He says if you see something like that, then you call for him. Let him deal with it. It is too dangerous for you.'

I hold my anger in check. 'Can you please ask him,' I say to Madani, very calmly, 'what he would've done if *he'd* got here first?'

M'Barak looks at me and then down, shaking his head. He says something to Madani, and when he looks up I can see that he is laughing.

'He says he hopes he would have done the same thing, but he thinks, *by God, maybe I would have been too scared!*' We are all laughing. 'He says you are a crazy woman but thank God, because if you don't do that, maybe one of your camels is dead now. But he also says please, please don't do it ever again, because he does not want to explain to your father why you die in the desert!'

We walk back up the hill, leading all four camels after us. By the time we are back at camp, M'Barak is mimicking for Madani the way that I got in between the camels, roaring with laughter and clutching the younger man's arm. 'And then she did *this*! And *this*! And the camels – they went like *that*! And I tell you, I never see a woman like this, by God . . .'

That evening we sit around the fire and have a conversation that will stay with me.

As so often happens, the dramatic incident with the camels triggers off a plethora of tales of dangerous encounters and hairy situations. M'Barak tells me tales of wild camels he has known, of camels he has smuggled over borders and wrestled into submission. Madani and I tell M'Barak how lucky we both feel to be walking with him, what an excellent guide he is and how we trust him. His ears turn pink at the compliments, and then he turns to me and he says, 'I have never worked for a woman before. When

I took this job, they told me, "It is a couple, but it is the woman who is the chief." I didn't know what to think. But then that night – you remember that night – when the storm came in the valley and the tent fell down?'

I nod. I remember, all right. It was the night Kadar turned up.

'Well,' he says, pointing into the sand to emphasise this point, 'that was the night I knew you were *chief.*' He stands up and mimics me, pretending to hold the tent.

'Drop the tent!' he yells, and he and Madani go off into peals of laughter, kicking their legs in the air. 'Get the camels!' They laugh even harder. I am laughing with them too, although uncertain if I am being criticised or praised.

'Did I sound stupid?' I ask Madani. He repeats my question to M'Barak, and at that point they both settle down and look at me. M'Barak turns to Madani and tells him something solemnly in Arabic, with great dramatic pause, as he always does when he wants to get his point across. Madani translates:

'Not stupid. Very much, not stupid. Before this, there is no leader. We do not know who runs it, this walk – if it is me or Gary or you. But this night you take control and tell us what to do, and then we know – it is you, the *chief.* Gary, he is very nice, very good man. But the *chief* – it is you.

'And then, in Tan-Tan, I think this walk is finished. I think you are too sad to stay, that it is too hard. Everybody, they try to cheat you. Kadar, he does the wrong thing. The police are bad; Madani gets in trouble. And I am sick of everyone. But then, no, you come back. You keep walking. I never, ever think you come back again after Spain. But you do, and you keep walking, and you learn Arabic, and you learn the camels. No, *lalla,* truly, you are Saharawi – and you are the *chief.*'

They both look at me earnestly. It is late into the night, far later than our normal sunset bedtime. We have stoked the fire up. The moon is late tonight and just rising, low and yellow, on the horizon. I look over at the two faces of these men who have been my companions for four months now and feel a rush of affection. I take M'Barak's words with a grain of salt; if there is one thing I have learned over this time, it is that exaggeration and lavish praise is a characteristic of Arabic communication. But I know that, at least in part, M'Barak means what he says. I am touched and appreciative that he has some understanding of the road I have travelled to here.

'You have been good friends to me,' I say in halting Arabic. 'I wish I could take you both into Mauritania.'

Madani translates M'Barak's quick response. 'M'Barak says he will find you the guide for Mauritania. He will not let anyone but the best of camel men go with you. You are as his daughter; he will make sure you are safe.'

M'Barak nods emphatically and I smile, but again I take it with some caution. Excessive promises are something else I have become wary of. Equally, as much as I am grateful to both of the men, I am eager to run my own show. I see ways now that would make things more efficient, and there are habits that I find annoying. I am a little like a teenager looking to leave home; I want to make my own mistakes. But while I am here, I intend to learn as much as I can.

As the moon rises and our tales get taller, I am led to ask M'Barak another question. We have been talking about the feral camels that roam the interior of Australia. This is one of the men's favourite bedtime stories. Their eyes widen and I can see their sheer disbelief that there could possibly be so much money running around at liberty, there for the taking. They always ask if there are people out there catching them.

'Let's say I wanted to go out there and get a camel,' I begin. 'How on earth would you catch one that is not hobbled or has a head rope?'

M'Barak and Madani talk over top of each other to answer, leaning forward to explain.

'It is very hard to catch wild camels,' Madani translates. 'And very dangerous. You need two men – strong men.

'You never come at a camel from the front; he will run straightaway. You need to approach him from behind, so he does not see you.

'Right at the last moment, as he sees you or before, you grab his tail. As soon as you do, put all of your weight, as hard as you can, back against him, like this.' M'Barak leaps to his feet, grabs the branch of the acacia tree and adopts a waterskiing pose, pulling back with all his might.

'But then, as soon as you have him like this, you must wrench the tail over to the side. Weight on his tail will unbalance a camel; like this he cannot run, does not know where to go. And when you twist to the side, you pull with your whole body, and he will come down onto the ground. But for this you need to be very, very strong – otherwise the camel will twist free and run, and then you have lost him.

'When he hits the ground, this is where you need the other man. He will run to the front and get a rope around the head and nose of the camel – like you have done when you mouth rope, yes?'

I nod – this bit I understand from catching the camels every day.

'As soon as you have a rope around the head and mouth, you control the camel. But until you have the mouth rope in or a ring through his nose, the other one stays holding the tail. Like this, you control the camel.'

As he finishes, M'Barak sits back down, having acted out Madani's story. He wags his finger at me.

'But this, *lalla*, is not something you ever try,' Madani interprets sternly. 'This is very dangerous. Too dangerous. Even worse than fighting bulls. M'Barak says to promise you will never do this.'

I laugh at them both. 'I'll never need to. But it's a great story.'

Before bed, I wander away from the camp and look back down the hill. In the glow of the fire I can see the cloud of the acacia and a couple of date palms silhouetted by the moon in the distant valley. I can just make out the outlines of my camels couched near our camp. Madani and M'Barak, robed and turbaned, lie on cushions. From this distance, the tableau looks impossibly exotic, like a scene from *Arabian Nights*. I look up at the incandescent sky and for the first time in so very long, I feel something deep within stir back to life.

I can do this. It's strange and weird and so unlike what I thought it would be; it's so much more than walking and camels and wells. But I can do this. I can learn it. I just have to keep on going.

Thank God there are so many kilometres of this beautiful place yet to walk.

Laayoune brings me back to earth with a thump.

After a tumble down a hillside, I've torn all the ligaments in my ankle. Left with little choice, I've limped along for the last few days until we are in the vicinity of the town. This stretch has taken nearly three weeks. At the first opportunity, Madani and I hitch in from our camp. We travel the seventy kilometres in yet another run-down contraband vehicle. I stay wrapped up and hidden the whole way. We race to our respective needs: Madani to find hash, booze and women; me to get my ankle examined, pick up money from Western Union and find the internet. M'Barak has water to last for a few days, but we are hoping to go back out to camp tomorrow. This is just an overnight stop to ensure I have done no serious damage to my foot and to buy the supplies we need, having run out of nearly everything.

Laayoune is overrun by UN-marked four-wheel drives and military vehicles. I've never seen so many in one place. It's also far larger and wealthier than most of the towns I've passed through. Perhaps due to the UN presence, there are far more cafés and restaurants catering to the European market. But I stay clear of those – I don't want to attract any attention. Although there is the same bustling marketplace as in Tan-Tan, Laayoune seems far more modern – there are proper shopping precincts as well as the lines of tin doors that open onto the street, behind which are a thousand tiny stores. There are no camels in the street here, or nomads driving a herd of goats along quiet laneways; there are motorbikes, expensive cars and Saharawi men dressed in Western suits. But the women are a sea of colourful *melekhva* – Saharawi dress – and it is this that reminds me we are firmly in the Western Sahara now. I feel a surge of excitement, as if I've crossed some invisible border.

M'Barak has family here, and we contact them on arrival – they will drive us back out to our camp. The downside of this is, of course, that I'm immediately absorbed into the heart of the family. While I appreciate their kindness and hospitality enormously, it's almost impossible to explain that I need to spend most of my time in the internet café – I must update my website, which takes hours on this connection. And, more importantly, I must communicate with Gary.

The family – and the women in particular – find it extra-ordinary that I could possibly need to spend so much time at the computer. I try to explain that I'm communicating with my family. They shrug and accept it, although not without silently inferring that I simply don't want to spend time with them.

Part of me seethes with frustration. I spend weeks on end in the desert, speaking only to M'Barak and Madani about camels and nomadic life – topics they are able to converse on. I have absolutely nobody to whom I can talk, in my own language, about my life or how I see things. While the two of them at least have each other, I am truly alone. Our lives are so very different that when I once tried to explain the concept of a diary to M'Barak, he laughed for hours and thought I was kidding. He thinks that mobile phones work or don't depending on how many people there are around. When I point to the towers we pass and a satellite in the night sky, and explain their functions, he truly believes I am telling a good joke. The world of aeroplanes, escalators, dishwashers and computers is so alien to him that they may as well not exist. A life where I have dead-lines and applications for funding to complete is beyond his comprehension.

So it's frustrating to get into town, where I can actually address issues such as funding and my marriage and be forced to sit through endless meals and fussing over in the homes of people who have little idea about life in the desert. They patronisingly try to teach me the customs they imagine are totally alien to me. The irony of this is that I have probably spent more time than any of them in the actual desert. The very customs they try to show me, like eating couscous with my hands, for example, have long since become second nature. They are nomadic people who now live in the town, and I find their society confined and oppressive, the women far less proud and independent than their 'less sophisticated' desert counterparts.

I sit in the internet café and have increasingly desperate email exchanges with Gary. I dread the contact as much as I desire it, never knowing what I will find when I open the inbox. Gary is in Australia now, and he talks about clearing his possessions out of our joint storage, talks as if our marriage is already over.

Somehow I thought that we could wait to do all of this, wait for the final discussions, until I am back in England. It kills me to think that while I am out here, he is already moving on. He even mentions drawing up divorce papers.

Every word drags me out of the desert and back into the horrible morass of my 'real life'. When Madani walks into the internet café to find me, I have tears streaming down my face and am trying to hide behind the computer and my *melekhva*. The men in the café are looking at me with thinly disguised curiosity.

I stumble after Madani and plaster a smile on my face for the next six hours with the family, where I have to make conversation with women who speak no French as they cover my hands with henna. I'm so tired and heartsick I can barely think. I'm longing to check into a hotel and simply close the door for a night, weep and talk to myself. Instead, I am paraded around the various houses of M'Barak's family as an honoured guest, drinking tea. We are committed to dinner every night for the rest of our stay.

Finally, we are driven back out to camp, where I play the part of traditional hostess for the men of M'Barak's family. We then walk for three days, around to the other side of town. We're in contact with family for the duration. I'm still waiting on money and various communications, and I go in and out of town more than I would like.

Being back in town brings back all of my fears about the future with crushing immediacy. I still have no word on the grant. Despite some good initial responses from publications, nobody has yet bought any of my articles. My book doesn't have a publisher yet. Apart from Kadar's payments, which are keeping me afloat, I have no money and no idea where any will come from. The thought of returning to the nightmare of divorce, penury and feeling that I have failed in my walk, is devastating. Above all, the sadness of losing Gary is suffocating. Once again, I feel the isolation; my only lifeline is my mother by email. It's my own private hell.

M'Barak, meanwhile, is tense about me being in Laayoune at all. He is worried that I'll run into trouble with the police and wants me to stay under the protection of family all the time. I understand his concerns, but I bitterly resent losing the only chance I will have for weeks, until Boujdour, to have a little personal space.

The following day is the last one we need to be in town; we are still waiting for the money to come through from Western Union. I have yet another dark exchange over the internet and tell Madani in no uncertain terms that I am getting a hotel room tonight, no matter what hassles I have with police. I don't care where Madani stays, although I offer to get a room for him too. I just need space.

I tell Madani that I'm going to the major Western-style hotel in town to have a drink in a proper tourist bar. We are staying in a run-down old guesthouse that suits our budget – rooms cost about two euros per night. I am happy to put the other twenty euros towards one bottle of nice wine and the chance that there may just be another tourist there for me to talk with.

Madani is anxious and insists on coming with me. I am secretly glad – I am used to having Madani around. Deep down, despite my grumpiness and impatience, his concern is touching.

We sit in a secluded part of the hotel. The maître d' sets up a place for us away from the main bar, which is packed to bursting with drunk, elaborately robed Moroccan businessmen. I know the types; I have seen them in every town. Corpulent, puffy-faced men with soft hands and clean, white, expensive robes, who drive nice cars and talk in hearty tones about their desert roots. I have seen enough of these men to know their character, and I stay well away while Madani goes to order the drinks.

But when he returns, it is with one of these individuals in tow. '*Lalla!*' Madani begins in tones of apologetic excitement.

'He knows M'Hamid! His sister was married to' – he looks confused for a moment – 'a cousin, I think, of my father's. Anyway, he is tribe. He knows the people I do.'

In the desert, this connection would be more than enough to greet the man as family. Despite my desire for solitude, *politesse* takes over, and I courteously greet the businessman, Mohammed, and invite him to sit down.

Within seconds he admonishes us for coming to the hotel – 'Bad people come here' – and tells us that his friend is a contraband dealer. He offers to take us to buy a bottle and says we should then go back to our hotel; we run the risk of finding ourselves in big trouble with either the drinkers or police if we stay here.

My hackles rise. If I were in my tourist clothes, in a million years I wouldn't go anywhere with this man. I would have written him off as a hustler straightaway. But I've been in the desert so long that my radar has gone haywire. I've been among people who offer everything, who treat me as family after three minutes on the strength of clan associations. I no longer know if my judgement is entirely correct. Although, after the debacle of M'Hamid, I am certainly more wary.

Mohammed goes to the toilet and Madani and I have a conference.

'He is fine, *lalla*, family. No problems. And he is right about this hotel.'

'Okay. But we go to pick up the bottle and then that's it, okay? Back to our hotel – no visiting anyone else, no arrangements for dinner or to meet up. No family favours. We pay him for his time, take our bottle and go. Got it?' Madani nods vigorously.

The three of us go outside and get into the shiny new Mercedes. Despite observing closely, I soon lose track as we swing down backstreets and into dark, dirt alleyways. We pull up in front of a typical contraband house – the ubiquitous mud brick, but characterised by a locked grill door through which the goods are passed.

Mohammed buys the bottle I pay him for and one for himself. We are no sooner back in the car than he opens his and imbibes in long, deep gulps. He had already had a few at the hotel. I begin to wonder just how inebriated this guy is, and I feel uneasy.

'Tell him we need to go back to our hotel now,' I say to Madani. I seem to be locked into a cycle of making poor decisions, usually involving alcohol and men, in a culture where I know I should stay the hell away from both. All I'd wanted tonight was just some goddamn *peace*. Just once.

He drives fast, but after ten minutes I realise we are on a highway – heading out of town. Nothing is familiar.

'Where are we going?' I ask him sharply. 'We really need to be back at our hotel. Could you take us back, please?'

Mohammed waves me away. His voice his slurred; he is taking us to his family's restaurant on the beach, he tells us. I look at Madani in horror. The beach is twenty kilometres away from town. It's nearly midnight.

Madani and I try to keep the conversation light-hearted, working together to convince Mohammed to turn the car around. The vehicle is weaving all over the road. The highway is deserted; dunes surround us in every direction, forming a wall of sand on both sides of the road.

We eventually reach the beachfront area. 'Oh,' says Mohammed blearily, indicating a restaurant with darkened windows. 'It's closed.' Madani and I cast grateful looks at each other.

'Yes, it's very late, *hoiya*,' says Madani, referring to him affectionately as 'brother'. 'We need to go home. Can you take us back to Laayoune?'

Mohammed stops the car and we all get out for a pee. I wander far away from the other two, wary of Mohammed. I squat in the dark shadows of a distant building. Mohammed begins to walk towards me. I think he's going to stop at the vehicle, but he keeps on coming. I am trying to adjust my clothing as he walks straight in front of me, breathing heavily.

'You should be ashamed!' I say and push past him, walking quickly back to the car. Madani is white and sickly looking; he sees my face and knows it is serious.

Mohammed is now muttering and rolling, too drunk to drive and shamelessly trying to grab my leg.

I do not want to get back in the car, but I have no idea what to do. Madani takes Mohammed aside and talks quietly to him. He comes back and says, 'He is sorry, *lalla*, he knows he is drunk and behaving badly. He will take us home now – he asks if you can you drive the car?'

Mohammed looks at me in repentance. I snatch the keys without looking at him.

I have gone only five kilometres when Mohammed begins yelling and moaning, grabbing at the top of my thigh. 'You cannot drive my car! I want my car back – this is *my* car, get out, get out . . .'

He is trying to take the wheel, groping at my leg, my body. I screech to a halt and leap out of the car.

'Go,' I say to him, shaking in anger. 'Just go. Madani – we will walk back to town. It can only be fifteen kilometres. Just get this maniac away from me.'

Madani looks at me in shock, and sees I am serious. Mohammed doesn't even wait for Madani to speak; he just gets into his Mercedes and roars away in a show of screaming tyres and weaving drunkenness.

We stand in the middle of the desert road, the sky high and clear above us.

'Fuck,' Madani says and sits down heavily. '*Lalla*, I'm so sorry.'

'Madani, this one isn't your fault. I knew better than this. I *knew*. What the hell am I doing? How could I have been so *fucking* stupid?'

I stand there in abject fury, all of it directed at myself. Of all people, I should know that when you are in a bad space, you attract bad things. I should not be drinking; I should be out walking, finding peace. I shouldn't be searching for 'my space' in a culture that does not understand that need. I should be wise enough to put this *shit* aside and run my camp and my walk with integrity. I think bitterly of Wilfred Thesiger, of T. E. Lawrence, of those honourable strong men. And then I look at myself, standing in the middle of the highway with a cheap bottle of red, out of my depth even with the supervision of good men such as Madani and M'Barak. I look at what I have dragged Madani into. I look at the hole I've dug for myself and feel so angry and humiliated that I could scream. And it is at that moment – something I'm sure he will regret for a lifetime – that Mohammed tries to finish us off.

In the distance we see the glow of headlights, hear the roar of an engine.

We look at each other for a moment; the vehicle is coming on fast.

'Get up into the dunes!' I yell at Madani. 'He's coming after us!'

But I am too late; as we run for the walls of sand and begin to race up them, the Mercedes comes flying over the hill, straight at us. We scramble through the thick, deep sand. Mohammed yanks the steering wheel, ploughing into the dunes just below us. We run, out of his reach, high up along the road. We crouch at one point, out of sight, but then he stops the car and begins to climb after us. We run on, so he gets back in and drives, keeping pace.

He stops again and gets out.

'Come down!' he calls. 'I'm sorry; this is stupid. I just want to take you home.'

We don't believe a word but, at the same time he calls, a Land Rover trayback – a proper nomad's desert truck – rounds the corner. Old, turbaned men are sitting in the back. It's the kind of vehicle that would always give us a lift.

We run down the hill, yelling for them to stop – they do. But before we can reach it, Mohammed is there first. We hear him ranting, and then the vehicle roars away before we can get to it. Mohammed turns to us, his eyes glinting maliciously. 'I told them you were a Western whore who flagged me down and then tried to rob me,' he says. 'No one will stop for you now.'

And suddenly – I just see red. And purple, and magenta, and every fucking shade in between. I know this mess is my own fault, but all I can see is Mohammed, and he has become the outlet for every bit of my anger, confusion and humiliation.

I walk over to him. There must be something in my expression that projects some of what I am feeling; I see a note of fear on his face. He is no taller than I, and he takes a step backward.

I lean forward and grab handfuls of nice, white robe. I yank him so that his face is barely an inch from my own.

'You listen to me, you bastard . . .' I start; and then out comes a torrent of vitriol with enough heat to melt a polar ice cap.

And menace.

I don't know where it comes from. Maybe I had it all along, but suddenly I know that the only way we will get rid of this bastard is to scare him silly. I loom over him, flash my knife and hold it to his throat. I tell him that if he comes anywhere near either of us – *ever* – that I will, without hesitation, kill him. Slowly.

And I mean it.

I come out of my haze and the man is choking and crying, cringing away from my knife. I shake him violently one last time, spin him around and shove him to his car. 'Fuck off.'

He does. The car is gone in seconds. This time, I know it won't be back.

Madani cowers on the dune. He knows that he just saw the face of madness, and he doesn't know what to do.

Another Land Rover comes along, and I step out and hail it down. Suddenly, my Arabic is better than ever before. 'I am a European tourist, and I was lied to by a man in town and taken out here. This man was trying to help me, and now we are both stuck. Can you please drive us back to town?'

The driver indicates the trayback with his thumb, and we climb in. We travel back to Laayoune in silence.

Back at the hotel, we look at each other in dumb silence. The adrenalin is subsiding, but the shadow of my madness hangs over the room like a pall. Madani drops his head, shakes it. When he looks up at me his eyes are filled with tears.

'You scared me, *lalla*,' he says softly. 'I was scared.'

I look back at him, and I cannot find the softness within. Something dark and ugly has grown hard inside me – I have humiliated myself for the last time.

'I have had enough of these men,' I say. 'I have just had enough.'

Madani nods. 'We should leave here tomorrow. It is a bad place, and if the police find us, there will be trouble.'

'I know,' I say. 'I will get the money, and we will go. Don't worry about the police. We'll get out of here.'

I try to smile, but he sees the hollowness in it. He leaves and I sit and smoke. I have nothing left. I don't know who I am anymore. The shame and self-loathing seethe in me, and I toss and turn in fitful sleep, desperate to be away from here, back in the desert space.

The police find me anyway.

Chapter Eight

I am walking down the road with Madani, fully covered, head down in my customary town pose. We're on the way back from the Western Union. There is a protest on; a large group of Saharawi are chanting outside the military headquarters. They are protesting the persecution of female political activist Amenitou Haider, who has recently been released from the notorious 'Black Prison' of Laayoune after international groups lobbied against her seven-month sentence. Despite the events of last night, I'm sparked by the scene. I'm fascinated by Amenitou and her case. I've heard her name whispered with near reverence by nomads from Tan-Tan to here. Amenitou, idolised by the Saharawi independence movement, is hated and feared by the Moroccan Government. She is articulate, educated, and outspoken about the abuse she's suffered, including horrific torture during her four-year illegal imprisonment from 1987 to 1991.

Surreptitiously, I take out my camera to photograph the women. While I appreciate the danger, I'm also desperate to get some images I can use in an article about Amenitou. I'm hoping that it may be possible to actually interview her, if I can find the right contacts. I feel that if I can just get something useful out of this hellhole, it will make everything worthwhile and somehow cancel out the horrible mistakes I've made.

Unfortunately, I no sooner pull the camera out than two men in police uniform appear. Madani and I are unceremoniously marched away.

We're separated. I'm shown into a bare, concrete room, and the questioning that I'm so familiar with begins.

But this time there is nothing benign, sleazy or lackadaisical about the interrogation. These are no rural idiots looking for a bribe. These guys are the higher end of the market – and not local. They're part of a rotating force that comes from up north; the man interviewing me is from Agadir. They have no understanding of the desert. To them, the Saharawi are nothing more than dangerous terrorists. By association, I too am suspect.

I later learn that Madani is fingerprinted and harassed. I am held for hours. They contact Kadar, who pulls in every favour he can find to make them understand that I'm simply a tourist. Stupidly, when he is initially contacted, he tells them I'm a writer. It takes me hours to convince them that he had it wrong: I am merely a teacher. This is what the police in Zagora have noted on my original papers. Fortunately, the man they deal with there is not the same one who tried to swap sex for a visa.

Kadar is the only person I'm allowed to contact, but I can't speak to him directly. The policeman makes the call while I'm sitting across the desk. I wonder if Kadar is fully aware of the gravity of the situation. I try to stay calm and think about how I can get out of this predicament. I curse myself for pulling out the camera; I curse even more the fact that I do not have any photos to show for it. This would make a brilliant story.

It is late when we are released, but the police are not done with us. They insist on driving us out to our camp. They want to inspect M'Barak's credentials. They also intend to shut us down; they merely scoff when I tell them of my plans to walk to Dakhla. They have no intention of allowing me to continue through what they see as country full of landmines, bandits and Polisario terrorists. They would be scared to drive an armoured vehicle through the territory – and rightly so. They cannot believe for an instant that I would be safe.

At the camp, M'Barak emerges, grey-faced and worried. Members of his family have already been out to tell him about our detention. He has been terrified that we would disappear, as so many activists have in the past.

The police look at his identity card and examine our camp. They question him closely and chide him for leading us into 'dangerous' country. They threaten to charge him for illegally guiding tourists.

But their curiosity is satisfied. We are no more than what we appear; we are neither international journalists nor drug smugglers. They drink tea with us, and their questioning turns from interrogative to merely curious. The danger is past.

Finally they leave, telling us they will return in the morning to ensure that we are making arrangements to leave the Western Sahara and to have our camels trucked back up to M'Hamid. They won't even entertain the idea that I will continue my walk.

We wait until their vehicle is a cloud of dust on the horizon, then we look at each other. We're all thinking the same thing.

'*Wahloo?*' M'Barak asks me tentatively. I start to grin. *Wahloo* is the local vernacular for 'gone', as in, *disappeared without a trace*. We use it every day, so I know what he means immediately. Suddenly, we are all laughing.

'*Allahi*,' I say. '*Wahloo*, tonight. Let's go.' And amid the odd, cackling cry of '*Wahloo!*', we quickly gather the camels and pack them with our baggage. As night falls, we walk off into the deep desert, far away from drunken men, from uniforms and families and questions, and into the one place they all fear – the one in which I feel safe.

The desert flowers are opening. The rain has gone, and in its wake the desert is littered with outcrops of brilliant purple and yellow blooms, thriving improbably among cold, rocky outcrops. The yellow flowers have a sharp, tangy citrus scent. As we walk, cavort and skirmish, their invigorating perfume wafts over us in waves. We thread them into our hair and tuck them into our clothes. The purple ones are stunning: cone-shaped and solid, they have myriad tentatively unfurling shoots. They look reluctantly brilliant, as if they could close up as soon as the weather turned.

The milder weather and new life breathe much-needed hope into my being. I'm tired. I've lost too much weight. Between the wind, the increasingly difficult territory, little sleep and emotional distress, we are covering ground slowly. In Europe with packs, I would think nothing of doing twenty kilometres per day – we'd usually aim for thirty. But now I'm struggling to get to twenty. Any more seems impossible.

I wrap my *melekhva* closely around my face, hiding in its folds as I walk, head down. I'm past grief about my marriage or worry about the future.

The flat nomad's sandals, with their nails that must be bashed into submission on a rock at least once a day, have left my feet in a terrible state. The pain beneath the arches is excruciating, and I know that the lack of support has done some kind of internal damage. After only ten kilometres they ache, and rising after a break is an exercise in willpower.

Our nights are increasingly tense. M'Barak scouts around, and we make our camps in well-hidden country. More than once we have all woken to the sound of a herd passing stealthily nearby and men hovering too close to our camels. They can normally be deterred by shouting a threat, but M'Barak warns me that if they slit the ropes hobbling the camels, they can disappear into the night in seconds. We live in terror of the camels being stolen.

For the first time since the big dunes outside M'Hamid, we begin to walk back into dune territory. Stunning as they are, dunes no longer represent the romance of the desert to me. They are simply obstacles to overcome, a hard day's walking and a lousy place to try to feed the camels. Since Tan-Tan, the camels have become the most important thing in my life. M'Barak flatly refuses to walk them hard. They're in superb condition, chiefly because he has nursed them along, refusing to allow me to walk the longer kilometres I would like. He insists we stop when there is good feed, whether we have walked four kilometres or forty. His diligence teaches me lessons about camels that I will never forget. If he drives me crazy at times with his habits and sexual banter, I've nothing but respect for the way he quizzes me on the names of plants, makes me choose a camp site and asks me why one place is better than another. From him I learn the first rule of true nomadic travel: *the camels come first.*

Wells are scarce, and we take a lot of our water from the large dirty puddles left by the recent rains. We strain the water through a turban to clean out the worst grit. Despite the brown colour, it tastes fresher than some of the murky well water I have drunk along the way. I walk and try to stay cheerful, try to muster the troops and keep a core of happiness in the camp, but I'm exhausted. No matter how far I walk, the emotional knot within will give me no peace.

The next day we walk through different country; it has suddenly altered yet again. The horizon is wide, the sky vast. In front of us stretches a seemingly endless series of small dunes.

'Do you know this country?' I ask M'Barak.

He shrugs. 'A little. I know which way to go.' But he eyes me with trepidation from under his turban. 'A lot of landmines here.'

'Let's go,' I say and flash a shadow of my old cocky smile. He grins back and walks on with a new energy. I slump back into my stupor. What he doesn't understand is that I no longer care if I walk over a mine. I am *hoping* to walk over a mine. For the first time in my life I can honestly say that I don't care whether I live or die – my preference seems to err vaguely on dying. I just don't have the strength to actually make the decision, so I'd be perfectly content to step on a metal disk and have the entire thought process taken out of my hands.

We trudge further into the dunes, which grow bigger and bigger. Several hours later I realise through my fug that I am in the depths of the largest dune sea I have seen since Erg Chigaga. I am jolted back to life as we shift from lethargy into business mode: me taking control of all four camels, M'Barak and Madani racing up and down dunes on either side, searching for a way through, searching for where the dunes end. I lead the camels on the path of least resistance. M'Barak doesn't need to tell me how to go now. He races far ahead, sometimes so far that I can only see a vague outline and his stick waving. As if by osmosis, I end up in the same places he does, find the same path through that he would choose, and gradually I feel my interest and life returning in tiny doses: *I can do this. I know how to walk through this country now – I'm a part of it.*

The heavy black cloud that has sunk me for weeks begins to lift in the sheer magnificence of this challenge, as the dunes go on and on. For hours, we struggle to find a way through, pulling the camels along almost by sheer mental force, communicating only long distance by waves and the odd shout. I lead the four up and over ridge and dune, unerringly finding the firm sand and gentlest passage. The camels obediently follow my every step, trusting me to see them right.

We emerge into scrubby country, the dunes now behind us. My legs are shaking from the strain, and the camels are breathing hoarsely. I've neither stopped nor paused for over five hours; there has been no safe place. Now the heat is up and the wind is vicious, and I know we're too tired to take a break. We need to find a sheltered place with feed for the animals – they're exhausted.

But there is no such place to be had. We stumble for hours through the sameness of bad country, passing nothing but low, bare shrubs. The only trees are withered skeletons. The scrub is lacking in the vitality the camels need. Habil goes down now every half hour and is becoming increasingly difficult to raise.

M'Barak and I spot the same lone tree – bare and pathetic, it is still the best we have seen thus far. Too tired to speak, we simply nod in accord and lead the camels over, couch and unload them.

Nobody speaks until after tea is made.

'This is bad country,' M Barak says.

'*Allahi*,' I say, rolling my eyes, gesturing. 'And the dunes! Huge!' I shout with laughter. Suddenly, the morose lethargy of the past weeks is gone, as we talk over each other about the dune sea we just crossed and what we were all thinking as we went.

'God, seriously, I thought I was lost,' M'Barak confesses. 'I thought I knew this way and then suddenly we are in the big dunes, where I did not want to go and cannot see the way out. Eeee!' He shrieks in gleeful relief. 'But, by God, I thought maybe we would die.

'And Toula, Toula!' He and Madani laugh and look at me with warmth and admiration, and shake their heads. 'You walk, and walk, like this' – and M'Barak struts about, imitating my hip-waggling walk, until Madani and I are convulsing – 'and you go over the big dunes, like a true nomad. True nomad.

'You walk those camels good,' he says, now serious. 'Truly, by God, you walk like a Saharawi. You hardly need M'Barak now. You know the desert. You know.'

There is no greater compliment he could pay me. For all that I have learned to be wary of M'Barak's flowery compliments, this one, I know, is sincere. When he shakes my hand in emphasis, I feel tearful and proud and embarrassed. I roll over and pull my *melekhva* over my eyes because I am tired and unused to talking now. The day is done, there is nothing left to say.

We emerge from the desert onto the piste track, about thirty kilometres from Boujdor. We've been walking for only half an hour when a vehicle approaches. We pull the camels over, away from the tracks, but the vehicle pulls to a halt and four men clad in military uniform get out.

I'm not sure whether to run or hide. I stand stock still – then suddenly Madani is racing forward and greeting the men. They are touching cheeks and embracing, and I realise with a rush of relief that they're family.

We couch the camels and sit down. The men collect twigs and make a fire, while I start preparing the tea. It has been a long time since we used the gas stove, and I will never use it again on a desert walk. Now we make fires every day.

'We heard about you being stopped in Laayoune,' says the leader, a relative of Madani's. The men all laugh and eye me curiously. But there is none of the insidious intimation I have become so wary of. These men are Saharawi, and family, and they look instead with the wonderful, twinkly warmth I see in the faces of so many nomads.

'Here, you don't need to worry,' he reassures us. 'The military – here they're friendly to us. They're local. And you have a lot of family here – we will look after you.' He engages M'Barak in a complex discussion involving strict directions to the best campsite, where there is loads of feed for the camels. They organise to come and collect Madani and me tomorrow, to do our usual range of chores in town. This will be our last stop before Dakhla. This stage of my walk is very nearly over. It's been two and a half weeks since Laayoune.

'The men here can give you good advice about Mauritania,' M'Barak tells me. 'They will know how to get you to Tomboctou, eeeee!' I laugh with him as we set the camp up.

Tomboctou looms large in my mind; it has done for months. It represents the first of my real desert goals. If Dakhla is the end of this stage, Tomboctou, on the Niger River in Mali, represents the first true milestone of the desert trek as a whole. It has gained in significance as I have walked, not least because in Morocco it has near-mythical status among the nomads. In tents going all the way back to M'Hamid, eyes widen and turbans are rewound with great energy at the mention of Tomboctou. Every nomad has a story about the glory days of the great camel caravans. The journey is one that captures everyone's imagination.

I am intrigued, not only because of local lore, but also by the fact that the place itself has such a romantic, intriguing history. The first European to return alive from the city was a Frenchman, René Caillié, in 1828. The faded desert town he found was a far cry from the city paved with gold of ancient repute, but there is no doubt that Tomboctou was in fact a centre of both trade and scholarship – several libraries and mosques remain there to this day. I have been intrigued by the history of Tomboctou for years, and in the back of my mind it has lurked as a potent lure, a symbol of success on this walk, just as Santiago de Compostela was to me so long ago in Europe. Tomboctou means 'real' desert. It means I have actually *got* somewhere.

M'Barak in particular is fascinated by my goal to walk to Tomboctou and beyond. He tells anyone who will listen and encourages me to speak to the men of Madani's family about it.

That night, one of the men arrives to take the two of us into town. Mahmoud is a veteran of the Polisario conflict, and his face is deformed where he was scarred by a landmine. He is a contraband driver now and has the quiet, lethal demeanour of a man who knows how to handle himself. Madani and I sit in his house and drink tea, talking.

'I know people on the Mauritanian side of the border who can help you,' Mahmoud says. 'All of our families – Madani's, mine – we have contacts on the Mauritanian side. But to get your camels through from here to there – this is the big problem.' His one good eye swivels up to me. 'Not impossible, you understand. Just not legal.'

I nod. 'But can I actually walk through from here to there – or will I also be stopped?' I ask. I've already been in contact with the Mauritanian and Moroccan authorities. So far I've been unable to get permission to walk across the border due to concern about landmines, and I'm certainly not allowed to take the camels. I don't want to go through with four-wheel-drive backup – I want my camels on the other side. Above all of these considerations, I still have no funding, so I can't really commit to anything until I know how I'm going to pay for it.

'In my opinion, you should stop here at Boujdour and pick your walk up on the other side of the border,' Mahmoud tells me. 'Between here and the border, the country is very bad. There are landmines everywhere, very few wells, and feed for the camels is no good. Nomads don't graze here anymore because of the mines. It is not good country for nomads or animals. I think that after here it will be very hard for you.'

Over the next few days, as we do the customary rounds of family visits, I hear the same advice repeated by every man I speak to. I'm interested in their advice, not least because all of them have done active military service and know the territory and the local authorities well – not to mention every smugglers' route in the vicinity. The overwhelming consensus is that I can certainly get the camels through illegally, if I choose, but this will put me in jeopardy with the authorities – and I run the risk of standing on a mine. I could also get someone else to take the animals through and go through legal channels myself, meeting the animals across the border. But this plan has several large holes, most of which involve how I, myself, will travel across.

But with every conversation I lean more and more towards taking a break from the walk anyway. I need to organise funding, visas and new equipment, not to mention my personal life. I never expected that I would simply walk straight on from Morocco to Tomboctou. I knew I would need a pause at the end of this training walk to organise the rest of the desert crossing. My conversations here are largely in the realm of research, but it is thrilling to be really talking about Tomboctou at last.

Boujdour itself is far quieter than the bustling modernity of Laayoune. Although the main road is bitumen, the rest are dirt tracks. The shops are rooms with tin doors that open onto the street, like Tan-Tan. Down one long track there are endless stalls selling grilled fish. There is an actual beach of sorts, dirty and rock-strewn, where boys play and swim and women wade ankle deep. I wander along the beachfront with M'Barak, but down here I'm fully clad in *melekhva*, and I don't feel comfortable doing any more than wading. Tourists are not part of Boujdour's fabric. It's the kind of town where people stop overnight before heading into Mauritania, not somewhere they come to sightsee.

After weeks in the desert, I wander the town, enjoying the simple pleasures of hot chips or a glass of fresh orange juice. The luxury of being able to just go and buy ready-made food, like barbecued kebabs or fresh salad, is a seductive treat I miss terribly. Small things perhaps, but it's the small things that I miss when walking – fresh fruit or tea with real mint.

It's slightly oppressive to always be accompanied in my wanderings. I miss the freedom of exploring places on my own. But I have been here so long now that I do not attempt to fight these restrictions – I know it's just not worth it. Sometimes I'm accompanied by the women of the families, and on these occasions our walk is a slow shuffle as they giggle and greet their friends, and stop at anything of interest. It's more a promenade than a walk, and it's an act of restraint to keep their pace. The women never stop at cafés or restaurants; it would not be proper. With Madani, I can stop at those places if I choose, but once I'm in *melekhva* I never feel comfortable behaving like a Westerner. And in Boujdour, I am clad in *melekhva* all the time, simply because it seems appropriate.

I check into a hotel for one night, despite the overwhelming family protests. I'm long overdue for a solid writing session, which I find very difficult in homes or while I am walking with M'Barak and Madani. Mahmoud looks at me with understanding from his good eye, escorts me to the hotel and checks me in. More than anyone else I've come across, he seems to understand my need for just one night of peace, despite it being entirely unorthodox for a woman to stay in a hotel on her own. I'm passionately grateful for the closed door. I throw myself across the bed in my knickers and spend the night lost in writing and on the phone to my family. It's heaven to remember my own life again.

In Boujdour, M'Barak and I have some serious talks.

'After here, *lalla*, I don't know where to go,' he admits. 'Of course, it is south and I know where to head, but I have never walked this way before, and it worries me. There are landmines everywhere. All the nomads I talk to say that there are only two wells – and that they are not good, often saline. There is not much feed for the camels. Nomads don't go south from here – we are at the end of the country they stay in. From here it is just bandits and military. I don't want to carry on.'

'But I need to go at least as far as Dakhla,' I say. There is over 300 kilometres between Dakhla and the border of Mauritania. I have accepted that I will need to sell my Moroccan camels on this side of the border and begin again on the other. Dakhla lies at the end of a peninsula. I plan to walk to where the road turns off, camp there, then do a day on foot into Dakhla itself, where I'll present myself to the local authorities. But M'Barak is not keen.

'Madani's family, all of the nomads, the military – they all say to stop in Boujdour,' he argues. 'They say it is really bad after here – very difficult walking, hard for the camels. *Lalla*, I do not want to go further than this.'

But I am determined. I feel that so many things have been taken out of my control. On so many levels, I feel that I have failed in this walk. After only a few days in Boujdour, I pack the camp up and we walk out.

We leave Boujdour in a sullen state. Madani and M'Barak had, I realise, expected me to acquiesce to their requests to end in

Boujdour. They are resentful about being forced to walk further. Madani wants to wallow in the sins on offer in town. M'Barak is tired of walking and wants to go back to his family. Both of them are uncooperative and think I'm being unreasonable.

I'm equally done in. All I really want is to call a halt, but it's a point of pride to make it to Dakhla. I push our band hard, making long distances each day, refusing to engage in discussion. Madani talks on the phone until reception runs out, taking calls from a dozen heartbroken females wanting to know when he's coming back to town. The other calls, somewhat less affectionate, come from his elder brother, demanding to know why Madani has not sent more money home.

Madani is a typical male in his early twenties: resentful of his brother's demands and out to have a good time. He wants to find a way to stay in my employ, avoid home and have enough money to spend on whiskey and women. Although I have considered taking him on with me into Mauritania, it makes little sense in the long run. At some point I have to strike out on my own. But I understand that Madani can see his opportunities for a new life vanishing if I leave. As he sees it, I'm deserting him to a life of misery back in M'Hamid.

We limp onwards in an uneasy, flat silence.

We camp one day close to the coast. I can actually hear the sea. The weather is hot now, high into the forties, and the lure of the cool water is irresistible.

'Come on,' I say to Madani in a rare attempt to lighten the mood. 'Let's go for a swim.'

He brightens up, and the two of us scramble like a couple of kids down the steep cliff to the wide, sweeping beach, where the Atlantic rolls away into the horizon.

It's deserted. We strip down, me to long cotton trousers and a T-shirt, Madani to his shorts and top.

We run into the waves. The feel of the water enveloping my body is the most liberating sensation I can imagine. We splash and laugh and play, and I feel torn between pure joy at being here and the strange awareness that I'm not really free. Not here.

As if to reinforce my thoughts, two armed police appear on the cliff path. They come down, order us out of the water and turn their backs ostentatiously as we dress. They go through the usual rigmarole of interrogation, taking our details. They warn us in stentorian tones that it is forbidden to swim here – particularly two members of the opposite sex. They follow us back to our camp and inspect everything suspiciously.

Suddenly, I've had enough.

We're still a few days from where the road turns off to Dakhla. We've not seen a nomad since we left Boujdour. The country is barren and uninteresting. Grazing is scarce, wells virtually non-existent. We're dodging landmines with monotonous regularity, and their increasing prevalence means we've had to exit our desert peace and follow the smugglers' piste tracks. We spend our days with vehicles roaring past, the drivers asking us interminable questions, and our nights disturbed by their headlights. We're terrified to light a fire in case we discover it is on top of a mine, and every time I go to the toilet I pick my way between live ammunition and pray to God I don't stand on a metal disk. I see them everywhere – there are several million unexploded mines out here, and I reckon I've walked around over three thousand of them. It's simply got to be a matter of time before my luck runs out.

I look around at Madani lying listlessly on his side, at M'Barak fretfully picking at his *djellaba*. I see in their faces the same exhaustion and emotional strain that lines my own. I look around at the windswept vista that carries on, in exactly the same form, for several hundred kilometres. I think of my empty bank account, the articles I've not written, the grant money that hasn't come through and the equipment I don't have. I think of all that I have learned and of the way I want to do things when I set it up again. I think of just letting go for a while, of going back and finally talking properly to my mum, of sitting in my friend Jo's kitchen and letting her fold me up in a huge hug.

I turn around to Madani and M'Barak. 'This is where we stop.'

Chapter Nine

It takes me nearly a month to organise my withdrawal from the Sahara. I rent a house in Boujdour while I do the research for the next leg in Mauritania. I talk to Kadar and arrange for him to truck my camels – now his once more – back to M'Hamid and pack all my gear into what I want to take with me and what I want to leave at his hotel. A local nomad stays with camels. M'Barak is exhausted and ready to go home. He stays in Boujdour for a few days and then takes off with some passing relatives. Saying goodbye to him is difficult. He clasps my hand and tears run down his face.

'*Zwina, lalla. Zwina. Hemdullah, hemdullah . . .*' he says, over and over. *Beautiful, beautiful. Praise God.*

In the end, he has shown himself a true friend – even if he does try to grab my butt as he leaves, cackling and whooping as he climbs into the back of a contraband vehicle, winding his turban around his face. The last I see of him are his skinny legs kicking the air as he begins telling the men in the vehicle about our walk.

I am dreading leaving and delay it until the last possible moment. I travel out for a final farewell with my camels. They look at me sideways and snort when I get sentimental.

I turn and look out in front of me. Madani and I mark the place on the road where we stopped with a cairn of rocks so big you can see it from the highway. I shelter my eyes and gaze south, into the distance where the border lies. I feel a tightening in my chest, a panic: a part of me wonders if this is it, the end of it all.

But then I look back behind me and think of the many months of learning, hardship and trauma that I've left in the sand to get here. I think of the unbroken chain of camps, water stops and fires. I think of the hurt and the fights and the nights I shook in terror, wondering if I was losing my mind. I remember the first time I walked through the dunes, clumsy and inept. I think of the last dune sea I crossed, and how I knew exactly where to go.

I think of the secret life I've led, the mental strain the isolation has wrought, and I chuckle at how I dreamed of desert peace. I've spent seven months in incessant company, barely finding a night on my own, let alone peace. The only peace I've had is in my walking hours, and they have been tainted with the tortured convolutions of my own emotional journey.

If the European walk was about doors opening in my mind, about conquering my own fears, this Western Sahara walk has been about splitting apart the fabric of my being, taking me as close to the mental abyss as I ever want to go. It has stripped me of every vestige of pride, security and comfort I possess, and thrown me into a whirlwind of confusion and mixed messages, into games I never dreamt of playing, governed by rules I didn't understand. I've been immersed in this culture so profoundly that I've almost forgotten my own, and in doing so, I've been pared away until only the barest essence of me is left, that tiny kernel of strength that has kept me company ever since I discovered it in the sunset clouds. I have made it through mines and hunger and pain and weakness. I have made nearly 3000 kilometres since I set out from M'Hamid, nearly 2000 since Gary took a bus from Assa.

I look at the desert lying in front of me and, although I do not want to hear it, a voice comes, unbidden, from the deepest pit of my guts, and I know it as my own.

I will come back to you.

And I know that this walk is not over, yet.

Marrakech is comfort, revelation and a staging post. I was going to stay a day or two then leave, but I can't bring myself to go anywhere. I'm not ready to move on, to go back the UK, but nor can I stay here.

I wander through the Djemaa el Fna in the early part of the day, before the square is full. The old henna ladies call me over, but not to hustle me. Instead, I squat with them and drink tea, and they examine the henna on my hands and cackle in appreciation. Whether it's something in my clothing or just that my face has become familiar here – very possible, given the intimate nature of Marrakech – I'm aware that I'm no longer treated by most on the street or in the souk as a tourist, but spoken to with more familiarity, particularly when I use Arabic. I'm still *other* and, after all these months, I know I'll never be anything different. In the end, I'm *not* Moroccan, *not* Saharawi – but for the Marrakshis, I'm also not a Western tourist either. In the shops, in the souk, I sit and have tea with the owners, and they don't harass me to buy. The orange juice merchants in the Djemaa el Fna call me over to their stands to talk about the weather and try to give me juice for free. They all say, 'You live here, yes?'

I've no appetite, often walking all day on tea alone. I make myself eat in the early evening. At one of the stands in the Fna, the owner is lovely and always gives me more than he should. The only thing I am hungry for is meat, and I eat a small plate and wander back to the hotel.

Most nights I sit up on the terrace and talk to other tourists. But I'm oddly shy and feel in some strange way as if I'm conning them. They seem to come from a different world: bright and carefree, making their plans to maybe take a bus here, maybe there. I don't tell them where I've been, just that I've spent some time in the desert. I want to cover the fading henna on my hands because to them, it's not beautiful. They want the black henna tattoos done in Western style – a rose, a Celtic pattern – that the crones in the Fna charge an extortionate sum for. They say they find the traditional patterns overdone and ugly. I want to tell them that Madani's cousins paid for the best henna lady in the village to do my hands – it was their parting gift to me and took most of a day to decorate both hands and feet. I felt so beautiful with my henna and new *melekhva* when I left Boujdour. Now both seem faintly ridiculous.

I listen to their conversations but I can't join in. Part of me is very content to simply sit and listen to them all talk, to melt back into my own culture. But I can't fully relax – I've more in common with the young Moroccan hotel workers who come up onto the roof to sleep late at night, sitting in their companionable circle a respectful distance from the tourists, brewing tea, smoking and laughing softly as they lounge on their mats. I want to go over and talk to them, but I would only be putting myself back in the trapped zone, back into the country. I know, somehow, that I need to pull out.

So I stay with the tourists and talk, and ignore the boys as the tourists do. The boys don't notice, because up here in a group, wearing jeans and having wine, I am just another white face. And that should be okay, but it isn't.

I don't know where I belong anymore.

Chapter Ten

I land at Gatwick and take the train into central London. I revel in the ease of everything – the voice in English over the loud-speaker; the Cockney friendliness of the ticket collector. I buy a pastie at Victoria Cross and almost swoon over the rich, meaty taste.

Laden down with my pack and worn camel-leather bag that has gone all through the desert with me, I walk down the street from Seven Sisters tube station towards Dan and Stefania's flat, friends of mine who have offered me a bed for a couple of weeks. I must look an oddity in my Moroccan clothes with faded henna still on my hands.

I walk past a group of Arabic-speaking men sitting outside a café. Almost without realising it, I lower my head and cringe into myself, trying to be invisible. As I pass I hear one, then another, call out to me, those calls I've come to so loathe on the streets of Moroccan towns: 'Hello! Hello! *Lady* . . .'

I'm so furious I can feel the hot sting of tears welling up. I'm in England, not Morocco. Why the hell can't they just leave me *alone*?

And then a girl with a headscarf runs up and tugs on my arm. 'Excuse me, Miss, but you dropped these,' she says politely. She is holding out the bag of my much-treasured and studied maps. They'd fallen off my pack. I thank her and turn to look behind me. The Arabic men are all looking at me in bewildered amusement: they'd been calling to me because I dropped the maps.

Somehow this throws me even further off balance, and I walk swiftly away, tears coursing down my cheeks. I'm shell-shocked, jumping at every noise, eyeing approaching strangers warily. My hand is curled around the knife in my pocket as I walk; I've just gone straight through customs carrying a sodding blade! I'm so accustomed to it I had totally forgotten, and in Marrakech there was no security screening. I feel tired and baffled. Everything startles me: the endless plethora of food outlets; the huge Sainsburys; the brand-new vehicles whizzing by; the wealthy, carefree people.

I arrive at Dan and Stefania's and we settle into an afternoon of amazing food and wine. Stefania is Italian, and every meal with her and Dan is a celebration. I eat but feel overwhelmed by the richness and plenty after months of a meagre, lean diet. We talk, but I barely take anything in. I'm so disoriented I want to touch them to convince myself that they are real, that I'm back among people who speak my language, with whom I don't have to be on guard.

The following day Dan flies to South Africa for a ten-day break. Stefania is working from home, and is flexible in her hours. She sits down with me in the lounge room that night, hands me a glass of wine and says, '*Talk.*'

And I do.

For the next ten days I talk from morning until night. I tell Stefania every single moment of the past seven months, leaving nothing out. Occasionally I stop and apologise, worrying that I'm being a self-centred bore.

'Keep going,' she implores. 'This is like reading a novel. It really is stranger than fiction.'

If I don't, if I don't tell all of this just once, I'm in real danger of falling through the invisible cracks of my sanity. I need to bring my experiences from 'out there' back into the present and make sense of them in this, my other life.

I could have no better, more understanding ear than Stefania's. She sits quietly, curled up, handing me cups of tea and listening intently as I cry and get heated and bury my face in my hands. For the first time in so many months I can let the mask fall, be human and soft. I can let go of the hard reins of control that I've held with such poor judgement at times. She hears my humiliations and my hurts, laughs at the incongruities and somehow understands me through it all. I'm so grateful that when I have finished, for the first time in months, I can fall asleep without holding the handle of my knife.

I go to stay back at Steph's, my landlady before I left for the first walk. She still lets rooms out, as does her next-door neighbour, Maria. The two houses operate almost as one, with everyone flowing back and forth, sharing frequent evenings outside chatting over the low fence with a glass of wine. Another friend, Steve, used to live in Steph's house; he now owns one just up the road. I'm passed between the three of them, depending on who has a spare room. I dub them the 'Bromley Road Crew'.

I'm completely flat, motherless broke. Dad sends me 100 quid, and I make it last for nearly a month. Steph, Steve and the others are unbelievably kind. Not once do they ever make me feel guilty for being dependent. They feed me, share their wine and fags, and let me stay for weeks on end. Their belief in me and the walk has never wavered. Now, as I cast about for ways to keep the walk on the road, they sit with me, endlessly talking through ways I could raise money.

Never in all my life have I been more grateful for my friends. All my London friends of old rally around and shower me with love and support: Joanne, who I stayed with for so long last time; Sarah, who travelled to Morocco with me years ago when I first met Kadar; the teachers from the school I used to work at; Dan and Stefania; my Aussie mates Jodie and Andrea. I stumble through those first few weeks back propped up entirely by their understanding. Sometimes my pride finds it hard to accept their generosity with grace and humility. There are times I feel unworthy of their faith, lost in a sense of failure.

My mum is still horribly ill. Despite having finished chemotherapy, and seemingly being clear thus far, she is having some truly awful fall-out symptoms. We will later discover that she has developed Ménière's disease, a condition of the inner ear. She is having dreadful attacks of dizziness and nausea that last for days, and suffers terribly from exhaustion. I'm beside myself with worry. I want to go home, but she continues to insist she's fine.

I go down to visit my dad in Cornwall. I can tell he's worried and negative about my chances to continue the walk. He urges me to return to teaching. I'm actually so desperate for money that I register for supply teaching, but I have to wait while my police clearance comes through. It takes weeks.

Nothing seems to be going right. Gary and I meet a few times, but it's clear there is no future for us together. My marriage is finished, and despite all that has gone in between, the horror of that still weighs down my gut like drinking a bucket of concrete. I almost wish I could simply walk away and be done with it, but the hopelessly deceptive sense of 'what could have been' – and what perhaps still could be – remains intense. It's hard to let go.

My book hasn't sold, and the pile of publishers' rejection slips grows ever higher. I find almost zero media interest in the story. One by one, I am declined for every grant I have applied for. I write article after article, and finally get a couple published, but payment is slow and immaterial. I buy tins of baked beans at Tesco's for eight pence a tin to eat on no-name bread. I walk endlessly, my brain churning, desperate to find a way to continue my journey. I wonder what is left of the girl who set out from Trafalgar Square with such hope and optimism.

I pore over maps. I know exactly the route I'll walk on the next leg. I want to pick up at the first point south possible from where I left off, about 300 kilometres away, just over the border in northern Mauritania. That point is a town called Nouadhibou on the Atlantic coast. I will then walk east, all the way across Mauritania, cutting slightly south and into Mali – to the legendary city of Tomboctou. From there I plan to follow the Niger River around to the city of Gao, then across to Menaka and into Niger. Turning north, I'll walk the fabled ancient salt-trade route from the Agadez region up to the town of Bilma and through the forbidding desert wastes of the Ténéré. Travelling north into Libya, I'll finally turn east into Egypt. I'll finish at Cairo, having made a complete west-to-east crossing of the Sahara. It is a journey of over 7500 kilometres, and I know it will be far harder than anything I have done before.

But the desert stretches out ahead of me on the map like a romantic, exciting novel, just waiting to be picked up. I've abandoned the goal Gary and I had originally: walking to Cape Town. The journey for me has always been about the desert. I may decide to continue on after that but, for now, I want to make a complete crossing of the Sahara. And I believe in my ability to make it. Just as I stretch my brain to think of ways of paying for it, I continue to contact people in the region to research the areas I'm about to walk into. This time I will be responsible; this expedition will be entirely mine.

I simply must make this walk work. I feel extremely focused – not least, I suspect later, because I feel I have nothing else left. Everything I am has become about this walk. And, for the first time, I want it to be a serious accomplishment: I want to be the first woman to ever walk, entirely on foot, from west to east across the Sahara with her own camel train and only local support.

Mariantonietta Peru crossed the Sahara from west to east with her husband, Michael Asher, some twenty years earlier by camel. I read their book long ago with fascination, especially the part when they went through war-torn Chad.

Mine will be a very different journey. They rode camels for a reasonable proportion of the trip, whereas I never do. Also, more than anyone, I know how very different it is being out in that environment on your own, as a woman, rather than as part of a married couple.

I never cared about records or 'world firsts'. But after everything I have been through, I suddenly feel like making my mark. Somehow – rightly or wrongly – I want this walk to count for something.

But even deeper than the superficial goals, I simply want to walk. In the middle of the night I wake up and stare at the ceiling and long for the crystal clearness of the Saharan sky. When I wander the streets of the city, I think of walking through the peaceful desert morning. When I have coffee with friends, I think of lying on cushions and drinking warmed goats' milk spiced with cinnamon, the thrill when I manage to have a whole conversation in Arabic. This adventure still retains the power to call me forwards. The walk is still my dream, and I retain some strange flame of hope. But then Mum calls, and everything changes again.

'You told me that I should tell you if I ever felt I needed you,' she begins. Her voice is quiet and I know what is coming. 'I can't cope on my own anymore, Paula. Would you come home?'

I step off the plane at Tullamarine airport, and look about in curiosity. My mother's friend, Mary, is there to greet me. We step out into the frigid crispness of a Melbourne autumn morning, and I'm struck immediately by the high, bright sky of the Australian dawn. I feel a rush of emotion. For the first time in years, I am home.

'She's really sick,' Mary tells me as we drive into town. 'They say it's just the Ménière's – but I don't know. She rarely gets more than a couple of days between attacks, and she's totally bedridden when they happen. She needs to quit work, and she needs help.'

I know it must be bad. I am grateful that she has at last admitted her own struggle, and I couldn't get on the plane fast enough. Somehow action is always easier than inaction, and to know that I can now come home and be with her, and help in some way, is an immense relief. I wish I'd done it months earlier.

I'm scared witless that the cancer has come back. But Mum's strength and determination is extraordinary, and in time I begin to absorb her quiet acceptance that what will be, will be. I also begin to comprehend how totally debilitating Ménière's disease is. Mum can no longer eat salt or drink alcohol – both things set off an attack of vertigo. Wracked with horrific bouts of vomiting, the attacks are brutal and leave her exhausted.

But despite her poor health, and all of her associated concerns about quitting work and managing financially, I sit on her bed and we talk about what life has been like for the past few years and the walk.

'I thought that you were a bit confused about why I'm doing this,' I tell her. 'That you would think I should just give up now, with everything that's happened.'

'Perhaps at the start I found it hard to understand,' Mum says. 'But as time has gone on and I've watched you achieve so much, I've begun to understand that you really need to do this. And I'm so proud of the way you have coped with everything and kept going through it all – I just want for you to succeed now. And I'm sure you'll find a way of getting back.'

Her unwavering support allays my doubts and fears, buoys me up.

Melbourne has never been a favourite place of mine. It is the city where I was repeatedly suspended from boarding school, where I dropped out of a spectacularly unsuccessful university career (twice) and suffered the predictable romantic disasters of late teens and early twenties. Always restless, I never felt I belonged here.

So it's a pleasant surprise to find I actually enjoy being back. After years overseas, it's almost a treat to feel so at home some-where – to be a local. I walk the city streets for hours on end, drinking coffee in the cute laneway cafés, absorbed in the familiar world around me.

I pull out my files and papers again, and start thinking seriously about sponsorship. I feel as though I'm now in a position to approach companies. I'm no longer an untested amateur. If the European walk left me with some nagging doubts as to whether or not I had really done anything noteworthy, the Western Saharan leg has been so incredibly tough, on so many levels, that I no longer have those doubts. I feel as though I have something real to take to the table.

But I've never seriously applied for sponsorship, and even the idea is daunting.

I find pieces of paper where I've made notes of tips and

strategies for pitching. There's an old sheet of paper left over from a night spent with Steph, who works in marketing; it has a complete phone-pitch script we devised together, along with advice about cold-calling. I actually have a lot of information and resources to draw on. I'm just terrified about beginning the real push for sponsors.

I remember Dad telling me I should practise my pitch on people I don't actually want to get sponsorship from, so that my confidence increases. But for someone who is reasonably outgoing, I can't bear to pick up the phone. Instead, I revert to my comfort zone and write a thousand emails. I'm uncomfortably aware that Steph and everyone else told me success never comes from an email. But I break out in a cold sweat when I think about dialling people and asking for cash.

I have two companies that I want to focus my pitch on: Dove Australia and Birkenstock Australia. I spend the next few days preparing in-depth proposals for each compay, tracking down the right people to talk to.

Dove has long caught my eye because of the groundbreaking 'Real Beauty' advertising campaign. I like the fact that they are driving a school-based program centred on educating kids about the media manipulation of body image in advertising. They have also set up a charity focused on eating disorders.

Of particular interest to me is Dove's association with the National Breast Cancer Foundation (NBCF). I've never walked for a charity before, but after Mum has been so ill I feel that I should somehow use my walk for a purpose greater than self-discovery. Dove draws together all the threads I'm interested in: self-esteem in young women; supporting breast cancer research; promoting strong, independent, *real* women.

After the problems I had with my feet in the flat nomad's sandals on the last stretch, I've discovered that I have developed a condition known as plantar fasciitis, which means I have inflamed the tough, fibrous band of tissue (fascia) connecting my heel bone to the base of my toes. It has begun to heal, but the doctor warned me that I will need to choose my footwear on the next leg with great care.

Having had mixed fortune with shoes all through this walk, I take a tactical approach and do substantial amounts of training walks in various brands of sandals. I trial over six pairs, and all of them leave me unimpressed, despite being touted as the latest 'space-age technology'. Eventually, I try a pair of Birkenstocks after long discussions with one of their salespeople. I leave rather concerned that I have forked out a substantial amount of money for yet another pair of dud sandals.

I rack up nearly 1000 training kilometres in those sandals, through every type of terrain I can think of. They are without any competition the most comfortable, durable and versatile sandal I have trialled. For the first time since leaving London, I don't feel the familiar pain in my arches. I can do long distances virtually pain-free.

I don't want to muck up the approaches to either of these companies. I need to employ every inch of persuasion. I know I have to do this. I simply have no more time.

I sit up late the night before I have promised myself I'd call. I'm shaking with tension, terrified of being rejected. I've no interest in pitching ad hoc to thousands of companies before someone says yes. I've chosen two companies that I truly believe are the right partners for my walk; neither will betray my integrity and the mission of the walk. I know what my budget is, and I believe Dove and Birkenstock can cover it. Now I just have to take my courage into my hands and make the damn call.

I pick up some old self-help book Mum has kicking about; I tend to loathe the things, believing them full of clichéd, trite one-liners. But I'm pretty desperate, so I start flicking through.

One simple line jumps out at me: *Always tackle the hardest thing on your list first, this way you give it the best of your energy.*

Excited now, I determine to pick the phone up first thing in the morning.

Two phone calls turn into two weeks of nail-biting, unbelievable anxiety. They don't say yes, but they don't say no either. Mum and I can barely stand to look at each other. The tension is so thick that the flat is claustrophobic; I walk so many kilometres around Melbourne that I wonder why I'm bothering going anywhere.

I could set a world record in my own city.

At the end of two weeks I get two phone calls in one day.

I have secured funding from both Dove and Birkenstock. It's August. I'm booked to leave in September.

My walk is back on.

'I heard you on the radio this morning,' says the voice on the end of the line. 'I've a bit of experience on expeditions. I thought I may be able to help you out on a couple of things, if you'd like to meet up?'

'A bit of experience' on expeditions proves to be a major understatement. In a bizarre twist of fate, when I'm interviewed on ABC morning radio, Graeme Joy, the first Australian to ski to the North Pole and veteran of over twenty expeditions worldwide, just happens to be listening. Within days I am adopted by him and his longstanding friend, Tom Daniel, who runs an online community for adventurers called www.feedtherat.com. These guys understand the adventuring world very well and have links to people and information that would have taken me months to find.

In their terms, my walk is unique. Rather than being out there for a few months in a carefully planned and executed expedition, mine is a long-range adventure, encompassing myriad challenges and unexpected obstacles that can only be planned for in the broadest sense. The more I explain what I do to Graeme, the more he shakes his head in amazement.

'I don't know anyone who has ever even attempted anything like this,' he tells me. 'It's so tough, on so many levels – you don't even know who your team is going to be until you get out there. Who are your guides? How will you find them? Buying camels, walking through five different countries, African visas, governments . . . I barely know where to start.'

He and Tom are invaluable in helping me get the exact equipment I want, and in dealing with sponsors and the various fine details important to be ironed out in contracts. They have endless good advice. I spend nights up at Graeme's going over my kit and drinking copious bottles of red while he cooks and tells me stories of his trips into the Arctic. Apart from being a member of the eight-man international Icewalk Expedition that skied to the North Pole, Graeme then solo skied to the magnetic North Pole several years later. Among other things, he co-led an expedition up Mount Vinson in Antarctica and kayaked in Greenland.

We look over my planned route, the enormous maps laid end to end on the terrace.

'So what do you think are the most difficult sections?' he asks. 'Which bits do you think are going to cause the most problems?'

I point to Tomboctou. 'Emotionally speaking, the stretch after here will be one of the toughest,' I say. 'It's like after I got to Paris. You reach one goal, which seemed so far away and almost unreachable when you first set out, and then realise that what lies ahead is far more daunting. This is the point where I'm in danger of being lax, of thinking I'm on top of everything and not recognising how tired I am. It's also where I'll need the most willpower to push forward – a new country and culture, everything totally different from before.

'Then after that, I think the next big challenge will be the salt-route stretch from Agadez to Bilma. The Ténéré desert region is notoriously tough – and, in essence, even after I reach Bilma, I'll still have another 700 kilometres of incredibly hard going before I hit the relative calm of Libya. I'll be tired and heading into the hot weather, even if I'm doing all the distances correctly. I'm resigned to the fact that if anything goes wrong between Tomboctou and Agadez, I may have to spend the summer holed up either in Agadez or Bilma. It may just not be possible to do the salt route if I'm running behind time.

'Niger will be extraordinarily difficult. Once I'm in Libya, I'm on the home stretch with less than 2000 kilometres to go. I might be tired and fed up, but at that point the end will be in sight.'

'How are you going to deal with those tough parts?' Graeme asks. 'What strategies do you have in place?'

For a moment I feel caught off guard.

'I guess the reality is that I don't have strategies,' I say slowly. 'In some ways it's enough for me to know that these will be the tough spots. If I know that, then when they happen I can just see them for what they are and push on through. My major concern is that my money will run out at one of those crucial points. My budget is incredibly tight, with no room for error.'

Graeme frowns. 'I see that as putting a lot of pressure on yourself,' he says. 'You don't need to be out there worrying about money.'

I know he is right. But I have no time left to try to raise more, and I'm anxious to get started early in the season. I shrug. 'I'll have to make do. I've always been short of money. If I put this off for a year, I'm afraid of losing my impetus.'

'In my experience, if there is any uncertainty, you're better putting things off than getting out there and finding yourself in a bad situation,' he says. 'You deserve to give yourself the best chance of success.'

Fundamentally, I see his point, but I have been consumed by the walk for so long that I can't bear to put it off. And besides, I can't imagine there is anything I can't handle after the rigours of the last trip. I talk through some of the logistics, but in the end I turn the conversation around to other matters.

Finally, there are no more maps to buy, no more details to finalise. I've got bags full of lip balm and sunblock, thin cotton pyjama pants and good-quality sports bras. I've my specially adapted Birkenstocks, fitted with a double sole to give me greater durability over rocky or inhospitable terrain, and a sack full of Dove products to share with the women in nomadic tents. I have the right maps, solar panels and camera equipment. I've bought Dad a plane ticket from London to Morocco to help me carry my baggage – it was cheaper than paying excess weight.

And I have, despite everything, forwarded some money on to Kadar. He is going to drive me down to Mauritania and help me to buy my new camels and choose my first guide. For all of our crossed wires and emotional quirks, I've grown to have faith in Kadar. In the end, he did the right thing by me in Morocco and paid me in full for the camels. I realised by the end of the last walk that he hadn't cheated me at all, financially. My only mistake with him had been a romantic liaison, but we moved past that. When I call him now, he is exactly as I remember him.

'So, you and this bloody walk! You are crazy, you know this, *lalla?* And this time, *God!* This time you make me drive to Mauritania and buy you more camels and get another guide. When are you going to stop with this crazy stuff, huh? And you realise this will cost you BIG money. Oh yes, this time, money for Kadar is HUGE . . .' And we both laugh, for we've been here before. But this time it is my money, my expedition, and I'm setting the rules. I know I can trust Kadar to deal with me honestly.

Mum and I set up banking and codes that will allow her to access my funds and send money through to me when I need it. She has begun to recover rapidly and no longer needs constant care. She has finally resigned from work and is taking care of herself.

I have nearly 8000 kilometres to walk. The desert cold season runs from the end of October through to the end of March. I know I will have to walk through the heat – it will be ten months at least, going hard, to get to Cairo. I have divided the walk into stages, and I know that this will be the hardest I've ever had to push. My first goal is the 2100 kilometres between Nouadhibou in Mauritania and Tomboctou in Mali. I've worked out the exact route I want to take, and know that I may well have to change guides several times to get there. I want to walk it fast and have set a time limit of 100 days, including rest stops. For the first time in the desert, I will simply have to walk between twenty-five and thirty kilometres per day in order to keep to schedule. It will all be far more structured and driven than ever before.

I look at the Michelin map of Northern Africa. I've been looking at this map for months. I have the bigger, aerial survey maps, the ones that show where the wells are and every contour of the land, but I can't bear to look at them. They're simply too daunting. I just look at the Michelin map, at the vast immensity of the yellow desert stretching right across, suck my breath in and think: *Good Christ, Paula, what have you got yourself into this time?*

Chapter Eleven

Dad and I land in Marrakech at two in the morning after a delayed flight. He begins to get stressed in the long lines for customs. I smile, knowingly, and tell him to relax. He looks at me as I sit on my pack and says, 'Well, girl, it's your deal.'

I negotiate with the taxi driver and give him directions. It's wonderfully familiar to be speaking Arabic again, to laugh with the driver and know where I'm going. Being with Dad gives me another layer of security. I feel charged and strong.

I take Dad up to the terrace of the hotel where I have stayed so many nights. I want him to feel the excitement of Marrakech. But it's late, and the Fna is quiet, the cooking fires at rest. I light a cigarette and we talk desultorily, but for Dad this is just another North African town. After so many months sailing up the East coast of Africa, he is far from enamoured by the culture, and unlikely to be seduced.

I sleep in the same room I always have and feel drawn back into the sordid homeliness of the sagging bed and cracked walls. I marvel that there was a time when this room seemed like Paris to me. From outside the wrought-iron window I can hear the late-night boys calling to each other. In the early morning I can smell the mint for the tea. I lie in bed, at once exhilarated and tired. Here comes the rabbit hole again.

We train up to Casablanca for my Mauritanian visa, and it's funny to be the local, explaining things to my dad. But I love having him here. It's bliss to share some of what I do with him and to have him understand, even a little.

In Casablanca we meet Kadar, and we all wait together for hours outside the embassy while they process my visa. Kadar puts his feet up and sleeps; I'd do the same, except Dad is here. He is impatient and annoyed, wondering what is taking so long. I try to explain that it's always like this here.

Later, after we have the visa, Kadar begins driving around. As usual, he does not explain why. I listen to some of the conversation in Arabic and tell Dad that I think they're going to see a man about the carnet for the vehicle to go to Mauritania. I have switched into deaf-and-dumb mode.

Dad says, 'I don't like being in a vehicle driven by someone I don't know, going somewhere I don't understand.'

I want to howl with laughter and say, *Dad, when you have been so desperate for a ride that you jump in with a stoned contraband smuggler who is driving an unroadworthy vehicle, THEN you know what it is to be scared. This? This is a calculated, careful risk. This is the normal rabbit-hole shit of Morocco – this is just how it is. Jesus, this is EASY. You think THIS is scary? Don't even begin to look at my life over the last year.*

But I say none of this. 'Dad, when you have been here as long as me, you know which risks are okay. Trust me, this one is fine.'

He looks at me and shakes his head. We are just about to drop him off to go back to London. 'Paula, I've only one thing to say to you.' Despite the fact that I'm over thirty, I roll my eyes and want to smack him. 'I never get myself into a situation I can't control. And on that note, I wish you good luck.'

I barely get to kiss him goodbye. And I hate what he said. I hate it because I know he is right. And those words will stay with me throughout the whole desert walk.

It's late at night. Kadar and I are driving on the long, straight road south of Tan-Tan, into the depths of the Western Sahara. Suddenly I see a familiar bit of landscape. I turn my head sharply, and in the light of the rising moon I see the rock pile that Madani and I erected long ago to mark the place where we had hiked to the road to hitch into Tan-Tan. I gasp and go to point, but we are already past it. And anyway, it would be no big deal to Kadar.

Dire Straits is playing on the stereo. I remember from the last time I was in Morocco that the only Western music I ever heard was Dire Straits, Bob Marley, Tracy Chapman or Celine Dion. Right now Mark Knopfler is singing 'Telegraph Road', and I look out at the Big Empty racing by – no song could be more apt.

The night sky is high and wild. The other driver is asleep in the back, and Kadar's turban blows in the breeze coming through the window. It is Ramadan time again, and we stopped in Tan-Tan so the men could break the fast. I have slipped into fasting as well, remembering how uncomfortable it is to be the only one eating when everyone else is eyeing you resentfully. It was wonderful to stop in Tan-Tan and gulp the water, drink the *harira* soup and eat a boiled egg, some dates and the ground, spiced-nut mixture eaten only during the month of fasting. Somehow I feel as if I'm being absorbed here again, slowly. But the world I am re-entering is all mine.

'So this time, *lalla,* this time it is all different,' Kadar says softly. He drives and does not look at me.

'This time, you are really alone. No M'Barak. No Madani. No me, either. Is just you. And for this, I am scared for you. The men, they will take one look, and they will all want you. Is dangerous for you. So this time, I want to say this: *You do not make yourself small.* Not for anyone. You are big girl, strong girl, strong in the heart.' He thumps his chest emphatically. '*You do not need to make yourself small.* No, you are not Saharawi. Saharawi woman, she stays in the tent; she wears *melekhva*; she looks after the family; and she does not smoke or drink. But she doesn't cross desert on her own, either. You have your own blood, *lalla.* You don't need to be Saharawi. What I want to say to you is: be good. Be good to yourself; keep yourself strong in the heart. Be true to your blood. Don't be crazy, yes? This time, you have to be smart. And me – I'm your brother. I am always here, on the telephone. When you get somewhere, you call me. If I can help you, I will.'

He reaches out and strokes my cheek, still not looking at me. 'I love you always, *lalla*.'

And I know that, in his own way, he means it.

Nouadhibou comes after we bounce along the rutted, sandy track that delineates the border between Morocco and Mauritania. One look at the border is enough to reassure me that I did the right thing in choosing not to walk it. Getting camels formally through the labyrinth of military posts, hustlers and hangers-on would have been nightmare enough. Had I chosen to try to slip through unnoticed, further inland, I'd have run a high chance of the landmines blowing me to smithereens.

The crossing marks the end of sophisticated, bureaucratically obsessed Morocco, and the start of African chaos. The decline is apparent even before we have stopped negotiating the various military posts. Things are not as clean or organised. Uniforms are ragged and dishevelled, rather than immaculate and worn with pride.

We are waved through the posts with alacrity as Kadar steps out of his brand-new four-wheel drive, imposing and wealthy looking in his clean, well-made robes. Mauritania is governed by the Saharawi. From being a second-class citizen in Morocco, Kadar is immediately recognised on this border post as a favoured son – and a successful one. He oils the palms liberally, and we drive past lines of frustrated tourists embarking on their Africa Overland odysseys, complete with gleaming vehicles adorned in sponsorship emblems. They glare in our direction, and I understand their frustration. But it's nice to be on the other side of the fence.

We see the beginnings of Nouadhibou long before the town itself. Several kilometres out, the roadside stalls begin. Roughly constructed, flimsy affairs, they seem made of whatever materials are at hand – wooden poles and hessian sacks, plastic bags, cardboard. They are little more than a shelter from the sun, and inside they sell anything from hair pomade to rice. They line the road in haphazard confusion, their inhabitants lazing on the ground in the shade, sleeping in the midday heat; or sitting on chairs, drinking tea with friends. Behind the shelters the rubbish creeps into the distance, and children run and play amid a sea of discarded plastic bags.

There is a far greater diversity here than in Morocco. Even before we reach Nouadhibou, I'm conscious of the black African women carrying round trays on their heads, tall and proud. Even the Saharawi women seem less restricted, their *melekhvas* falling away to reveal flesh, sometimes even, to my shock, a breast. Unheard of in Morocco, here the women seem to wear *melekhva* over their naked bodies, often with no more than a skirt beneath. I'm so accustomed to wearing many layers of clothing and never allowing my arms to show above the elbow or my leg above the ankle, that by comparison the women here seem almost naked. I press my face to the window and watch in fascination as we go further into the town proper.

At first sight, Nouadhibou resembles so many desert towns I've already seen: an endless sea of mud-brick, low-roofed buildings topped with a plethora of satellite dishes. There are the usual mosques on every corner and shops that directly front the street, their entrance the typical heavy iron doors that are opened all day. But as we continue in, I'm surprised by the number of modern, expensive-looking buildings around as well. There is a row of posh hotels side by side with the same humpy-type constructions I saw on the road into town.

Our accommodation – even the bottom level of budget hovel – is ridiculously overpriced. So is the food, and of a far inferior quality to that available in Morocco. In fact, cigarettes are the only thing that are cheap.

The contacts Kadar and I have set up prove to be opportunistic and full of hollow promises. Within twenty-four hours we have recognised their worthlessness and got a feel for the town itself.

Nouadhibou is in the chaotic, heady stage of development. There is money to burn; I see more men driving brand-new four-wheel drives than I ever did in Morocco. Everybody is starting a business, making a dollar, constructing a deal. But the

Mauritanian soul is different from the Moroccan – there is no sense of community here, no family to protect and nurture you. In Mauritania everyone is out for himself, brother against brother. Loyalty has a different meaning. Life is far harsher, more ruthless.

I'm grateful Kadar is with me; I need someone who can mix in. I might be more than capable of making my own choices but, here in the border town of a new country, a Western woman choosing her own camels and guide would make so much of a splash that I'd be lucky to get three kilometres from town before running into problems. Kadar is my insurance. He will make it clear that I'm as his family, and he'll be the 'front man' for my expedition.

We drive out to the camel market on the edge of town. The camels are penned in wooden holding yards, and their nomadic guardians lounge in the shade, drinking tea and chatting idly. The market is not as big as in some Mauritanian towns. Camels are not such a huge stock in Nouadhibou. But Mauritania is fundamentally Saharawi, and it was built on the camel trade. There is no town in the Saharan part of the country that doesn't have a camel market.

Within moments, I spot the first of my camels. Kadar sees it at the same time, and we converge on it and grin at each other. 'This, he is *very* good camel,' Kadar whispers.

'This is the one,' I whisper back. When we're not being watched, I make the camel couch and rise, walk him around and inspect his mouth. He's a white bullock, broad in the chest and about twelve years old. He has a calm temperament – I run my hands beneath his gut and around his genitals, and he barely grunts and doesn't move. He is stocky and strong and fits every word M'Barak ever said about what makes a good camel for long-distance travel. I want him.

The second one we spy is equally outstanding. Another white bullock, this time taller and leaner, but still strong. There is something in the face of this one that I like. He eyes me warily but doesn't pull back from my touch. When another camel gets too close, he rounds and roars at it, but doesn't bite. He couches and rises obediently, but he seems to barely tolerate us, going down and up as if to say, *Oh, all right, but only because I know I have to. Actually, would you all just bugger off and let me eat my lunch?* There is something slightly humorous and lively about him.

'I really like this one,' I say to Kadar.

He strokes the hump and runs his hands down the legs. 'This one, he is strong. But he needs to eat a lot.'

It is Kadar who spies the third. It's a tall, brown bullock, and to me he seems light in the chest, not wide and solid like the other two.

'This is a good camel,' says Kadar confidently. 'This the best of all three, I think.'

I look at it doubtfully.

'I don't know,' I say. 'He doesn't look so strong to me.'

'Trust me,' says Kadar. 'When I'm not sure, I look at a camel's face. This one, you look and tell me you think he is not so strong. For me, I look at his face and I say to you, this will be the best of your camels. Trust me,' he reiterates.

I look again but I don't see what he means about the face. Unlike the other two, I actually feel totally unmoved by this camel. But picking camels, I think impatiently, is not a popularity contest. Kadar knows more than I do; I should defer to him.

And so I shrug and, despite my misgivings, acquiesce.

Kadar and I squat in the sand with the two nomads, who are the dealers. The dealers do not actually own the camels. The animals usually belong to bigger herds out in the desert owned by wealthy, town-dwelling Saharawi. In a culture built upon the camel, no businessman in the Sahara is without a herd roaming somewhere in the desert, guarded by nomads such as these. A man's wealth and prestige is still judged by his camels, and at these markets the professional dealers trade animals and take their cut. It is a rich and lucrative business, and an excellent source of black-market income.

The dealers look at the ground, and so does Kadar. He takes a stick and slowly, after giving the impression of deep thought, draws a figure in the ground in the local currency – the Mauritanian ouguiya. The dealer gives a slight smile and shrug, and comes back with his own figure. There is nothing dodgy or frustrating about the exchange; it's slow and considered, and I know the exact point when a satisfactory price has been reached. Kadar glances at me and I nod. He spits on his hand and they shake.

When all the negotiations are complete, I've paid nearly a thousand dollars for each camel. It's what I was expecting, and I'm thrilled with the quality of the first two camels. The third I remain unconvinced about, but my faith in Kadar is great.

So now the hunt for a guide begins.

Kadar and I chat with the nomads at the market for a while. We're looking, ideally, for someone who will walk right across to Tomboctou with me, but this is rapidly proving impossible. The prices quoted are so ridiculous as to be laughable, and one look at the men offering to walk me there is enough to rule them out. I've been in the desert long enough now to tell the workers from the charlatans – these guys are all talkers, not doers. As soon as I ask questions about how far between each well and what distances they travel in a day, I can pick the lies and inconsistencies.

I've already established the route I want to walk to the next town, Atar. There's a train line running east for more than half of the distance. One route is to follow this line and then drop down to the south at a town called Choum and on to Atar. This is easy for water – there are wells all along – but it means walking more kilometres. The way I want to go is to drop diagonally down, directly into the dune country. The distance between wells will be longer, but according to my maps it is totally doable – and would cut out nearly 200 kilometres. My questions are specific. It is apparent to me in seconds that the men we are speaking to know only the railway-line route and are not true desert men at all.

Again, after talking to over a dozen men, Kadar and I are beginning to despair. The one lone man who seemed a genuine proposition backed down in horror when he realised I was a woman travelling alone. 'My wife would never let me go,' he says. 'And I cannot be responsible for a woman on her own out there. It is too hard for women.'

I sit beneath a multitude of hessian humpies, drinking tea, surrounded by curious robed men for whom I offer a diversion from their daily boredom. They question me about my walk, and laugh and shake their heads in disbelief when I tell them where I've been and where I want to go. But none of them are guide material, and all of them seem negative about my chances of finding one.

I'm anxious and growing impatient. I need to move my camels out of the holding yards the next day, and Kadar needs to get back to his family for the end of Ramadan celebrations. I'm on a deadline and want to get going. Above all, the route ahead is so simple that I'm certain I could make it to Atar without any need of a guide at all. I mention to Kadar that he could accompany me out of town, so it seems that we're walking together, and then I could continue on alone. He is horrified and flatly refuses. I'm annoyed that he doesn't trust me and feel hemmed in. I make a decision that I will simply hire anyone who seems moderately intelligent and is prepared to walk – and then do exactly what I want.

I'm aware that this may not be the most responsible or practical decision. But I make it anyway.

And it is thus that Harraba enters my life, and in doing so very nearly ruins my walk before it has even really begun.

Chapter Twelve

On the outskirts of Nouadhibou, in the cool of dawn, I sit on a mullocky dune, surrounded by my baggage. The Atlantic twinkles over my shoulder; the western terminus of the African continent. I'm at the beginning.

The women of Harraba's family fuss over my belongings, putting a last-minute stitch into a camel saddle, repacking food into what they think are more efficient bundles. They sit in a chirruping circle, drinking endless glasses of tea, going through everything I own. I find their presence intrusive and annoying, but I'm accustomed to the first-day trials. I smile sweetly and play along, taking photos and generally trying to relax.

We're waiting for Harraba, my new guide, who is walking the camels out from the market. In a fit of desperation, we offered him the job late yesterday afternoon. He is a hanger-on at the camel market and says he knows the route to Atar well. I know with one look that he is neither a true nomad nor a cameleer, but I no longer care. I want to walk. Harraba, with his dull features but genial manner, seems a reasonable, safe compromise.

The sun is high in the sky when Harraba shambles into camp. From being entirely unconcerned with his capabilities when we struck a deal at the camel market, I suddenly find myself feeling nervous. He looks anxious and unsure, nothing like the clear certainty of M'Barak. We begin to pack the camels, and I can't bear to watch what he is doing. Everything, in my opinion, is being loaded incorrectly.

'Don't interfere,' says Kadar. 'They do things differently here. It is not like Morocco. You need to let him pack the camels his way and learn from him. He is nomad, he knows what to do.'

'But he's taking forever, and the load isn't secure,' I say in exasperation. 'It can't possibly work like this. The stuff will fall off.'

Kadar dismisses my concerns with a wave. 'I think you should trust him, *lalla*,' he says.

I've been packing camels daily for months on end. Yes, I never took full responsibility for it – M'Barak was always the ultimate authority – but I participated and learned exactly what *not* to do. I may be slow at tying knots, and seemingly clumsy, but I'm certain that my technique is better than Harraba's.

I'm not interested in making a big scene on the first day, in front of his family. But one thing I learned from last time is that it is vital to assert my authority at the beginning. At the first opportunity I will let Harraba know exactly how I expect things to be done. I look over his dull expression and wonder if I will have any luck. I'm now thinking that his face has a slightly mean, petty cast, and I feel extremely uneasy.

The brown camel is behaving appallingly. He will not rest in couched position, and as we try to pack him he is lurching onto his feet and roaring indignantly. Even after being double knee-tied and his head roped between them, he is obviously disgruntled and shifts in frustration. I don't like his style at all, and once again I doubt the wisdom of buying him. The other two, however, are model citizens.

I watch Harraba lurching about, and I have a pang of longing for the busy, scurrying M'Barak, darting from here to there with such surety. Harraba seems obsessed with small detail but misses the larger picture. He will spend minutes tying an excess piece of rope out of the way, then realise he needs it to tie on another piece of kit he has forgotten. When I enter the ring to participate, he chuckles patronisingly and pushes me out of the way.

Harraba speaks only Hassaniya Arabic, the dialect of the Saharawi and the only Arabic I've learned. I know enough to communicate, especially when it comes to the desert and camel-related topics. But Harraba is not a natural communicator, and he does not make an effort to understand or be understood.

Finally, the camels are packed and ready to go, but I don't feel an ounce of comfort. I remind myself of the mental deal I struck when I hired Harraba, but this was contingent on me being able to run the camp my way. I am getting the feeling that he will insist on being boss. It is not a battle I want to fight.

I think, fleetingly, of calling the deal off and waiting in town to find someone more suitable. A part of me sees this as being the more measured, sensible course.

I weigh it up and think of the long kilometres ahead. I'm confident in my own abilities after walking so long with M'Barak. I know how to spot good grazing, how to run my camp out there. I'm not scared of being left on my own, although I do feel daunted by the size of these new camels, all of whom loom at least two feet higher than my old ones and seem far more aggressive. But I don't want to waste time and money in a town where nobody understands the desert anyway. I also see the danger of rejecting Harraba after a deal has been struck; it wouldn't bode well for my chances of hiring another guide.

I decide I will just have to wear the consequences of my decision-making, and so I turn and pose smilingly for the photos Kadar takes and bid Harraba's family goodbye. Kadar takes Harraba aside, and I know he is giving him 'the talk', about me being family and the need to treat me with respect. I've learned something Kadar has not: the only way my honour will be intact is by the strength of my integrity – but it doesn't hurt to have a head start.

And then the rope is in my hands, and I turn and face east, away from Kadar, who is smiling and waving. I walk into my new adventure, leading my three camels into the Sahara of Mauritania.

At first it seems remarkably easy. For the first time at the beginning of a walk, I slip immediately and comfortably back into my rhythm. The camels follow calmly, and within half an hour of leaving Kadar and the others, I feel as though I'm back in the Western Sahara again. I half expect to look to my right and see

M'Barak bouncing along on Ali Baba, laughing with Madani.

I don't feel clumsy or awkward in my *melekhva* and sandals. They're familiar now, and there's something comforting about wrapping up again, feeling hidden and cocooned. I like the spicy scent of incense that lingers in the folds of my new *melekhva*. From the feel of the material on my face, I can tell it will become one of my favourites. The sky is wide open and luminous. For these first two days we are, strangely, heading north since Nouadhibou is at the bottom of a peninsula.

But it doesn't take long for my illusion of familiarity to be shattered.

The camels are skittish and the method Harraba has used to tie the baggage on is illogical. The bags fall off with monotonous regularity. Unfamiliar with how he's tied them on, I find it difficult to fix the problems when they occur. Harraba walks too far ahead of the caravan to be aware of the baggage problems and rarely turns back or rejoins me. He is irritable and sharp, often contemptuous in his tone when we are packing up.

I want to like him. I understand that I'm a strange breed to him. I also appreciate that he is trying hard to appease me, by putting up a shade cloth in the afternoon for me to rest under, pointing out features of interest or telling a funny joke. But his efforts are offset by the way he works with the camels and even more in the peremptory, often dictatorial, tone he takes with me.

I'm now facing the consequences of not being more firm with M'Barak on the last walk. There are things I simply don't know how to do. I may know exactly how to balance the baggage and where things should go, but I don't have the skills with ropes to tie them firmly in place so they won't fall off. I know how to mouth rope the camels, but I've never used the nose rings and am not sure how to tie the ropes securely. I'm also concerned that things work differently here, that the ways I learned aren't the same as Mauritanian ones – perhaps it's me who's in the wrong.

But most of all I'm angry at myself for my lack of confidence. Surely I am competent by now and can assert myself calmly? I berate myself and determine that I won't be some silent passenger on this walk.

These are my camels! Harraba will leave me in Atar. There will be guide after guide, country after country. I'm the only one who will go the whole way, and it is I who must be responsible. This is my camp and my expedition, and I MUST run it the way I know is best. There is no room for these temper tantrums. I must just swallow my pride, ask for help on the things I'm not sure about, and insist on the things I know. I must do this.

But the funny thing about resolutions is how easily they can come undone.

At the end of a week I'm forced to take stock of my situation.

As a direct result of poor handling and packing, the bag holding all of my satellite equipment took a shocking fall – I'm now without my laptop or internet connection. I've developed a hideous urinary tract infection. I can't imagine a worse, more painful infection to get while walking. I've no specific medication for it, so I use my general antibiotic. Despite every effort on my part to change course – even down to actually walking off on my own – Harraba has persisted in taking the route I didn't want, along the railway line, stacking a further 200 kilometres onto my walk. It's completely clear that he has no idea about desert travel.

But worse than all of these things, I am now suspicious of his motives towards me.

Two days ago we stopped at the home of some of Harraba's family. I was relieved of a vast amount of my supplies by a combination of wheedling on Harraba's behalf – and straight-out begging – from the women, something I've never encountered in the desert before. But this was just a minor annoyance, something to laugh off. Today, however, when we stop, Harraba smiles silkily at me and proffers a gift – a small spearhead he found while walking. He is watching my face eagerly. When I dutifully admire it, he hastily pulls out his ID card. This jogs a memory from Morocco. The first step in wooing a potential bride is to present proof of one's earning capacity by showing the profession written on one's ID card. And then the warning bells go off.

He is sizing me up for wife material, I think incredulously. I wonder if I could possibly be right. Seconds later, he informs me with a snicker that he was too tired to make love to his wife last night. *Right. Thanks for that.*

I meet his comments and advances with a steely rebuttal, but the damage is done. I'm desperate to be out of this situation.

It's the tail end of the hot season. The temperature is still in the high forties by ten in the morning. I'm sunburned and dehydrated, despite slathering myself in sunscreen. My lips are chapped and peeling. My body is tired and stiff, unused to launching straight into such long distances. Now, in addition, I can feel the infection in my pelvis like a leaden weight, and I fight against the incessant urge to urinate, knowing it will hurt like hell.

I have to face facts. I can't continue with Harraba; that much is plain. I don't trust him on any level. I feel vulnerable, as he obviously knows people along here. He told me last night that he used to labour on the train line. This figures – he's a town worker, not a nomad. While I'm not necessarily worried about him robbing me or putting me in harm's way, I can see a pattern emerging after the episode with his family. I'm sure that I can look forward to an endless parade of needy acquaintances along the line, and I know I will be at his mercy.

The infection is getting worse by the hour, and I suspect it may well become serious. The brown camel is difficult to handle, and I doubt my abilities to handle all three alone. Because I had assumed I would always be walking with another nomad, I have set the expedition up with two thirty-litre jerry cans of water and two twenty-litre ones, rather than a series of smaller containers. These are difficult to manage alone, although not impossible if I cut down on the water I'm carrying. Nonetheless, the operation would take considerable readjustment to make it workable for one person.

I'm sure I could navigate through the dune country. But I'm worried about my skills with tying the baggage on. And I can't be sure that I won't find myself in serious ill health. I know just how hard dune walking can be – no place for a sick person with poor handling skills and a recalcitrant camel.

Nonetheless, I pick a well on the map a few days hence that's near a minor settlement. Unless I find another solution, I decide that is where I will give Harraba his marching orders.

We're camped on a dune near a small settlement, and I'm cooking dinner. Harraba is lounging on one of the mattresses, smoking and talking to three of the men from the settlement, who have come to visit. I assume they will stay for dinner. Nomads usually do, and I like the custom.

I'm trying to keep an eye on the camels and cook at the same time. I cannot trust Harraba to track the direction the animals move in when they graze. I have three rocks balanced around the fire, and the pot is sitting over glowing coals, the water and rice bubbling. I stir it as I watch the animals.

It's only a week or so into the walk and I'm exhausted, sick, fed up and now injured. I can't see a glimmer of light.

But just as the sun slides down over the horizon, the men stand and face east, robes billowing in the breeze. The eldest stands out in front and, in a melodious tone, he begins the evening prayers.

Behind him the men intone the responses and bow their foreheads to the earth in obeisance. In the brilliant glow of the dying day their silhouettes make a deeply evocative picture, and I feel moved by the richness of their worship. Although I'm accustomed to seeing Muslim prayer, in Morocco praying tended to be a much more personal exercise. Here in the devout Islamic Republic of Mauritania, prayer and ritual is a much more integral part of daily life. As the dunes spread around us and my camels graze below, the scent of tea brewing on the fire, I feel the comfort of their faith surrounding me. As we eat, hope steals into my bones once more.

This isn't the last walk, I suddenly think. *You can make this right. You're dealing here with the shadows of old patterns, old insecurities. You need to stand up and change this reality. Recognise your mistakes. Be strong. You can do this – you know how to do this. You have to.*

Over the next few days, the UTI worsens. I'm passing blood in my urine and running a terrible temperature. It hurts like hell to walk. I can often cope for the morning stretch, but it's the afternoon leg – the one which Harraba continues to insist on despite my protests – that turns the pain from being a bearable irritant to an all-consuming haze of agony. The antibiotics are possibly doing an okay job, but without the space to rest I simply can't heal. I can't quite believe that I'm unable to control the situation. The infection intensifies; the baggage falls off; Harraba is increasingly obnoxious.

I keep my bedroll notably distant now, and I watch his actions carefully. I'm feverish and paranoid through the nights. My lower back hurts, and I think the infection has gone up around my kidney area. I wake constantly, worried that Harraba will decide to try his luck.

We walk to the well, and I'm only just hanging on. I'm still unsure what to do. I sit under a tree and make tea, and Harraba says he will go fill the jerry cans.

I normally go to the wells. But today there is a settlement, and the well is surrounded by people and livestock. I can't face the inevitable storm of attention I will cause, so I agree to stay behind.

As he leaves, I pull the tea glasses out. In Nouadhibou, I bought six new glasses. I love those glasses; I picked them carefully and packed them so they wouldn't be damaged. Harraba has already broken two. Today I lift the container and discover that he must have had an accident while I wasn't watching – there is only one glass left.

One glass. After only a week. So far, this guy's stupidity has cost me a laptop, my RBGAN remote satellite connection, five tea glasses and my sanity. I feel the slow burn of my anger rising.

I hear a yell. Harraba is returning from the well and, once again, he has tied the jerry cans on in a stupid fashion, relying entirely on the camel not shying or moving its weight for them to remain balanced. I have asked him repeatedly not to do this. The jerry cans are covered in a rope mesh, which can easily become tangled around a camel's legs if the containers slip. I have shown him how to attach them when the camel is not wearing panniers, and I can't believe that he has simply ignored me.

He yells again, and I realise that exactly what I had feared has happened. The tallest and strongest of my camels is shying madly, bucking and weaving in an attempt to rid himself of the clinging, heavy containers, which have slipped under his belly and are now rocking. One comes loose and hangs down to the ground. The dangling rope immediately tangles up and my camel goes down on his knees, madly scrambling to free himself from the swaying encumbrances.

Harraba has run up with his knife out, ready to cut into the rope around my camel's legs. Before I can think, before I can even imagine what is about to happen, I am on my feet and running, screaming at the top of my lungs to let the camel go, to just *move away*. I have my knife out and catch the attention of every nomad in the vicinity. I must appear so terrifying that Harraba is simply too stunned to move. He has his fingers tangled with the ropes and looks up, frozen in an expression of surprise.

I reach him and the camel, and literally push Harraba out of the way. His finger was caught in the rope when the camel bolted, and he is shoving it under my face, moaning that it is broken. I say, over and over, 'First the camel, then you. First the camel, then you . . .'

Carefully, I unwrap the cord from around the camel's legs and tie him down. I cut away the tangled rope and release the jerry cans, then slowly move them away. I soothe the camel before bringing him to his feet and checking for injury. He is shaking and blowing hard, skittish to the touch. I walk him over to the other animals and couch him with the rest.

Throughout the entire process, Harraba keeps up and his angry monologue, moaning about his finger and blaming the accident on the camel. I ignore him outright.

I set about packing up the baggage and begin saddling the camels. Harraba eyes me in confusion.

'But I am hurt,' he says plaintively, 'and I want to have a rest and some tea.'

I look at him, the fear and indecision gone. He has not only cost me equipment, he very nearly cost the one thing I cannot, under any circumstances, afford to lose: one of my camels.

'I'll walk alone from here,' I say calmly. By this time there are several nomads gathered around. They look at me in astonishment and start to laugh and scoff among themselves.

Harraba just looks at me in bewilderment.

'You can't walk alone,' he says flatly.

I stop what I'm doing and look at him steadily. 'You don't work for me anymore. I won't walk another day with you. From here to Atar, I walk alone.'

Incensed, Harraba runs off, muttering and obviously distressed. I gather that he's gone to find someone to attempt to change my mind. I don't look around at the small crowd that has gathered; I just start packing my camels – exactly as I like them packed. At one point a lad comes forward to help me. I let him help lift the jerry cans on, then wave him away, along with the others who offer help. I don't want anyone else to interfere. They stand around awkwardly, watching my every move.

Harraba returns minutes later in the back of a pick-up truck filled with men. They all jump out, and the driver saunters over and addresses me in French. Harraba has found someone to 'reason' with me.

I calmly explain what has happened. I'm surrounded by a group of men, all crowding in, straining to hear what I'm saying, thrilled by this freakish deviation from their normal day. I address the man who spoke to me in French.

'I will speak with you and Harraba,' I say, 'but the others need to go away. There are too many people here.' I'm familiar with excitable mobs from my time in Tan-Tan, and I know that Harraba is anxious to garner support and incite the crowd in his defence. I want nothing to do with that kind of scene, and as I stand my ground the mob melts away to a reasonable distance. I am left with Harraba, who is looking slightly shamefaced, and the French speaker.

'But what will happen to Harraba if you have an accident? What will he tell the police?' I want to spit in contempt – after all the trouble he has caused me, the only concern Harraba has relates to his own self-interest. His question confirms my decision.

I write out a note and read it to them both, absolving Harraba of any responsibility towards me, asserting that the decision to walk alone is entirely my own. Harraba in no way has harmed or deserted me.

I'm no more than halfway through the letter when Harraba

begins shouting aggressively at me, moving into a physically threatening space and spraying me with spit. '*My money! What about my money! I want my money, all of it!*'

I've already thought of this. I calmly hand him his bag, in which I've placed the full amount I promised him from Nouadhibou to Atar. He counts it and then demands the Birkenstock sandals I'd said he could use for the duration of the walk, since his own had broken. I give them to him. I can't be bothered arguing. I simply want him and his incompetence away from me and my walk.

The crowd has drifted closer again. Harraba is ranting to them, complaining about my stupidity, demanding that everyone here recognise that it is my decision to walk alone and he's done nothing wrong. I keep my head down and continue packing. But the crowd won't let it go and, like the mob I faced in Tan-Tan, I know they want more, some kind of final act to the theatre.

I start to speak to one young man in particular, who keeps throwing me questions. I smile and calmly say, 'I have no problems with Harraba. He's been an *excellent* guide. He's managed to guide me all the way along the railway line!' The men look at me quizzically, not sure if I'm making a joke or simply stupid. 'For Harraba, I think he's tired now and has had enough of all this walking. He was so tired when we stayed with his family a couple of days ago, he couldn't manage to make love to his wife – he told me!' At this, the bulk of the men begin to see my sarcasm and crack up laughing. Harraba's face is dark and his thunderous rant gains in volume and expletives. But I've actually started to enjoy myself, and the audience is mine now.

'Harraba and I don't agree about how to pack camels,' I say, holding my hands up in supplication. 'After all, I'm a stupid tourist, and Harraba, he's a true nomad, he tells me. But unfortunately, since Harraba has been packing my baggage, I've lost more than I started with. I have only one glass left out of six!' I hold up my tea box. 'So even though perhaps I am stupid, and might have big problems out there in the desert, I think for now it is better for Harraba to go home to his wife and for me to pack my own camels. And thank you all so much for your help and concern; I am very grateful and you are all very kind.'

I smile around, beaming, and the men all laugh, smile shyly back and retreat to a comfortable distance. They watch with concern as I tie my camels together and begin to walk away. A couple of them call after me, asking if I will come have tea with their families, but I wave them off and keep walking. Only one young guy continues to run alongside. He is the one who helped put the jerry cans on the camels. I say nothing, just continue to walk until the well is several hundred metres behind me and the men have disappeared in the desert haze.

I am shaking. The young man says, 'Please, stop here at my hut by the railway line and take tea with me.'

I hesitate for a moment and then stop. 'Thank you,' I say.

I sit inside the small humpy for half an hour. It's the only time I have ever left my camels laden and waiting for so long, but I need a moment to calm myself. I can't quite believe what I've just done.

The humpy is no more than a couple of wooden poles and some hessian sacking. The young man has a thin mattress on top of some cardboard on the dirt floor and a fire outside for cooking. He makes me delicious tea and offers some biscuits and nuts. I'm touched and bring some of my own supplies in to supplement his.

He works on the railroad, checking for faults up and down this stretch. He also guards a small herd of his family's camels. He tells me he would love to walk with me and is so sorry I have such trouble, but he can't leave his post.

He leans forward and frowns. 'Everyone around here knows Harraba,' he says. 'He is crazy, you know? And he isn't a nomad. Very stupid, crazy man.' I nod wearily. I wish I'd been smart enough to see that.

I get up and say I must go. He comes out and helps me tie the camels together. He puts the biggest white one at the front, followed by the medium white one. The skittish, uncooperative and volatile brown one, he places at the rear.

'You always walk with them like this,' he says. 'This one' – he points to the big white one – 'he needs to be in the front; he is a leader. If you put him behind, he will cause troubles. This one' – he points to the medium one, who I have begun to call Zaina, the Arabic word for 'beautiful', because of his calm nature – 'he doesn't matter. Anywhere you put him, he is easygoing and no problem.'

He points to the last one, whom I've simply begun to call Hammad Kasool – 'Brown Lazy' – and his face darkens. 'This camel is problems,' he says solemnly. 'He will always give you problems. You need to watch this one, but maybe behind the others he will be okay.'

We shake hands and I walk away, leading my little caravan.

I head straight into the dunes to the south-east. It's too late for me to follow the diagonal route down to Atar, and I don't feel confident heading into that territory on my own. And I'm still ill. I know it's safer for me to stay by the railway line, where I can find help if I need it and water stops are regular. But I don't want to walk anywhere that people will see me, so I head about five kilometres into the dunes, away from the line, and walk parallel to it. At least tonight's camp will be solitary. I want to be nowhere near the well I left – or Harraba. I don't trust him.

I find a place and couch the camels. I knee-rope them all with extra care before unpacking them, which I usually don't do, but I'm on my own now. I'll have to exert far more caution than I normally would, particularly with the brown camel. I unpack and hobble them. I watch as they shamble off into the dusk, noting the direction they are taking and where they are likely to head during the night.

I walk over to a neighbouring dune and strip off. For the first time since I left Nouadhibou, I have a proper wash without wondering whether Harraba will suddenly pop his head around the corner. Splashing and scrubbing in the dying light, I look around and take in the country around me.

There are tall rock formations on one side of me, brilliant ochre in the late rays. The sand is golden and rich, undulating gently in low, pleasant dunes, dotted with the rich green *sabay* grasses the camels love. The air is clear and still, the afternoon winds at rest, and the desert is peaceful in the rosy gloaming. I draw a breath and sit down abruptly on top of the dune; I feel the Big Empty coming back to me.

That night, just after I have eaten, Harraba turns up accompanied by the young guy I had tea with and a policeman. I'm surprised and unsettled that they tracked me here. The policeman is calm and relaxed, though, and listens respectfully as I explain my wish to walk alone. If I'd been in Morocco, this would have spelled the end of my walk. But here, I get the feeling that the policeman is reluctantly present and only too happy to leave me in peace.

Harraba glares at me resentfully throughout. I barely glance at him. I'm finished with that episode.

The young man whispers to me as they prepare to leave: 'I'm sorry I brought them here, but they were going to round up a big group of men and a truck and search for you. I thought this is better, and safer, for you. Tomorrow, you go further into the dunes – they won't find you. I will come and help you pack up at dawn.'

I clasp his hand gratefully. I was worried about packing, and I'm not too proud to accept help when I know I'll need it.

I go down to check on the camels. They have been eating all afternoon and are resting. I decide to follow M'Barak's example, which I haven't since being in Mauritania, and knee rope them for the night rather than relying on hobbles. I can't face a long episode of tracking them tomorrow morning.

I tie them down close to my swag. The moon is still high and bright. I lie looking up at the sky, taking comfort in the familiar sounds of the camels snuffling and snorting close by, trying not to jump at shadows. I'm grateful that I've passed so many peaceful nights in the desert; the tally of those nights is reassuring and allows me to drift into sleep, secure in my mind that the desert is benign, as it always has been.

I wake early and begin to saddle and pack the camels. I'm all but finished by the time the young guy comes running over the hill. He helps me to tie the last of the jerry cans on and checks my knots and the loads. He offers to walk a way with me, but I refuse. I need to go alone now.

He mentions a settlement a couple of days up the line, where I can get water. He also says that there are good nomads there, family friends of his. If I need help, then stop there.

We shake hands and I walk away into the desert.

It's not the clean, easy break I would have hoped for.

The brown camel is recalcitrant. Already yesterday I had some trouble with him; on several occasions he pulled away from the others, and I had to lunge for his head rope. I've been worried about losing him or having trouble with baggage falling off, given his sudden movements, so I pack him with only unimportant foodstuffs and one soft bag that can fall safely – the one in which I have stuffed my money and passport.

All day he is belligerent and difficult, repeatedly pulling back on the rope so that I have to finally untie him from the end of the line and lead him in my other hand. This is awkward, as it puts him directly next to the big camel, whom I have begun to call Bolshy Sod – he is a brave, strong camel, but he doesn't take kindly to being usurped or challenged in any way. I have both of them on short leads, but every time their paths get too close they snap and snarl at each other, taking fright and jumping out of each other's way. They jerk their heads and growl. I try tying Bolshy behind Zaina, but this only leads to more problems as he increasingly tries to trot up the inside, between Zaina and Brown Lazy, who both jump.

I cover very little ground, incessantly stopping and readjusting ropes and baggage. I'm also increasingly worried about the nose rings. The holes for the nose rings on both the Brown and Bolshy are bleeding. I've only ever tied camels through the nose to let them drink, having been taught to always mouth-rope them. I accepted Kadar's initial assessment that these camels were too big and strong to rely on a mouth rope alone, but I can't see that the nose rings are working.

Harraba would simply tie their lead ropes around their necks at night. When I watched them feed, I could see the ropes getting caught in tree branches, constantly tangling and tugging on the rings. It was one of the many things we had argued about. Last night, I took the head ropes off while the camels grazed. I relied on the hobbles and a length of rope I tied about each one's neck, then ring-tied them again this morning. I'm worried now that, despite my safety measures, the holes will become infected.

I'm tired, frustrated and terribly insecure. Have I been kidding myself about being able to do this on my own? I've been walking since shortly after dawn, yet by early afternoon I've covered barely fifteen kilometres, stopping over and over to try to instil order and calm on the caravan. But the stops unsettle the camels – they are fractious, snarling and biting at each other, growling at me.

I decide to simply call it a day and rethink the way I'm doing things. I find a place and go to couch all three camels.

Zaina and Bolshy go down without bother, and I knee-rope both. But just as I tug at the Brown's rope, he jerks his head back and, to my horror, the nose ring tugs straight out of his nostril. I'm left holding a dangling rope with the ring on the end as he bucks and cavorts his way across the bowl where I'm camped, dislodging much of his baggage, which further enrages him. Unfortunately, I realise as he walks up the ridge in the dying afternoon sun, he is still carrying my soft bag.

The one holding my passport and money.

For a moment, I simply stand there and watch him go, numb and frozen with inaction. Then I bolt across the bowl and make a desperate lunge for the camel, trying to get a rope over his neck and restrain him so I can head-tie him. But he is far beyond reason now and stays well out of range, his unhobbled legs carrying him far faster than I can run. Even with a great deal of stealth, I can get nowhere near him.

I watch to note the general direction he is heading and go back to where Zaina and Bolshy are resting so placidly. I quickly unpack them. I want to simply hobble them and leave them to graze, but I'm too afraid I'll come back to find them gone. I knee-rope them close to a large stand of *sabay*, so they can hop limited distances amid the feed. Then I take a five-litre jerry can, my compass, GPS, rope and headtorch and start out along the tracks the Brown has left in the sand.

I've left my baggage in a loose pile, covered with the camel blankets. I must simply trust that it will be safe, along with my camels. I've no idea how I'm going to catch this rogue camel with no hobbles or neck rope, or even if I'll be able to catch up with him. But equally, without a passport or money, I'm going to have one hell of a time trying to get out of the country – particularly in a small desert town. Besides, I think, almost choking on a short burst of nervous laughter, what kind of officials would ever believe the story of how I came to lose them?

I follow the tracks for an hour or so. Every now and then, I catch a glimpse of the Brown on the horizon, the unwieldy baggage making his an unmistakeable silhouette. Occasionally, I come across parts of my kit that have fallen out of the panniers – a bag of rice, some flour. I put them on top of a rock cairn and mark all around so they are easy to find.

Gradually, I realise the camel is making a large, lazy turn, following a haphazard feed line. To my horror, that line is heading north. Within the next hour, we cross the train line and are heading straight into the heavily mined territory of the Western Sahara.

I'm not entirely sure just how thick the mines are in this area. All I know is that at one stage, the entire region on both sides of this seemingly invisible border was littered with explosives. When I asked the nomads on the Western Sahara side about smuggling camels through this zone, they shook their heads and said it remains no-man's-land, that the sands have shifted now so that the chances of ever clearing the territory of mines are nil.

As I watch the Brown heading deeper into the oddly shaped mounds a couple of kilometres north of the tracks, somehow profoundly different from the more defined, low dunes I have just come from, I glance at my GPS and see that I'm right on the border – and right in the midst of the territory the nomads spoke about.

I wonder what the hell I'm doing. I've no idea how to catch this camel, even if I get close to him. But then what on earth is the alternative? I think about having to leave my camels and walk to the train, going back to Nouadhibou only a week in and the horror of calling my family, my sponsors and Graeme: 'Oh, look, sorry guys, I just couldn't hack it – everything went wrong!' I would rather be blown to smithereens than suffer that humiliation.

I pause for a minute and sit down for a drink. I carefully reach around and sweep the sand away, hoping I won't uncover a mine.

Then the futility of my actions overwhelms me, and I start to laugh – seriously laugh – at my circumstance: I'm sitting here in the growing darkness with a horrible urinary tract infection, tracking a stupid camel who just happens to have buggered off with my money and passport, straight into territory I have done everything to avoid – and on top of all that, I just might be done for if I sit on a sodding landmine.

I sit and light a cigarette, cackling so hard that my whole body shakes and the tears run down my cheeks. I think that only I could manage to dump myself in such a ridiculous position, right at the start of the walk. I look back and see all the little things I've done wrong that have led to this point: settling on Harraba when I instinctively knew he was no good; allowing Kadar to overrule me about the Brown; not being entirely sure of my knots and packing before I set out; putting my money and passport on the one camel I know to be unreliable. I see all of these mistakes, and a dozen others, with crystal clarity, and I allow myself for a moment to be angry that I did not foresee disaster.

And then I stand up, shake myself off and start following the tracks again. If I've learned one thing over the last few years, it's that the only way out of the dark 'MIG zone' – 'mistake-induced guilt' – is to learn from the mistakes. And then do it better next time.

I walk and walk. Occasionally I get close enough to the Brown to sneak up behind him, or lie in wait behind a bush, and attempt to ambush him with the rope. I lose count of the times I have near misses, or even part successes: I get the rope over his neck or head, but it is torn out of my grasp before I can draw the ends together; I get a lucky throw straight over his head, only for his violent contortions to undo it; I get within feet, only for him to suddenly sense me and bolt, bucking in fury to the next dune.

For hours we play a frustrating game of hide-and-seek, and I'm yanked off my feet, knocked sideways and left in the dust. I start talking to myself, talking to my friends and family, having whole conversations, which usually end in semi-hysterical laughter, imagining their replys. And then I have one conversation that brings me up short.

I imagine myself talking about this night over the fire with M'Barak, him leaning forward on his side with his legs curled beneath him, drawing in the sand and listening intently, his eyes never leaving my face as I explain how I wound up here. And then I imagine myself saying, 'But what would you do?'

And I suddenly remember a night just like that, the one after I got between the two fighting camels. M'Barak explained exactly how to catch a wild camel, if I were to try it in central Australia.

I stop in my tracks and play the conversation back through my brain in slow motion. Yes, I can remember every step of what he told me to do. There is only one hitch: he said it would take two strong men.

Unfortunately, men of any description are noticeably absent.

I think for a moment. Hard. And then I look at where the Brown is grazing, just fifty yards away, eyeballing me occasionally in amused contempt. I think, *Fuck it. Why not?*

I dump my water bottle and other possessions behind a bush and creep forward, using the *sabay* as cover to approach the camel directly from behind. He grazes on contentedly, oblivious to my approach. I'm now within reach, directly behind him, only a metre and a half away. My heart is going like a triphammer drummed by sparrows; I can barely breathe. I pause, frozen in an agony of indecision, and then I see the camel's head rise suddenly. I know he has sensed me. If I don't make my move, he'll be gone forever.

I leap from behind the bush and land right behind the Brown, both hands wrapped around the top of his tail in a vise grip. With every inch of my strength, I sit back and dig my heels in, my thighs and upper arms straining beyond anything I knew possible. I take every bit of the big body I have often wished I didn't have and throw it left with all the force I can muster, hauling that animal as if I was a mother turning a truck off her baby.

It has all happened so fast that I'm still half-expecting to get a stinging kick from the side and watch the camel bolt into the Never-Never. But to my sheer astonishment, his rear legs go straight out from under him and he hits the ground with a stunned thud, hindquarters first. He's so severely off balance that he is already rolling onto his side as he lands, the hanging baggage unbalancing him even further.

For a split second I've no idea what to do. Deep down, I had never really expected even this much to work. And then I remember that this is the moment when the second bloke is supposed to be at hand, roping the camel's head. Before the Brown can gather his wits or my conscious mind can assess it too much, I literally launch myself onto the camel's side. In a stumbling run that keeps the animal off balance and on the ground, I make it to the neck in three clumsy lunges. I throw myself down over the neck and head and, just as he is finding his rear legs and going for the escape, I pull the slipknot from my wrist and get it right over his snout, wrapping the other end over the top of his head. It's tight in seconds. Although the Brown is now on his feet, pulling and squealing, he has nowhere to go. In moments the rope is tighter and more secure and I get him back on the ground and knee-rope him. I grab one of the other ropes from the dishevelled baggage, make a mouth rope out of it and get it in his mouth. Despite the knee rope preventing him from going far, I am angry and pumping adrenalin at the end of it all. I'm squatting fifty centimetres from his nose, holding both ropes tightly and forcing his head to the earth. His eyes roll and he snorts and squirms beneath the restraints. We eyeball each other, but I have won this stand-off – and we both know it. I may be trembling just as much as he. But I won.

I hold the ropes tightly and continue staring at that animal until at last my breathing calms and I feel the mad, trembling strength subside and the weakness come. Then I collapse on my backside and shake my head dumbly. The moon is on the wane and has risen late, but I can see enough so the tracks and signs of our recent skirmish are plain in the sand. I wish I had my camera so I could photograph them. I want some record of this night, of this memory, because already I can't believe it has happened, that I *did* this. I remember every motion of my body with spellbinding clarity, yet I remember the camel as nothing more than a squirming blur beneath me. The whole struggle could have taken no more than ten seconds, from the leap until the final mouth rope. It feels like it was an eternity.

I stand up and rearrange the baggage. My soft bag, thank God, is still hanging on, and still contains the money and passport. Very little besides the couple of pieces I found on the way have been dislodged. Despite being unbalanced, the kit is remarkably stable. I adjust it all and retie it. Then I pick up a big, solid stick, untie the knee rope and hold on tightly as the Brown scrambles to his feet and fights me for a moment. I clout him over the head until he subsides into groaning mutiny, and we begin the long walk home.

It is close to dawn when I crest the dune where I left the camels. According to my GPS, I've done a round trip of nearly forty kilometres. My exhaustion nearly turns into tearful relief when I see not only the camels, right where I left them, but also the young bloke from a couple of days ago, sitting patiently by their side.

He rises and rushes eagerly to meet me.

'I was worried. I felt bad about leaving you to walk alone, and so yesterday afternoon I started to track you. And I could see that you are having many problems, stopping a lot. The Brown one is a big problem, yes? And then I got here and I see that you have left to track the brown one, and I thought: *well, I will wait here tonight and then, if she does not come back by sunrise, I will go to look for her.* But here you are – and with the brown camel! What happened?'

I talk so fast the words just spill out. While I talk he makes tea and listens, laughs and nods in all the right places. I'm not sure he understands when I tell him about catching the Brown; he looks up quizzically. In the end, I simply say that I managed to catch him after a lot of problems. Then I ask him to show me how to make a nostril rope.

I'm unbelievably glad to find him here. As the sun rises and day breaks, I feel drained and exhausted, the events of the night leaving me shaken. My nocturnal wandering seems surreal, like distant dream. I feel unable to deal with the reality of the coming day. I cannot even think about trying to pack up and walk again.

'I think you should go to the settlement further up and find someone to walk with you,' the young guy says. 'You can't make Atar alone.'

I'm angry and despondent; I feel as though I haven't even had a chance to *try* to make it alone. But I also feel the sheer truth of his words.

I acknowledge something I have hidden from: right now, I don't have the skills I need. I may be able to navigate; I may know how to pack, or saddle, or find a good camp. But my camels are not handling well, and I'm not confident in my own abilities on a range of levels. Being out on my own has taught me exactly what I don't know. Now I need to learn.

I look at the young guy.

'Let's go to that settlement now,' I say.

Later that day I'm lying in the shady cool of a low mud-brick house that is part tent, part solid construction. For once I'm sitting with the men only – something I will become more accustomed to on this journey. My walk is no longer run by men. Now I *am* my walk, and it's the men whom I belong with. On this occasion I am in the home of a man called Mohammed, and the others are his brothers and sons.

One look at Mohammed is enough to fill me with reassurance. He has a lively, intelligent face; a manner that is unfailingly calm, smiling and polite. He greets me as family and his wives and children are open and welcoming. I am served tea and food immediately, nurtured as I would be in a Western Saharan tent, and at once I am at home again. I am in surroundings I understand.

I do not talk a lot about Harraba. Within minutes of the meal and tea being completed, Mohammed and I reach a financial agreement that is far fairer than what I paid Harraba. I am anxious about the camels, which I unpacked and left just outside the door, knowing they have not eaten all night. But Mohammed summons one of his sons, and within moments the camels are driven away to graze on rich acacias close by. Another son is checking my jerry cans and asking if the camels are watered. I feel close to tears at the show of kindness and support. A spark of defiance insists that I should be out there on my own doing it. But I am too exhausted for pride. Common sense tells my pride to go to hell.

I'm still here. I'm still walking. I have time to learn; right now, I have to take care of myself and my camels.

In the early evening I follow the young guy to his other temporary humpy, a replica of the first, close by the tracks, which he shares with some other family members. I try to donate some of my food, but he smiles and declines. He cooks a large plate of pasta, and he and the other men, thin and undoubtedly hungry, stare and grin at me, insisting I eat the majority of the plate. One of them brings me a heated pail of water after dinner, and all of them tactfully withdraw, showing me a place behind some hessian where I can wash.

When I come back to the humpy, they've laid my swag out a respectful distance from the hut. All of them press small gifts onto me – an old spear head, a beautiful rock, a hollow stone that threads onto a necklace. From around my neck I take a necklace I put together before I left, the one that holds all my good-luck charms. I take off the three charms – a crystal, a medallion and an old decoration I was given in the Western Sahara – and give one each to the three men. I attach the hollow rock in their place. We all look at each other, smiling, and they all touch their hearts as they wave farewell.

I lie down in my swag and pass contentedly into a deep sleep, not even stirring when the slow, long coal train rumbles past in the early hours.

The remainder of the walk to Atar is uneventful and immensely reassuring. The infection begins to lift almost immediately as I change back to my old routine of walking only once a day, for about six hours. Mohammed and I agree totally on how to pack the animals, and we laugh together as we get the job done in a fraction of the time it took with Harraba. The camels begin to settle, and the days pass easily and without incident.

Chapter Thirteen

I'm sitting beneath the shelter of an African-style rondavel, in a rough-hewn wooden seat, drinking a cold beer and talking to two French pilots.

I feel like I've landed in heaven.

I'm staying in a camping ground in Atar run by a strange couple – she German, he Dutch. They both have the jaded, weary air of people who have been operating under tough circumstances for some time. While they are helpful to me in my efforts to get replacement equipment sent through and organising various logistical matters, I'm aware that every traveller who passes through – and there are many, arriving in a variety of manners from traditional overland four-wheel drives to motorbikes to tours – has a problem that needs to be solved. The couple have little patience and answer the same questions often.

I'm trying to find a guide. For a day or so I've been inter-viewing a variety of hopefuls. I even drove twenty kilometres out to the desert with one particularly helpful local who thought he'd found the perfect man for me. But thus far, none have impressed me enough to hire them and, after the Harraba experience, I am cautious. My camels are with Mohammed and a nomadic family just outside town, so I'm in no rush.

'How do you choose a guide?' one of the French pilots asks. They are wonderful company and have insisted on sharing their beer supply with me. It's bliss to chat and relax. Three weeks into this walk, I discovered on arrival in Atar that I have lost over fifteen kilos, and the trial by fire of the first leg has left me shaken and lonely.

'I have just about honed my questioning now, I think. Before I start the conversation, I work out exactly where I want to go – for example, the next leg is from here to Tidjikja. I examine my maps and work out how many days it is between each well and how long it will take to walk the entire distance, allowing a little room for error. So then when I sit down, I essentially let the prospective guide do the talking – I say where I want to go and then ask him to tell me how he would do it: Which direction would he take out of town? How far does he walk each day? How long will that take? How many days in total does he think it will be to the next town? Et cetera. It's interesting how quickly most of them eliminate themselves.'

'How so?' asks the Frenchman. 'How do you know if they are incompetent?'

'Well, I got it so wrong the first time that I don't know if I'm qualified to answer that,' I say ruefully. 'But now there are certain details that are easy to spot – like if they say that from here to Tidjikja will take one week, when I know simply from looking at the map that it will be at least two. Or if they mention vehicles – in other words, they are planning to simply follow four-wheel drive tracks, which I never do. Or if they talk about walking ten hours a day – they may be able to do this, but I choose not to. I don't put my camels through that kind of distance when they have so far to go.

'Some of the hints are easy to pick up on: perhaps they are very overweight or have soft, unmarked hands. Both of those are dead giveaways that they are more accustomed to guiding from the comfort of a four-wheel drive than walking anywhere. And then there are the men who eye me like meat on a butcher's hook. They get short shrift straightaway.

'The worrying thing is that no matter whom I ultimately choose, I will never really know if they are any good until they're actually out there walking with me. That's the gambling part, I guess.'

They shake their heads in amazement and we laugh. I sound so cavalier; but I certainly don't feel it. The first leg has been a baptism by fire, and I feel wary and tremulous about the future. I'm waiting for a laptop my dad is having couriered out, in the hope that I'll have satellite communications as I planned. None of my equipment works, even when plugged into the mains, eliminating the faint hope I had that the problems were solar-panel related.

The stretch ahead is one of the most isolated and difficult in Mauritania, a 400 kilometre stretch that passes through a vast dune sea. The alternative is to walk around it, taking the overlanders' route. But this will cost me time and kilometres, not to mention the added unpleasantness of sharing my journey with vehicles. I need an excellent guide. I'm determined that I will choose someone this time who can teach me the skills that I still don't have and improve the ones that I do, so that I'm never caught short again.

I spend days having endless rounds of interviews and telling the story of Harraba's sacking, which has mysteriously leaked into town – I suspect via Mohammed, the lovely nomad who walked the last few days with me. He'd never tired of hearing the tale, and now it seems every nomad in Atar is anxious to drink tea and howl with laughter. '*Wahid cas! Wahid cas!*' They wheeze, slapping their thighs in appreciation. '*Wahid cas*' is Arabic for 'one glass', and it's how the story becomes known – the tale of how being left with one glass was the final straw. I tell that story so many times it becomes rote.

But I don't say too much about losing a camel. The terror of that experience is still a little too raw. I remain ashamed of my incompetence and worried about my ability. And there is no way I want to hire a new guide who thinks I'm not up to the task.

I talk with another Frenchman, Jean, who suggests I meet with his guide who has been recommended to him by a friend. The man, Khabuss, is said to be ex-military and a local topographer. Jean tells me he is, apparently, 'the best'.

I'm sceptical but agree to go to the man's house for tea. We walk through a thousand back alleys and sandy lanes until we arrive at a ubiquitous tin door and are welcomed by a smiling

Saharawi woman who reminds me of those I knew in the Western Sahara. As she ushers us into her home and begins the tea ritual, I'm struck by how familiar and comfortable the whole process is.

The contrast of Jean's obvious discomfort furthers these feelings. In denim and boots, he is awkward sitting cross-legged – and he made the mistake of offering the woman his hand upon entering, which she smilingly declined. He is lovely and well educated, and I understand entirely what a mind-blowing experience all of this would be.

I remember back to the first meal I had in Kadar's home and feel a bittersweet nostalgia. Back then I longed to understand this place, to be a part of the culture. Now a part of me mourns the loss of a tourist's naïvety, the feeling of being the Other. Familiarity has bred a dual reality: while I take comfort and pride in being at home here, I no longer see my surroundings with wonder or fascination.

After a moment Khabuss sweeps in. Tall and heavy-set, his face is open and intelligent, lit with good humour. I sense in him an element of hardness. His manner is somewhat egotistical and overwhelming. But as we talk, I gradually begin to relax – he answers every question of mine with dead-set accuracy and, if his boasts are to be believed, he knows exactly what he's doing.

'I spent five years walking in the desert around here,' he tells me. 'I wanted to make proper maps of it all – maps local people can understand.' He brings them out to show me, colourful affairs with pictoral representations of geographical features. I will come to truly appreciate the wonder of these maps, but at the time I'm more concerned with the fact that they are indeed topographically accurate. Khabuss is obviously very knowledgeable about the local terrain.

He agrees with me immediately about walking the dune sea route, but warns that it is a tough walk and that he doubts Jean's ability to make it through. Jean and I have come up with the idea that he will walk with me through to Tidjikja, thus saving him the cost of hiring camels and allowing me to halve the price of a guide. I'm wary about walking with anyone else, but Jean is a gentle character, and I'm horrified by the kind of quotes I'm getting from prospective guides – more than four times per day what I paid M'Barak in Morocco.

We agree that Jean will walk the first few days, and then if he is struggling, Khabuss tells me there is a final camp before the dune sea where it is possible to change guides – he assures me he can find someone there to help me.

By the end of the night I agree to hire Khabuss. He is so charismatic and self-confident that he reminds me in some ways of Kadar, but with a steadier, more practical bent. Although I'm aware that I'm taking a chance, I feel more confident that it's a good one. Khabuss's military background is reassuring – he spent twenty years in the army, rising to a senior position. Perhaps it's this experience that gives him the aura of hardness I noticed when we met.

'He is an egoist, but I think he is also bloody good at what he does,' I say to the Dutch owner of the camping ground, who knows Khabuss. He has made a few disparaging comments about the character of my prospective guide, and I sense a longstanding feud between them.

'Oh, he'll get you there, all right,' the Dutchman says sourly. 'He definitely knows what he's doing. And you certainly won't have any trouble with bandits.' He looks at my questioning expression. 'Anyone messes with that bastard, he'll just kill 'em.'

It's a measure of my mindset that I find this pronouncement oddly reassuring.

It's midmorning and we're packing the camels together for the first time. The nomadic family I paid to mind them is sitting in a huddle, watching proceedings with immense amusement. Khabuss and I are packing as Jean stands and watches. I am reminded of Gary's and my first day watching M'Barak and Madani. I can sense his frustration at being extraneous to proceedings.

Things are slightly tense as I watch Khabuss and show him how I like things done. His pride doesn't take kindly to being corrected by a white woman in front of his peers and, after one or two exchanges, I withdraw entirely and decide to wait until we don't have an audience. It's hard for me to let go after the problems with Harraba, and I'm also keen to show Khabuss that I at least know what I'm doing. But I stop, take a deep breath and recognise my pride and insecurity for what it is. The fact is that while there are things I do know, there are plenty I as yet do not, and I need to accept that simply because Harraba turned out poorly doesn't mean every guide will. Until I see any differently, I should assume that Khabuss is everything he says he is and just watch and learn.

Even so, it's difficult, as we walk around the outskirts of Atar, to remain calm. He orders me about and rushes around anxiously when a vehicle approaches. I know how to handle my camels and already have them on short leads, well off the road. I resent being treated as an idiot. But I swallow my retorts, mindful that the first day is always painful.

I can't fault his walking pace. He sets a fast stride and maintains it, for at least thirty kilometres, over rough terrain. I had eyed his impressive girth with a little scepticism, but by day's end I have to confess he is as tough as his boasts suggested. As we make camp he leads the camels off into the distance where the feed is excellent, and I can tell he is far from tired.

Jean is a mess. He collapses onto the ground and virtually passes out, rising only to eat a little dinner, groaning with abject exhaustion. I remember my first days with the pack – even the first days of this walk – and have complete sympathy. I can't also help feeling a sneaking satisfaction at his discomfort – it is, vicariously, somewhat reassuring.

Within days I have totally relaxed. I have long conversations with Khabuss about the problems with Lazy Brown and the infections around the nose rings. We discuss it all, and he shows me how to remove the nose rings and use only the ropes through the unaffected holes on the other sides. He also agrees with me about mouth-roping, and we switch to this method. We are in accord about tying a permanent neck rope that is not connected to the nostril, so their noses are only used when they need to drink, thus eliminating the rope getting entangled when they eat. Just these simple changes leave me heartened, and I quickly find myself talking with him as I would M'Barak.

By the time we reach the last camp before the dune sea, though, it's obvious that Jean will not be able to continue.

'I cannot do this,' he groans to me that night. 'I'm already sick. I know if I go one more day, I'll be very sick. I have a fever and I can't eat. It's too many miles and too hard. I'm just exhausted.'

My heart sinks. Just as I'm gaining faith in Khabuss, I'll have to say goodbye to him. I always knew that he was essentially Jean's guide and that if it came to a separation I would have to make do with someone Khabuss chose for me.

But later in the evening Khabuss comes and squats beside me. 'I've told Jean that I cannot go with him,' he begins. 'We've walked together for three days now, and I know that you will continue. Maybe at the start I thought you were a little crazy and just playing around but now, after some days, I know you know what you are doing, and I can see you are very determined. I also think that there is a lot you still need to know, and I don't want you to get into trouble. I want to walk with you and teach you, properly, and help you pick another guide to get you further on your walk. I don't want you to have more trouble like with this Harraba.' His face darkens as he mentions the name of my last guide; Khabuss has heard my stories with rising disgust.

I am stunned by his offer – and deeply touched.

'I can't afford to pay you what Jean and I offered,' I say straight-away. 'I just can't afford it. I will understand if you want to go with him for the shorter trip.'

Khabuss looks straight at me. 'It is a matter of honour for me now,' he says quietly. 'I will walk with you for nothing if you can-not afford it. I cannot let you cross those dunes with anyone else – no one knows them like I do.'

I look at Jean. 'Are you okay with this?' I ask.

'Now, after I walk with you for a few days, I understand a little about what you do. I think you need Khabuss more than I do,' Jean says, nodding. 'I will go with one of the nomads here who Khabuss knows – mine is just a little tourist circuit, riding the camels for a few days. I want to see the dunes and take photos but, to be honest, I don't want to go right into the dunes with you. I just don't think I could do it.'

I shake my head in amazement at his kindness and generosity, and thank him profusely. Khabuss and I discuss money for a whole five minutes. He promptly accepts the first offer I make, eschewing the traditional bargaining process, and shakes my hand. It's the last time money is a topic between us, something I never forget about him.

Our final mission in the camp is to swap my brown camel for a different one. While the other two have settled, Lazy Brown has remained recalcitrant and vicious. Khabuss told me promptly that he will never make it through the big dunes. Although it worries me to be collecting a new camel at this stage of proceedings, I am totally fed up with dragging the Brown like a sack of potatoes behind me and dealing with his belligerence while being packed or handled in any way. He goes down at least four times a day and is difficult to raise. He has been eating well and should not be struggling, and I, too, have no faith that he will make it anywhere remotely difficult. I wish I had stuck to my instincts at the camel market.

But his replacement is the last camel I would have picked.

'He's tiny!' I exclaim.

'Yes, but look at him,' Khabuss says. 'He is perfectly trained. And this camel, he has been with nomads all his life – he is used to being ridden for miles, day after day. He knows how to work hard, then rest and eat, and then work again. This camel will follow you until he drops dead from exhaustion. I promise you, this camel you will not regret.'

It's a straight swap for me, so there is no financial inducement for the nomads or Khabuss.

'The nomad knows your brown camel is no good. But we are family, and he does this favour for me,' Khabuss tells me. I'm a little sceptical about this; my brown camel may be bad for an expedition, but he will still fetch a good price in the market. I doubt that the nomad is actually losing on the deal.

The swap is dependent on the nomad being able to actually ride my brown camel, so we all watch in amusement as he saddles him, then gingerly mounts while his brother holds the lead tightly so the camel can't budge. The tense rider nods and takes the mouth rope.

As one, all the nomads leap back as the man lets go of the head rope and the camel jolts to his feet and cavorts about. I hold my breath, and the men whoop and laugh, but within moments he comes under control. The nomad nods in satisfaction.

I look over at my new fellow. He is the smallest camel I've ever seen, but fat and stocky. He eyes me placidly, and I could swear he smiles. He might be tiny, but I like him already.

We walk hard and fast. The landscape changes from mullocky dunes to rocky hamada, deep ravines to stony soil, then back to flat plain. We cover the kilometres in amazing time and come up fast on the wide expanse of dune sea.

I'm walking back into my desert peace at last. Secure with Khabuss, I'm more engaged in my walk than I've ever been. He doesn't allow me to travel as a passenger; I'm constantly being called on to define our direction, choose the camp or say why a certain path is not the right one. He doesn't guide, but rather checks my navigation. In the morning when we pack the camels, he watches all I do, makes me shift things when they are wrong or retie a rope that is not secure. Not one piece of luggage moves all day after we've tied it on.

For the first time, I feel that I'm genuinely learning the skills I need to operate alone. Khabuss sees it as his job to teach me, test me and train me in everything he can. In the middle of the night when a herd of camels passes close by, we rise together and, as the wind swirls and the tracks of our camels begin to fade, he insists that I find the tracks and rope the camels on my own. Even when I walk some distance in the wrong direction, he just follows, allowing me to make my own mistakes. Only later will he tell me where I went wrong. He tests me with military discipline, and tolerates no error.

On the days when the walking is easy, I drift into the meditative space I treasure, sinking into the enormity of the Big Empty. I feel the earth pass beneath my feet in that ancient, reassuring rhythm that has carried me so far. Without consciously examining it, I begin to retrace the steps of the last walk in my mind, gently probing at the hurt and calamity of those long, lonely days in the Western Sahara. I think about Gary, Kadar, M'Barak and Madani. I think of the mistakes I made and the humiliations I put myself through, and I shake my head. And as I walk further into myself and this wild place, I feel comfort steal over me and the haunting reality of the true desert sink into my bones.

One day we climb high into the big dunes, winding and weaving, in and out, around and over. Khabuss races away, like M'Barak used to do, but he rarely corrects my course. We communicate by gestures, until he signals from the top of a tall, golden dune to join him.

At the summit I draw a deep breath and release it in amazement.

As if God has taken an enormous paintbrush, a line is drawn straight through the heart of the dunes. On one side – where we are standing – the sand is a pale-gold, bright and plain. But on the other side of the line, every dune rippling off into the distance, as far as I can see, is burnished russet – a deep, rich red like the pindan of Western Australia. The contrast is breathtaking; I can't imagine what created such distinct colouration.

'It's beautiful,' I say.

'Not many people ever see this,' Khabuss says softly. 'This is deep desert.'

My gaze is unwavering.

It's unlike any desert I have ever walked before. Our camp that night is only a sparse patch of grazing, and this dune sea takes some time to cross. But a few days in this haunting, windswept heart of the Big Empty seems an eternity. Time stretches before and behind me, a hollow, echoing loneliness.

With Khabuss, I learn a lot, too, about the nomads of this country. I had come across few nomads with Harraba, since we had stayed in populated areas. On the way into Atar I'd been so ill and pushing so hard that I'd barely noticed the type of people we came across. But as we come out the other side of the dune sea, Khabuss and I begin to encounter nomadic settlements, and I start to get a feel for Mauritania.

The first thing to strike me is how very much poorer the nomads appear than in the relative wealth and fertility of Morocco. The tents are shabby, with usually only one to a family. There is none of the multi-tent set-up I saw in Morocco, nor any of the implements that make cooking or housekeeping easier – no portable gas burners or low table to eat from. When tea is made it is in cheap glasses, sitting in the sand – the gorgeous silver trays I'm used to are gone.

The women are clad in tattered *melekhva*, usually with breasts poking out the sides. They have none of the smiling sweetness of the Saharawi, but rather a tougher, coarser approach. Whenever we camp close to a settlement, the women arrive in hoards, trying to sell me any one of dozens of 'artefacts' – ancient stone tools they have found in the desert or simply stones shaped like tools. There are old, broken spearheads and more recent crafts: woven bowls, simple bangles.

When I don't buy, the begging starts. Although I'm accustomed to giving what I can, the Mauritanian women harass me with belligerence. No matter what I give, it's never enough and they can become quite rough, actually delving into my bags to look at my possessions. After a long day walking, this is exhausting and frustrating.

Khabuss is a great help in dispersing the crowd and often diverts their attention by showing them his maps, pointing out the topographical features in their region. The nomads gasp in delight. I watch nomadic men remain intrigued for hours in this way, gradually connecting the images on the map to the land they walk through. For most, it's the first time they have ever seen a map; it's like watching a new world unfold and they are entranced.

But I find myself oddly disassociated from the culture around me, unlike the last desert walk when I'd found myself endlessly absorbed by the minutiae of nomadic life so profoundly different from my 'other' life. Now, my obsession to perfect my camel loading and survival skills eclipses my cultural curiosity. When Khabuss and I lie on the mats at night, looking up at the stars, I want to practise my Arabic and learn how to navigate by the night sky. I want to know how to read the landscape with surety, guided by instincts. I want to pack my camels correctly and understand what I'm doing with them.

I'm obsessed by the actual mechanics of my walk – the urge to do it *right*, to be independent. When we come into camps I feel impatient and unsociable, anxious to be back in the Big Empty. I feel no empathy towards the women.

One night when we're talking, I allude again to the stars, as I have so many nights before.

'How do I find my way to Tomboctou?' I ask idly.

Khabuss stands behind me and raises my arm to the stars. 'Do you see those two – *there,* and *there*?' he asks, using my arm to point towards two sets of two stars, which angle down to a point in the sky.

'Of course. I see them every night,' I say.

'Tomboctou lies between those two lines. If you walk towards the point that is right in the middle of the two lines, you will find Tomboctou,' he says. I shake my head in a gesture of cynicism.

'Months ago, M'Barak told me that if I just kept *that* star behind me, I would also find Tomboctou. His exact words were, "Keep that star between the cheeks of your arse, and you will find Tomboctou."'

Khabuss is rolling around laughing. 'Your M'Barak – he knew what he was saying. Keep that star behind you, and walk towards the meeting of those two lines, and you will get there. Believe me.'

I look high at the stars and fix their position in my mind. I want more than anything for his words to be true. I imagine coming upon Tomboctou and seeing it lie between those stars. I dare not even believe I will see it like this.

We stop one day to buy a goat, and Khabuss slaughters it and hangs the meat. He goes through the process patiently, and sits by me as I clean the intestines in a bowl. I tell him that I'm not mad keen on the usual stew people make out of the intestines. While I devour the offal these days, I've never liked the metallic, chewy taste of the intestinal tubes.

Khabuss holds up a finger, eyes sparkling. 'Ah, but I will show you a way to make the intestines that is so good, you will want to eat it every day.'

Sceptical, I watch as he deftly plaits the cleaned tubes into neat, thick ropes. He takes the stomach bag (tripe) and stuffs the ropes into it, along with some onion and seasoning, then folds the corners over and uses a green twig to thread it into a neat package. He digs down into the fire and places the package into the coals, then covers it over with ash.

'We leave it here tonight; in the morning, this is delicious,' he tells me. I've watched every movement and am intrigued.

The following day we have been walking for several hours and are ready for a stop when Khabuss pulls the package out of his robes. He hacks a piece off with his knife and hands it to me; it is thick and rich and divinely satisfying. We eat hunks of it as we walk along, and that day there is no need for our usual stop.

This experience typifies what I like about the Mauritanian desert, as compared to Morocco. In many ways Morocco was a soft desert experience. Although I was at times in very isolated areas, we found fresh supplies in each town and good stores of meat. I never really worried about being stuck without food. But out here, the only meat I eat is what we buy from nomads and slaughter ourselves. The settlements are poor and hungry, and there is rarely anything other than some weevilly rice for sale. Nomads here do not eat bread with every meal like Moroccans, so I rarely make it. Breakfast is a few biscuits; lunch, perhaps some sardines in pasta. Dinner is rice and onions, with meat when we have it. Often lunch does not exist at all. I drink endless mugs of a maize drink called Gofiya, a powder I mix with water and sugar. It's my staple. Khabuss jokes in the morning when I get up, greeting me with, 'Bonjour, Gofiya?'

It's also on this stretch that I begin to gain immense respect for Mauritanian men. Accustomed to finding honour among the women in Morocco, but having developed a wary respect for the men, I'm pleasantly surprised by the role reversal in Mauritania. The men are wonderful, almost without exception. Polite, proud, funny, intelligent and courteous, they are devout Muslims who pray five times a day in beautiful sing-song cadence. They inevitably greet me with shy goodwill and eat quite happily from the same plate. Frequently they will enquire bluntly as to whether I am married. When I reply that I am, which I always do, they never overstep the line of familiarity. I often find myself, during my time with Khabuss, engaged in quite complex conversations with the nomads we meet about Islam and Catholicism, the similarities and differences.

On one occasion Khabuss invites the men from a neighbouring tent over to enjoy dinner with us, since we still have some meat left. One of the men is old and an obvious student of the Qur'an, highly esteemed by his fellows because he can actually read it rather than simply recite it.

'We are always happy to eat with People of the Book,' he tells me. 'All of this confusion between Christianity and Islam, all of the arguments between the Jews and Muslims – this is stupid. We share your prophets. Yes, we who follow Islam know that Mohammed is the last and truest prophet, but Mohammed himself said that the People of the Book are our companions, our friends. Our history is the same. Of course, I would like that you see the way of Mohammed and take him as your prophet, but you are still my friend.

'This is why Mauritania still has an Israeli embassy. All the other Arabic nations evicted the Israelis. But when they spoke about doing that here, the imams called a nationwide Friday prayer to talk about it and decided that if Mohammed said that the Jews are our friends, we have no right to do anything different. So the Israelis stayed, and we honour their presence.'

We talk late into the night, and I am humbled by the almost mystical nature of their Islam. It reminds me of what I have read of the Sufis, the spiritualist Muslims who share some traits with the peaceful Zoroastrians of Persia. I'm touched by their humility and warmed by their inclusiveness.

'But the women!' I say to Khabuss later. 'They are strident and loud and rude. They are so dictatorial to their men – and lazy! I haven't seen a Mauritanian woman lift a finger since I got here.'

Khabuss's face darkens.

'Mauritanian women *are* lazy,' he says abruptly. 'They lie around and drink milk to get fat. They like money, and they expect their men to make it. If they don't get what they want, they divorce. *Pah!*' Khabuss spits to the side. 'It is hard to find a good woman in this country.'

If I heard it from any other man, I might be sceptical. But Khabuss's assessment tallies with my experience. They drink so much milk that I can actually smell it coming off their bodies, and the majority have enormous rolls of fat that spill out of their *melekhvas*. They complain at the slightest exertion. I read months later that a new government initiative in Mauritania has begun to tackle obesity, due to the high rates of diabetes among women. It does not surprise me.

Three days out from the town of Tidjikja, where Khabuss and I will part ways, I become tense again. I have been out with him for fifteen days. I've learned more in that time than ever before and feel for the first time that I'm on top of the detail I need to run my camp correctly. I'm dreading his departure and the process of breaking someone new into the role.

'Don't worry, I will help you find your next guide,' Khabuss reassures me. 'And if we don't find anyone – I'll walk with you myself. I will not leave you alone.'

I'm touched by his concern, but also ashamed of my weakness. I want to simply stride off into the desert on my own. I now feel as if there is nothing I cannot do by myself. But I don't need Khabuss to point out how stupid such a move would be. Simply tracking the camels and packing them every day on my own would be exhausting enough. But even if I was happy to take that on, the most vital role that has emerged is the guide running interference between me and the nomads we come across. While I'm always happy to entertain people at my fire, to share my tea or food, I'm simply exhausted with answering the same questions every day after thirty kilometres on foot and fighting off the women, their incessant demands and attempts to reach into my bags.

Khabuss has been incredibly effective as my protector. But I remain wary of finding a new guide. However, in his overwhelming manner, Khabuss solves the problem before we even arrive.

It's late afternoon and we've just walked through a tiny desert oasis town. I walk out with some relief; we stopped to buy some bread and cigarettes – Khabuss smokes more heavily than any guide I've ever walked with – and were immediately swamped by local children, fascinated by a white woman with three camels wearing *melekhva*. We wound our way through the quiet dirt streets and filled our jerry cans at the well. Now we're making our way out of the valley, past lush date palms and carefully planted gardens. After the weeks of barren dune country, it is almost indescribably green and rich. We are only two days from Tidjikja. The end of another stretch is in sight.

I look behind us and in the distance I see a shambling old man leading a tired old camel. He seems ancient from this distance. He walks with his head down, stooped. His beard is white and his body weathered. But he walks in a sprightly enough manner and keeps pace with us from a distance.

After a few kilometres we halt to make camp, and within seconds he catches up. He and Khabuss exchange greetings. I'm already making tea and lunch for three when the old man couches his camel. It would be unthinkable not to share our food.

He is courteous and shy with me, but very proper in his conversation with Khabuss. There is something quite noble about him, even with his shabby clothing and lone bottom tooth.

He walks away to attend to his camel and Khabuss says, 'I think we have found your new guide.'

I look at him in stunned disbelief. 'You have to be kidding! That guy is nearly ready to fall over dead! He must be eighty! He's lovely, but how can he walk the distances we do?'

Khabuss chuckles. 'No, no. This man is from an old family, one of the first tribes. We have relatives in Chinguetti in common.'

I've been here long enough to understand the significance of the Chinguetti connection. There are several towns of old scholarship in Mauritania, of which Chinguetti is one, where the first of the Yemenis settled when they originally crossed the desert. Racial ties and pure Arabic blood are highly prized in Mauritania, and Khabuss's family is right up there on the tribal ladder. It's no small thing for Mohammed to be of the same tribe.

But still. The guy looks like he would blow over in a sandstorm.

'Do you really think he's up to it?' I ask.

'Absolutely. This man, he will be a wonderful guide. But I haven't asked him yet. Maybe he can walk with us tomorrow, and you can see what you think.'

I watch him that night. When it's time to bring the camels in, Khabuss frowns at me to stay, and they walk away together. I watch how the old man handles the camels, and I feel a pang for M'Barak – this man has the same gentle, calming manner, the same wiry sprightliness. We sit together around the fire and I'm touched again by his possessions, the way he has every last thing – his pipe, his things for tea – in perfect order, wrapped carefully and stowed in tidily stitched sacks that he repairs unconsciously as we talk. Again, habits that remind me of M'Barak.

Although he is shy, Mohammed also has a sense of humour. We tell him about Beiyal – the little white camel, who we have begun to call 'Henry' since he seems to fancy himself a man rather than a camel – often comes in to sleep right in the centre of camp. Mohammed giggles, shakes his head and tells us about the personalities of my camels as he sees them.

'Beiyal, the little white one – he is the little clown with a big heart. He will walk forever, and he likes people. Zaina is the worker of your group. He will go anywhere you need and never jump or flinch. This is a strong, good camel.

'Bolshy Sod' – Mohammed calls him Thurra Thurra, meaning 'one who talks too much' – 'he is the leader. He will be your best friend, but he has a temper. He needs to be in control. He is the big man. But he will never let you down.'

My eyes widen: in less than half a day, he has summed each of them up perfectly. I cast a look at Khabuss, who nods knowingly. He had it right. This guy is perfect.

It takes the whole of the next day to convince Mohammed to take the job. He is worried that we will have trouble communicating, given my limited Arabic and his total lack of French – and he is worried about the responsibility.

But Khabuss lays it on pretty thick, invoking tribal loyalty and masculine honour, saying sorrowfully that if Mohammed doesn't take the job that he, Khabuss, will have to continue on with me. Finally we get around to talking money and settle on a reasonable amount without any fuss. We determine that in Tidjikja my camels will stay with Mohammed and his family while I stay in town for my customary few days to do the usual internet and communication stuff. I have a guide, and I haven't even had to go to town. Mohammed will walk with me to Aayoun el Atrouss and, as Khabuss strictly instructs, even further if I can't find anyone else.

On the outskirts of town, Khabuss and I take our bags and hike in the last few kilometres. Mohammed shambles off to his family tent, my camels obediently following behind.

Khabuss and I sit on a rock for a final smoke and I hand him his money, plus a good tip. He doesn't even look at it. I know that this was not about payment for him.

He looks at me, his tough, strong face twinkling, and he says: 'You will be all right with this man. And he will find you another one. But Paula, do me a favour. Please. Stop at the end of Mauritania. Mali – it is full of Tuareg, full of bandits. And Niger? These are dangerous, bad places full of crazy people. What you've done is already incredible. Don't die doing this – stop at the end of Mauritania, yes? Promise me?'

I smile. 'You know I won't promise you that, Khabuss. But you have taught me so much – surely I can make it from here? Don't you trust me?'

He shakes his head sorrowfully. 'It is not you. You know all you can know now, and you are very smart. But these people – Mali, Niger – you don't know what they are like. Crazy. Be careful, please. And when you think it is time to stop – just stop. Finish this. And I will pray for you on the way.'

We walk the final bit into town, where he sees me to a hotel run by his friends and instructs them to take care of me. And then he is off, in the back of a Toyota trayback with old military mates, waving at me as he lies back and lights a cigarette. I'm guessing that none of those men will get a word in for the duration of the ride.

I hoist my pack and enter my room.

⋊⋉

I don't want to stay for long in Tidjikja, despite having several tasks that require internet and phone connection. The phone lines only work at certain times and cut out in the middle of a call. The lone internet point, courtesy of a local dignitary, works sporadically.

One day a vehicle of French tourists turns up; they immediately launch into complaints about the phone, the roads, the accommodation, the food. For me, these three days of rest inside a closed room, the ability to have a shower – even if it's cold – and to simply lie down and close my eyes without fear of losing camels or being surprised by nomads is sheer bliss. I can't relate to their complaints and quietly disappear from the communal space back into my own room. Once again, I'm deep in it now, back in the ritual isolation and focus of desert walking.

I stay in the quiet bungalow room and write, or look at photos from the walk. I study myself and think about where I've been, where I'm heading. I treasure the time out from the walk to put it into perspective. The stop is made sweeter knowing that, thanks to Mohammed, I have nothing more complicated than supplies to organise.

On the fourth day, I go down to the general store and pick up the supplies I've ordered and paid for. The boys carry them up the street for me, and I see Mohammed ambling down the road towards us. He has walked twenty-five kilometres from his family's tent into town and is barely breaking a sweat. He eyes the supplies and asks if we're going to carry them out to the camp. There must be eighty kilos of stuff there, at least. I laugh and tell him I've organised a vehicle to take us out.

We bounce our way out to the tent, Mohammed guiding the driver unerringly across the terrain, far from any track. When we arrive, it is to the kind of tent I am accustomed to in Mauritania: poor, crowded and hungry. But Mohammed's family is warm and generous, and we eat together on the night before we will set out. I'm slightly concerned by the hacking coughs and deep, rasping snuffles of half the family, and so I sleep outside in my swag, even though I know it is unsociable. In the morning, I'm woken by one of Mohammed's granddaughters placing a bowl of sweetened goats' milk by my bed. She sits back, waiting for me to drink.

We pack the camels and, for the only time I can remember since I began walking, the first day is not traumatic. Mohammed and I laugh and joke as we calmly pack the animals, who in turn are settled and cooperative. The job is done in excellent time, and we stop for a final glass of tea before we set off. Mohammed doesn't turn to wave to his family. As soon as we are out of earshot, he turns to me with a look of relief and says, 'It is good to be in the desert again.'

We laugh together, and I'm reminded again, so very strongly, of M'Barak, who used to roll his eyes when he talked about being stuck at home with his family.

Abruptly, the desert landscape becomes achingly beautiful.

Mohammed leads me over and down a treacherous, rocky mountain pass. We weave our way cautiously through, often coaxing trembling, weak-kneed camels through terrifyingly narrow passages.

The country beneath opens up as we round the pass. Surrounded by sheer drops, we are heading down into a deep, peaceful valley. Whereas we're descending a rocky pass, the valley wall on the far side is made up of gently undulating sand ripples – not the peaks and troughs of dunes but symmetrical rows of soft mounds on the wall itself. At the top of the wall there are layers of rock, rather like thin biscuit slices atop a marshmallow cake. The valley floor is perfect camel country – firm underfoot with endless clumps of acacia, *sabay* and other rich desert shrubs, all of which the camels love to eat.

I look at Mohammed, happy. 'How long does the valley go for?' I ask.

'We follow this nearly all the way to Aayoun el Atrouss,' he tells me. 'Good country. Very good. Wells everywhere here.' He nods in satisfaction.

The immense stillness of the valley fills my soul, and Mohammed's own calm seeps into the walk and camp, so that by the end of that first day my rhythm is already established and the camp takes care of itself.

With Mohammed there is none of the late-night, campfire tales and conversation that there was with Khabuss, yet there's something else, something lovely and special. We walk companionably, at the same pace and, although we do not talk a lot, every exchange is filled with gentle humour and goodwill. We agree on places to camp with a nod between us, just as I did once with M'Barak. We notice the same things at the same time – an unusual set of tracks, a piece of baggage falling off, a camel behaving strangely.

We're lucky that we have such a silent understanding, for it is on this stretch that we enter the field of demons that will torture my walk for the next 1500 kilometres – *uniti*.

The rains in this part of the desert were particularly heavy last year. On one hand, this is wonderful for grazing and wells – there is an abundance of food and water deposits are everywhere. But the rains brought forth growth of another kind, this one not so appealing. *Uniti* is the Arabic word for what I know in Australia as 'bindis'. The tall, stalk-like grasses grow to over waist height, and the tiny balls covered in fine prickles fall from them with every wave of wind or brush of material. Within minutes of walking each day, the *uniti* are stuck to everything: clothes, camel ropes, shoes. Cousins to the *uniti* are the rather more spiteful three-cornered jacks, which are harder and spikier. These can be so fierce as to drive right up through my sandal. When they gather between the sandal and my foot, they pierce the skin and need to be plucked out.

But the three-cornered jacks are immediately noticeable, and thus less dangerous – once removed, they fall harmlessly away, despite hurting like hell. The *uniti*, on the other hand, are insidious and persistent. They gather in my sandals, and I walk until the accumulated piercings are unbearable, at which point I empty them all out. But as I brush them away, or pull them out of where they have tangled my *melekhva*, as if it were rolled in velcro, their tiny spears detach and embed themselves in my fingers and hands. My feet are like pincushions. At the end of each day, or whenever we sit down to rest, I use tweezers to pluck them out from wherever they have entered. But I always miss one or two, no matter how hard I search, and these in turn become swollen and infected.

Worst of all, the *uniti* become embedded in the blankets and ropes. Mohammed's bedding must be plucked free every night. The blankets all need to be combed and plucked before they go on the camels so that the animals are not uncomfortable, and the camels themselves need brushing down with twigs each morning. But the ropes . . . The ropes are sheer agony.

To pack a camel well, ropes need to be pulled so tight that nothing moves – saddles, panniers, bags of supplies. No matter how many hours I spend plucking the ropes free of prickles, inevitably by the time they have dragged a little on the ground or come in contact with other baggage, they're saturated in the little spears once again. The *uniti* rip into our hands every day as we pack the camels, leaving them covered in prickles, which once again must be pulled out. I must be aware every day, when leading the camels, of holding the lead rope high and tight out of reach of the grasses, or else it becomes clogged again, leaving me unable even to grasp it.

Our hands are so painful from the endless piercings that, for the first time, we both have to use spoons instead of our hands to eat from the plate – the heat in the rice stings, making it impossible to ball the hot rice in our palms. I frequently wake in the middle of the night to find that one of the missed spears has become infected, and the area is hot, swollen and throbbing. Then I have to find my needle, disinfect it, pierce the fluid bubble, and dig the prickle out. I do this perhaps every second night and sometimes three or four in one night, if we've been through a bad area.

Finding a camp is often about walking until we find a patch of ground unafflicted with *uniti*. Once we do, neither of us move out of the small area unless we absolutely have to. I could never have imagined that something so seemingly insignificant could cause quite so much discomfort. My walking rhythm changes to adjust to these new conditions: ten paces, stop, pull the prickles out. At the end of each day, the soles of my shoes are entirely made up of the embedded barbs, which need to be pulled out to stop the deterioration of the shoe. I often think that I should have brought boots to wear on this stretch, but even boots and gaiters would not have offered significant protection, although they would certainly be an improvement. The reality is I'd never come across prickles like these before – I didn't even know they existed in the desert.

You don't know what you don't know, I guess.

But Mohammed and I laugh through it all, and his calm good humour is an immense comfort. He, just as M'Barak once did, picks up on 'fuck' as an epithet from me. After only a few kilometres, I will hear him muttering and I call out, 'Mohammed! How's it going?' To which the inevitable reply will drift back painfully: 'Fucken *uniti!*' It never fails to crease me up.

Surrounded by one of the most stunning, serene stretches of desert I've ever walked through, I can't help but shake my head at the irony of how many other things suddenly become difficult: the *uniti* torment us day and night; both Mohammed and I come down with raging head colds, which rapidly turn into hacking, chesty coughs; and the cold descends at night accompanied by bitter winter winds.

I'm terrified for Mohammed. No matter how tough he may be, he is also a thin, elderly man – he thinks about seventy. I swap bedding arrangements and make him sleep in my swag and sleeping bag, filling it with as many blankets as I can. But his cough wracks his whole body, and for days he runs a temperature, despite me putting him on a general antibiotic. I insist on one rest day near a well, but he flatly refuses, protesting that he is fine. I'm humbled, over and over, by his unthinking kindnesses towards me even when he is ill. When he hears me coughing harshly one night, he comes over to my bed with a hot drink he has made. In the mornings, he still gets up to pray and lights the fire. He is the only guide I will ever have on this second desert trek who makes the fire in the morning. On the few occasions when I begin to do it, he waves me away with a smile and says it's part of his job.

Of course, it does occur to me that maybe he just thinks my fire-making is rubbish compared to his. Which, I cheerfully confess, is true. Mohammed, like M'Barak, can make a fire out of thin air in the middle of a sandstorm.

Regardless of the prickles and illness, I've never experienced such deep peace as I do on this stretch. I'm not looking forward to reaching a town, not measuring my walk by how soon I will get to the next point. No matter how difficult it is out here, I love the stillness and solitude. It feels to me as if I'm more a part of this place than I ever have been. I immerse myself in a book of T.S. Eliot's poems, *Four Quartets*. I've never read much when I'm walking. But out here, Eliot's descriptions of internal struggle match my own. He keeps me company.

After two weeks of this strange juxtaposition of tranquillity and pain, we walk to a place only six kilometres from a small town, Tamchaket. We're not planning to go to the town; despite the fact that our supplies are dwindling, we've enough to make it to Aayoun el Atrouss. The only thing we are hoping to buy is a goat. After a steady diet of rice, biscuits, Gofiya and sardines, we are both craving meat.

We make a camp, spying a tent in the middle distance. What neither of us realise is that directly behind us, just over the valley wall, a small settlement of about eight families are camped.

I wander off in the afternoon, just after we've made tea, to have my customary daily wash. It's one of my 'self-indulgent' pleasures in the desert, to find a private place, strip down, wash away the sand and prickles, and brush my hair. But today I've no more than set down the jerry can when a small face pokes around the scrub; it's followed in rapid succession by another ten.

I smile and go through the greeting process, but I'm met with dumb, shocked stares. This is one of the more remote parts of the desert, and no vehicles come this way. Tourists in a four-wheel drive would be strange enough. One lone white woman stripping off for a wash is entirely inconceivable.

I give up on my wash and walk back to camp, trailed by a motley entourage of curious kids. By the time I have rejoined Mohammed, the crowd has swelled to about thirty, as the women inevitably turn up and crouch in a circle around my camp, fluttering and twittering to each other from behind their *melekhvas*, shouting out the odd smart comment to Mohammed.

I begin to make tea, as hospitality requires, but I feel bored and annoyed by the incessant cackling of the women at my efforts.

They can't imagine that I could know how to make tea. While I understand their incredulity, it has overtones of early white explorers being astonished by any display of intelligence on the part of the native tribes they discover. There is a large element of cultural superiority inherent in their attitudes and, after two months in Mauritania, I'm becoming tired of it. Funnily enough, Mohammed, whom I've nicknamed the 'Zen King' in honour of his superhuman calm – is also displaying signs of impatience.

'Don't make them any more tea,' he says to me in a whisper. 'These women are not good.' I agree with him.

When the inevitable demands for presents begin, I'm ready for them – I've a few *melekhvas* that are damaged from the prickles but still very serviceable. They're clean and I've folded them neatly in readiness for such an occasion. I dole them out, along with some of my fast dwindling supplies of Dove products, tea and sugar.

The women fight over the gifts like wolves. It would be amusing to watch, if not so appalling. These aren't hungry women or children – they are fat and well clothed. They sneer at the *melekhvas* I hand out and insist I must have better ones in my pack.

We ask about buying a goat. One of the women comes forward and magnanimously states that she will give us a goat as a 'gift'. Feeling embarrassed by my previous, seemingly unfair, judgemental attitude, I smile my thanks and wait eagerly as she brings over a tiny kid. It's smaller than any animal I have ever bought for slaughter, no more than a few days' worth of meat. But I'm grateful for her gift, and Mohammed takes it over to the side and slits its throat in halal fashion.

The woman waits until the knife falls before turning to me with her hand outstretched. '*Cadeau?*' she says, using the French – not Arabic – word for 'gift'.

I look at her in astonishment. In all the time I've been in the desert, never once have I been given something as a 'gift' and then been asked for payment. While I nearly always reciprocate in kind, and often with goods of a higher value, it's never been expected. More often than not, particularly in the Western Sahara, it has been haughtily declined. When it comes to buying an animal for slaughter, I'm accustomed either to having a good-natured barter – or having a family slaughter an animal and invite us to eat, after which I will always contribute other foodstuffs to the family stores.

But to offer an animal as a gift, and then demand payment? I'm shocked and affronted.

Mohammed is watching the exchange in embarrassment. He speaks gently to the woman, and I understand the conversation: he is reminding her of custom and manners, and reprimanding her. But the woman rebukes him sharply. She doesn't realise I under-stand much of what she says. She maintains an ingratiating smile as she tells Mohammed to stay out of it, because, 'You are already making money out of the "white" – let us get what we can, too.'

Mohammed, in a reaction entirely typical of the gentle Mauritanian men, will never openly confront a woman. He backs off in the face of her greed. I'm disgusted with her.

But then I think of the unstinting honour I've witnessed so often in the desert, the quiet pride. And, despite the fact that our sup-plies are close to finished, I go to my bag, open it and begin loading the woman with foodstuffs. I keep a smile on my face and I hand out flour, biscuits, oil, sugar and tea. I give her bags of rice and the pasta at the bottom of my sack. I keep nothing but what we will absolutely need for the next few days. Included in that are the last three packets of biscuits, our staple for breakfast and during the walks.

The woman holds up the flour. 'But what is this?' she cries to Mohammed. 'What am I supposed to do with this?' He explains that it is flour, and she exclaims again that it is useless and tosses it to one side so it breaks open. She gestures to the last few packets of biscuits in the bag.

'What about *those*?' she asks, a hard look in her eye.

I explain that they are our last few packets until we reach the town.

'But you are only six kilometres from Tamchaket. You can buy more there,' she says.

I look at her and smile. 'But so are you.'

'They're expensive! I can't afford biscuits!' she scoffs at me. I look at her. She is wearing a *melekhva* of a quality I never see in the desert – straight from a Nouakchott market and worth fifty times the cost of a packet of biscuits. Her children are clad in store-bought clothes and are wearing proper shoes. I looked over at her tent earlier, when she brought the goat, and saw it is shabby and ill-kept. She hasn't stitched the tear in the roof, nor is the mat on the floor clean. And suddenly I've had enough.

'This is all I have,' I say, gesturing to the supply bags nearly empty on the ground. 'I've no more money until I reach the next town. We've been walking a long way. But if you feel that you need what I have, then please help yourself.' And I stand away from the bags and turn my back.

Mohammed looks at me in horror and makes to drive the women back, but I wave him away. The women descend onto the bags, literally knocking each other out of the way as they tear at what little is left. When they have emptied the sacks, they begin to wander away, casting covetous glances at the closed bags containing my personal possessions and the technical equipment.

One last woman hangs back. She holds out her hand pitifully to me; embedded between the thumb and forefinger is one lone *uniti* spear. It's barely even swollen. 'I need medicine,' she moans. 'I am very, very sick.'

Mohammed and I look at each other and start to laugh. We hold out our hands, which are ripped and bleeding, and point to our feet, which are messes of cuts and swelling.

'Sorry – we have no more medicine for these,' I say.

But my words have no effect. She simply turns her nose up and walks away up the hill without another word.

Mohammed looks at me curiously. 'Why did you give everything away?' he asks. 'Now we will have to walk to Tamchaket – and I don't know how much we will be able to buy there, anyway.'

I try to explain, but my limited Arabic makes it difficult. After so many months of unstinting kindness and honour, I'm accustomed to behaving in the way I've been treated. It's difficult to explain that it is some queer point of inverted pride that, no matter what the pressure, I continue to behave that way. Rather than slice off some piece of my seemingly immeasureable fortune, I want to give in the spirit that I have been shown – to my last bit of food. Perhaps also, and somewhat less nobly, it is about trying to humble those who would see me as a cash cow, to shame those women, who are so proud of their culture and lineage, into recognising to what depths they have fallen.

There has been something quite revelatory about the last few weeks in the desert. The long stretches, the unceasing rhythm of packing up and walking, the still nights and empty days; the frenzied pace of learning with Khabuss giving way to the serenity of Mohammed – all of these things have pushed me into a more contemplative state than at any other time since I left Trafalgar Square.

The immediacy of the prickles and the stark beauty of the terrain have made me think endlessly about simplicity, the daily struggle with small things. This walk has been such a metaphor for life: just when I thought I was on top of everything, had a good guide, understood how to make my camels and camp work and was in beautiful country, the prickles came along to test me every second. I've written in my diary more than once in sheer frustration: *will this walk ever give me a break?* But I know that life will always test me, no matter how ideal the circumstances.

I'm left seeing how really unimportant all of these small battles are – these perceptions that the women have of me, or the way I see them. I may not have money to burn, but I honestly can't be bothered anymore with fighting about a hundred bucks' worth of supplies – not today. We won't starve, and I can buy enough to see us through. So I shrug and laugh, and Mohammed shakes his head in bemusement.

But the following morning I insist that we walk straight through the centre of the family tents, right as they are all waking up. Everyone there knew we were not planning to walk to Tamchaket; I make it clear, by our direction, that we have changed our minds. We now need supplies. Most of the women stare and a few go back inside their tents. I sense an air of discomfort. As I reach the end of the tents, the woman who asked for medicine comes running after me. She is holding a small artefact in her hand, one of the many rocks that nomads collect and sell to tourists.

'*Cadeau! Cadeau!*' She calls to me, indicating that the rock is a gift. I slowly draw to a stop and wait until she is right up in my face. I look to the rock and then slowly up at her, and I let all of my contempt from the previous day flood my features until her eyes fall away.

'No, thank you,' I say quietly in Arabic. And then, invoking the lines and custom I have heard so many times, I say, 'God has given us all we need. Praise be to God, everything begins and ends with Him.' And with all the dignity I can muster (and a bit more for show) I walk away without looking back.

We are barely over the hill when Mohammed begins to kill himself laughing. 'Did you see her face? Oh, shame on those women! They were so bad! "*God has given us all we need!*" Oh, shame on that woman, on her family, shame. But her face when you said that . . .' We laugh together and I see that he gets it.

That night, after we have bought a sack of rice and some biscuits in the settlement, three men ride to our camp on tall, beautiful camels. They sit and drink tea, and then one of them hands us a package. It turns out they are the men from the tents we passed; they had been away with their goats. They're embarrassed and humiliated at the treatment we received, although they do put it in so many words. Inside the package is a loaf of bread with camel fat baked into the centre, a delicacy I haven't had since Morocco.

We thank them and they wave us away. They tell us that we should come back and stay with their families so they can entertain us properly – they will slaughter a goat. We tell them we must keep going, and they leave with courteous *salaams*.

'Do you think they were ashamed of their wives?' I ask Mohammed.

'They should be,' he mutters darkly. 'But Mauritanian women, they never listen to the men. Talk, talk, talk, and they take everything. They don't work. They don't make money. Just lazy, in the tent all day, and then like with you. Not good.'

We camp on the outskirts of Aayoun el Atrouss, and I go to a phone booth to call my family. Dad tells me that both a satellite phone and replacement satellite internet connection have been sent out – one from England, the other from Australia – to meet me in Nouakchott, the capital, along with some treasured goodies like replacement antibiotics and other medication to alleviate the recurring urinary tract infection. My mother, it seems, has become fed up with worrying about me dying on my own in the desert and has hired a satellite phone so she can rest assured that I have a method of communication.

Nouakchott is about 800 kilometres away, and it requires a staggered journey of two Grand Taxi rides, the old Mercedes that operate throughout Northern Africa.

Mohammed offers to stay with the camels on the outskirts of town for four days, giving me a chance to get to Nouakchott, stay a couple of days to pick everything up from the various courier offices and test the new equipment. He is happily ensconced next to a very hospitable family tent – which just happens to have two nubile young wives who, in contrast to my recent negative experiences of local women, are hard working and warm. I buy some supplies for him to share with the family and know he will be well fed and looked after for the duration. We agree that he will look for a guide in the area over the next few days, and if he doesn't find one, we'll search together on my return. I pack a bag and we walk into town together. He stays with me while I buy a place in the taxi and agrees to meet me at the taxi rank in four days' time.

After my months in Morocco, I am well accustomed to the vagaries of long-distance rural travel. One simply wears comfortable, loose-fitting clothes; carries something to cover up with in the event that sleeping somewhere is on the agenda; and always takes a decent water bottle. Apart from that, a good dose of patience – no time limitations or expectations – are an important factor, as is the view that anything can and will occur, from breakdown to accident.

In another life, a Grand Taxi would seat four passengers and one driver. In Mauritania, they seat six passengers and one driver – seven if someone is small enough to fit. Two go in the passenger seat in the front and four squash into the back. It usually takes outside help to close the doors, and baggage is stowed beneath feet when the boot fills up.

I'm decently clad and my head is covered, but I'm not wearing *melekhva*, as I know I will be exiting in the modern city of Nouakchott. As the taxi fills up I become a little uneasy that I'm the only woman, and then I sigh with relief as a typically round, loud Mauritanian woman named Mariam turns up.

The relief fades within seconds. *Oh, Lord, save me from these women.*

The driver wants her and me to sit in the front. It makes sense. As the only two women, it gives the men in the back breathing room and us our own space. I'm keen to take him up on it, no matter how cramped. But Mariam refuses, point-blank. Instead, she takes up residence behind the passenger's seat. She orders me to sit next to her; the middle seats are the most uncomfortable on long rides, since there is nowhere to lean to doze, but someone has to sit there and it doesn't bother me much, so I acquiesce. Two men get in the front. Another man sits next to me – he is going all the way to Nouakchott. The fourth place is reserved for villagers travelling from one stop to the next.

Mariam informs me that her place will not change for the duration of the journey. Nor will the fourth place ever be beside her – I'm to stay seated where I am. When she has finished speaking, she hawks and spits with such ferocity that she nearly beheads a poor sheep standing nearby. Her expectorations then go on ceaselessly until the car sets off. She will hurl an ever-increasing amount of bodily fluid out of the car at regular intervals.

From her body emanates the dank, milky scent now so familiar. Before we have even left Aayoun she has ordered one of the men travelling with us to go and buy her a litre of milk, which she promptly gulps in one go. Mariam will not move herself to buy something. She simply taps the shoulder of the closest man, hands him the money and gives the order.

We set off, the customary '*Bismillah*' uttered by us all as the taxi lurches out of town. I often think that it's at times like these that the Arabic intonation of '*Inshallah*' is at its most appropriate.

Nobody is ever really sure that anything will actually work for long enough to make journey's end. It really is in God's hands, because nobody ever bothers to actually check that the car is road-worthy enough to make it. I utter it with as much fervency as anyone else these days.

From the moment the vehicle sets off, Mariam is talking. She barely stops to draw breath for the duration. We're subjected to her opinions on everything from the camels we pass to the state of the government. The men nod politely and bow to her opinions, even though one of them is a teacher of international politics who has recently been lecturing in France. I'm amazed at their toler-ance. Before Westerners decide that women 'behind the veil' are timid, marginalised creatures, they should have a look at the way they are running the country of Mauritania. It would be easy to argue that, although they are cosseted, the women in fact have few rights outside of the home, but this too would be entirely inaccu-rate. Women are employed and largely represented in politics. Their vocal stance is by no means limited to private exchange. I've simply never seen anything like it – the women rule this place.

In this taxi, Mariam has stretched her copious physical presence to occupy nearly half of the back seat. This is why she insisted on sitting there. If I squeeze back, she simply elbows my breast with ferocity and glares. No way am I messing with her bulk. She'd crush me like a gnat.

We stop at a roadside eatery: a hessian tent propped up on wooden poles beneath which hangs a large carcass. We indicate which pieces we would like, and the owner hacks them off and cooks them on a brazier. I eat in a tent with Mariam, separate to the men; she continues her conversation with them even through the hessian divide.

In the early hours of the morning the driver halts for the night, and we all troop into a rough concrete shelter next to another car-cass hang. After more meat and tea, we all roll out our various sleeping covers and doze off. Throughout the night other taxis arrive, and their inhabitants enter to eat and sleep. The light never goes off and the parade never ends. Mariam's voice is not silenced all night, except when she is drinking milk.

Nonetheless, I became accustomed to communal sleeping long ago and manage to pass out for a few hours. In the morning we all wash in the ritual fashion: face, mouth, arms, hands and feet. The passengers pray. I look at a clock on the wall and realise with a shock that it is Christmas Day.

I hadn't given it a thought. Certainly nobody else around me has.

We trundle the remaining few hours into Nouakchott, where Mariam is let off first, to the gasping relief of everyone else. We all stretch out and the men light their pipes with contented grunts. Mariam had outlawed smoking in the taxi. The conversation is genial and humorous, and I finally have exchanges with my fellow passengers. Up until now, we'd all been beaten into silence by the other woman.

I check into a modern hotel and spend a couple of days playing with my replacement equipment. It all seems to work, although after the traumas of the last few weeks I remain sceptical. I meet a couple of South African pilots in the hotel and we have a lovely evening – speaking in English.

'We are both divorced,' one of the pilots tells me. He shrugs. 'AIDS.' I try to keep the surprise out of my face as I nod sagely; then I see the twinkle in his eye.

'Africa Induced Divorce Syndrome,' he explains, and we all crack up.

'I can top that,' I say. 'Mine is Adventure Induced Divorce Syndrome.' It feels good to finally laugh about it, to be sitting here in some bar in the back of beyond, and cackling amid the madness. Rather than trying to relax in a culture not my own, it's actually okay for me to have a drink and enjoy a good conversation. And it's Christmas to boot! When I travel back to Aayoun, I feel refreshed by the pilots' company.

On the return journey, we pull into another roadside barbecue to eat, again in the early hours of the morning. I'm tired and uninterested in the attempts of the loitering men to draw me into conversation. I sit with the men from my taxi to eat; they are, as ever, protective and courteous. We're travelling together – I'm their responsibility. They dissuade the other men with frowns.

But one young man is particularly persistent. He sits alone, robed far more completely than any other Mauritanian I have seen. He wears a cowl-like robe that hides much of his face. His expression is pinched and hostile, and he eyes me with contempt.

'You! You are not Muslim,' he finally says, pointing at me.

'No, I am not.' I smile politely and continue eating. 'I'm Catholic.' This is untrue. I am Church of England – and lapsed to boot – but all Muslims know what a Catholic is. Claiming I'm Catholic has always been enough to politely arrest this type of conversation, but my new acquaintance seems particularly persistent.

'So, why do you think all Muslims are terrorists? Do you think *I* am a terrorist?' He speaks loudly, jabbing the air with his finger. It's nearly three o'clock in the morning, and I've been in a crowded taxi for over twelve hours. I'm exhausted and hungry; the last thing I fancy is an in-depth discourse on international prejudices or Western politics.

'Of course I don't think you're a terrorist.' I speak without looking up, hoping to close down the conversation. The men I'm eating with frown at the young man and his bad manners, but he carries on.

'If I were born in the time of Moses, I would be a Jew. In the time of Jesus, I would have been Christian. But now it is the time of Mohammed; he is the last prophet. How can you be a Christian? You will burn in hell. You are in a Muslim country; you eat with Muslims. You must surely see that you should be Muslim.'

He is working himself up; worse, others are looking around at us. Even the men at my table are looking at me curiously. Although they're too polite to say so, I can see they believe the young man has a point. I think despairingly that this is an unfortunate – for an outsider – reality of Islam: some of its more fundamentalist adherents believe so fervently in the inherent rightness of their doctrine that they feel it remiss – are indeed instructed that they are remiss in their religious practice – if they don't seek to convert.

As far as the majority of people I meet here are concerned, I'm to be pitied for coming from the West. Whereas there was a certain envy in Morocco for the wealth and perceived freedom of Western countries, here in the Islamic Republic of Mauritania, there is only a superior, detached curiosity.

In the critical rhetoric of the cowled young man, I feel the intractability of the cultural gulf. I think of how international governments and communities in countries such as my own try so earnestly to 'understand' the Islamic world. I think that it looks more like two teams playing cricket by entirely different rules. The fundamental problem is that we're not Islamic. And no matter how generous, curious and hospitable the people I come across may be, deep down that distinction can never really be overcome. Islam is not something that people choose to take pieces of. It's a way of life, a mental state governing every aspect of the individual's life.

The following day, when I arrive in Aayoun el Atrouss, my head is whirling with this thought of the seemingly inevitable conflict between Islam and the West. It's a thought I've had for a long time, certainly since my dealings with Moroccan men. And just as it has started to coalesce in my brain, I walk into a storm.

'Look at this!' cries a young man as I walk into a general store in town to buy some meat before heading out to my camp. He is gesturing at the television. On the floor mat, a group is huddled, the women rocking and crying in horror, the men shaking their heads and muttering darkly. It's the afternoon before Eid al-Fitr, the feast of mutton – the most important date on the Islamic calendar. The town is full of people buying final supplies for the following day's feast.

But on television, Al Jazeera is showing Saddam Hussein with a noose around his neck. Even worse, the next shot is my very own Prime Minister, John Howard. Out of every international leader, he is the only one to openly commend the execution, basically stating that Saddam is getting what he deserves. His comments are played in full, on a loop.

It's not a good day to be Australian in Mauritania.

I walk out of the store, my head reeling. I can't believe that the powers that be are unaware that Hussein is being executed at the Muslim equivalent of Christmas. Equally, I'm sure that the majority of citizens in Australia, or indeed any Western nation, would have no idea of the provocative significance of that act. But for every Muslim worldwide, it must seem a cruel, sadistic insult and a direct jab at Islam.

'He was a bad man – we all knew that,' one of the women in the shop had cried. 'But he was tried by the Americans – we all know it was really them – and now they are killing him. On the day of the festival!' I remember the seething bitterness of those around her, and I think, *This is the reality they all see. And is it so far from the truth? Do they not have a right to be angry?*

But I feel wearied and saddened as well. On that pivotal day, as if the future of world relations suffers an enormous blow, I think of how many people will be sitting in their lounge rooms in Europe, England, America and Australia watching Saddam die, largely with little feeling. I'm sure there will already be a multitude of jokes circulating on the internet. And there will be those who, like me, oppose the death penalty and will be saddened by the taking of a life, no matter what the circumstances. But underlying those feelings will be another, more primal one: justice has been served. After all, didn't Saddam wage mass murder and violate the human rights of thousands?

But in Mauritania today, several million Muslims are watching a brother Muslim be executed by a foreign power, on a holy day. The same foreign power that their televisions have shown bombing and shooting at Muslim innocents for months now. They see a humiliated, debased brother crying '*Allah Akbar!*', defiantly maintaining the faith to the end. Above all, they see another Muslim.

And therein lays the gulf.

I feel vulnerable and guilty, and more than a little scared. I scurry back to the camp in full *melekhva*, my head down. The streets are empty and the atmosphere is ominous. From open doors I hear the blare of a multitude of televisions and the odd shouts. When people do meet, there is an air of disbelief. It reminds me of the atmosphere I heard about on the day Kennedy was shot. From a payphone at the edge of town, I call my father.

'Did you hear? About Saddam?' I ask breathlessly.

'I think I've heard them all already,' my dad says dryly. He thinks I am about to tell him a joke.

'Dad, it's not funny here. It's really serious.' He picks up on my tone straightaway.

'Jesus, I hadn't thought about that. Not much of a sense of humour about the whole thing, huh?'

'Dad, did you see what Howard said?'

'Yes, but the guy's an idiot. Everyone knows that. The execution was condemned almost worldwide.'

'But nobody here knows that, Dad. They didn't show anyone but Bush and Howard. And even worse, the next clip they showed of Howard was one where he was stating in some press conference months ago that Australia remains opposed to the death penalty. The hypocrisy was hideous! The rest of the world could have sobbed their hearts out – but here it plays as if we are all cackling with glee. And Dad, did you know it is Eid al-Fitr? Did they report that?'

Dad is silent. He was moored in Port Sudan for months, and has spent a lot of time in Muslim Northern Africa. He understands the significance.

'Nobody reported that. Christ. You better head out of town. And don't tell anyone you're Australian.' He is silent again for a moment, and then he speaks. I can almost see him shaking his head sorrowfully: 'And I thought we had freedom of press.'

Back at the camp, Mohammed is lying peacefully beneath a tree, mending one of the rugs. As I approach, I feel touched and reassured by the sight of his calm demeanour.

I sit down and we greet. He puts tea on the fire.

'Did you hear about Saddam Hussein?' I ask.

Mohammed shakes his head sadly. 'There is but one God and that is God,' he says in the ritual fashion. 'It is not good. Not good.'

'Do you think our governments are bad for killing him?' I ask bluntly.

He looks at me and puts his head to one side. 'The Qur'an says it is wrong to kill. What does your Book say?'

'Thou shalt not kill . . . But we both do,' I add. 'What did you think about the planes in America?' I never normally get into these discussions with my guides, but today is special. I need to know what he thinks.

'This is wrong. It is terrible! It is never right to kill. God tells us this.'

'I agree. And I don't think it was right to kill Saddam either. But today I felt like everyone hated my country. I don't agree with my leader, you know. I didn't vote for him.' I feel like a child, but I desperately need to explain that Westerners are not all as they appear on the television. I guess a few million Muslims worldwide must have felt the same way after 9/11.

'It is wrong to hate,' Mohammed says softly. 'Every Muslim knows this. It is wrong to kill, and it is even more wrong to kill in the name of religion. You and I have walked together for weeks. You are a daughter to me. You are Catholic – Christian. I am Muslim – what does this matter? Saddam Hussein was a bad man; he killed many people. Now his country is hurting because of his bad deeds. There is no God in any of this. God has nothing to do with it.'

'No, just bloody oil,' I say gloomily in English. Mohammed looks at me curiously. '*Gasoline*,' I explain. 'It's all about gasoline.'

Mohammed nods and laughs quietly. 'There is one God and that is God,' he says again. I look at him and smile.

There is Islam, I think, *and then there is the Islam of the Bedouin.* I look at Mohammed's calm, serene face and reflect on the million kindnesses he shows me every day, even as he sits here mending one of my rugs. And I think that faith – any faith – is in essence simple. This is perhaps why the Bedouin have such a pure, wise expression of Islam. The simplicity and hardness of their life means that faith is a source of comfort, rather than a weapon. It is something to provide warmth and kindness both to the adherent and to all others encountered.

In the early morning sunlight, we sit and drink our tea, the Big Empty benevolently shining on our silent accord.

Later that afternoon we discuss the issue of a new guide.

'I will come into town with you, and we will ask around,' says Mohammed. 'It may be hard though, since the festival is tomorrow, and all this stuff with Saddam. I think we should wait a day or two.'

Two days later we enter the town and go through the now familiar ritual of calling into every supply store, talking to the 'fix it' men who are always lurking in corners watching for opportunities. We place ourselves in a prominent place to drink tea and await the applicants.

Late that afternoon we are introduced to one man who seems to fit the bill. He's another Mohammed. His full name sounds like Mohammed Le Min.

He's a big, strong man, and looks hardy. He tells me he's worked in the military. After Khabuss, this is reassuring. There is something in his face I don't much like, but he seems to be able to answer all of my questions. We agree to meet at his family tent that afternoon with all of my camels. It's just out of town in the direction I'm headed.

'What did you think?' I ask my old Mohammed, whom I've nicknamed Mohammed the Good.

He shrugs, and the first alarm bell goes off.

'Perhaps he is all right. I am not so sure.'

'You think not?' I ask, beginning to worry. 'I thought he was a bit thick; but he seems to know the way there.'

'I don't think he is ex-military,' says Mohammed bluntly. 'His ID card – it says he is a nomad. If he was ex-military, it would say so. I think he is lying.'

I look at him sharply. 'I didn't like his face. I think I might have made a wrong choice.'

I haven't actually hired Mohammed Le Min yet; the trip to his family's tent is by way of a test for me. Although I'm anxious to get going, I've no intention of repeating the Harraba experience. But equally, I'm concerned that Mohammed will be too harsh a judge – he is, after all, the most exceptional yet of my guides. His standards of care and responsibility are high. I may not always be so fortunate, and I'm prepared to get by with less if I need to. So, I reserve my judgement.

In the tent of Mohammed Le Min, I'm less than impressed. Although we are fed and offered hospitality in the ritual fashion, when I offer his wife a *melekhva* by way of a gift, she tugs at the one I'm wearing and demands I give that to her instead, as it is better quality. In fact, she's wrong – the *melekhva* I'm wearing is an old one from Morocco that I used for walking. It's comfortable and her request is rude, so I refuse and give her some bolshy comments in reply, albeit smilingly. She laughs back; I'm beginning to learn that this is the only way to deal with Mauritanian women. Just be as rude as they are, and smile the whole while.

I question Mohammed Le Min quite closely. Mohammed the Good watches carefully. He has all the right answers, although he is overly cocky, preening in front of his audience of cronies, all of whom are impressed that he will be hired for such an important job. I honestly cannot make the man out. He seems to know what he's doing, and he handled the camels well when we came into the camp. He appears fit and can look me in the eye. But there is still something I just can't put my finger on.

During the course of the conversation, I'm offered a special cushion to sit on. I'm comfortable where I am and wave it away, but everyone insists. As I go to sit down, the whole tent watches me in breathless anticipation. At the last second, I look beneath me.

The cushion moves.

Predictably, I leap into the air, and the entire tent breaks up. In fact, the 'cushion' is a pet tortoise. Apparently they are kept for their shells, which are made into jewellery. Practical joke over, the owner stands and leads the tortoise out on a leash. I laugh along, but somehow I don't find the joke that funny. Seeing the tortoise shuffle along in the dust on a leash just makes me sad.

Mohammed the Good and I walk back to our camp. I have struck a financial deal with Mohammed Le Min and made a down payment. He will walk to us in the morning before I set out.

'What do you think?' I ask Mohammed again. He asked many questions of the other man and scrutinised him as he answered.

'Honestly, I have to say I am not sure. He knows the route, this much is certain. And he understands camels. But I do not like his family, or his conduct. There is something about him I don't like.'

'Me, too,' I say. 'But I've hired him now, I guess.'

'Well, in the morning, I will stay in the tent with his family and have some food before I leave,' says my old protector. 'If you need me, I will be there.'

In the morning, Mohammed Le Min arrives late at the camp. We've already finished packing the camels. It's an inauspicious start and I glare at him. Mohammed the Good shakes his head in disgust.

Le Min and I begin to walk. Mohammed the Good waves goodbye; I watch him heading up to the tent on the hill and want to call to him to stop. I feel tense and angry. I am already cross with myself for striking a deal with this guy. If Mohammed the Good had felt right from the outset, this guy seems all wrong.

We've walked no more than 300 metres when Le Min drops the rope from the camel and squats. I'm used to all of my nomadic guides squatting to pee. Usually they simply face away from me and open the slit in their pantaloons, while I hang back a prudent distance. But Mohammed Le Min is dropping his pants to defecate. Right in front of me.

This is an insult unheard of in all my time in the desert.

Defecation is the ultimate unclean act, one that's hidden and never discussed. Even farting is the height of rudeness. I've never even *heard* one of my guides mention the word. And here is this idiot shitting right in front of me.

I turn away, shocked. He is still smoking.

Eventually, he stands and begins to shuffle onwards. I'm striding at my normal pace. When I turn around, he is fifty metres behind me.

'Hurry up!' I shout. 'We need to walk faster than this.'

He shambles over, laughing. 'Calm down, there is no problem, no problem, slowly, slowly,' he says in a patronising tone. 'Now I need to stop for a smoke.'

'Stop?' I say in amazement. 'Stop? We haven't even started!'

'I am a bit tired. It is the first day. Let's just rest for a while.'

We're right on the side of a track; we aren't even out of the town yet and into the desert. I am desperate to get the camels off this shoulder – they're unsettled by the rowdy, crowded African trucks thumping past us. Right at that moment, I spy another one coming. There's no room between the road and the acacia trees, which are low and will easily tangle in the camel baggage. I yell out to Le Min and back the two camels I'm leading right up hard against the trees and stop, holding them tightly. But he just keeps on plodding along, leading Beiyal, the little white camel, perilously close to the road.

The truck comes level and toots its horn, so close it leaves the camels skittish. Beiyal leaps into the air and nearly hangs himself on a tree. Freaked out by the thorny branches clinging to the baggage, he cavorts and jumps about, breathing heavily, confused and scared.

I'm ready to kill.

I walk over to Le Min and say quietly, 'Give me my camel.'

He makes the very big mistake of laughing at me. 'No problem, Paula, calm down, slowly slowly, no problem . . .' But he doesn't hand over my camel, and he looks uneasy.

I can feel the rage rising inside me as I did with Harraba. I'm as disgusted with myself as I am at Le Min.

I rein in my temper. This is far from being a crisis – I'm still on the edge of town.

On the other side of the road I can see two young boys playing. I beckon them over and hand them some money.

'Run. Go to the tent of Mohammed Le Min.' I gesture to the man. 'Do you know where that is?' The boys nod solemnly. 'Run there and ask the old man inside, Mohammed, if he would come here. Can you do that?' The two boys nod, ignoring Le Min's protests.

'Run!' I yell, giving them a little push. I'm suddenly gripped with fear that Mohammed the Good will have already gone.

I walk the camels off the road and unload them. All the while, Le Min is cajoling and laughing, trying to engage me in conversation, chain-smoking and squatting to pee every five minutes. At least I think that's what he's doing. I try to ignore him.

Fifteen nail-biting minutes later, I see the figure of Mohammed the Good approaching. His head is bent towards the two young boys as he listens attentively to their chatter. He draws close, and looks at me enquiringly.

'He walked 300 metres and had to stop for a rest,' I tell him quietly. 'And then he left Beiyal on a long lead when a truck went by. He is useless.'

I don't need to say anything else. Mohammed the Good asks a couple of brief questions of Le Min, and then I hear a harsh note enter his voice and see Le Min back down.

'He says he wants to keep the money,' Mohammed the Good tells me, shaking his head. 'I have told him he is no longer needed, and he needs to pay you back. But he is arguing that he is just a little unwell – he ate too much at the festival – and he will be fine. But I don't think so. I think he is no good.'

'Me, too,' I say. 'I should have seen it before. I'm so sorry, Mohammed. Thank you so much for coming to help me.'

I am embarrassed that I should need help so badly so soon. But Mohammed the Good shakes his head and smiles.

'Me, too. I should have known better. I thought this man was no good. But I just wasn't sure. Don't worry. I am just glad I am still here. I was too scared to leave in case this happened!'

And we look at each other and laugh. Then Mohammed resumes talking to Le Min. For a peaceful man, he sure does a good impression of being pretty damn tough. Le Min backs down and shuffles off back to his tent.

'He is going to get the money,' Mohammed tells me.

An hour or so passes, and a figure walks towards us. But it's not Le Min – it's his wife. Mohammed and I look at each other and can barely contain our laughter. He has sent his *wife?*

The rotund figure bustles self-importantly to the fire and sits down, barely exchanging courtesies and refusing my tea. She waves a lurid orange purse at me.

'We cannot pay your money back!' she starts indignantly. 'It is just after the festival! We have had to pay for many things – this money is gone already! You must take Mohammed Le Min back as your guide – he is very good and will be a good guide to you. This is not fair! I cannot pay you!'

I look at her in contempt. 'He could not walk more than 300 metres,' I tell her. 'He went to the toilet right in front of me. He is rude, and I don't want to walk with him. You need to get my money back.'

'But he is sick! He ate too much!' For every transgression, she has an excuse.

And she may well be right. Perhaps Le Min was ill and had diarrhoea he could not contain. Perhaps he is an excellent guide and knows just where everything is. But I've been through all of this before. I don't like the guy, and I don't trust him. And whether that is fair or unfair, I'm the one who will be stuck out in the Big Empty for weeks on end. And if I've learned one thing, it's better to be on my own than stuck out there with someone incompetent. In addition, there is no sob story regarding money that I've not heard a million times over in Mauritania. If she doesn't have the money, her family will. One Mauritanian would never cheat another like this, and I'm not about to be treated any differently.

So I look at the woman and address her sternly.

'You need to get this money back,' I say. 'I won't walk with your husband, and I won't leave. If this gets more serious, I'll simply go to the police.' Her face falls. She sullenly hands over the money, still in the same canister I gave to her. Without a word, she stands and walks away.

Mohammed looks at me and his lip curls in disgust. 'He sent his wife? This, he is not a man.' He shakes his head, and repeats the phrase. 'He is not a man.'

Then his face brightens, and he looks up at me.

'So, where are we walking to now?' And we both howl with laughter.

I'm aiming for a town called Nema. It's the last town before the Malian border, and I'll need to find a guide to Tomboctou. Mohammed is out of territory he knows, so for this stretch – 500 or so kilometres – the navigation by map and GPS is strictly mine. This is not at all unsettling for me, as I keep a close watch on navigating anyway, but it's difficult for Mohammed. He has no understanding of maps or modern navigation, no understanding of where Nema is. I tell him it is fifteen days away and wells are clearly marked. While he is happy to walk with me, he is uneasy and worried that I will lose our way or not find water for the camels.

There is a road that goes to Nema, but I never follow roads. And anyway, it would take us several hundred kilometres out of our way. The difficulty for Mohammed is that all of the nomads we meet tread the route north from where we are, rather than east in the direction of Mali. Every time we stop to talk to a nomad, Mohammed asks about wells, grazing and direction, and the nomads continually point north. He wants to follow them. I keep pointing to the map, showing him that there is indeed a valley with good grazing and watercourses to the north, but this is not where I need to go. Then he asks why we don't follow the road. I explain that there are no wells on the road, that I never walk there – we are some hundred kilometres north of the road by now anyway. But I can tell he is distrustful of my abilities.

In addition, the *uniti* prickles are worse than before. We're hacking through shoulder-high grasses for much of the day, and the terrain is continually undulating. It's hard work. Finding camps is awkward and time-consuming.

I'm absorbed in navigating, checking my compass every half hour and the GPS every hour. Although it's a straightforward walk, I need to zigzag to locate wells, and I'm aware of not losing my concentration in case I miscalculate. The first time I actually lead us directly to a well, Mohammed's face lights up.

'There are the tracks! Look!' he cries when we are about one kilometre away. I feel a rush of relief – although I knew the well must exist, I'm still grateful to see the familiar signs leading off exactly where they should.

We enter the small clearing and are immediately surrounded by curious nomads watering their animals. I go about silently preparing the camels to drink, as Mohammed engages in conversation. The women squat nearby, covering their faces, giggling at my exertions. Occasionally, one of them calls to me. I smile and return greetings, but I do not engage further. I'm tired of being the centre of attention.

Three small boys arrive in ragged clothing, riding donkeys. The donkeys are laden with jerry cans and empty goatskins ready to be filled. They have obviously ridden in from their desert tent to pull water for their family. The eldest could be no more than eight, the youngest about four. But they squat patiently in the dirt with the men and drink tea as they wait their turn at the well. The eldest expertly packs a pipe and smokes as he exchanges information with the older nomads.

When it's their time to haul the water up, the eldest hitches his donkey to the fifty-litre bucket at the end of the rope and pulley, and the youngest boy chases the donkey out at a run. The eldest boy works like a man three times his size as he manhandles the huge bucket, watering the animals and filling the containers. The muscles on his skinny back stand out like ropes. He moves with a sure, rhythmic grace, laughing with his brothers as he works.

When he is finished, he beckons to me and shyly offers to draw my water also. I try to help, but he won't allow me. He and his brothers water my camels and fill our containers. The youngest boy approaches Mohammed and hands him a bottle of camel milk. Mohammed drinks deeply and gives it back with his thanks. I pull some biscuits out of my bag to give the youngster and he takes them eagerly, grinning at me. When they have finished working, he ties the half-full bottle of milk onto the side of one of my camels. He nods at me and smiles. We walk away and I am touched, yet again, at the thought that those boys have just given us the one sustenance they arrived with. They have perhaps a twenty-kilometre or more round trip to go today – and yet their first thought was to give what they had to someone else on a long journey.

I am humbled by such small acts of kindness.

For days the wind blows with a chilling permanence. The hollow roar doesn't slacken at any point. We walk with our heads down into it, plodding through the prickles and over hills for twenty-five, thirty kilometres – then camp, eat, sleep. Never have the days dragged more slowly than on this stretch to Nema. Every day when I check our location and mark the kilometres on the map, I can see we are covering good ground. But each step is laborious and painful. I feel as if the wind is carving me out, emptying me. I feel flayed thin by the world around me. I feel tired.

Worse, my laptop and satellite connection are not working again. I'm baffled – they worked just fine in Nouakchott. I try everything I can think of, to no avail.

Every afternoon, as I mark our location, Mohammed hovers. 'How far did we go today? How many days until we get there? Are we close yet? Is there a well nearby?'

It's a strange experience. I'm always walking through country I don't know, so I've become sanguine and relaxed about the unexpected. I cover my bases and make sure, as much as I am able using maps, that I am walking through terrain which affords lots of options for wells. I talk to nomads as I go, or use my guides to do so, and hire people who know the local area. But essentially, after so many years walking, I'm used to the process of embarking on an unknown stretch and perhaps having to take a day or so more than I thought or deviating my route for some reason or another.

Normally any questions I ask amuses my guides. They know the terrain so well that they have nothing to worry about. It's a stroll to the shops for them, a wander in their own garden. But for Mohammed this is impossible, and it's almost amusing. He is out of his comfort zone, and suddenly he's worried and fractious, checking and double-checking the map even though he doesn't understand it. He's suspicious of my well-finding every time, until we actually get there. Our relationship remains friendly, but his unease in many ways highlights the enormity of what I'm actually doing.

It strikes me that nomads are not necessarily experts on the desert. They are experts on their particular piece of it. But beyond those confines, they are uneasy. When we stop at wells, Mohammed boasts to other nomads in no meagre terms of how far he has come, and yet he has no real comprehension of how far I came before that. I wonder how he would feel if I dumped him in the middle of Melbourne with some money and told him to walk to Sydney.

An unfair comparison, I know, but it nonetheless, reminds me that nobody is infallible. There is no real omnipotent nomad out here who is utterly at one with his environment, who simply glides through the Sahara as his home. We're all simply individuals who understand and know our own place. For everybody, there is somewhere new, somewhere unknown.

We talk about it one night.

'You come from Australia,' Mohammed says to me. 'That is part of America?'

'No,' I tell him and take out my map. Then I realise the futility of it. 'You know France . . .'

He nods, his face lighting up. 'Of course! So your country is in France? But I thought America is in France?'

I laugh. 'No. In France they speak a different language to America – it is a whole other country. Australia is many, many kilometres away from France and America.' I see his confusion. 'You know when we are walking through the country from here to Nema, and you tell me that the people here are not your tribe – that their dialect is different, and they are different from what you know?'

Mohammed nods intently.

'So – you've never been to Mali, right? But you don't think that the Malians are like you.'

Mohammed shakes his head vigorously. 'No, they're totally different. Malians! They are Tuareg, completely different, different language, everything. Nothing like Mauritanians.'

'Right!' I say. 'It is the same for us. You see, in Australia nobody would see any difference between you and the Tuareg in Mali – because they would think that you all live in the Sahara, that you are all nomads, so you are therefore the same. But you know that you're totally different.' Mohammed looks at me in disbelief. I know that he is thinking: *But how could anyone think we are the same?*

'So, it is the same for you,' I say. 'You meet a white person, a

Westerner, and think we are all the same – that we all speak the same language, live in the same place, live the same way. But we are all totally different. If I travel to Northern Australia, I am like you are here – I don't know where anything is. And if I go to France, I am just like you in Mali – I don't speak the language and feel totally lost. Your world is a lot like mine. I understand why you feel lost here.'

Mohammed looks at me thoughtfully.

'But I've been in other places for a really long time, now,' I conclude. 'And so I guess I don't get so worried anymore, because there's always a way through, and people are always kind. People don't change that much from one place to another. We all need to eat, and drink, and sleep. So I know it's strange for you to walk through a new place, but please, trust me. We will be okay.'

Until I said all of that, I didn't realise how true it was. I've been walking for so long now that I see different places, enter into them, but ultimately I press on through. In some ways this saddens me. I wonder how much of my original goal, of truly being *in* a place, I am missing now. Maybe I would be better served by simply stopping, living here for some time. I remember feeling the same way about the Western Sahara. But it is the end goal that draws me onwards, and this is also not my place. I have no reason to stop here.

Mohammed looks at me. 'I like being in my own place,' he says quietly. 'I would not like to voyage like this, always new places, never know where you are really. There is no stillness.'

And for a moment I wonder when it is that I will find my own stillness.

We camp on the outskirts of Nema, five kilometres from town. Mohammed is extremely grateful to see signs of life. Until we reached the actual perimeter of the town, I know he was sceptical as to whether we would arrive at all.

I'm exhausted. The two weeks from Aayoun to here have been unbelievably wearing. The cold I got a few weeks ago lingers in a deep, hacking cough, and my feet and hands are a stinging mess from the prickles. Tomboctou is still 650 or so kilometres away and, although I'm making good time, I feel the strain of looking ahead, the weight of kilometres yet to be walked.

Mohammed and I hobble the camels, draw blankets and ropes around the baggage, and walk into town to find a guide.

Nema is a bustling, seething mass of people. I have never felt so instantly averse to a place in my life.

There is something slimy about it. Perhaps it's a classic border town: illicit activity thrumming alongside the perpetual transfer of people and goods. The buildings are run-down. Men lounge about in Western gear and the women are all wrapped entirely in *melekhva*, shuffling in their ponderous, chattering groups, eyeing me suspiciously. Unusual for me, I remain wrapped in *melekhva*. I don't feel overly safe here.

Mohammed and I make our way to the market and begin the familiar hunting process. Within seconds, we are surrounded. I'm poked and prodded, and arrogant young men dressed in muscle T-shirts yell that they will walk with me – they know every road to Tomboctou! Mohammed is confused by the hustle and out of his depth. I'm tired and too fed up to smile.

An older, more soberly dressed man approaches from a reasonably wealthy-looking produce store and greets Mohammed respectfully.

'You're the white woman who wants to walk to Tomboctou?' he asks me quietly.

I answer that I am. The man disperses the curious, invasive crowd and guides us into one of the hessian-and-pole tents that serve tea. We sit down on cushions, grateful for the peace.

'Where have you walked from?' he asks. I run through some of the history of my walk, and Mohammed interjects frequently, anxious to impress upon the stranger the scope of my walk. One of the advantages of the past couple weeks is that Mohammed has a new appreciation of what I do. He is effusive in his descriptions of the hardships and insistent that he won't leave me with any guide he deems inadequate.

Finally, the man tells us that he knows someone who can

help, and he leaves us to go and get him. For half an hour, Mohammed and I sit and drink our tea. Beyond the opening of the tent there are lines of people crouching, watching us in open-mouthed fascination. I am so used to it that I just continue drinking my tea. Mohammed keeps telling them to go away, waving his arms. They momentarily rise like a flock of seagulls, then land again at a slightly greater distance.

The man returns. With him is a lithe, cheerful little man, who looks to be in his sixties. He greets Mohammed warmly and exchanges the long and courteous greetings appropriate between older men. Mohammed looks more relaxed by the second. The newcomer seats himself in an unobtrusive place in the tent, not trying to prove anything in the positioning, which wins him another point with me. He shakes my hand firmly, holding my eye, and smiles as he introduces himself as Ali.

He has almost won me over before he even starts.

He listens carefully as I talk about my walk and does not mention money. He tells me a little about himself, and I find that he speaks fluent French, a relief after speaking only Arabic with Mohammed.

'Years ago, I used to travel to the salt mines in Taoudenni, north of Mali,' he says. 'But I've not done that for over thirty years. I began working for the oil companies, guiding their four-wheel drives through from here to Mali. Sometimes I've worked for the military. But recently that work has stopped, too, so in recent years I've been working for a tourist agency, guiding their groups.' He proudly pulls out a card, and I recognise the name of the company – I've actually contacted them more than once for information. They are well known and respected in the area.

Still, I usually don't like working with registered tour guides. In my experience, they tend to be used to travelling by vehicle and having a cook and various other helpers along for the ride, making them somewhat averse to actually working – or walking, for that matter.

'I walk every step of the way,' I say firmly. 'I do all the cooking and most of the camel work. I need someone who knows the route very well, particularly between here and Tomboctou, as I know it's a difficult one for water and there are bandits. I expect you also to help with all the work around the camp – collecting firewood, tracking the camels in the morning when I'm packing up. There is nobody else along for backup, and I walk over twenty-five kilometres every day.'

I am slightly ashamed of how abrupt my tone is. M'Barak would have been horrified at my rudeness – but then, Mauritania is not Morocco. And I have developed a healthy fear of making bad guide choices. I need to know that I've left nothing unsaid, no avenue open for confusion.

Ali smiles at me, and I sense a hint of wickedness in his merry eyes. I really like this guy.

'It has been a long time since I've made a trip on a camel. I think my backside will be very sore after just one day, eh?'

I laugh with everyone else, but I answer him directly: 'I don't have a camel for you to ride, unfortunately. You will have to walk.'

Ali waves me away. 'I will buy a camel to ride. I'm too old to walk this far, and I've an injured leg. I have family in Mali, and Mauritanian camels sell well there – so I will buy one here and sell it at the other end. This is not a problem. I know the route so well I can walk it with my eyes closed – I know every step.' And without missing a beat, he rattles off the name of every well between here and there, and how many days between each one. I have spent night after night studying well and region names on my big map, and I know he is spot-on, down to the exact place where the route splits into two alternatives.

We agree to take a break and meet again that afternoon. Mohammed and I wander off to discuss Ali.

'My only concern is his ability to work with the camels,' I say to Mohammed. 'I know he knows the route, and I think he's a good man. But it seems that it has been a long time since he worked with them.'

Mohammed is nodding in agreement. 'He is not a nomad,' he warns. 'But I agree he is a very good man and knows the way very well. Perhaps he should come out to the camp – I will watch him with the camels and then we will make up our minds.'

In the evening, Ali comes out with us and helps pack the

camels. He has told us to come and camp further in and around a bit from the town, a place he says there is good grazing. Mohammed and I are a little sceptical – our camp site is fine – but his suggestion is a good way to see what he is made of with the camels.

He watches closely as Mohammed and I pack.

'I have never seen camels packed like this before,' he says, gesturing at the panniers. 'I've never used these. Can you show me how you use them?' I keep him with me as I pack one of the camels and then gesture to the third camel, which has the baggage piled beside it. 'You do that one,' I say.

I don't want to be caught out again.

Ali is a little taken aback, but slowly and methodically goes about packing the camel, occasionally asking advice. His knots are solid and logical, and the kit sits flat and stable on the camel. He handles the animal well. Mohammed and I look at each other in satisfaction.

We walk to the designated spot, which indeed does have good grazing and better shelter from passers-by. We have tea and negotiate the terms of our deal. Like Mohammed and Khabuss before him, Ali does not drive a hard bargain and we agree on the exact sum I had discussed with Mohammed beforehand. Again, this is the only time I discuss money with Ali.

We agree to set out two days hence. I need to buy a lot of supplies for this stretch, as it will be over twenty days in the wilderness. I also need to make phone calls and try the internet. Despite every best effort, my equipment, after functioning for one day, has packed it up again. I'm at my wit's end to know what the problem is.

Ali offers to take me into town and find somewhere for me to stay. Mohammed flatly refuses my suggestion that a nomad should guard the camels temporarily. He's become quite protective of my camels and wouldn't entrust them to what he sees as incompetent town-dwellers – a description I'm inclined to agree with.

The only hotel in Nema is entirely booked out – the Paris–Dakar Rally is due in town over the next few days. Ali tracks down a small eatery – I would hesitate to use the word restaurant

– that has a room out the back. It is normally used for travellers to eat, pray and sleep for a few hours before continuing their journey. There is no bathroom or any privacy, but Ali says the owner will agree to let the room to me exclusively for two nights, which will at least give me a chance to do my washing and use the internet and phone across the road.

I pay an extortionate amount, and so begins a catalogue of disasters so humiliating they eventually begin to amuse me. Albeit in a slightly hysterical fashion.

The room does not lock. Although the owner continually reassures me that it is for my use only, he has yet to inform anyone else of this situation, which means that the door is constantly opened by people who enter and gawk at me unashamedly until the owner comes bustling back and yells at them. He explains in a whisper that this is *my* room now. I feel embarrassed and uncomfortable when I realise the situation and say to the owner that I'm more than happy to lower my paid price and share the space, as long as I have somewhere secure to leave my electronic equipment, which was the only reason I wanted a lock-up room in the first place. The owner declines – he already has his money. So I put up with the insulted stares and miffed customers and head over to the internet place.

Which, of course, doesn't work. Except for ten-minute intervals at unpredictable times of day.

I go to the biggest store to order my supplies and find myself being charged nearly triple what I'm accustomed to. I argue with the guy behind the counter, and in the end I simply refuse to pay and storm off to another store. Then another. In the end, I eat humble pie back at the first. He is in fact the cheapest and has by far the widest variety of goods. More importantly – he has the only operative phone in town for international calls.

I try to phone everyone I can think of in an effort to sort my equipment dramas out. But the phone works for minutes and then cuts out, and the conversations are stilted and hard to hear. I give up and decide to do my washing.

I ask the owner if he can point me to where I can find a water source. I have brought my own bucket and soap. But he shakes his finger in remonstration and walks me around to another hole in the wall where several young men sweat and strain as they wash enormous loads of robes and clothes by hand.

I don't want a laundry service. The bulk of my washing is knickers and bras and, even if I thought it was acceptable, I've no desire to hand over my underwear to a Mauritanian man. My washing is wrapped in an old *melekhva*. The owner keeps trying to yank it from my grasp to give to the laundry boy. I'm equally determined to keep hold of it, and try to maintain a smile as I explain through gritted teeth that all I want is some water and a place to wash them myself.

But the owner doesn't understand my Arabic and is insistent. The flimsy material of the *melekhva* suddenly gives way, and my grungy pile of worn and stained knickers cascade to the floor in wide-open public view to an audible gasp.

There are maybe ten men standing around now, and none of them know what to do. I lunge forward, my face flaming, to scoop everything up. One of the laundry boys is there first; he obviously thinks that I expect him to wash this stuff.

He picks up my dirty undies and, with an expression of extreme distaste, prods them aside, one by one, keeping what he will wash – trousers and *melekhva* – and daintily returning the others. I sit there silently dying in shame as one after another my poor old hard-worn knickers is shown in all their filthy glory to the curious crowd of men.

When he is finished I make a flying grab for the rotten pile and exit with as much dignity as my total humiliation will allow. I want to turn on the owner and scream, particularly when he mumbles to me that there are certain things laundry boys *don't* wash and that he will show me where the water is for these.

That's all I wanted in the first place, you idiot! I want to shriek, but I just scurry away to wash my clothes.

Of course, I then have no place to dry them but the room I'm staying in. There are no words to describe the abject horror on the faces of the local men that evening when they enter the room to pray and find my knickers strung up along the walls. I'm past caring.

I'm so dehydrated that I haven't thought about peeing the whole day. But it's past dusk, and too late to go outside again, so I cast around for the squat toilet.

There isn't one.

Out the back door of the room is an empty block, which faces onto a busy street. It's where I washed my knickers today. Occasionally, I've subconsciously registered people entering and exiting. I now realise why: it's a communal toilet. I go outside and squat down under the cover of *melekhva*, but a white woman is obviously far more interesting than a local one, so my activities draw a bit of a crowd. At least I've water in my bottle left over to rinse off.

In the morning I decide to cut my time in Nema short. My night was a joke – the owner's goat stayed in the kitchen and spent every second voicing its disgust at the meagre quarters. In a concrete room, the sound was deafening. I'm filthy, tired and heartily through with the town. At first light I organise a vehicle, pay for my supplies and bail out back to Mohammed and the camels. He rocks in silent laughter as I repeat the trials of the previous day, cringing in sympathy with my laundry predicament and waving me away with affection as I go to have a decent wash. As always, the sheer telling of the events makes them funny and harmless, and my spirits are immediately restored.

Ali races out that afternoon in a panic, having visited the café to find me gone. We agree to meet at the well in town early the next morning. He has bought a new camel, which he is very proud about – and also a gun, something we agreed on and that I paid for. I'm not overly happy about carrying a firearm, but Ali was insistent that it was advisable on this stretch, as a protective measure. I've never agreed with the idea that carrying a firearm is a preventative to any kind of violence, but I gave in this time, perhaps out of weariness as much as anything. I'm also entering that uncertain mental space that comes with a new country. I tend to rely on Ali's judgement rather than my own. It will become a recurring theme, although I see it only vaguely at the time.

That night is the last I have with Mohammed. We sit up late around the fire, eating good meat and vegetables for once, and talk. We do the thing that always happens at the end of a stretch: discuss what has been, laugh at what is now over – for Mohammed at least: the prickles, wind and navigation anxiety. I tell him stories of M'Barak, Madani and me in the Western Sahara, and he laughs and nods in understanding. I've spoken to him often of M'Barak; of all my guides, Mohammed is the most similar to that funny, staunch, wiry old nomad. Mohammed says to me, as the fire burns low and we are ready for bed, 'I would like to meet this M'Barak of yours one day. He is a real nomad.'

I think how proud M'Barak would be to hear those words. I wish I could sit the two of them down around a fire.

I look at the kindly old man and say, 'You have been just as M'Barak to me – a true friend, a wonderful guide. Just like a father. Thank you so much.'

And Mohammed, with his gentle, calm nature and with more graciousness than I expect he feels after walking over 500 kilo-metres longer than he intended, says, 'It has been an honour.'

Slightly embarrassed, I take out the money I picked up from Western Union today and hand it to him. It's double what we orig-inally agreed, plus a tip. When I give him the roll of bills, he looks at me in wonderment and says, 'But this is more than we agreed.'

'You walked double the distance,' I tell him. 'Did you think I expected you to do that for free?'

He looks at me solemnly. 'It is a matter of honour, not money,' he says. But then his old face creases into a smile and he says, 'But this is very good for me! Thank you!' He tucks the bills away and we laugh, all awkwardness forgotten.

Every manner of flashy, loud, four-wheel drive roars past us at great speed as the Paris–Dakar races into town. Left with no choice but to follow the same road, Mohammed and I hang on tightly to the camels as they cavort and snort in terror when the smoking, fluorescent-painted beasts pass. The drivers stare at me dumbly. Occasionally, one frowns and looks back as their vehicle races past, unsure if it was a white woman they just saw hanging on to camels.

Hounded by vehicles and jeered at by bemused locals, Mohammed and I make our flustered way into the bustling market square. Within seconds we're swamped by a nigh on hysterical mob, who are trying to touch me and the camels. Well-trained though they are, my camels will not stay couched while they are prodded and harassed. They rise indignantly to their feet and, when one particularly shrill woman persists in poking Bolshy, he lashes out with a leg – the first time I've seen him do so. I could kiss him.

I don't want to leave Mohammed, but I can't see Ali anywhere.

'I need to find Ali, so we can get out of here,' I say, and he nods in resignation. I tear off at speed through the crowds and walk one length of the market to another before I locate him. He is surrounded by a similarly fascinated crowd, his camel packed and ready, looking just as uncomfortable as we are. His face lights up in relief when he spots me, and he and the camel are on their feet in seconds, following me back to where Mohammed is fighting off the manic crowd with a look of abject weariness.

'We're going to get out of here,' I tell him. There is no time for niceties. He presses my hand once and smiles with his whole face – and then he's gone, off into the crowd with his small bag of belongings to find the first of a series of bush taxi rides home.

I feel suddenly bereft. The crowd pushes in on me, grasping at my clothes, face and camels. Somebody jolts Beiyal, and a small jerry can falls off. The crowd jostle each other in competition to tie it back on.

'Get away!' I roar, to even my own surprise.

Momentarily shocked, the crowd backs off and I quickly tie the jerry can on properly. The onlookers nudge and mutter to each other, fascinated by my every move. I look at Ali, who nods. He sets off. I take all three of the camel leads and walk behind him, not game to tie them in their usual formation with the giant entourage following us.

On the other side of the square, a series of outlandish four-wheel drives have pulled up, the Paris–Dakar in action. They're all but ignored and, indeed, they seem as fascinated as the rest of the crowd by our little caravan. It strikes me as somewhat ironic that in a desert border town, my expedition draws more attention than the money-laden Paris–Dakar Rally.

Before I know what's hit me, we're heading out of town and up a steep, rocky path. Unprepared for this and focused on the crowd surrounding us, I hadn't seen the ascent coming or stopped to fix the baggage for a steep uphill climb. By the time I realise that we're on quite a treacherous path, the baggage is beginning to shift. Then, partly due to the unbalanced kit, one of the camels goes down. In tense silence, I have to totally unpack him, turn him around and reload before we can continue. So soon in, I don't trust Ali with the camels. It's an hour or so until we reach the top of the incline and are away from the hubbub of town.

Ali and I have barely spoken a word to each other. Now we're suddenly at the top of the hill, surrounded by relative peace – if I disregard the vehicles screaming by at close quarters – and I turn to look at Ali. He is pale, his face strained. How unpleasant all of this must be for him. It's the usual nightmarish first day, albeit more stressful than most, and he must be wound up like a spring with worry – not to mention put off by my hostile silence. I suddenly see the funny side and start to laugh. He looks up hopefully.

'By God, what a mess!' I exclaim. 'I haven't had breakfast yet, and I'm sure you haven't either. Why don't we just sit down and relax for a while with some tea?' By the time I am finished, Ali is grinning madly and nodding his head in agreement.

'*Allahi! Allahi!*' he breathes fervently, and we settle down and sit in the early-morning cool. We drink our first proper tea together, laughing every time one of those God-awful vehicles goes racing past.

Unknowingly, and like his predecessors, I indoctrinate Ali into my language. By the end of tea, when the next vehicle races by, he looks at me slyly and says, 'FUCKEN' Paris–Dakar!'

Chapter Fourteen

I am on the way to Tomboctou.
   The words run through my head like a mantra whenever my mind is empty. After months of walking towards an almost mythical goal, I'm on the final leg. Even though Tomboctou represents not even the halfway point of my west to east crossing, it's lurked in my subconscious for so long that it has assumed Everest-summit proportions. At night I look up at the pointer stars that Khabuss showed me and wonder if they will indeed lead me to Tomboctou. I eagerly check the map, marking off our kilometres as the tiny dot along the Niger River comes closer and closer.

Life feels good. The prickles are still hell, and getting worse. The walking itself is no easier. But I'm fit, my camels are strong and happy, and there are prickle-free camps every day.

Ali is a joy to be with – cheeky, irrepressible and reliable. Like M'Barak, he has something of an obsession with larger women. He has already bombarded me with questions about Western men and their preference for the slender female form.

'I see all these tourists come, and the women – they very short hair, like a man, with strange colours. And they are skinny! And the men – *they* are fat!' Ali screws his face up in revulsion that any man would allow himself to get fat; in his culture, it's not seemly for a man to be obese. It's an indication of laziness, a lack of discipline. Fat is for women.

'But the men tell me they don't like fat women, and this, I really don't understand. Why would you want a motorcycle when you can have the comfort of a LandCruiser?' He indicates with his arm span an imaginary woman so enormous he would drown in her flesh. When I say this, he rolls on the sand cackling.

'Yes! Yes! A woman so big I can dive in and disappear!' He crows. 'But why do your men like skinny women? They may as well have sex with boys!'

It's not an unfamiliar theme for me – M'Barak would always comment with great enthusiasm when we passed a larger than normal nomadic woman on the size of her *zerfal* – her butt. It got to the embarrassing point where I would actually eye the butts up myself as we passed, then await the comment. In fact, it became such a bad habit that I had to focus on *not* looking at women's butts when I last returned to the UK.

'In your country, do they think you are fat or skinny?' Ali asks me. I bite back my laughter – his tone is entirely serious.

'I would certainly *not* be considered skinny. Most people would probably describe me as 'large' or 'big'. Generally, people would think I could lose a bit of weight.' Ali looks amazed.

'But you have a *petit zerfal!*' he says, and now I can't help it and begin to laugh out loud at his consternation. 'Well, you do!'

'What – you have been watching my *zerfal*, Ali?' I say, shaking my head in mock reproof.

'No, no!' he cries and cracks a grin. 'Well, yes, a bit, because I ride my camel, you know, and you are far up ahead of me leading the camels. And your *zerfal* – it goes like this, you know?' And with his hands he demonstrates my pronounced hip waggle.

'And so I can tell if you are having a good day or a bad one, because on a good day the *zerfal*, it goes like this' – and his hands show a rolling, fluid action – 'but if the prickles are very bad or you are grumpy with the camels or something, then your *zerfal* is like this.' His hands describe a sharp, clipped movement, exactly the way I know I walk when the prickles are forcing my legs stiff or I'm pissed off.

I'm howling with laughter at the descriptions. 'I never knew that my *zerfal* said so much about me. Maybe instead of asking me how I am every day, you should just talk to the *zerfal*, huh?'

Now Ali is gasping for air as he points at me. 'Exactly! "Good morning, *Zerfal*! How are you feeling this morning? Is everything good for you today?"' We are both rolling around on the sand dune, hysterical, and every time our laughter begins to die down, Ali indicates my arse and says something like, 'Are you having fun yet, Mr *Zerfal*? Do you have anything to say?'

For the rest of the trip to Tomboctou, Ali will continue to talk to my arse as if it is me. It never fails to jolt me out of a state of discomfort or make me smile – not once do I feel that there is another agenda. Ali simply has a wicked sense of humour and a true gentleman's appreciation of the female form. Bliss for Ali would be a few bouncy, nubile wenches, a handful of good camels, a night on the dunes under the stars, good meat and a stealthy bottle of whiskey when nobody was watching.

Perhaps in the wake of Mohammed the Zen king, I'm deep into a calm, meditative state of mind on this stretch. My camp has never come together in a routine so quickly. Ali and I work together without any fuss. At night the camels often come and graze close to the camp, and Beiyal, the one I began to call 'Henry', exhibits even more human-like qualities. One night, I wake in a shock to find him stretched out right next to my swag, virtually eyeball to eyeball. He opens a lazy eye and chews his cud – I swear that if he thought he could fit into my swag, he'd try it.

Ali leaves me alone when I walk, not trying to talk to me, as some guides do. He understands the pace of the walk and the peace I find in it. He knows how to be still. Despite the continual needling of the prickles, I go deeper and deeper into myself on this stretch, lulled into contemplation by the long, quiet days, interrupted only very rarely by other nomads.

I think of reality and how fickle it is. I can only *truly* experience where I am at any one time. England and Australia seem so far away that they almost cease to exist; I think of the Melbourne laneways, the smell of coffee in the morning, dinner in Lygon Street with friends. I think of high heels and make-up and searching to find the right colour top to go with some trousers. Then I look around me at the stark expanse and wonder if it's possible that this other life can still actually be happening while I'm here walking.

I've often been asked what I think about when I walk. I've usually blown the question off, flippantly answering that I think about sushi, or a cold beer, or sex. Although those responses are calculated to raise a smile, they have their own truth – some days, visions of watermelon hang in my mind with such clarity that I can taste them.

Beneath this swirl of mundane thought lies a more intuitive layer that I begin to tap into over days and weeks of uninterrupted walking. These subconscious thoughts gain strength and coherence without deliberate effort. Once, after what feels like days of mental meandering, I'm walking along when suddenly a thought of almost dumb simplicity pops into my mind.

I am just here, I think with sudden clarity. *That is all. I am just here.* For a long, still moment, I have an overwhelming sense of the inherent truth of those words, an indescribable feeling of understanding and synergy. And then it is gone, and my conscious mind tries to probe what it meant. But the wonderful thing about walking is that the conscious mind soon lapses back into somnolence, and the subconscious whispers: *it's enough that you felt it.*

I write the episode in my journal when I stop walking, but I know that it has already lost its potency. As I lie in my swag that night looking again up at the brilliant stars, I think that as long as I am walking I don't have to work this stuff out. I can just let it wash through me, wait for another of those moments and know that they are important simply to *have*. Perhaps understanding them is not the point; maybe it's enough just to know them for what they are and retain even a piece of that sense of the infinitesimal.

My mind goes so far away when I walk through the Big Empty that I barely know what is real and what is imagination, and when I know it is time to stop I draw myself reluctantly out of dreaming. Some days I think I could simply walk forever, until I reached the end of this place, whether I had water or food or not. I could just quietly put one foot in front of the other and live in the dream state, that it would somehow sustain me until the end.

I understand the djinns, the feared ghosts of the desert. I understand how they are as real as the sand itself, for things live out here that in other places exist only in fairytales. What is within the dark recesses of the mind somehow finds form here; and the djinns, I believe, are the echoes of a thousand lost souls, wandering through this great haunting place. The djinns mirror what we become when we are of the desert.

I dread coming out of it, the return to the mundane, the tight faces of society, the petty boundaries. I dread leaving the clean, stark wilderness, leaving behind the glimpse of my true essence and drawing on the 'material' layers once again. And no matter how I crave it, I dread having to talk when I am used to the silence.

Talking about my walk feels in many ways like a lie. I can discuss the quotidian details: the guides, camels, routes and wells. But the real revelation is this strange subconscious thinking. It's this that profoundly changes me, moves me, makes sense of the darkness that has already passed and shines a light into the future. It gives me hope and purpose. When I'm out here in the deep desert, I feel so strong that I'm afraid of nothing. When I walk in that subconscious place, I know myself; the seas within are calm. There is no self-concern. It is a precious epiphany, which is at the same time unknowable. I rarely recognise the gift of it until I'm in another town, and it is no longer there.

Right in the middle of the calm, I'm forced to address one harsh reality: the water is nearly finished.

Two days ago, Ali and I had a conversation about wells; there was one marked on my map just a few kilometres out of our way. Ali waved my request away, saying that there was another one just a day away, right along our route. I consent reluctantly. After the training I received from M'Barak, Khabuss and Mohammed, I would never walk past known water if my stocks were low. But Ali is so insistent, almost insulted at my mistrust. And I, in turn, have faith in him.

Before I agreed to pass, though, I had a good look at my map and calculated that even in the worst-case scenario – that there is no water at the next well – there are two water sources within a ten-kilometre radius. The situation isn't life threatening.

It's midday when we reach a prickle-free hill and make camp. Ali tells me the well is only four kilometres away. I always go with the camels when they drink, but I'm struggling hard today with infected feet. There is only half a litre of water left in one of the small bottles. I have never allowed water to get so low, and I'm not at all happy. Ali is apologetic, and as it has taken a day and a half to reach a place he assured me was only a day away I decide that I'm not going anywhere and flake out under a tree.

But by dusk Ali has still not returned. It should have taken him no more than three hours at the most, even if he sat and had tea with nomads at the well. I'm deeply uneasy.

I don't even want to suspect Ali of foul play – it would make no sense – but I look at what he has left behind anyway. I can see all of his personal baggage, his camel saddle and the rifle. He certainly wouldn't abandon those things. In addition, Ali is a certified guide. His entire income is derived from word of mouth and good practice with tourists. There is no way that the price of three camels could ever make up to him the loss of his reputation if things somehow went wrong for me. I feel reassured to eliminate that as a possibility.

I'm left with two thoughts. One is that the well itself was either dry or saline. In that case, he would have had to make a round trip of over twenty kilometres to get to the next closest well and back again – he wouldn't return until later tonight.

The other possibility is that Ali has somehow met with either an accident or violence. Handling four camels at a well if there are other animals around can be tricky, and accidents easily occur. Equally, there are bandits everywhere. We have taken precautions with our fires every day: cooking our main meal before nightfall and tamping the fire out before it can be seen at night. We do not camp in obvious places and avoid encountering anyone. There is no guarantee that Ali hasn't met with someone more interested in acquiring my camels than drinking tea.

Either way, I can't know. Night is falling and there is cloud. Even if Ali manages to find his way back in this direction on such a dark night, he will need to be guided in. Despite the danger it may be seen by someone undesirable, I light a big fire on the hill and roll my swag out under a bush nearby.

I've very little water left – perhaps 300 millilitres. I've sipped it sparingly today, which is hard after I walk: I drink little while actually moving and tend to put a lot down when I stop. Instead, I've eaten one of my prized tins of fruit, of which I carry only a few. In the back of my mind I'd always thought they may come in handy if I was ever stuck for water; it was bliss to open one of the tins; eat the soft, wet fruit and drink the syrup.

I'm leaving the last of the water for as long as I can. I may need to get through another day out here on my own and then walk through the night to one of the neighbouring wells. I don't want to use the water until then, since I'm far from seriously dehydrated.

I try to sleep, but at every noise I wonder if Ali is approaching and leap up to wave him in. In the middle of the night I hear a herd of camels rush through at great speed and the urgent, hushed sounds of men driving them onwards. They have to be bandits – nobody legitimate would drive camels at that pace so late at night. My fear for Ali's wellbeing ratchets up a notch.

By early morning there is still no sign, and I begin to seriously consider my options. Oddly, I'm not afraid – but I'm mightily pissed off. To be so close to Tomboctou and to consider actually failing seems a cruel twist of fate. If I can't find Ali or the camels, I may at best have enough equipment and cash to swap for two camels, enough to get me to Tomboctou if I can find a nomad willing to trade. But it will leave me skint financially and in a precarious position. Besides, I *like* my camels. I want them back.

I know there's no point at all in leaving my current location during the day. Anyone who has ever grown up in Australia knows that the first rule of survival is to never leave the car. My camp is the same as the car. I have tinned fruit, shade and a little water. I could exist for days here if I needed to.

But I also know, without any doubt, that there is a functioning well ten kilometres away. It was the backup one Ali would have gone to if the four-kilometre radius one was dry. We had spoken to a nomad two days before who watered his animals there. I also know there are some tents in that direction, since he was heading back to his. The well is marked on my map, and I could see by the way the land was falling anyway where it would be. If Ali is not back by this evening, I will take the water bottle and GPS and head to that well, leaving him a note. The other nomads close by will also help me find him.

Having made my plan, there is little to do but lie down in the shade, conserve my energy and wait.

Close to midday though, I call Dad briefly. I have agonised over whether or not it's a fair thing to do, but I feel it's also important to give him my GPS points and those of the well I'm headed to. He takes it all on board with immense calm, as only someone who has sailed solo from Australia to England could, I guess. I tell him that I will call briefly to confirm my movements.

And then I lie down to think.

But my thoughts are a long way from being maudlin or sad. Instead, I feel a strange kind of triumph. Without even being aware of it, I'd actually been observant of the features around me – wells, tents and direction. While I could curse my stupidity in letting the water go so low in the first place, at least I know how to take care of myself. If this had happened in the first three or so months that I walked with M'Barak, I would have been terrified with no idea where to go or what to do. But now I'm so comfortable out here that finding a well seems no more alien to me than finding a supermarket in a backblock in France.

But I'm still pissed off and worried to hell about Ali and my camels.

Late in the afternoon, I make out the tired-looking caravan walking into camp. I'm buoyed and curious. But I don't rush down or say anything, just put the tea on to boil. Whatever Ali's story, he won't want a shrieking banshee interrogating him when he is obviously exhausted.

The camels are tired, I can see it. We hobble them quickly, and I lead Ali over to the shade. He has a cut head and is covered in prickles. His face is grey with exhaustion.

Neither of us says anything until he has pounded some snuff in his little bowl, sniffed and drunk some tea. He had no sooner arrived than he proffered me one of the jerry cans. The first word he said to me was 'drink'. I made a show of not sculling the water; I don't want him to know how worried I was. Now we sit and he indicates the water over and over, telling me to drink. I do.

Finally, he looks at me, and to my surprise I see that his eyes are watery. His voice shakes and he says, 'Twenty years ago I left my brother in a camp just like this while I went for water. I got lost. When I got back, three days later, he had wandered off to look for me. We found his body. He had died of thirst.' He shakes his head, and I can see that his whole body is trembling. He looks up at me again, and I can hear the fear in his voice. 'I thought you would leave. I thought you would try to find me. I was so scared . . .'

I'm lost in sympathy. I think of how he must have panicked through the night – what would have happened to him if he had lost a Western tourist for whom he was responsible? His business would be finished, his reputation in tatters. But even worse, he would have suffered the same trauma twice. It must have been a torturous night.

'What happened?' I ask.

'I rode to the first well, but it was dry,' Ali starts. 'I knew there was a chance that would happen, so I was okay, just turned the camels around and headed for the other one. I got there in the late afternoon, which was fine. But just as I rode up, a large herd of camels came along with two men.' He looks at me. 'They weren't good men.' I nod, almost sure it was the same group who came past last night; the timing would fit.

'One of them shot off a gun and scared Beiyal, who I was riding. I fell off and almost knocked myself out. I was very dizzy.' He touches the nasty looking cut on his forehead. And then he cracks the ghost of a smile. 'But your camels – ha! They're so good. As soon as I fell off, all the camels stopped dead still, and I could get hold of all their cords. Even though there were many camels, all running around and nervous, your camels all stood dead still. When the men tried to take them, I could hold onto them. And I had my knife. They didn't want a fight; in the end they left.'

I'm torn between horror at his ordeal and ridiculous pride in my gorgeous camels. They are so well trained now that they respond to the flick of my fingers to get up or go down, and even in the madness of Nema they didn't bolt or panic. Hearing their behaviour praised so warmly is like having one's children admired.

'I watered the camels and filled the jerry cans. Another nomad turned up, and he wanted me to come back to his tent, because I was wounded, but I knew you had no water. I told him my friend was back at camp with no water. He said he would send his son, but I didn't want them to know there was a woman here on her own. He was asking a lot of questions and seemed a bit strange. I got suspicious, so I said I had to go.

'I set off in a roundabout way in case he followed me, but then it was night and the clouds came over and I didn't know where I was. I didn't want to get lost, so I just lay down to sleep, but as you can see' – he indicates his prickle-infested robes – 'it was bad prickle country! In the end, I realised this morning I'd gone a long way in the wrong direction, and to be honest I got lost a few times before I found my way back.' He hangs his head.

'I'm very sorry, Paula. We should have stopped for water two days ago. I've been too long guiding people in cars – I forget about how important water is with camels.'

Any residual anger melts away inside me with those words. I know that he means exactly what he says, and I know also that he has a point. It's easy to forget the immediate need for water when the next town is only ever a few hours away by car. I'm just so pleased to see him and have my beautiful camels back that I could dance a polka.

'I got a bit worried,' I say. 'But my *zerfal* was totally calm, so it was fine.' Ali looks at me, and we chuckle quietly. He clasps my hand in affection, and we sit in silent relief and watch the night fall.

One day Ali gestures to a lone tree, just before a sand dune.

'When we pass that tree, we are in Mali,' he says. It's hot and my feet hurt. I look at the tree and wait, as I always do at such pivotal moments, for some kind of internal shift or external lightning bolt.

Something to mark the passing of a frontier.

But it never happens. The lines we have drawn on maps to divide up land never mean very much to the land itself. I watch as two nomadic children come skipping over the invisible boundary, taking their animals to water. I'm quite sure nobody ever mentioned to them that they are passing from one country to another. I imagine a small hatch opening in the tree and an officious little man sticking his hand out and saying, 'Passport?' to the kids each time they pass. The image tickles me.

But the changes do become apparent quite quickly. The nomads we meet now are Tuareg. Although a few of them speak Arabic, the majority speak only Tamashek, the Tuareg language. Ali teaches me the most basic of greetings – '*Maygan. L' Hadagaas?*' – but I find I have less enthusiasm for learning the language than I do with Arabic, in which I'm still only barely capable. It's frustrating and depressing: I'm in a culture and environment with which I'm entirely familiar, but once again totally unable to communicate.

The nomads themselves look very different from those I'm accustomed to. A parallel would be the 'ferals' from *Mad Max Beyond Thunderdome*. The men have mad, untamed hair, which sticks out in corkscrews or in tangled, matted shocks. They wear brightly coloured clothes rather than Saharawi robes – tunics in bright purples and greens, turbans of even more vivid shades. They wear long knives and swords with tassels, and their sandals have fur trimmings, beading and turned-up toes. They're littered with jewellery and adornments, even this far out in the desert: heavy rings and detailed necklaces from which hang decorated pouches. The women are clad in simple black *melekhva*, but beneath the covering their hair is often braided in elaborate sculptures. Here, the men's finery far outdoes the women's.

I sense a new freedom almost straightaway. The men seem less curious, less aware of me as a woman than anywhere I've been before. Ali tells me that I can stop wearing *melekhva* and just wear my cotton trousers and a long top. I actually see women clad in similar dress, and with a sigh of relief I discard the extra material that has been catching in the prickles for so long.

We buy a goat from a nomad and the price is nearly half what

I'm used to paying in Mauritania. I'm curious to notice, as we drink tea, that the method the old man uses is rather different to what I am used to – the ritual seems less pronounced, the tea coarser and cruder, and he doesn't worry about staying for three glasses. Although this is not uncommon for nomads who are passing, I sense a difference in the general demeanour of this man that is in line with what I have been observing the last few days. They just seem wilder, and it feels strange to walk into a different culture when my whole desert experience has been Saharawi.

I'm lying in my swag, trying to ignore the throbbing in my swollen feet. Two days ago my left foot suddenly erupted in a series of angry, oozing infections; it seems the prickle overload got to it. Despite my efforts to clean and treat the wounds, the infection is worsening. I'm in a race to get to town, where I can rest.

Suddenly the night erupts in a blinding flash of light. For a second, the world is floodlit, every detail of the landscape laid bare in the harsh brilliance. Then the initial incandescence fades, and above me a meteor burns a fierce bright-green streak across the sky for long, breathless seconds. The light fades away, and then, just as I turn to yell to Ali, a deafening BOOM sucks any other sound out of the sky. The reverberations die away, and I realise it must have landed very close by.

'God! Ali, did you see that?' I cry, sitting up. Ali is upright, saying '*Allah Akbar*', over and over.

'Someone important died today,' he says solemnly. I have heard this before – M'Barak always took meteors as a sign of a dead soul passing. With a meteor that big, it must have been one hell of an important soul.

I've seen a lot of meteors in the desert – some nights it's like a fireworks display – but I've never seen anything of this magnitude, and I say so.

'Me either,' says Ali. 'And I think it must only be about twenty-five kilometres away, judging from the time between the flash and its falling.'

We both sit there in awe, discussing the sheer immensity of it.

I cannot help but wonder if there were any nomad tents beneath that huge, natural bomb. I feel unnerved and excited by the scale of it, by the reminder of the wider, wilder natural universe out there, and my own isolation is highlighted yet again.

My foot gets worse. It's swollen like a soccer ball, and I can see the lines of infection beginning to spread up my leg. The pain is blinding. I stagger along holding the side of the camel baggage for support, scared to stop in case I just can't get going again. Ali begs me, even going so far as to get angry, to ride one of the camels. But I am horribly stubborn. Whenever I feel slightly tempted, I imagine how awful it would be if by some bizarre chance I got back after all of this and somebody said, 'Oh yes, I saw that woman – but she was riding the camel, not walking!'

After walking every step, all this way, I would rather fail than suffer that kind of misunderstanding.

Oddly, the more ill I become, the more polarised this becomes in my mind.

Walking becomes an excruciating agony. The last seventy kilometres into Tomboctou seem impassable; I wonder why it's *always* the last stage before a goal that is blisteringly difficult.

But, eventually, we make camp only four kilometres from town. Ali says we will walk in tomorrow morning. From here, I can see nothing, just the overgrazed territory that tells me we are close to a town. Night falls, and I am tremulous with excitement about being so close to Tomboctou. But my foot hurts like hell, and my happiness is tinged with sorrow that I will be saying goodbye to Ali, who has been such good company.

Suddenly he grabs my arm and points into the middle distance.

And I see it. Right beneath the confluence of the two sets of pointer stars, exactly where I've been looking for months, I can see the lights of Tomboctou beaming into the night sky. It's exactly as I imagined it would look.

I plonk down heavily onto the sand, fix my gaze where the sky and the incredible reality of those town lights meet, so choked that I cannot talk. After years of holding Tomboctou in my mind as some kind of talisman or holy grail, to be finally staring straight at it is overwhelming. I have fought hard, through so much.

Ali is delighted at my reaction.

'Ah, it is good, yes? Tomorrow, Paula, the *zerfal* is *very* happy; no more of this *ba-bing!*' And with his hands, he indicates the unbalanced limp I have struggled with over the last few days as the infection in my foot worsened.

I laugh, too, although I can feel the tears of relief and achievement thick in my throat behind my smile.

'Oh, my *zerfal* is *so* happy, Ali! And tomorrow night, the *zerfal* will be sitting on a bar stool holding a cold beer! And yours – your *zerfal* will be tucked up with a Malian princess, hey?'

'Eeeee!' he shrieks and kicks his legs in the air, just like M'Barak so long ago. 'Tomorrow, our *zerfals* have found paradise! And they need it, after all of these prickles – yes, I'm too old for journey like this by camel. I'm glad it is finished. And your *zerfal* needs to rest. Tomorrow, I will take you to my family, and then I will find a woman, and you will get some of your "medicine", and then I will buy a sheep and we will eat meat together with my family. And I will make sure you get the liver!' Ali knows just how much I love the rich goodness of the offal.

'A few days in Tomboctou, and Paula's *zerfal* is like the LandCruiser with the meat, hey? Ha! No more petit!' And, delighted with that thought, Ali rolls over to sleep.

I lie in my swag and look up at the glorious sky that has led me here, right to this spot. I give thanks to every deity I can think of – and some I don't know – for this wonderful confirmation of natural wisdom. I thank them for somehow proving that in a world that can be so unforgiving and hard, there are these moments of small miracles, the confirmation of a long-held faith. I look back at M'Barak's star and there it is, right between the cheeks of my *zerfal*. And up ahead, the stars point, like divine arrows, down to my first goal – and further on to my future. I forget my throbbing foot and growling stomach and lie back in deep contentment.

Chapter Fifteen

We enter Tomboctou quietly, just past dawn, winding our way through dirt laneways, past low dwellings that sit behind fences made of entwined thorn bush. The houses are much more stereotypically African than anything I've seen before: low tents made out of woven fibre, usually connected in part to a squat mud-brick building. Although there's evidence of more grand homes, similar to the large, square concrete-and-earth houses I've seen in big towns all through the Sahara, the majority remain cast in the more traditional mould. In the yards, beautiful African women clad in brightly coloured cloth use long, heavy poles to pound grain in wooden bowls, and the early morning echoes with the hollow rhythm of their work.

'It's customary to enter Tomboctou in secret,' Ali tells me as we walk down the street. 'Traditionally the camel caravans arrived back from their trading journeys late at night, and unloaded in darkness, so that nobody would know what wealth they had brought back. Tomboctou is a town that keeps its business to itself. It is dangerous around here to let people know what you've got.'

I've heard of a Canadian man who made a similar journey to mine, four years before me. In various places I've heard nomads speak of him. He refused to travel with guides and had many troubles along his way, from all accounts. But in Tomboctou he met with more than just trouble. After couching his camels in the main street, the story goes, he entered the Western Union to pick up cash. He resupplied in the town – drawing attention from every onlooker – packed his camels and walked out into the dusk.

He was found the following day with his throat slit, all his possessions gone.

No, Tomboctou is not a place for ostentation and, for all that it has long become a tourist curiosity, it remains the centre of mystery it always has been.

But on the first day I enter, it seems little different to many of the desert outposts I've encountered. Ali takes me to his family home, where I collapse gratefully in the cool shade of the woven hut and drink goats' yoghurt sweetened with sugar. Ali introduces me to Mahmoud, his cousin by marriage, whom he assures me is a brilliant guide and will take me all the way through to Menaka – a journey of over 700 kilometres.

Mahmoud does not immediately impress me. He is Arab rather than Tuareg, but his habits are more African than any of the Saharawi I've ever walked with – and his manners are coarser. When I begin to make the tea, he removes the makings from my hands and shakes his head patronisingly, telling me that I must watch and learn. I look over at Ali, frowning, but he winks. I take that to mean he will need time to talk with Mahmoud in private.

After my good fortune with Khabuss, Mohammed and Ali, I feel quite safe to take his suggestion of a guide. In addition, the infection in my foot is appalling. I'm anxious to see my camels safely entrusted to a local nomad for grazing and myself into a hotel and medical care. We agree that Mahmoud's son will take the camels and that I can leave the bulk of my baggage with the family. Ali understands that I need a few days to sort out visa issues, get my foot seen to and generally rest in a hotel without family fussing about. He has worked with tourists enough to appreciate my desire for privacy, but also understands that I am more than happy – indeed eager – to meet them and share some food and time.

Mahmoud and I agree to meet in Ali's company in a couple of days to talk in depth about the upcoming stretch. I still don't like him much.

Ali's relative drives us up through the town. The roads are thick with deep sand, and I remember reading that in this part of Mali creeping desertification is a real issue. Whole towns are being subsumed by the ever-increasing sands.

Before I even go to the hotel, I go straight to the gendarmerie to sort my visa out. I'm terribly nervous. The Malian embassy I consulted advised me that, since I didn't know the exact date of my entry into Mali and tourist visas are only valid for one month, I should present at the gendarmerie in Tomboctou and pay a fee to have my visa issued there. I had endless conversations about this and never really got a straight answer. In Nouakchott I had planned to get a visa and let it expire, just so I had one in my passport. But I had since met several African old hands, and read on the internet in travellers' hubs, that it is indeed a simple matter to get a visa in Tomboctou. In the end, I decided to take my chances.

I'm stunned by the simplicity of proceedings. A friendly African man greets me in fluent French and shows me into a clean, orderly room. He asks me no more than a few simple questions, informs me gently that the fee is about twenty Australian dollars – and stamps my passport without any further ado.

The entire episode is over in ten minutes, and he has granted me a two-month visa instead of one.

'Enjoy your time in Mali,' he says as he smiles and waves me out of the door. I was even given a glass of tea.

I check into a hotel and revel in a hot shower and a closed door. My foot is so painful that I have to sit on the shower floor. It is throbbing with a deep, heavy pulse, and the lines on my leg run nearly up to my groin. I know I have a blood infection and I know it's serious.

I limp out to the foyer to ask the man on reception where I can find medical treatment. A large group of American tourists has arrived, so I take a chance and approach their tour leader.

In great coincidence, it turns out to be an Italian man who Ali has worked with on a number of occasions. He has been working in Tomboctou for over twenty years – and has even heard of my trip. It's a wonderful feeling.

One of the tourists in the group is a doctor. He takes one look at my foot and orders me into my room, where he arrives with a medical chest that would save a Third World country. He hands out horse-strength antibiotics and tells me not to move anywhere until the lines disappear and the swelling goes down, then advises me on the best way to clean and dress the wounds. It's almost a relief to be forced into inertia.

In my room, I take out my journal, maps and GPS and do the maths of my journey so far.

When I made my original estimates on the floor of Mum's flat in Melbourne, I'd planned on taking 100 days in total from Nouadhibou to Tomboctou. I'd taken the distance from the map as being 2100 kilometres and had planned to make the distance in seventy walking days, with a margin for error meaning it could take ninety, plus rest days that could – at worst – mean 100.

I've had so many delays, setbacks and problems that I had been almost scared to think of how my progress had been affected. So I'm stunned with satisfaction to realise that, despite everything, the walk including rest days from Nouadhibou to here has taken 102 days; the distance I have covered is in fact 2400 kilometres; and I have done the lot in only seventy-eight walking days.

For the first time since this walk began, I've set concrete targets and stuck to them – the two-day alteration in total days notwithstanding. Despite feeling on so many occasions like I was getting nothing right, I am right on time. My camels, if a little tired and thin, are travelling well. My health is not fantastic, but I'm on the road to repair. And, better than anything, I feel mentally and emotionally strong. Life is good.

A couple of days later my foot has shrunk to a manageable size, and I exit the shelter of my room and go to explore the place that holds such a legendary status, both in my mind and in history.

After Mauritania, entering the vibrant, distinctly African colour of Tomboctou is akin to walking out of a strict Catholic girl's school and into a Bohemian nightclub. The women are tall, black and dressed in exotic panes of multicoloured fabric. They wear bright twists of material on their heads, on top of which they carry whatever it is they need to: water, produce, a sack of flour. Their arms are bare, and the panes of material part to reveal flashes of leg as they walk. They are confident and sexy, laughing and chattering. When they pass me on the street, they meet my eye and greet me cheerfully.

Although there are also Tuareg women clad in black *melekhva*, they, as their Arabic counterparts did, scurry away into their homes and remain largely hidden. But even their dress is less confined than the Arabic women. They are rarely fully veiled and their *melekhvas* are worn far back on their heads, showing thick ropes of plaited hair.

The women fascinate me. For months, I've been accustomed to coming into towns and finding women clad in the dark, tie-dyed shades of *melekhva* favoured by Saharawi. Although there are often colourful patterns, they remain swathed, hidden women. The life and colour of the culture has tended to be found either in the tents of the desert or behind closed doors, where the women have more power and exuberance. On the streets, I've been accustomed to being studied with latent curiosity by lounging men through cigarette smoke and the women being inaccessible, heads lowered and veiled.

In contrast, Tomboctou resounds with a vibrancy and diversity. Funky Malian rhythms and melodies blare from open doorways, rather than the wailing discordance of Arabic tunes. People laugh. Everywhere, I see wide-open smiles and heads tossed back in laughter. The roads are full of chattering men and women, neatly dressed adolescents and simple *fun*. It's almost like being in the middle of a perpetual carnival.

The roads are lined with shacks made of any material at hand – hessian, plastic bags, corrugated iron – and within them people sit to eat kebabs and sweet-potato chips, or whatever stew is on offer. The women sit and eat with the men, laughing.

I walk the street in my cotton trousers and top and attract no more than cursory attention. Despite its isolation, busloads of tourists arrive in Tomboctou regularly from the south, and the town is full of hustlers and salespeople accustomed to conning each new arrival. Several words in Arabic is enough to see me left largely alone; Tomboctou is also a place in which news travels quickly, and within a day it seems most of the hustlers know who I am and why I'm here.

I sit outside on a rough wooden seat in a cheerful African bar. The small courtyard is lit by tiny bulbs that glow as evening falls, and more local music is piped from a good stereo system. I can sit alone at last, undisturbed. There are several groups of tourists and Africans. I feel neither uncomfortable nor conspicuous.

I order my first beer in three months and sit back. I can smell meat being grilled in a clay-fired oven just around the corner, a mixture of dust and spicy richness. Tuareg men enter the bar and swish past me, nodding politely, leaving a pleasant aroma of incense in their wake. The table is chunky and roughly hewn, and a candle in a jar sits in the centre – such small things comfort me.

I become aware of voices speaking in English and turn around. A group of three girls are chatting excitedly around a table. They are about the same age as me, obviously here on holiday from London. I wait for all of a minute and ask if I can join them.

The girls are all fascinating, well-travelled artists and musicians, and good company. I feel instantly at home. We chat and laugh, and I feel the loneliness seep out of my bones.

Several times during the evening I am interrupted by Arabic men who have heard of my walk and have come to find me. They ask questions with great curiosity and treat me with respect. Some of them know Khabuss or Ali and are thrilled to talk about the country I have walked through. They ask me about who I met, and, in some cases, ask for news of tribe or family. I feel a real sense of pride in my walk. Perhaps it's a leftover from the long weeks of isolation, but I feel sure of my place here.

When I leave, it's with a promise to catch up with the English girls in a few nights. One of the gentle Tuareg men they have befriended drives me back to the hotel on his motorbike and wishes me goodnight politely. I wander into the hotel and have a good chat with the bartender before falling asleep in a haze of beer-induced contentment.

Four hours later, I wake up feeling as if a cattle truck has invaded my head. I drag myself to the bathroom and lie moaning on the floor, my pounding head resting against the cool tiles to ease the splitting pain. I can never remember hurting from alcohol so much. It seems that abstinence, hard work, antibiotics and beer really don't mix.

How surprising.

Tomboctou becomes a wonderful stop. I'm held up waiting for a parcel that has been sent through from England, containing yet more replacement satellite communications equipment. I visit Ali's family and eat the long-promised meat. Even better, this close to the Niger River, there is fresh produce. I taste my first fresh, crispy salad in months, savouring every mouthful. Ali and I meet up most evenings, whether I'm staying at his home or at the hotel and giggle in the bar over a beer or two. Ali is intrigued by the English girls and in awe of the generous backside of one in particular. The second he meets her, I have to stifle my amusement at the look of wonder and appreciation that spreads over his face.

He offers to sell me his camel, but I decline. I'm sure my camels have plenty of distance left in them, and the price Ali is asking is out of my budget. I gift him the rifle and a generous tip, since his care and good humour has been a boon for me throughout this stretch.

My budget was always tight but, only a third of the way into the trip, I've blown it out dramatically. The price of guides has been four times what I budgeted, largely because I'm paying danger money through the bandit areas, but also because in recent times tourism has exploded and is being exploited mercilessly. The bottom line is that a tourist in a four-wheel drive will pay thirty to fifty euros a day – simply for a guide to sit in the passenger seat and point out the sights. I was paying M'Barak and Madani five to ten euros a day each. Here, I'm trying to find good, hardworking guides who are prepared to walk and help with the camels for under forty euros a day – and struggling.

I'm aghast at how low my finances are. Mum is already dipping into her savings to keep me afloat. I'd originally planned for the purchase of new camels twice through the walk, and thought

I would buy the first in Tomboctou. Due to the blow-out in guide expenditure, I just can't afford it. I try to push money out of my mind; I can't remember a point when it *hasn't* been a problem. I just have to have faith it will turn up, somehow.

One night I eat with the Italian tour guides and their American group on the terrace of a house of one of the wealthier Arabs in town. We are seated at a long table with rich cushions placed on benches, surrounded by torches. It's an exotic scene of almost unimaginable luxury to me, and I feel privileged to be a part of it.

We are served a dish of lamb stuffed with couscous and fruit. I'm amused by the caution and hesitancy of the group as they mutter among themselves about whether the food is safe to eat or not. I have to restrain myself from scoffing it with abandon.

Between the Italians and our Arabic hosts, I hear anxious mutterings regarding the state of affairs in Niger. Tuareg rebellions against black African governments have been an ongoing feature in both Mali and Niger for decades, and have resulted in protracted and bloody conflicts. Both countries are in uneasy truces, but rumour suggests that turmoil is once again brewing in Niger. The Italians have stopped their tours there, although no firm news has come through.

Everybody is worried about bandits. When I meet Mahmoud once again with Ali, he talks in dark tones about the country we are about to walk through. I study his face on this second occasion and listen closely, trying to get a measure of the man. He seems to me a dour soul, looking for the negative aspects in everything. There is none of the twinkling humour of Ali or the calm easiness of Mohammed. I wonder uneasily if I should tell Ali that I want to renege on our initial agreement. But I also think that perhaps this is just the changing of culture, a new way of being. I have no experience of life in Mali and am not certain if Mahmoud's demeanour is more characteristic of cultural difference than personal fault.

He does seem very knowledgeable about the route, and Ali has known him for years. I'm assured that Mahmoud is a very hard worker. I watch him once loading up some camels of a relation, and he is obviously highly competent. I suppress my unease and agree that we will leave in a couple of days.

Ali bids me goodbye the day before I am due to leave. Satisfied after his nights with Malian wenches, and having delivered wealth to his Malian family, he is heading back to Mauritania. I can see by his face that he would far prefer to stay.

We part with promises to stay in touch, and I sadly watch him go.

I've left my camels outside of town to graze: they were looking thin after the Tomboctou haul. I want them to rest and fatten up so that we can head into the next long stretch fresh and fit. But I'm not worried about feed for the camels. After all, this next leg will have us close to the banks of the Niger River, and surely feed will be plentiful there.

Chapter Sixteen

We walk out of Tomboctou on a bright, sun-filled morning, trailed through town by a procession of the English girls I met and a crowd of laughing, playing children. It's a farewell to a place I've thoroughly enjoyed, but already a nagging presentiment is dogging me.

The camels are far from well. After delivering them into what I thought were the trusted hands of Ali's relative, it's plain to me that they haven't been grazing on good feed, but rather scrabbling at the meagre weeds on the edge of town. They're thin and drawn, in no better shape than when we arrived – worse, in fact.

'Your camels are tired,' Mahmoud muttered with a pessimist's satisfaction as we packed up that morning. 'They have walked too far. They might not make it to Gao.'

I'm still seething over his comments as we make our way out onto the plateau, leaving the town behind. I'm familiar enough with my own faults so I recognise that part of my anger is directed at myself. I *knew* that my camels needed to eat well, and I should have gone with the nomad to ensure they were grazing on the rich feed ten kilometres from town. Instead, I'd been so tired when I arrived in Tomboctou that I was all too willing to delegate the responsibility for their welfare to someone I didn't even know.

My camels are not exhausted, but they were certainly losing condition when we arrived. I've seen this before, in Morocco, and I know that ten days of solid rest and good feed can make an enormous difference to camels when they are still in reasonably good condition and used to long journeys. But conversely, when they are tired, camels can be listless in their search for food and need to be led to good grazing. I'm deeply concerned about their welfare.

My self-criticism is not restricted to the camels. From the moment we began packing this morning, my initial scepticism regarding Mahmoud's character has grown by the hour. If I'd thought Harraba abrasive and uncooperative, Mahmoud is proving downright aggressive. Before leaving town, we've already come into direct conflict on a number of occasions, and on each one he has confronted me with belligerence and contempt.

Already, I know I've made a mistake by hiring him. I feel a wave of despair within: *how, after the debacles of Harraba and Mohammed Le Min, could I have made such a stupid error – particularly when I had felt uncomfortable from the start? When am I going to begin to trust my own instincts?* I walk along wondering when I will ever get it right.

We walk in an uneasy silence, Mahmoud running off in various directions, carrying his axe over his shoulders, hacking at a tree root here and there in search of a good piece with which to construct his *dhabuz*, his walking stick. Both the camels and I find his abrupt movements unsettling; I can feel my animals jumping with shock when he abruptly cries out and races off or suddenly pops up beside us again. He's not interested in walking close by the caravan, but instead often walks so far ahead of me that he is a mere blur in the distance.

We stop and make camp. Mahmoud waves me away impatiently when I begin to make a fire for tea. Not, as Mohammed would, because he wants to save me work. He thinks I don't know what I'm doing.

He makes a small, finicky fire, muttering in frustration. He snatches the teapot from my hands, tells me I'm doing it wrong and proceeds to make a pot of thick, bitter tea. He criticises the way I have constructed the camp and rolls out his own woven bamboo mat, setting up an entire little section for himself in the most sheltered area. I'm pushed out in the wind and forced to create a new section for myself.

I serve the tinned sardines, bread, nuts and biscuits that usually constitute lunch. Mahmoud won't eat with his hands from the same plate as me. He has brought his own large wooden spoon. I had read that this is not unusual for Tuareg, but Mahmoud is an Arab, and I find his actions – even if they are unthinking – deeply insulting. I had seen him eat with his family from the same plate with his hands, and he has been made well aware of the way my camp runs by Ali. There is a thinly veiled hostility in his every action.

As I serve the meal, Mahmoud holds out his own large cup and shakes it inches from my face.

'*Dilly hoon! DILLY HOON!*' he insists, indicating that I should pour him some water. The jerry can is actually right next to him; I wonder if I've perhaps misinterpreted his meaning. I reach for the water and pour. He sits back and slurps with loud, grunting satisfaction. When he looks at me, I see a gleam of triumph in his eyes.

Oh no, I think with growing dread, *I'm in real trouble with this one.*

No more than an hour passes before he taps me on the shoulder. 'When is lunch?' he asks, frowning. I look at him in bemusement.

'We have eaten. I will cook dinner on sunset,' I say. He stares at me in disbelief. Suddenly he throws his hands up in the air and begins to spew vitriol.

Do I expect a man to work on an empty stomach? He needs two proper meals a day! Tinned sardines and bread is not a meal! He needs a proper pot of something. He is not walking all the way to Menaka with no decent cooking. I am lazy and inconsiderate, and he is a MAN, do I hear him? A MAN! I am a woman – now *cook!*

I am so stunned my mouth actually hangs open.

In all the time I've been in the desert, never once have I been spoken to like this. In fact, no matter how deeply I may have unwittingly insulted people at various times, it has been a notable characteristic of nomads whom I've met to neither take offence nor reproach me with anything but embarrassed, apologetic tact. In turn, I've learned to mask my annoyances or irritation and approach any potential conflict with a great deal of calm and humour. I may not always have entirely succeeded, but the exceptions have been rare and regretted immensely.

I just shake my head.

'The supplies are there,' I say quietly, indicating the baggage. 'Please feel free to take what you need and cook what you want.' And I get up and walk away.

As I go, I can hear Mahmoud raging at my incompetence and laziness. He bangs the pots and shrieks his discontent to God, lamenting his own inability to cook and my uncaring nature for leading him into the wilderness and leaving him to starve.

I go to commune with the camels.

They are lying in the sparse shade of the scraggly trees around us. This is another point of tension that has already arisen: the feed here is terrible. Earlier Mahmoud had suggested we make camp here. I wanted to continue to better country, but he had waved his hands helplessly and said that this is as good as it gets for miles. Now I can feel the tension in my belly morphing into a stone of worry.

I try to think things through calmly.

I'm already slightly behind schedule and do not want to return to Tomboctou and try to hire another guide. If worst comes to worst, the town of Gao is only a couple weeks' walk away – I can sack Mahmoud there. I have paid him half of the agreed fee in Tomboctou, with the other half to be paid in Menaka; if I drop him off at Gao, I need pay no more than the initial half. In the meantime, I need to break down the dangerous barrier that has risen between us and attempt to be conciliatory yet firm. The task of running the camp effectively is up to me. I need to find solutions rather than sulk.

I return to the camp and begin to cook dinner.

'I understand that you are accustomed to eating two hot meals a day,' I tell him. 'I've never worked that way in my camp before, and I've not bought rations to cover it. However, I'm happy for you to eat the pasta and tinned sardines that are in the stores, if you don't mind cooking for yourself. I try to keep the tuna for the dinner meal, so I would appreciate it if you stuck to sardines at lunch. But if there is anything else you would like from the stores, what is there is yours. Does this make it easier for you?'

Mahmoud grunts and shakes his head in disgust, but he can see that I'm extending an olive branch.

'Yes, I suppose that will be fine,' he says reluctantly. 'I'm a man, you know. I need to eat.'

'I understand that,' I tell him. 'I'm sorry that I didn't ask you about meals before we left – I thought Ali had explained things to you. I should have checked.'

On sunset I make the tea, which is usually drunk after prayer and before the meal. Mahmoud has been praying loudly and with great enthusiasm for twenty minutes. All of my guides pray with differing levels of commitment, but I've never known one to go into such detail as this. I sit and wait, the tea getting cold and my usual enjoyment of the quiet dusk disturbed by his passionate supplication to Allah.

He ends his prayers by stepping back and forth in a ritual fashion across the fire. I find myself fervently praying he will fall in.

When he finally sits down, it is to criticise the tea (again); refuse to eat from the same plate as me (again); and to snort in disgust at the meal over which I have laboured with particular care. I look at him in something akin to desperation.

'Mahmoud, why won't you eat from the same plate as me, with your hands?' I ask directly. 'In this camp, we are family. All of my guides have eaten with me as family. I am confused why you will not.'

Mahmoud barely looks up as he answers. 'You are white. You are a woman. And you are not Muslim. I cannot eat with you.' He turns his back on me and eats in silence.

And that's it – that's the sum total of Mahmoud's opinion of me. I settle back into my lonely, windy corner and eat my small plate of rice and tuna.

It's going to be a long haul to Gao.

⇛⇚

We're walking through poor, scrubby country. The feed is too sparse to sustain the camels. Some days we walk miles further than I would like in search of better feed. We never find it.

I'm caught in an ongoing, futile debate with Mahmoud over our route. I want to walk close to the Niger River, where logic tells me vegetation will be more plentiful. The other alternative is to cut up north about fifty kilometres, into deeper and wilder desert – my map shows a good valley and waterholes in that area.

But Mahmoud insists on taking a course that is halfway in between. He is afraid of the northern route, saying that it is bandit-ridden and dangerous. He believes the route close to the river, along which are clustered small villages, will attract too much attention.

I feel stifled by his negativity and sceptical of his analysis. We are walking close to all the major routes through the desert – the worst place to encounter bandits, in my experience. I would prefer to either head into the deep desert of the north or take my chances with the villagers and know there is good feed.

On occasion, I simply change course, heading down towards the river. Mahmoud and I come close to blows at these times. As the camels become increasingly worn and thin, my reaction becomes more desperate. I try to think things through logically, to find a solution to the dangerous stand-off that is developing, but there is a fundamental fault in our working relationship that I have never – even in the depths of my experience with Harraba – encountered.

Mahmoud considers me beneath his contempt. In his opinion, I am out of my depth and attempting an impossible feat. The chain of communication has been broken. Where Khabuss informed Mohammed, who in turn informed Ali, of the background to my walk and the distances I have travelled, it is plain that Ali did not pass the same degree of information on to Mahmoud. Or, if he did, Mahmoud simply discounted it as lies.

Only once does the confrontation become truly dangerous between us.

I've been away from the camp, sitting with the camels as I do every day now. In the late afternoon I walk back to the camp, and Mahmoud bursts upright and runs over to me.

'Where have you been? I have been looking everywhere for you!' he is shouting in my face.

'I was with the camels. I told you where I was going.' I speak calmly, holding his eye and my position.

'I couldn't find the rice! I haven't eaten! You stupid, stupid woman. You don't just walk away from me.' He is breathing hard, spit at his mouth.

For one very slow, clear moment, Mahmoud raises the hand that I have watched with wariness ever since we left Tomboctou.

I can see in his eyes that he is quite serious about slamming it into my face. I have seen this coming for some time now.

I step an inch closer, not taking my eyes away from his face, and for a second I let him see the anger and strength that I have kept well hidden these past days. At the same time, I put my hand to my belt and show the knife hilt grasped in my hand. I almost will him to do it, to go ahead and hit me. Right at that moment, I know I would happily stick him and watch the stupid pride and fury leach out of him.

But he wasn't expecting it. A sudden light of awareness dawns on his face, and he backs down. He actually puts his hands up in a gesture of defence.

I do not move an inch. I force a neutral expression on my face, but he has already seen everything he needed to in my eyes. He backs away, muttering, and stamps off back to the camp.

I'm shaking, but I'm not afraid. He needs to know that raising a hand to me is never an option, and I'm not sorry it has come to this. I know I will need to sleep with one eye open from here in, but I also know that it is time for him to go – pronto.

But I'm in a remote section of the desert, and the village-dwellers in along the river herd cattle; they're black Africans from the Songhai tribe who grow crops and fish. They're not camel men. In addition, I do not speak Tamashek, the Tuareg language, or any of the multitude of African dialects. It would be very hard for me to enter one of the villages, sack Mahmoud and hire some-one else. And without the language of the region, I do not feel comfortable walking alone.

Mahmoud himself makes no secret of his desire to finish

walking. He complains every time we stop. 'I am too old for this,' he moans. 'In Gao, you find another guide. I am too tired, too sick. I cannot do this anymore . . .'

I'm quite sure that he does not mean to relinquish the money he has been promised when we reach Menaka. He just wants to be paid in full and leave before the job is done. But I have other ideas.

I think incessantly as I walk, trying to find a rational response to the dilemma, to apply analytical thought to a problem that feels as if it's sucking me under.

The country itself is dispiriting.

One day, we come across a small hut not far from a well. For days we have been passing huts full of children suffering with malaria. I have given out nearly my whole supply of chloroquine, but I know that for many of them it is just too late. At this hut, a skeletal woman stumbles out, holding her small son in her arms. He is naked and burning to the touch. She puts him on the ground, begging for help, and he squats to defecate.

Half of his intestine falls onto the ground.

It's all I can do not to vomit. I kneel down and cuddle him, handing his mother what medication I can. I give her some food supplies and tell her how to prepare a thin gruel that he may be able to stomach. But I know it's already too late. The woman's face is resigned. She tells me it is the fourth child she has lost this season to malaria.

I walk away feeling ill and helpless, ashamed that I walk through this country as a tourist – that I'm on *holiday* – amid such misery. The sheer helplessness of the situation rolls over me like a tsunami. It's so hard to imagine that there is simply no help to be had, no hospital that will magically make something better, no doctor in a white coat to wave a wand and heal that child.

I've dressed so many horrible wounds now – me, who has always hated that stuff. I'm a 'Westerner' here, and that means I'm a shop, doctor, charity and bank, all rolled into one. I dress serious burns on children who have fallen into fires; infected prickle sores that are festering for lack of treatment; deep wounds from mishaps with knives or other tools. There are children with malnutrition, eye infections and a dozen varied, serious illnesses that I cannot identify. Half the time I just hand over some aspirin and act reassuringly.

As the days roll by, my sense of helplessness combines with travel weariness, and I find myself very despondent. The camels are emaciated and utterly exhausted. They won't even eat, just lie down in defeat, like I feel like doing. I don't even know if they will make it to Gao – they have nothing left. If I had money, I could buy more from the nomads camped here, but I don't and I can't. I feel like I've failed those animals and myself, and I can't see a way forward. I walked out of Tomboctou lulled into such a false sense of security; I felt so on top of my game. I feel as if I should be past this kind of stuff now, and it shakes my confidence.

I can't find the exotica in the things I used to. I read over my old diary, from the first time I was in the desert, and remember how thrilled and excited I was in those initial months, how it felt as though I was finally doing *exactly* what I was meant to. In many ways the landscapes and cultures are more exotic now, and yet I am unmoved. I am too worried about camels and baggage and wells and Mahmoud to stop, take a picture and just *breathe*. I have become a woman on a mission rather than a traveller and, although I see the necessity of it, I don't always like the compromise. No guide or tough stretch can extinguish my love of the desert – just cloud my appreciation of it for a while.

But so much of it here is trodden and occupied; I sometimes think there is no corner of the Sahara that man and his beasts have not infiltrated. I miss the sense of complete solitude that you get in the Australian bush. Right now, I miss life in Australia full stop. Every bit of the laid-back ease of it.

We are walking along a well-worn four-wheel-drive track. I've given up arguing about this. Mahmoud knows I hate walking where vehicles are likely to pass but insists he feels safer here. I don't. I've seen too many vehicles passing us carrying men dressed in military uniform and carrying guns to feel any level of security. Mahmoud tells me they are army. I don't care – they look dicey.

Far ahead an old four-wheel drive trayback is hurtling toward us. It's weaving erratically on and off the track, and I can see dark-clad men leaning out of the sides of the tray.

I can also see a machine-gun mounted on a tripod perched over the roof.

Mahmoud, as usual, is way off to the side, making his usual mysterious forays into who knows where. I can't see him, and I start leading the camels off the track and away from the path of the vehicle.

There is no scrub to speak of and I'm dangerously exposed. I lead the camels in a sharp angle away from the road, but the vehicle alters its course and comes screaming in my direction. I look around and see Mahmoud sprinting towards me, bellowing something, but his words are already lost in the roar of the vehicle.

For a moment I think the trayback is just slightly off course, but in a horrible, slow-motion reality check it's clear that he's aiming straight for me. I put my head down and just keep walking. I've been the object of overt curiosity many times; in my experience, head down forward motion is the best defence.

The vehicle screams alongside, about twenty metres to my left. From the corner of my eye I can see three men in the front seat and six in the back. They wear a ragtag combination of old military-style fatigues, turbans and odd clothes. The vehicle doesn't look like government issue; I'm almost certain it's contraband. But smugglers are usually low-key and rarely sport mounted machine-guns. In fact, every one of these guys is holding a weapon.

The men are yelling and waving their guns. The vehicle performs several crazy doughnuts on my left side, then slowly loops around behind me. I walk on and hope they will just keep driving, but I hear the roar of the motor coming up behind me again, and they pass on the right side, circling closer.

Mahmoud is frantic now.

'Bandits!' he screams. 'You need to drop the camels and run!'

I look at him in contempt. 'Just keep walking,' I say through gritted teeth. No way in hell am I dropping my camels and running.

He looms over me and spouts in voluble Arabic, swearing unintelligibly. I tune him out – I'm watching the vehicle.

About fifty metres ahead, it turns again and races straight for us. The camels are jumping and unsettled, but walking steadily enough behind me. Again, the vehicle passes and loops around. Again, it is closer. I can actually see the face of one man in particular; he is standing up in the back and instructing the driver. His eyes have a wild, manic look. I've seen it before; I would swear he is coked up.

As the vehicle once again turns to face us, Crazy Man suddenly aims his machine-gun at the sky and lets off a round. It takes me a second to equate the sharp popping noise with the weapon in his hand. To my complete amazement, the camels don't falter for a second; they don't even seem to hear it. For some reason, this will always be the main thing that I remember from the incident.

I don't know what I'm supposed to feel. I've no real idea what to do. But it seems to me right then that if I stop, if I show fear, it will go badly for me. For thousands of kilometres now, I have walked through it. Suddenly all I can do is exactly that. I put one foot in front of another, head down. In my mind I hear the words like a mantra: *don't make eye contact, don't interact, don't show fear. Just keep walking, keep walking, keep going . . .*

The vehicle slowly approaches. My legs feel like jelly and I can't bear to look up, but some instinct tells me that to turn and run would be fatal – this is still a game to them.

Twenty metres out, Crazy Man aims the mounted machine-gun and lays down a row of bullets right in front of me. The dirt flies up where they hit. He is telling me to stop. The others are laughing, but there is an edge of fear in their voices. Some of them discharge their weapons into the air, others off to the sides. They are all whacked on something; their movements are jerky and uncoordinated, their faces uncomprehending.

I come slowly to a halt, but I still don't look up. Mahmoud is holding is hands out placatingly, trying to talk to the men in a variety of languages. But they are not interested in Mahmoud; they're staring at me. I can feel them.

Crazy Man leaps down from the vehicle and swaggers over. Three of his friends get out of the back and lounge next to the tray, smoking, weapons pointed loosely at the ground. Mahmoud stands in front of me and suddenly his calm tone turns to one of belligerence. I want to scream at him to shut up, just *shut up* and let me handle this, but he won't. He just gets more and more hysterical.

Abruptly, Crazy Man punches him in the face and knocks him to one side. It's the careless violence of his actions that unnerves me. I still don't look up.

The other men come over and push Mahmoud between them, laughing. They take idle swings, punching him in the face. He's weeping now and begging them to stop. He's also telling them that I have money and supplies, to take what they want.

Crazy Man points his gun at me.

He says something in a dialect I don't understand. Then he makes the unmistakeable gesture of rubbing his fingers together, right in front of my face, and says in French, 'Money'.

'I have some money with me,' I reply, not looking at him. 'I can get it for you. Please leave my guide alone.'

He doesn't understand me and yells out to his friends in the same dialect. I tell Mahmoud what I mean in Arabic, and he translates.

Crazy Man gestures towards the camels.

I couch Bolshy Sod. In Tomboctou I sewed all of my extra cash into the saddles, except for emergency money of about AU$400, which is in an easily accessible bag on Bolshy. I have Khabuz to thank for this precaution; he had advised me to do it months ago, but I only just got around to it.

I take out the AU$400, which is in Malian currency, and proffer it. I try not to look at where Mahmoud is cowering, his face bashed, nose streaming blood. I've no idea what the men are going to do. I'm on a weird autopilot and all I really feel is anger, but I don't want them to see it burning in my face, in my eyes. I'm scared of what they will do.

Crazy Man counts the money and stuffs it in the pocket of his fatigues. He pokes me in the chest with his gun and says something. I understand by his actions that he wants to know if there is any more money.

I hold my hands out in a gesture that says, *This is all I have.* He begins to scrabble through the baggage on Bolshy, but it's a feeble attempt. After seeing there is simply stores in most of the bags, he gives up. I'm grateful that the strongbox with my digital equipment is at the bottom of the panniers.

He backs off, then raises his gun into the air and shoots again, a sudden burst of fire that makes my heart stop momentarily, then thud in my chest. Now is the dangerous time, I know it. *Is he going to shoot me? What the hell is he going to do?*

I turn around and get Bolshy Sod up. I feel that if I just deal with the camels – do *something* – that I will be all right.

Don't look.

I begin to lead the camels slowly again. Mahmoud is copping a few kicks off to my right. I don't look at him either. I can still hear him saying in Arabic to take *me*, that he is one of them. I don't care right now if they kill him.

I walk right next to the vehicle and the men sitting in the cabin stare at me as they smoke. I keep my eyes down.

From behind me I hear another burst of fire, and the back camel, Beiyal, skitters about. For the first time, I'm blindly furious. *If that bastard kills my camels, I'll have him*, I think, and it's like a red curtain of rage comes down in my mind.

I keep walking.

I'm past the truck. I can hear them chattering and Mahmoud pleading. I hear someone scurrying up behind me and I tense, waiting for the attack, wondering what the hell to do when it comes.

But it is Mahmoud, wiping his face and hurrying, telling me to drop the camels and run.

I keep walking.

His pride won't let him run without me, so he falls in step. Behind us I can hear the sounds of the men climbing back into the truck. As the engine starts my heart begins to thud again, and I wonder what will happen now.

The vehicle circles us. Once, twice, three times – close enough that I could touch the sides. The men in the back are screaming and laughing, firing into the air, waving their guns.

And then suddenly they are gone.

For long moments I walk with my head down, listening to their engine fading into the distance. Even when I can hear it no more I keep walking, ignoring Mahmoud's flood of speech, blank to everything. I just walk until I'm sure I cannot hear that vehicle anymore, until I'm sure they are gone.

And then I pull off into the first bit of scrub I find and unload the camels.

'That's why I don't like to walk close to roads,' I say to Mahmoud. He looks at me incredulously. They are the first words I've spoken to him since we saw the men. Over an hour has passed since they left.

He begins to scream at me, waving his arms in the air, indicating his wounds and his terror . . .

And I can't look at him – I can't even think – all I can do is make a fire and smoke cigarette after cigarette and drink tea. I listen to my heart pounding in my chest and think: *Thank God they didn't kill my camels.*

And I don't know why, nor will I for years to come, but I don't think for one moment about whether or not they wanted to kill me.

Mahmoud and I are done. He knows it; I know it. We talk little about the incident mainly because I simply refuse to. The little I do glean is that the bandits were from another African country – Guinea, Mahmoud says – and were running drugs. They certainly bore no resemblance to any nomad I dealt with in the Sahara and were probably nothing more than opportunistic criminals.

The one and only thing Mahmoud makes pointedly clear is that he does not want me to ever mention the incident to anyone else. He gives me many reasons for this, most of them to do with honour and patriotism. I assure him I will never speak of it to another guide nor write about it on my website. I will stay true to my word the entire duration of my walk.

I was angry and fed up with Mahmoud before the incident, and
it only gets worse in the days after. Every trivial annoyance feeds
my frustration.

Very quickly, though, I make my mind up. No matter what
other life-and-death issues we have faced, I've simply had enough.
It's time I smiled again and took control. This is my walk and my
life, and only I can fix it.

I leave Mahmoud and the camels in a patch of good feed with
the bulk of the supplies. There is a village nearby, and the local
nomads have told us there's a transport truck that runs from there
to Gao every market day, which is today. I walk the ten kilometres to the village. It's time to go to Gao and get another guide.

The vibrant bustle of the village cheers me immediately. The sight
of the river itself is the first thing that lifts my spirits: a great,
silvery swathe of glistening water, teeming with stock and fisher-
men. It is bounded in some areas by desert sand and in others by
green growth. It seems so incongruous after the barren wasteland
I've walked through, and the scent of it alone is thrilling.

The market is a chaotic mass of the usual makeshift humpies,
beneath which any manner of wares are for sale. Fresh produce
jostles alongside folds of brilliant cloth. The brightly coloured turbans favoured by Tuareg men hang next to fanciful slippers. One
entire section is devoted to men sitting on blankets with piles of
different grades of tobacco and snuff before them.

I'm fascinated by the villagers. If Tomboctou had seemed a
mélange of Arabic and African culture, here I feel deeply immersed
in black Africa. Only rarely do I see the telltale dress of a desert
nomad. Most of the people here are river-dwellers. Fisherman walk
past carrying their catch tied to long poles or in wire baskets.
Children run around with trays on their heads, selling fresh fruit and
deep-fried treats in plastic packets. It feels impossibly rich for a desert
town, so unlike the scrabbling settlements I am accustomed to.

Like Tomboctou, I sense a general lack of sexual tension – the
African women openly breastfeed, young women are clad in tight

wraparound long skirts and short-sleeved tops. Everything is bright and cheerful.

I find the truck that is going to Gao later that afternoon. It's a standard cattle truck – just an old engine with a wooden-based stock crate on the back, covered only by a few metal bars over the top. I've often seen these passing me, ever since Morocco, but have never travelled in one. The men begin to load it. Sacks of grain are thrown in, hen coops tied to the metal bars at the top. I eye the growing pile of stores warily and wonder where it will all fit. I'm informed that we won't be leaving for a few hours.

After several experiences with African transport, I decide to eat a good meal and stock up on water before we leave, not to mention have a wash and go to the toilet. I find a meat stall, the carcasses of beef hanging from a wooden pole. A tall Songhai man hacks at the beef with a machete, his cigarette dropping ash onto the meat, and shovels the pieces into a clay oven. I pay him for a kilo and he serves the roasted meat on paper with chopped onion and spices. I sit on the woven mat floor and savour every bite – especially the dripping rich fat, which I never ate on meat before I began walking.

A gaggle of boys hangs around the tent, watching me shyly. One of them comes forward and hands me a glass of tea to wash my meat down. I smile and proffer some money, but he declines, giggling, and he and his friends squat and stare as I eat.

I wash my hands and wander over to the truck, where the driver and his young assistants are sprawled beneath it in the shade. They move over and offer me some space, and we chat in French about good places to stay in Gao. One offers to show me a bungalow and camping place favoured by budget travellers: Camping Bangu. When they spy my camera, the boys come to life and begin to pose, asking me to take photos. Within seconds, I'm surrounded by villagers clamouring for portraits, pointing and laughing when they see the digital result.

Finally, the boys begin to load the truck in earnest. One of them shows me a place up at the front of the stock crate, where he has placed some softer sacks, and tells me to get in. It's still some time before they will be ready to leave, but I know he is trying to secure me a good seat, and I climb in gratefully.

An hour later I'm more grateful than ever. The loading of stores is done, and the crate is piled more than halfway up the sides with everything from machinery to blankets, goats, chickens and boxes of produce. Containers and sacks overhead. When people begin to climb in, they jostle for every square inch of space. I find myself jammed up against an oddly shaped piece of machinery wrapped in an old cloth, my knees up against my chin, water bottle in my lap. I'm surrounded by three women, all with babies, one of whom immediately thrusts the younger of her children onto my lap with a big smile. I clasp the precious bundle with a rush of happiness; the beautiful little girl stares up at me with big, placid eyes, coos contentedly and goes back to sleep. Her mother clasps my hand briefly and all the women beam. I beam right back.

Men stand behind me, holding on to the steel poles overhead for support. There is no room for them to sit.

I can't see anything but the sky. The truck rattles to life, and I hear the sound of a dozen hands on the sides. The standing men yell encouragement to those outside, who are pushing the truck forwards. The engine catches and the vehicle begins to lumber heavily on its way. The young men run alongside, then swing themselves up onto the steel poles and settle in on top of the cabin, hanging on precariously. There isn't an inch of the truck that doesn't have someone dangling off it.

In the late afternoon, the heat in the crate is intense. As long as we're in motion there is some air movement, but for the most part I slip into the half-doze I have become so accustomed to assuming on long trips, swaying in the heavy press of bodies with the movement of the truck, letting the sweat gather and pool where it will. Only when I move slightly do I notice that my body is soaked in sweat. Any movement means one's neighbour is disturbed, so I don't tend to shift.

Opposite me, a large black women occupies quite an amount of space. She is loud and cheerful, and the men respond to her obviously bawdy humour with smiles of deference. Within moments of settling in she has taken responsibility for several of the children around her, arranging them in a crook of her arm or on a knee.

Her hands intrigue me – they are enormous, gnarled and tough. I have never seen such capable hands on a woman. When I was younger, I always disliked my own hands. 'Peasant hands', an old workmate of mine once referred to them jokingly. I longed for the tapered, elegant fingers of a piano player – the slender, oblong nails – instead of the square stockiness of my own. But I look at the magnificent paws of that woman and imagine just what they have done in their time, what lives they have held and the unceasing tasks they have managed. How shallow Western perceptions of beauty are in the face of such competent, wise toil.

The truck trundles laboriously through the afternoon and into the dusk. Above me the sky fades into the pastel velvets I love, and for once I've no dinner to prepare and can just sit here and enjoy the change. We stop on sunset for prayer and climb up and over the sides of the crate, handing babies from one to the other so everybody can scramble down and relieve themselves.

It's on rides like this that *melekhva* makes total sense, and why I chose to wear a sarong with cotton trousers beneath. On the side of a lonely desert track there are rarely bushes to hide behind. African women just squat, the copious folds of material providing adequate privacy. My sarong performs the same function. Like the Muslims all around me praying, I wash in the ritual manner, using my jerry can – hands, face, neck, arms and feet – then put on some of the scented oil I carry in a small bottle wrapped in my headscarf. I found long ago that staying clean and smelling nice is the difference between discomfort and good cheer on these journeys.

Through the dusk and into the evening we trundle, stopping at every small settlement – sometimes where there doesn't seem to be anything at all – for a family to jump on or a bundle to be dropped off. When the truck bogs in deep sand, the boys leap down from the roof and run in front, laying down the sand traps then pounding the cabin when the tyres are clear. They swing themselves back up, their muscles standing out like iron cords; they are rarely still for more than ten minutes.

Above me the stars emerge in pinpricks and the sky sinks into inky blackness. I rock against the women, and the baby lies quietly asleep. Every few hours she wakes up, and her mother breastfeeds her and hands her back. Occasionally I shift her position and she reaches out with tiny hands and kneads my skin, snuffling happily. Over the course of the journey I acquire a couple more children, who stare at me sleepily before passing out across my legs.

We stop and eat at roadside stalls, fresh fish grilled and stuck in bread. I can hear the river and smell its salty heaviness. It strikes a note of nostalgia deep inside, and I feel suddenly homesick for the pungent, thick mud scent of big rivers like the Murray at the end of a blistering summer's day.

There's something wonderful and reassuring about being a part of this passive journey, of just sitting and being transported from one place to another, with no effort on my part. In the middle of the cool night breeze I wonder idly what it would have been like if I had simply chosen to travel Africa like this, on local transport, bouncing along from one place to another. I wonder why I have to be such a hard-nosed purist.

In the early hours of the morning we reach Gao. A journey of 200 kilometres has taken ten hours.

I kiss the women and babies goodbye and take a taxi to the Camping Bangu, where a sleepy young boy shows me up onto the earthen terrace. He waves off my offers of money until the morning. I wash from my jerry can, roll my swag out and fall asleep immediately.

I rise before dawn. I'm on a mission and don't want to waste any time.

As day breaks I'm sitting in the central part of the *auberge* grounds and, as soon as they arise, the young boys who work places like this come over to ask me what I'm doing here, what I'd like to eat – the usual tourist-related questions.

I pick the most senior, communicative guy and explain that I'm looking for a guide; it's a matter of urgency. I describe exactly what I'm looking for and say that I'm going into town to spread the word. He assures me he knows some people, and we agree to meet back at the Camping Bangu that afternoon so I can talk with his friends.

I walk along the dusty road into Gao. It's a big, prosperous city, more so than Tomboctou. The centre is full of proper shops, and some of the roads are sealed. There are restaurants and bars, and a market that sells every provision I could want. The relaxed attitude is similar to Tomboctou but, like the previous village, more African than Bedouin in nature. While I stand out because of my colour, it is again obvious that the men don't have the same level of intense interest, despite the fact that the majority are Muslim. Gao feels like another more sensual, light-hearted culture than in Mauritania.

I eat breakfast from a street stall overlooking the bustling river's edge. Everywhere are women cooking stews in enormous pots and big trays of freshly caught fish. I eat some deep-fried, donut-like balls, sweetened with sugar, and imbibe the world around me. It feels so rich and interesting, and I'm glad I will be coming back to Gao to stay for a while.

I talk around town, targeting the more obviously Arab men I see, simply because I have the language to communicate with them. This approach is not overly productive, given I'm looking for a Tuareg guide.

I'm more firm in my decision to hire a Tuareg because of the racist currents running through the exchanges I have with the Arabs. To a man, they are scathing in their assessment of both the black Africans and the Tuareg. The Arabs are here for business and have no interest in, or respect for, this culture. Also, in the conversations I have with these men, I feel conscious once again of myself as a woman – scrutinised and assessed. I find plenty of Mahmoud's dismissive contempt.

I head back to the camping ground.

I'm greeted eagerly by the camping boys, who push forward a young, wiry Tuareg bloke dressed in modern clothes. He greets me quietly in French. His name is Moussa and he is from Menaka, the town I'm headed to after Gao.

Moussa speaks all eight of the local dialects, including Arabic. His French is fluent and he has worked a lot with tourists. He has travelled from where I'm camped back to Menaka many times, grazing his family's herds. His family is originally from the Kidal region of Northern Mali – the centre of the 1990–95 Tuareg rebellion against the black African government. Moussa himself was involved in the conflict. Many of the local bandits are people he knows. In short, he is exactly what I'm looking for.

Most importantly, I like him. He meets my eye and talks calmly, without false pride. He readily admits that he has worked more with donkeys and goats than camels; he knows how to handle the animals, but doesn't pretend to be an expert. This doesn't bother me, since I'm more than comfortable now with the actual handling of the camels. My questions revolve more around grazing routes and camp habits. I question him in great detail. I don't mention the shooting incident with the bandits. I'm almost certain that Mahmoud won't bring it up, either.

'You are used to the walk?' I ask, using the French term, *le marche*. I always let my guides know from the outset that I walk twenty-five to thirty kilometres a day. I need to know they are accustomed to such distances.

Moussa laughs. 'All my life, I make *le marche*,' he says. 'This is easy for me.' I'm reassured, for now.

We agree to a deal, and he doesn't demand an extortionate price. I tell him about Mahmoud and that I'm expecting a degree of hostility when I relieve him of his duties. Moussa chuckles as I explain, as diplomatically as possible, why I need to sack him.

His manner reminds me of Madani. I know that he is a young man and perhaps a little addicted to town life – he chain-smokes and drinks several beers while we talk, and I can sense the rascal in his chatter with the others. But I'm vastly relieved to be travelling with someone who is at home in the country and culture, and I feel as sure as I can be of his good nature.

We agree to travel back to the camp in the vehicle of his friend, Omar, the next day.

I've been quite honest with Mahmoud about going to Gao to find a new guide. He has complained incessantly from Tomboctou that he is too old and sick for the journey; not a day has passed when he hasn't moaned that he's struggling with the distance and the trauma of hard work. He was more than happy to be left with the camels, lying about idly for a few days and eating my supplies.

What I've not mentioned is that I won't be paying him the other half of his agreed fee. I decided that in the interests of wanting to come back to find my camels safe and my baggage intact, this is one detail that's best left until the last minute. Right now, Mahmoud is laughing, thinking that he will be paid in full for a job only half done. A good deal, from his perspective. I'm not looking forward to breaking the truth to him.

Moussa grins and tells me he is sure we will handle it between us.

We drive back to the camp in a relatively new four-wheel drive in less than a third of the time the truck took. I've paid for the petrol and a nominal fee – it's worth it to get us back to the camp in good time – and a good mental state.

Mahmoud makes a big show of greeting us, but he eyes Moussa with disdain, which the younger man cheerfully ignores. I wryly note that Mahmoud has already bundled his belongings up, ready to leave. In the bundle I spy two of my camel blankets and several bags of stores.

I calmly hand over the roll of bills that constitute his fare back to Tomboctou and a small tip. I know better than to leave him with nothing. I'm sure he has left all his money with the family back in Tomboctou in anticipation of the second half of his pay.

I walk away and wait beside the car for the inevitable eruption.

Seconds late Mahmoud walks over to me, his face a screwed-up picture of alarmed bemusement.

'What is this?' He asks, shoving his hand beneath my nose. 'Where is my money?'

'I paid you half of the agreed price in Tomboctou,' I begin, already knowing how this is going to play out. 'You've walked less than half the distance to Menaka, so I've given you the money to get home, plus a bit extra because you stayed here with the camels for a few days without me. I'm not paying you the money I would have paid to get from here to Menaka, because I now have to pay Moussa to walk there.'

Mahmoud gets right up in my face, screaming and pointing.

'So you get rid of this stupid little Tuareg! I walk with you to Menaka! Come on, let's go! We walk wherever you want to go, and *you pay me my money!*' I can feel his spit in my face. I stand my ground in silent contempt. It is a replica of the situation with Harraba, down to the exact lines, and I have no intention of playing the game.

Very quietly, I say, 'You were the one who told me that you didn't want to walk any further. You told me to go to Gao and hire a new guide. You said you couldn't walk any further, that you were too old. I've hired a new guide. I've already paid you more than half of the money, and I'm not even halfway. I will not pay you any more, and I don't want to walk with you any further.'

He looms over me, and I can see in his eyes the same look I faced down in the desert a week ago. He wants to hit me so much he is crazed. I feel not a scrap of fear. Just as before, I almost want him to do it, almost want the chance to hit back. But I know this anger; it is an old acquaintance from Morocco. I know it's nothing even to do with Mahmoud himself, just the edge I constantly live on here, grounded in my own fears and doubts. I will never let it better me again. I've come too far. I may well have made a mistake in hiring Mahmoud, and I may have to suffer to rectify that mistake. But I will do it with dignity.

Both Moussa and Omar realise what is happening, and they rush to intervene. The discussion predictably deteriorates into a screaming argument, from which I extract myself. Moussa attempts to explain and cajole; Omar tries to placate and reason. But Mahmoud is furious and goes so far as to throw himself across my baggage and refuse to move. It's almost comical.

Eventually they all look at me: Moussa and Omar with pleading helplessness and Mahmoud with triumphant challenge. I shrug.

'So – we go to the village and talk to the police,' I say. 'No problem.'

Everyone is aghast. Nobody in Africa willingly draws the attention of the authorities. But at the centre of Mahmoud's ire is the written, witnessed contract I had drawn up in both Arabic and French in Tomboctou. Having one is something that Khabuss taught me always to do. It states the exact terms of the arrangement: Mahmoud will walk all the way to Menaka and be paid half in Tomboctou and half on arrival in Menaka. It also clearly states that I have the right to terminate the agreement at any point. It does not, however, state whether or not I should then pay the full amount – an oversight I won't repeat. It's signed by all parties concerned, and Mahmoud is now waving his copy around in righteous indignation.

'No need for police! It says right here that I walk all the way to Menaka!'

I just load the camels and say, 'We'll let the police sort it out.'

Moussa takes me aside. 'I need to stay out of this. I fought as a Tuareg during the rebellion. I don't want anything to do with the authorities.'

I tell him that's fine, he can wait on the outskirts of town. My only concern is that Moussa will be so alarmed by Mahmoud's antics that he won't want to take the job. I apologise to him for the drama.

'It's fine,' he says. 'That man is crazy. Even if you weren't paying me, I wouldn't leave you alone with him – I think he was actually going to hit you!' He shakes his head in astonishment, then mutters darkly in French, 'Fucking Arabs.'

I look at him and he smiles mischievously. I'm beginning to grasp the depth of the racial chasms in Sahelian Africa far more clearly than any history book could have described.

In the drab, concrete block of the gendarmerie, we're kept waiting for some time. Mahmoud paces opposite me, muttering in anger. Within minutes, he has gathered a small crowd of sympathetic Arabs as an audience. One in particular becomes heated upon hearing the tale of Mahmoud's misfortune and appoints himself honorary advocate.

Omar remains with me, and we ignore the increasing stream of insults and accusations.

Eventually, an official comes out and we give our respective sides of the story. Among the crowd that has gathered, there's a tall, well-dressed Tuareg man. He stands close to us, and I notice that the official greets him with respect.

I present my story with calm brevity, taking care to address the official properly. He is polite and respectful, and listens to both sides. It is the voluble Arab who speaks on Mahmoud's behalf in a passionate torrent of Arabic. Mahmoud interjects often, pointing accusingly at me. I'm reminded of the angry mob I saw surround the thief in Tan-Tan – every dispute here is public property, and we have drawn quite a substantial crowd by the time we are finished.

The official holds his hands up for silence.

'We will need to consult the *commissariat*,' he says. 'I will go to his house now and ask him to hear you. Wait here.'

The Arabic contingent turns to me triumphantly, their gestures and comments saying, '*Yeah! NOW we'll see what happens!*' It is turning into grand farce, a scene reminiscent of playground fights.

I sit in the shade of the porch, and a shy official brings me some tea. I chat with Omar and the well-dressed Tuareg, who I now understand to be the nominal head of the Tuareg in the village. He is polite and speaks fluent French. We restrict our conversation to my journey thus far, where I've been and how I've travelled. I feel very comfortable with him.

I occasionally catch snippets of the conversation in Arabic; one line makes my spine stiffen in disgust.

'She just wanted a young boy to fuck,' Mahmoud tells his captive audience, and they chuckle knowingly. 'I wouldn't fuck her – that is why she wants me to go.'

The men with me look away in embarrassment, unsure if I have understood or not. I look at the elder Tuareg man directly. 'I'm here for my work,' I say. 'I have a man at home. I do not search in Africa for men, just to do my walk and take my pictures. He should be ashamed.' He nods at me and smiles.

I'm aware that there is more than the odd Western woman who arrives in Africa with a double agenda. Ali, among others, told me numerous stories of being propositioned by wealthy tourists, particularly women of a certain age. In Tomboctou, the tour guides were constantly involved in casual liaisons. It could make for a plausible story from Mahmoud, and I need to make it clear that I've no such goal in mind.

The official returns and we're taken to the home of the *commissariat*. A crowd of at least fifty trail us down the road. When I enter the low, mud-brick dwelling, as many as can fit crowd inside. The rest hang through the open windows and door, following every piece of the action.

The *commissariat* is an African man, from which tribe I don't know. He is dressed in an elaborate uniform, although from his dishevelled appearance I suspect he was roused from his afternoon nap to hear our dispute. We sit in a circle on a woven rug with embroidered cushions. Mahmoud and I have four people sitting between us, and I'm glad he is not opposite me.

Beside the *commissariat* is the Tuareg man I spoke to earlier. There are two other, obviously senior, men of the village by his side. The *commissariat* informs me that we will need to wait for the *marabou* to arrive, the village imam.

Another man arrives. He is tall and elderly, flanked by respectful juniors. He has an elaborate headdress, and hung about his neck is an impressive collection of medallions. He carries a staff. I don't need to be told that he is the Songhai chief of the village.

The *marabou* arrives and proceedings begin.

Once again, we tell our respective stories, and the *commissariat* looks over the paper that Mahmoud is waving in protest. Again, it is the Arab advocate who speaks, hushing Mahmoud's attempts at outright abuse.

We are asked a number of questions, all pertaining to the route we have taken and where we are heading.

The *commissariat* eventually shrugs and hands the paper back. 'This contract states clearly that the white woman can terminate the agreement. I don't see the problem.'

At this, the screams of protest from Mahmoud's camp are tinged with real hostility. I'm lost and look to the tall Tuareg man, who eyes me back with a mixture of amusement and apology.

'They will not accept the decision, because there is no Arabic leader here,' he tells me. 'We've just sent to the next village for the Arabic *marabou*. Ours is Songhai, and the Arabs don't trust him.'

I restrain from eye-rolling and sit back and drink some more tea. Outside the crowd chatters excitedly, and I suspect bets are being taken on the outcome of the debate. The African chief sits in splendour, and the *commissariat* listens in wise silence to the general points of wisdom thrown onto the floor by onlookers.

We've been in the house for over two hours when the Arabic *marabou* arrives in the police vehicle. He steps out, garbed in the whitest, most starched Saharawi robes I have ever seen. With a tall staff in his hand, he sweeps into the dwelling with an authority that obviously supersedes all others.

I go through the traditional Arabic greetings, and he responds by asking every formal question I've heard.

When we're finished greeting, he speaks in turn to Mahmoud. When the advocate begins to respond to his ritual questions, he simply raises his hand to signal silence and frowns slightly. The advocate subsides and Mahmoud is forced to speak for himself. Every aspect of his body language is defensive and sullen, and he doesn't meet the Arabic leader's eye. I'm encouraged by this. When the leader turns back to me, it's obvious in his expression that he has taken Mahmoud's measure.

Once again, we tell our stories. The leader looks at the contract. He asks Mahmoud a few short, sharp questions in Arabic so fast I can't understand. The advocate continues to try to answer, and each time he does the leader cuts him down harshly. Mahmoud answers in a plaintive tone, shaking the paper. I understand his Arabic well enough: he has a contract and wants his money.

Finally, the leader holds his hand up to silence Mahmoud and turns to me. He asks me something nobody else has, in French, 'This man is happy to walk to Menaka with you. Why don't you want to walk with him?'

It's a difficult question to answer. Everything I've learned from my experiences in the desert warns me against making personal allegations – preserving a man's honour is paramount. But equally, I need to make it understood that I *cannot* continue with him.

'We have argued many times about the best route to take,' I begin slowly. 'I have my own opinion about the best direction to walk, in terms of grazing for my camels. I may be wrong, but

I have walked many kilometres in the desert now, and ultimately the responsibility of my expedition lies with me. I am paying Mahmoud well to walk with me. Although I'm happy to accept advice, I need a guide who will work with me, no matter what his opinions are.'

The leader looks at me curiously for a moment and then says, 'But now, after this, he will do what you want, I think.'

Mahmoud nods frantically when the comment is translated by his whispering advocate. I am under the hammer; everything turns on my next answer.

'Perhaps you are right,' I begin. 'But tonight, when I walk out of this place, it will be just Mahmoud and I alone in the desert together – with over 500 kilometres to go until Menaka. Unfortunately, once we are away from the environs of the village, I do not share your faith that Mahmoud will continue to defer to my wishes. He has had many chances to do so, and has chosen not to. He has also made it clear that I am a very unsatisfactory employer. Nonetheless – I *am* his employer. And he is no longer my choice of employee.' I look at the leader, and for a moment let my serious face fall and allow a small expression of humour to creep through. 'You know, sometimes people just don't get on.'

He has watched my face with intense scrutiny throughout my talk. But it's this last expression that breaks the spell. He sits back and raps his staff on the floor.

'This is very simple,' he says. All around, the crowd stirs and I know that this is the ultimate judgement. 'The white woman has the right to terminate this man's employment. She has paid him the money she owes him, and she does not need to pay anything else. I think, perhaps, that it would be a nice gesture to give this man a small present, though, something to take home to his family.' He looks at me enquiringly. I've been waiting for this – I knew from the outset I wouldn't get away scot-free. This has always been about negotiating the price. In my pocket I have CFR50,000; I'm hoping to get away with paying 25,000.

'I have already given him 10,000 on top of the agreed price,' I say. 'I am happy to give him another 10,000.'

There are cries of outrage from the Arabic camp, but we are in familiar territory here. We haggle furiously for a few minutes, and eventually it is settled that I will pay the 25,000. And then comes the clincher.

'Can you shake hands, please,' the leader says. I lean forward immediately and put my hand out. For a brief moment Mahmoud hesitates, and my heart stops. If he does not shake on this, the entire process is essentially null and void, and neither I nor my camels are safe anywhere near this village.

He slowly leans forward and, for the barest second, allows the tips of his fingers to touch my hand. Then he sits back in disgust.

'It is done,' says the leader. He stands and briskly leaves the hut.

The moment he departs the Arabs erupt into verbal abuse.

I walk up the street with Omar and the older Tuareg man. The whooping, jeering group of Mahmoud's supporters follow closely behind. They are spoiling for a fight. The comments are sexually accusatory and racially vile. I need to get out of here.

Moussa is waiting by the camels, and we pack up quickly. The Tuareg elder takes me aside, and says, 'You need to get far away from here tonight. He has shaken your hand, but his friends have not. Once he leaves town they might decide to impart some justice of their own, and there is nothing anybody here can do to stop it. You need to walk a long way, understand?'

I nod and he goes to tell Moussa the same thing. I'm embarrassed by Moussa's chaotic introduction to my camp, even though part of me was expecting trouble. I know that the only way through is to simply hold my head high and not dwell on past troubles, but I'm tired and it's late. It's so hard to always be contained when I really want to scream out the tension of the long day's proceedings and talk through every nuance of the encounter. But that is my stuff, not Moussa's, and discussing it further will do nothing to move us forward.

We walk out of the village in the late afternoon, Beiyal limping on his bad foot. We walk until late that night, past several other villages, and camp high on a hill where we can see any approaching crowd.

I fall asleep, relieved that the dark cloud that hung over my walk has been blown to another place.

Chapter Seventeen

M oussa and I follow the course right by the river. It's the desert as I have never known it, a place of settled people, crops and endless water.

Sometimes we walk right alongside the river itself, waving and smiling at the women washing their clothes or to the men and boys fishing in long, narrow pirogues. The villages themselves are a curious mix of pretty woven African rondavel tents and mud brick. On one side they front the river; on the other, tall spectacular dunes rear majestically. On the far side of the river I see gentle green pasture left over from the flood rains. Animals – horses, cattle and sheep – graze contentedly. From the cooking fires I smell fish grilling with spices.

The lush greenery of acacia trees and other, more verdant species softens the mud brick that in the desert towns can seem so barren. The settlements appear tranquil and cultivated.

I'm actually enchanted in a way I never really have been in the desert itself. Life moves at a more placid pace. Everything is easier; there is fruit and the animals are fat. People have whole gardens to grow their produce. I think back to the small, miserable tents I've passed recently, wracked by malaria and inhabited by gaunt, starving figures, struggling to maintain a handful of goats. Here on the river I see no cases of malaria at all – although perhaps they are hidden indoors where I do not go – and plump, smiling children. It's a different way of life on many levels to that of the desert nomads I'm accustomed to. Although the African tribes here are predominately Muslim, it's a more relaxed, sensual Islam than any I have seen. The women cheerfully wash naked in the river, and the men simply look away. I rarely hear the mosque calling the faithful to prayer.

We water the camels every evening directly from the river and hobble them tightly beneath rich boughs of acacia. They eat better than they have since Tomboctou, and the villagers never complain about our animals grazing on trees so close to town, even though there are many herds of camels in the area.

Moussa and I fall into an easy routine. He helps pack the camels and then makes the running with the villagers we pass, conversing in a variety of languages. I'm grateful for his linguistic expertise and ability to recognise every person by tribe before they even open their mouths.

I do notice, though, that Moussa is increasingly quiet and withdrawn. He goes so far as to be noticeably reticent one day. I begin to worry. I suspect he is in pain, but he won't talk to me. I'm surprised by his choice of footwear – just a pair of rubber flip-flops – but I've seen nomads walk in less.

His desert familiarity is indisputable. I watch him with the fire, the camels and other nomads, and I know he is at home here. He picks good paths along different terrain and is gentle with my animals. He also doesn't interfere with how I do things and actually shows interest in learning. In turn, I've learned a lot from him about local plants and wood, some species of which are different to what I'm used to.

But there's no denying his level of discontent. In the afternoons, he lies far away from the camp and smokes, speaking only when I approach him, and then with little humour.

Having just endured one of the worst guide traumas of the whole walk, I can't bear to think that I may be involved in another. And if I am, then perhaps the problem is me? Maybe I'm just expecting too much of these men.

We're walking along a difficult path, through volcanic rock and down a deep ravine surrounded by dunes. The wind is howling, an incessant gale that in less sheltered terrain would mean a serious sandstorm. We wind down into a valley and shelter in the lee of a rocky cliff. As soon as we're in the boundaries of the rock bowl, we're cut off from the wind as abruptly as if we closed a door to a house. We throw ourselves down to make tea.

'We're coming into Bourem today,' Moussa says. I'd already figured as much from my map and nod. 'It's just over that hill.' I nod again.

Moussa obviously has something on his mind. He shakes his head in a gesture of irritation and wanders off. I drink some tea and eventually say, 'So – should we keep moving?'

The sandstorm is bad, but not enough to halt our progress, and there is no good feed around here. I don't see any point in wasting time. Moussa takes the lead of one of the camels and sets off without a word. I feel very uneasy, and for a moment I consider asking him what's wrong, but I think that deep down I don't really want to know.

Moussa walks far ahead. We're on a narrow path with increasing traffic. I have never walked like this before: trapped between the outskirts of a village and the river itself, walking alongside donkeys carrying bundles of feed and women balancing trays on their heads. It's also difficult trying to negotiate muddy patches – the camels hate them.

Moussa is walking fast and doesn't look back. He turns off the river path and begins to follow a winding, tricky passage between houses into the town. He may well know every turn in the road, but I'm confused and the camels are upset by the sudden onslaught of humanity. There are motorbikes whizzing past, children calling to me, women sitting open-mouthed on their doorsteps as I pass. It's like walking through a small Australian country town leading three exotically clad elephants.

We arrive in the town centre, a bustling marketplace that I would normally avoid like the plague. I can't understand why Moussa has led us here, nor why he has stopped. We've plenty of water and no need of supplies. I am harried, and the camels are jumpy with the press of the crowd.

Moussa couches Beiyal, and I see him untie his small bag. I look at him, bewildered. 'What are you doing?' I ask.

'I can't do this,' Moussa mutters, shaking his head. 'You wait here and I will find you someone else – but I am not doing this anymore. It's horrible.'

I'm floored. The wind is howling around my ears, and the centre square is a frenzy of people, animals, vehicles and market stalls. Things are flapping and squeaking in the storm. I have absolutely no idea why Moussa wants to leave.

But I know one thing.

After the events of the last few weeks, and all I've gone through with Mahmoud, I'm not about to do it again. I don't care if there are bandits laid end to end from here to Gao. I don't care if my camels and I starve to death. I just can't stand here and have another traumatic, heated debate in a public place, defending myself or trying to plead with Moussa. I don't want a new guide. I don't want a guide at all.

To hell with it, I think. I look at Moussa and shrug.

I pick up the ropes for the camels and, without turning back, head off in the direction that I hope leads out of town.

I ignore the catcalls and stares of the villagers, and hustle the camels along as fast as I can. They plod calmly behind me, as if understanding my shock and urgent need to get out of here. I'm walking along the dirt road that leads out of town, and at any second I expect to see a vehicle roaring past with Moussa in the back.

I'm too despondent to think on his reasons for leaving. I'm afraid that I'm just too difficult to work with, too hard to please and dictatorial. Perhaps I'm completely unreasonable. Perhaps all the lovely guides I had in Mauritania were just freaks of fortune. I'm worried about nursing my tired, thin camels to Gao, through territory where I don't speak the language to explain that I need to graze them overnight. I'm worried about how I'll find another guide when I get there. If I've lost not one but *two* guides and word spreads, who will want to walk with me?

I walk a few kilometres out of town and couch the camels out of sight of the road. I sit down on a rock and, for the first time since I left Nouadhibou, tears well up. I always knew that the stretch after Tomboctou would be a low point. But this – this is far beyond low.

In the distance I can hear a shout and look up. Moussa is running up the road towards me, his skinny little figure struggling under the weight of his bag. I'm so happy that I could kiss him. Instead, I give him an enormous, teary grin and stick out my hand. He shakes it, pumping it up and down, and sits down beside me.

'I am so sorry. Of course I won't leave you,' he says.

'But why did you want to go?' I ask. 'I have no idea what's wrong. Please tell me, and I can find a way to change it. It's not good for you to be so unhappy.'

Moussa doesn't look at me, and his face reddens. I can tell he is embarrassed. I look at him curiously.

'When you said in Gao, about *le marche?*' he begins, and I nod. 'I thought you meant, you *travel* twenty-five to thirty kilometres each day. Like, *le marche* being the journey, you know?'

I'm beginning to see where this is going.

'And all my life, I ride donkeys and camels all day, so when you say twenty-five to thirty kilometres, I am thinking, *No problems.* Normally, I go like forty to fifty in a day. So this is really easy. But I didn't understand that you meant actually *walking* all this way, that you don't ride the camels. My feet – they are so sore I can hardly stand up. I have never walked like this. It is very hard for me. I thought you had tricked me into coming out. I felt very angry, because if I had known that it was all walking I would not have agreed to come. This – it is horrible for me, you know?' He looks at me earnestly. 'I am Tuareg! We *ride* the camels!'

I look at his expression of indignant pride and then down at his poor, tired feet, and I cannot help it: I crack up with laughter.

'I thought you just didn't like me!' I tell him between gasps. 'I am thinking, *I met this lovely smiling young man in Gao, and now I'm stuck with a sulky man who hates me!*' Now Moussa is laughing too, and his face lights up into the twinkling character I first met.

'I can just re-pack the camels,' I say. 'We don't need to carry much water, and supplies are low, so it's easy for you to just jump up on Bolshy Sod. And in Gao, I can buy a donkey for you to ride to Menaka if you like. They are cheap here and handy at wells to pull the water bucket up. No problems.'

Moussa looks at me gratefully. 'My feet are so sore,' he says. 'I am sorry about saying I would leave you. I should never do that. My father would kill me if he knew. Can we not mention this back in Gao?'

I stick out my hand again. 'I am just so glad you came back, Moussa. I honestly didn't know what to do. I think this one is just between you and me, hey?' We grin at each other and shake. I'm so glad to have him back, I could skip the entire distance to Gao.

After Bourem we arc back out into the desert and away from the river.

The walk into Gao is straightforward and slightly boring, as we plod into villages every other day to stock up on water. The camels find plenty to graze on and Beiyal's foot begins to heal. But they remain thin and tired, listless in the afternoons, and I know that their time is close to up. I'm hoping to get them to Menaka, Moussa's home, where there is a large forest for them to graze in and a renowned camel market. I plan to rest them in the forest around Gao for a week or so, then push through to Menaka and trade them there if I need to.

Moussa and I talk endlessly about the options. He says I can stay with his family in Menaka for a week or two, and his father will help me trade the camels. I trust his judgement and family to do the right thing by me, and it also works in well with my schedule – Menaka will be the last stop before Niger, and I need to travel back to Gao and perhaps down to Bamako, the capital, to organise my visa and try once again to replace the technical equipment that still doesn't work.

The day before we enter Gao, we pass a village in the grips of a lavish festival to celebrate the triumphal visit of the Malian

President. The road is lined with women in their best wraps and men robed and adorned in all of their finery, riding horses or sitting solemnly. I know that in Tuareg culture it is customary for the men to veil rather than the women, but this is the first time I've seen so many men wearing colourful turbans and hiding their faces so that only their eyes, underscored by indigo powder, show.

The chief of the village greets us and is very excited when he sees my digital camera. He tells me that he has a house in Gao where he'll be staying this week and asks if I could take some photographs of the villagers and print them out for him. I agree, and in turn am given carte blanche to photograph all of the village inhabitants. The chief walks around with me, sternly telling the villagers to pose. I take many photographs in the hessian shelter where all of his wives are resting – I lose count of how many there are after meeting five.

I photograph women hiding behind scarves, Tuareg women in dark *melekhva*, laughing young Songhai girls in vivid wraps. I take several of the chief standing solemnly with the horsemen of his village. He tells me that horse riding is a vital part of Songhai tradition, and the men are really proud to have a chance to show off their horses clad in finery.

Every time a vehicle approaches, the crowd erupts into a ululating, clapping mass of song. They wave flags and jump up and down – even though none of the vehicles is actually the president. It doesn't matter. It *might* be, and that's all that counts. I love this crazy festival on the roadside, even if to an Australian eye it seems an unusually enthusiastic welcome for a politician. Moussa explains that the president is incredibly popular, having recently opened schools, hospitals and roads in the region.

We eventually pack up and Moussa exchanges mobile phone numbers with the chief, who tells me he will invite me for dinner at his home a few days hence.

We're on the final stretch into Gao. I had thought it would take just over two weeks; instead, it has taken over three to walk the 400 or so kilometres. I will have to take time off in Gao to rest the camels, and even more in Menaka. The dreaded stretch of low energy and slow going I had foreseen back in Australia is proving to be every bit as tortuous.

And I was wrong when I discussed this with Graeme. Knowing that it would be difficult makes it no easier to accept.

We walk through the back streets of Gao in the early morning, chased by ragged groups of kids. We wind our way through the back streets to the tin door of the Camping Bangu, and Moussa calls to the boys inside to open the double doors.

We enter the courtyard to a clapping welcome from Moussa's friends and, for the first time, I unpack my camels directly in the courtyard of a tourist accommodation stop. I need only pile the bags in the corner – no storing of equipment or discussion about where things need to be left. It's an enormous relief.

But I feel ambiguous about being back in Gao, in another town, so soon after Tomboctou. I had originally planned that my next major town stop would be in Agadez, over 1000 kilometres after Tomboctou. But since then I've stopped as much as I've walked. I don't feel as though I deserve another town break, another period of slothfulness. I feel frustrated and itch to get on with it.

I know that the camels need to rest and eat; there is no sense in pushing hard when they are tired. I know also that there are no camels to be bought here; I need to get my camels to Menaka to trade them. I understand all the rationales. But I have the same sense I did many months ago on the first European walk, of wasting time and somehow failing by stopping so much.

I walk the camels back out to the forest I had spied on the way in. I have paid a friend of Moussa's to watch the camels out here for the week, and I want to make dead sure he takes them exactly where the food is plentiful. But it isn't cheap. Mali is even more expensive than Mauritania. It seems that the poorer the country, the higher the price for everything.

I contemplated staying out with the camels myself, but I need to do the usual rounds of internet communication, photo processing, supply buying and, hopefully, organise my visa – there is an embassy outlet in Gao.

The first night I'm in town, the chief of the village phones to invite me for lunch the next day. Moussa drives me there on his motorbike.

We are shown into a large mud-brick home with beautiful woven mats on the floor and nice cushions. The chief has at least two of his wives here, both of whom greet me with warm smiles and clasped hands. I've had the photographs printed off and blown up to eight by tens. They are the first photographs I feel really proud of, and the chief seems equally pleased.

Before we eat, a young American girl turns up on a bicycle. She says hello and, to my astonishment, starts speaking in fluent Songhai to the chief, who obviously knows her well.

'Hi, I'm Brie,' she says to me. 'I work with the Peace Corps in Gao – I've been out here for about six months now. I had to come and see you for myself – the chief told me that you walked here from Tomboctou with camels! Are you serious? I honestly thought he was kidding.'

After the last three weeks of strain, I'm delighted to be talking to someone in English. Just as with the girls in Tomboctou, I can't get my words out quickly enough. I'm impressed by her grasp of the language, as I listen to her talk to the chief. It turns out that they have been working together on developing a monthly festival to celebrate the culture of horsemanship in Songhai culture. Brie herself is an avid horsewoman and has bought a horse locally to ride. It's one of the reasons why she is so interested in my walk – she has plans to do a few long-distance rides herself.

The chief ends our visit by presenting me with a woven mat and a book of the Songhai language. I'm honoured by the gesture.

Despite my impatience at being stopped, I try to enjoy Gao, wandering through the bustling market and down by the riverfront. I meet up with the Peace Corps girls and some of the other workers from various NGOs operating in the area and thoroughly enjoy their company. I admire the decision the Americans have taken, at around the age of twenty-two, to come all the way over here, learn another language and live in local homes. Although some travellers are disparaging, writing the Peace Corps off as do-gooders, of all the NGO workers I meet in Africa I find them the least precious and most interested in where they are. It's no small feat to truly live *in* a community; most NGO workers I meet have their own home, a vehicle and servants. The Peace Corps kids get allocated a bicycle and a family.

Their kindness and enthusiasm are infectious. I also use their knowledge of Gao to help with some sticking points.

One is my own health. The urinary tract infection I developed right at the start has never really gone away. I have used all my own antibiotics and gone through another course that I purchased in Tomboctou. Although I can reduce the worst of the symptoms, every few weeks it comes back with sudden, painful savagery. It's only a matter of two or three hours from when I feel the first symptoms before I am passing blood in my urine.

The girls take me to a pharmacy, where I have long discussions with the girl behind the counter. In this part of Africa the pharmacists usually double as rudimentary doctors. All drugs are available over the counter, so one either needs to know exactly what to get or hope the pharmacist does. I explain my symptoms and show her the last antibiotics I took. She confirms my theory that I have built up a resistance to the drugs and gives me some new ones that she says are stronger. I buy two courses and ask her to give me anything she can think of for prevention. I have become quite scared of the infections; they leave me exhausted and crippled, walking doubled-over in agony. I worry even more about what kind of long-term damage is being done, if they are recurring and this severe.

I try to get my computer fixed, to no avail. I also attempt to track down the Nigerienne Embassy, which is supposed to have an office in Gao. It's permanently closed and a sign refers me to Bamako. I try to contact the embassy by phone, and I talk to the police, but nobody seems to know what's going on. Other tourists mention that they simply got their visas on the border into Niger, but I don't trust this method.

I decide to go to Bamako after reaching Menaka, since the camels will be resting there anyway. I'm extremely unenthusiastic about taking yet more time off, but I try hard to accept that this is part of the process. Once I get into Niger I will have to move very quickly in order to make Bilma before the hot season, so perhaps I should just enjoy the rest while I can.

I had always accepted that I may need to hole up in Bilma for the worst of the hot season. I figured that if I could make it into Libya before May, I would be prepared to carry on through the heat just to finish. But it is mid-March now, and there are 1700 kilometres between me and Bilma. With the scheduled pause in Menaka, I can't imagine under any circumstances making Libya by May. With luck, I could possibly do it by June, but I know just how hot it will be by then. Walking the great wastes of the Ténéré at high speed will totally do my camels in. Worse, I know that there are no camel caravans travelling the salt route this time of year. It would make far more sense to wait until October and push on, but I feel reluctant to call a halt on any level. I just want to get there. I'm scared of losing momentum. I feel as if I already have.

It is in Gao that I also begin to become culturally worn down again. It's the usual time frame for mental weariness – I've been out here for over five months, going hard for most of the time. The myriad boys who hang around the camping ground looking for tourist work are nice but tiring. They are all after a buck and vie for any work I can throw their way, like ferrying me around on their motorbikes when I have errands to run or finding a particular piece of equipment. I don't like to leave the camping ground much – since as soon as I do it costs me money – so I find myself drawn into the family dynamic of the Camping Bangu. It's not long before every member of the owner's family has taken me aside and confided that they have a child's school fees or sick brother or broken motorbike – could I help? I am well used to this kind of interaction from my days in Morocco and know how to be kind but firm. But it's exhausting to feel that every time I stick my head out the door, someone else will be asking for money.

In the middle of it all, I come back to the camping ground to find a dreadlocked, unmistakeably Australian cyclist unpacking his battered kit. His name is Lachlan Prouse, and he has been cycling for *four years*. He is also the most wonderful bloke I could have imagined running into, particularly since he has, like me, lived in Broome.

'I started travelling in Asia, but after a few months I just thought, *Stuff this*. I wasn't seeing enough. So I bought an old bicycle, set it up with some kit and started cycling. I've been all through Asia, Russia, India, the Middle East, Europe . . . fifty-three countries so far.'

We sit and talk late into the night. I am astonished by Lockie's tales of dragging his bike through the snowdrifts of a harsh Iranian winter – 'I carried it more than I rode' – and sleeping in yurts in the Gobi Desert. He's the only person I've ever met who has travelled in a similar way to me: day in, day out; solitary progress; immersed in other cultures and in one's own company for weeks and months on end. He has been shot at on African borders and showered with kindness from strangers, and he cycles his way through it with humility and strength of will. He is a gentle, kind soul, but I am reassured to find that he also has his moments in dealing with locals.

'In Africa it's far harder than anywhere else I have travelled,' he tells me. 'It's hard not to get frustrated and fed up with being ripped off everywhere you go and begged for everything you have – especially when you have very little to start with.'

I talk to him about the ongoing dramas in the desert, particularly in Mauritania, with the women literally pulling the clothes from my back and how much it upset me to be constantly having to say 'no' simply because I had given everything away that I could spare. I say how selfish and rude I felt – but also how hurt I was at being perceived to be both of those things. Lockie laughs quietly.

'You know what I came to in Mauritania?' he says, looking at me slyly. 'I know this sounds bloody awful, but honestly, you have to find a way to laugh sometimes. I don't speak French, so most of the time on borders the guards look at me as if I'm a total imbecile, which can get really tiring. So in Mauritania I am having the same difficult conversation for about the fiftieth time, and this bastard is laughing with his mates at how stupid I am. I had cycled 120 kilometres, was exhausted and filthy, and just dying to chuck the tent up somewhere and have a wash. To be honest, I felt pretty close to losing it.

'And then I really looked at this bloke, with his rotting teeth, and I thought, *Hey, brother, in another year I get to take a plane out of here back to the best country on earth. Twelve months from now I'll be sitting on a beach drinking a cold beer and feeling some nice bird's boobs, and you'll still be sitting on your donkey with no future and no way out. So, brother, laugh away. I can give you that much.*'

We clink our beers and laugh, but the laughter has a sombre undertone. As politically incorrect as he sounds, I feel comforted and uplifted by his words. The fact is that the weight of the poverty here is a quicksand pulling everyone under with it. I feel so overwhelmed and helpless in the face of it.

So something in Lockie's words gives me back my sense of humour – and also my self-worth. I remember for the first time in a long time that this is *not* my home, and everyone I meet is *not* my responsibility.

'Sometimes I feel as if I'm bursting with the impressions I have of life here,' I say. 'But they are the kind of things you can't say – or feel you can't – because the other travellers I meet are having a totally different experience. I either meet Lonely Planet dreamers, who are lovely, but tend to hold the view that "It's all about the *culture*, and their poverty is our responsibility"' – Lockie chuckles with me when I say this – 'or else I meet the hard acts, the long-term ex-pats who are angry and resentful and hold the view that "Africa's stuffed – they are all lazy bastards and all this is their own fault."

'I guess I kind of lie somewhere in between the two. I get swindled out of more money than the hard acts, because I don't *want* to be a hard act – and if it costs me a bit more, so what? I have to pay big money no matter how hard I bargain, so being overly hard only makes life more traumatic. I don't hate Africa or Africans or Arabs, but I do dislike the racism between the cultures, and, particularly with the Arabs I meet in Mali, the contempt for Western society. On one hand there is a greed for the material benefits of our society. But on the other, there's contempt for who we are and the way we operate. I sometimes get frustrated with what seems to me to be laziness – groups of men sitting around drinking endless glasses of tea and moaning about how they are so poor. Yet I've had the experience of offering those same guys two weeks' paid work walking with me – and they will turn it down because it's "too hard" to walk every day!'

These feelings have been bottled up for so long. I feel guilty telling anyone about the underlying racism I dislike so much – walking down the street and hearing, 'Hey! *Le blanc!*' – 'The White' – called out to attract my attention.

'There is one thing I know for certain,' I tell Lockie. 'And I would never have thought it before this walk – in Mauritania and Mali in particular: I couldn't live in Africa. No Western person truly belongs here. We're not welcome, not accepted, and definitely not understood. Sure, we are tolerated, for the tourist dollars and charitable funding we bring. But deep down there is an inherent contempt for our society. Particularly in the case of the Arabic, Islamic population – there is a true sense of superiority. I never felt this in Morocco, but here I know – just *know* – that every smile is underscored by a layer of mistrust and thinly veiled contempt. Although I still meet good people, and have no doubt that they are interested in welcoming me, I feel always on guard here and, unfortunately, unable to truly be open with people. I find it dispiriting and disillusioning.'

'Oh, God yes,' says Lockie. Having felt like I just uttered heresy, his calm acceptance of my negative viewpoint is an enormous relief.

'That's why I couldn't handle what you're doing – the whole guide aspect of it, I mean. Sometimes I will stay with a family for a day, or a couple of days, but to be honest, I'm dying to get out of there by the time I leave. I look forward to being back on the road, back in my own space and company, just on my journey. It would be so bloody intrusive to be stuck with someone else in my camp every day – especially someone who you are paying to be there and who may or may not do things the way you want them done. After years of cycling alone, I've got a whole routine set up. I find it difficult even cycling with someone else for more than a day or so – I'm just used to doing it my way.'

His understanding is incredibly comforting. I look down at the ground and, without meeting his eyes, say, 'Sometimes I really wonder if I'm going to be able to do this.'

'I know, sister. I know,' he says and pats me on the shoulder. 'But I reckon you will.'

Those five words mean more to me than anything anyone has ever said. So often I find messages on my email or website from people saying, 'I know it's hard but don't give up! You can do it!' And despite my sincere gratitude, I think dully, *Mate, you don't know me, and you don't have any real idea what it's like out here. And I seriously DON'T know if I can do this anymore.*

But Lockie is different. He's been doing this stuff for years, and he knows exactly what it's like out here. Talking to him reassures me that I'm doing okay, that my fears are normal, and my walk *is* as tough as it feels sometimes. Deep down, I've worried that I make it hard for myself, that it's not the world around me that is causing me problems – *I* just get it wrong at every turn. Some part of me seems to think that I should be cruising through this walk, focused, determined. I should have goals and outcomes and strategies for every possible problem. That I am, somehow, a rank amateur here under false pretences.

I don't know why these insecurities keep plaguing me; they just do. But there is comfort in being able to share at least a few of my fears with someone I really trust.

I make the most of every day with Lockie, eating good food and wandering through the market. We drink cold beers in the evening and talk about everything from our love lives to why we do what we do. I relax a bit and enjoy things I never normally would – like getting my hair braided and buying some earrings.

On the day that I'm due to start walking to Menaka, Lockie uses my digital video camera to record Moussa and me packing the camels. I've carried the camera since Nouadhibou and have been promising myself that I will start using it to make a daily video diary. But it takes Lachlan to actually interest me in the process. I vow to myself that, on this leg, I will talk to the camera every day.

I take one last phone call from Graeme, who has been a lifeline of help and information since I left. He relays the concerns of one of the prospective sponsors I have contacted about further funding. Things aren't good. I've been very frustrated by the conversations we have been having and feel that we have reached a bit of a stalemate.

The comment went something like, 'But how do I know that she will actually *make* it to Cairo? After all, she started off saying she was walking to Cape Town, and now she has changed that. There has been a diminution of the original journey. How do I know she won't just give up on this one as well?'

Even as I'm packing, those words are ringing through my mind. I feel gripped by an almost blind fury. I try to put it aside until I am out in the desert and have time to walk with it. I don't know quite why the comment should touch such a raw nerve, and I understand myself well enough to know that it must be because, secretly, I fear exactly what was said.

I say goodbye to Lachlan, knowing I've found a real mate. He's heading down towards Cape Town, travelling across into Niger then down into Nigeria. Our paths won't cross in Africa, but we promise to meet up in Australia.

I'm glad to be leaving Gao and on my way again.

Chapter Eighteen

After being enchanted by Mali when I first entered, by the time I am halfway to Menaka it has lost a lot of its appeal.

This desert is unlike anywhere I've been before. This is the furthest south I will go, and it's more Sahel than Sahara. Sometimes there are thick, tangled forests, which are wonderful eating for the camels, who are so tired now that they can barely muster the energy to eat at all. The weather is becoming incredibly hot, and it's a different heat to the dry Saharan winds I'm used to. There's something heavy, almost humid in the air. Frequently our camps are overrun by ants, which climb into my swag and drive me mad all night. There are mosquitoes and scorpions – a lot of scorpions. Although I've seen them before, I now find them almost daily and become very wary about where I sit down.

I have a lot more encounters with officialdom. I'm stopped by many of the military vehicles and give the same details over and over. All of them appear to be sizing me up, and I'm never sure if the encounters are about to erupt into violence. More than once I'm grateful for Moussa's talent with languages and charming manner. He gets us out of more situations than I can count.

At wells, I find people wanting to actually charge me for water. The first time it happens I get quite hostile. Moussa takes me aside and says that it is normal here for people to pay, but I don't believe it. I don't see any of the other nomads paying for their water. There is none of the easy acceptance I was given by desert nomads in Mauritania or Morocco. The nomads here, who are chiefly Tuareg, seem secretive and closed to me. Although they appear less fazed by my gender, my colour immediately seems to place me in the category of someone to be taken advantage of. Not being able to speak the language doesn't help, and I wish I'd taken the time to learn Tamashek.

For such a straightforward stretch, I spend every day wondering if we will actually make it. Halfway through, I'm forced to take the ropes out of the camels' mouths and thread them through the nostril holes, just to keep them walking. Bolshy is hauling the others along behind him. Beiyal, that gutsy little man, occasionally falls to his knees in exhaustion. Once I have to twist his genitals to make him rise. I don't have any choice. If I leave him here, he will simply die.

I am willing the animals on. Moussa and I are entirely united in our efforts, and he is a true companion. One night, when I'm afraid that the camels simply won't make it through the hard heat and wind to the well the next day, Moussa takes the donkey and four jerry cans, rides ten kilometres to the well and fills up – just so we can water the camels. In the quiet of the night, they slurp the cool water gratefully, and I wonder if his actions just saved their lives – Beiyal in particular.

The walk through to Menaka takes thirteen days, but by the time we reach the small town I am literally dragging my camels behind me. Beiyal has had it – he simply can't go on any further. I sell him the first day we arrive, to Moussa's cousin.

The other two are taken straight out to the vast forest bordering Menaka. For the last few days, I've been whispering in their ears that I'm taking them to the best feed they have seen since the Tomboctou stretch, that they will graze and get fat and drink from a stream that runs through the forest. I have whispered it to them like a mantra, praying that they would make it just this bit further.

They take one look at the great valley, teeming with rich acacias and every kind of shrub they love, and eyeball me in what I would like to think is gratitude and awe. But they are camels, so they are probably just telling me to sod off. They plunge eagerly down in to the cool shade and begin tearing off great hunks of the lush green foliage. I'm tearful just watching them.

Moussa's family welcome us, and I'm immediately comfortable with them. We've missed the market by one day, so I will take off for Bamako in a day or so and make the market next week. In the meantime, I sit in the evening cool in the sandy courtyard of the home, and one of Moussa's little sisters shyly brings me over a chilled ginger drink.

Moussa's mother runs a small shop from the back of the house. She and her daughters mix up vats of flavoured drink – ginger, raspberry, lemon – and pour it into small plastic sachets. Moussa recently bought her a freezer, so she freezes the packets and sells them to the local children, along with cold flavoured-milk packets. I love the frozen ginger drink and buy one after another. Used to long days of heat and dust, I can't believe how refreshing they are.

During the day, the interior of the mud-brick house is cool. But, as evening falls, the heat is released and it becomes unbearable. Moussa's sisters – the eldest of whom can be no more than thirteen – are all incredibly competent. They drag the wooden bed frames out of the house and place mattresses on them. The frames are a couple of feet off the ground, which lets the breeze move underneath the mattresses. They set the beds up in different areas of the courtyard – the parents under a woven shelter, the brothers at one side of the yard, the sisters the other. They thoughtfully put my bed on the opposite side of the woven shelter that people rest under during the day so that I have a little privacy. I'm especially charmed by one of Moussa's young sisters, who, aged only five, always comes to put a pillow under where I am sitting and makes my bed up every night. She won't let me do anything and jumps at the slightest hint that I may want something. She is gorgeous, and we laugh a lot.

The elder daughter astonishes me with her hard work. From the moment dawn arrives and the call to prayer has everyone out of their beds and prostrate on the ground, that girl is working. She sweeps the yard down with a stiff twig broom, lights the cooking fire, prepares the breakfast and tidies the beds away. She washes the family clothes and by midmorning is preparing lunch. After that is cleared away, she will begin on the evening meal – or on any of the myriad chores such a large family generates, including bathing her younger siblings.

She works cheerfully in brisk, efficient movements. Only a very young teenager, she is running the whole house.

Daina, Moussa's mother, has done her time of that kind of drudge work. Her jobs now are looking after the smallest children and her grandchildren, making the tea, and enjoying her guests. She is rotund and friendly, and speaks a little Arabic. We talk in a fashion and I like her.

Moussa's father is a learned man who speaks French as well as Arabic, Tamashek and the local African dialects. He is often involved in deep discussion with other men in the village regarding the current political situation and various NGO-funded projects in the region. People seek him out for advice.

Just inside the entrance to the house, bullet holes scar one of the doors.

'When the army came during the rebellion, my mother hid here with my sisters,' Moussa tells me. 'After the rebellion finished, everyone wanted me to get rid of the holes, but I said 'no'. It is important that we remember these things, I think.'

'Do you think the rebellion up in the north will reach here?' I ask.

'It isn't around Kidal, my home, at the moment,' Moussa says. 'But it doesn't look good. The government just says we are bandits – but it isn't about that. The Tuareg just want equal rights like everyone else in Mali. The government keeps trying to ignore us, and they can't keep doing it forever.'

I wonder if it is the lot of the indigenous inhabitants of a place to be persecuted and feel disenfranchised. The real victims of the Western Saharan conflict are the nomads who have roamed the area for thousands of years, first interbreeding with the invading Arabs and then being judged alongside their original conquerors when the territory went under dispute. I think of how the Aboriginals in Australia, the Native Americans and the Inuit are also dismissed by the ruling power. And now the Tuareg. There seems no end to it.

During the day, a solar panel charges up a large truck battery.

Just on evening, the television is brought out and placed on a low table and hooked up to the battery. All the chairs and mats are arranged in front of it. Just before six o'clock the door opens and half of the town streams in, sitting wherever they can. At six o'clock a hush descends and the torrid strains of *Barbarita*, a Colombian sitcom dubbed into French, are heard.

I've seen the odd episode ever since I arrived in Mali. The workers at the camping ground in Gao were obsessed with it. It's an amusing, titillating mash of high passion, unbelievable drama and unspeakably poor acting. In one episode, three women all gave birth in a half-hour slot, one of them as a plane was going down and another with a knife held to her throat. The women are sexy without revealing too much, and the men are always under the thumb of domineering mothers. Nobody drinks alcohol – or if they do, they are bad. The women are caught in all the problems relating to arranged marriages, and everything is high passion without actually being explicit. If anybody is kissing, mothers immediately clap their hands over the children's eyes. It's so bad it makes *Days of Our Lives* look like Shakespeare, but every eye is glued to the screen for the duration.

As soon as it's finished, everyone clears out and goes to bed.

I end up staying a few days, as there is no transport out of Menaka. One of the reasons time seems to pass so slowly is that there is an unrelenting sameness to every day. There is no difference between week and weekend or between individual days. The only time things change is on Friday when the main sermon is delivered at the mosque. I have one conversation with Moussa about weekends; he says he has heard of them. It's one of the more disorientating sensations – a rhythm that has governed my life since childhood simply doesn't exist here. The shops are open every day except Friday afternoon, and even then they open in the evening. School runs on weekdays, but there are also classes on the weekend. Not that they matter much for the girls. Moussa's two sisters don't attend, although his brothers do, even up until their late teens.

Eventually, Moussa organises a ride on the transport truck, and we load into the heaving wreck for another long ride.

We arrive back in Gao early the next morning, after yet another interminable ride. This time Moussa arranged for me to ride in the cabin, but I think I would rather have been in the back. I was jammed in the middle of three others on the front seat, as well as the driver. There was nothing to hold onto and nowhere to stretch. I'm so stiff I can barely move when I get out. It's not helped by the fact that having this damned urinary tract infection means that every bump is excruciatingly painful. My lower back is seized by a deep, dragging pain, and I'm once again passing blood.

We stay the night with friends of Moussa's, a warm-hearted African family. The matriarch makes us a fresh salad and grilled fish, and insists on washing my hair with a soapy brew of dried mint in water, which is refreshing in the somnolent heat. Afterwards she braids my hair tightly. All the girls sit around and watch, laughing and chattering.

I sleep up on the terrace with the boys. As I prepare for bed, I pause for a moment to think how accustomed I've become to the smallest things here. For example, the toilet and wash area are the same; there is a concrete base with a hole in it, surrounded by mud-brick walls. One simply goes in with a bucket of water, strips off and has a wash into the hole. The hole itself is covered by a wooden plank, as it is teeming with cockroaches. When the plank is removed, a stench is released. I never squat too close, aware of the fat insects beneath. But such things are small nuisances now. I'm thankful just to have a private place to wash.

In the morning we catch the bus down to Bamako. It's a typically long, bumpy journey, all of us packed into the old bus with no standing room left among the livestock and baggage. At every tiny settlement along the way, swarms of people converge outside, selling everything from sliced papaya to chocolate biscuits. We hand our money through the window and the goods are passed up to us. In many ways Africa makes you lazy; there is always someone else to do things for you. I don't even have to get out of my seat to eat.

Every prayer-time the bus stops somewhere there is a water outlet so people can put water into their little plastic kettles and perform the ritual ablutions. In the evening cool I exit with everyone else and stretch out on the gravel, a wonderful feeling after being seated for so long. Since I am going to a city, I'm wearing my old Western clothes that I have not pulled out for so long – light trousers and a long cotton top. I had to buy a belt in Gao to hold my trousers up. The material billows around my form and my top keeps falling off my shoulders. I have lost an awful lot of weight.

I'm feverish and exhausted with the infection. When we roll into Bamako after twelve hours on the bus, all I want is to check into a room somewhere and find a doctor. But we're collected from the station by Moussa's relatives, and I spend the first half of the day in their home, eating and watching television as Moussa catches up on family news. I know there is no point in rushing this process, but I eventually say I'm catching a taxi to the Catholic Mission, a tourist accommodation I had searched out on the net before leaving Gao. I wave away the usual protest that I should stay with family; I no longer take on board obligations of hospitality. I am essentially paying for Moussa to be here, although it is not a formal arrangement, and I don't owe anybody anything.

I collapse on the iron bed in the hostel and lie for an hour in peace beneath the whirring fan. I then have a cold shower, where I realise that I'm trembling with fever, spots dancing before my eyes. I have a tremor of fear and wonder just why I'm so ill.

I report to the hospital in Bamako and spend a frustrating half day trying to be seen. A lovely young Indian doctor finally examines me and takes a urine and blood sample. I can get the results of the urine test today, but the blood results will be a few days.

I wait in the corridor, sitting on a bench between two large, vibrantly clad African women fanning themselves.

After a few hours the doctor calls me back in and frowns.

'You have a very acute urinary tract infection,' he says. 'I will need to wait for the blood test, but the bacteria count is extremely high. I'm going to give you some very strong antibiotics, but you need to wait in Bamako for the results of your blood test. The infection has climbed up around your kidneys and is very serious, although it is not actually a kidney infection yet. The problem is when infections are this severe, the chances of it actually going into your kidney is very high . . . What is it you said you've been doing?'

I tell him about my walk, and he shakes his head in bemusement. I have the feeling he doesn't actually believe me. I am used to this by now. I guess they see a lot of slightly off-the-wall tourists, and he is not to know whether I am high on drugs and living in fantasy land or not.

'Well, if you are walking, as you say, this is the worst thing you can do for this infection. You *must* rest. It will not get better if you are walking. You must also prevent against fatigue and dehydration – both things will exacerbate your condition. You will need to come back in three days for the results of your blood tests. In the meantime, *rest*.'

I go away with the antibiotics and medication to alleviate the symptoms. I understand that I must take it easy, but I only have a few days in Bamako. I'm trying to get the visa for Niger, as well as have my laptop fixed and pick up a new solar panel. I'm so tired by the time I get back to the hostel, though, that I just lie down and slip in and out of a feverish sleep.

The next day the antibiotics seem to have kicked in. The worst of the pain has gone, and I set out to organise the visa issue.

I arrive at the address for the embassy, which is a short walk from where I'm staying. Bamako is a modern city. Over the river there are high-rise buildings and people clad in suits. But on my side, there are open-carriage African transport buses and dirt roads. Shacks selling the usual array of goods sit side by side with trendy bars where white people drink beer and eat pizza.

The embassy is closed. There is no notice on the door explaining why. According to the old sign announcing operating hours, it should be open now. I ask some of the people trading in the vicinity what's going on, but they all shrug, smile and tell me to come back later.

I go to see the police at the central office and wait for hours before anyone will talk to me. Finally, an impatient official tells me that he has no idea why the embassy is closed – maybe they have gone to lunch? – and there is nothing he can do. He also says that I shouldn't be so bothered – I should be able to get a visa on the border.

I go to the internet café and get onto the Lonely Planet Thorn Tree forum, asking if anyone has had issues with their Nigerienne visa. I also go onto the African travellers' forum, The Hub, and see what the word is. The information varies. Some people as recently as last week found the embassy open. Others tell me they got their visa in Gao. Still more say that both outlets were closed and they obtained visas on the border itself.

I explain that I will not be passing through the road border, but entering the country some 500 kilometres north of there, so that the first town I come to will be Tillia. I don't like my chances of walking into a small desert outpost without a visa, especially if there are Tuareg rebel issues in the north of Mali. I phone the Nigerienne Embassy in London for advice, and they tell me that the Bamako office should be open. I phone the police in Gao and ask if the embassy outlet there is open; they say it has been closed indefinitely.

I've no idea what's going on and feel increasingly uneasy. It is the first rule of African travel not to turn up in a country without a visa. I got away with it once, in Mali, but I don't fancy my chances twice. I decide to just turn up to the embassy several times a day in the hope of finding someone.

The days slip into an annoying round of checking the embassy, the internet and trying to find solutions to my equipment problems. I meet Moussa most days for lunch in a funky little restaurant down in the river quarter, where stalls selling every imaginable piece of useless junk are cheek by jowl with tourist restaurants and souvenir shops. Moussa himself is ostensibly trying to 'help' me locate what I need. But I soon recognise the signs of Madani from long ago: I represent a meal ticket, someone who will pay for his lunch and a few beers. I politely excuse myself from his company. Bamako for Moussa is party time away from the family; his days are rounds of friends, bars and hustling for more tourist business.

I want to be seduced by Bamako, but I'm too worried about my visa, equipment and health to really enjoy the place. I go to the market, but only to buy some material and have it made into usable clothes to replace my worn-out walking gear. I'm more interested in finding stationery than sightseeing. It is a practical rather than pleasure stop and, although I enjoy wandering around the bustling market or eating at one of the roadside stalls, I feel impatient and frustrated.

Moussa turns up one day shamefaced and morose – he has gone through all of the money I paid him for the last stretch. He tells me that some more was stolen. In short, he's broke and needs help. I say that I'm sorry to hear about his troubles and give him a small amount of cash – enough to eat for the next couple of days. It's not the generous hand-out he expected, but I've already paid his wages, a tip and money for his family. I won't be taken for any more, particularly when I know he is pouring it down his throat in a series of bars.

The day before I'm due to leave, I arrive at the hospital for my blood results. But the doctor has left the hospital and nobody seems to know where my results are. I'm feeling infinitely better anyway, after minimal walking and the antibiotics, so I basically give up and decide to take my chances.

Later that day, I take the same approach to all the things I came to Bamako for. I can't find the solar panel I need; nobody can fix my laptop. I am getting nowhere with the visa issue, and all the tourists I meet tell me not to be so uptight – Niger happily issues visas on the border. I look at how much I am spending to simply stay in the city and decide to call a halt to the whole thing and get back to my camels and walk.

Chapter Nineteen

I arrive in Menaka late at night. Moussa is still in Gao and has given me the number of a friend to contact on arrival, but no one answers. I have no idea what part of town I'm in, nor where the house is from here. One by one, the passengers are picked up or wander off, until I'm left standing alone.

I see a street kid hanging around the bus; he was trying to sell cigarettes to the passengers. I beckon him over and mention the name of Moussa's family. I wave a note in front of his face and he grins widely. He hoists the box of produce I have brought back from Gao and leads me away through the silent, dirt streets.

It's times like this when I marvel at how far I have come. I trail a kid no more than eight years old for half an hour through pitch-black backstreets, and never once do I worry that I'm being led into a trap. Maybe I am stupid and naïve. But I also know that fear is the mother of all trouble. If I retreat into fear every time I'm faced with a challenge, I won't achieve anything.

He raps on the tin door I recognise as Moussa's, and I'm welcomed by one of the girls, who is rubbing sleep blearily out of her eyes. I politely decline her efforts to make me a bed and collapse on the dirt on top of my swag for the last few hours before dawn.

Tomorrow is market day.

Standing in the midst of Menaka's market bustle, I draw more attention than a space shuttle landing in downtown New York.

I wander from camel to camel with Moussa's father, couching them, walking them around. The Tuareg nomads, many of whom have come into the market from the deep desert, eye me in fascination. When I take the lead of a camel and couch it, they squat and make noises of disbelief, and they laugh and shake their heads when I insist on feeling beneath the camel's belly for his genitals, to see if he will jump or not. I open the mouths to inspect teeth, and at least a dozen men jump up and admonish me to be careful. They soon retire again when they realise I know what I'm doing.

I don't want to be shaken by their scrutiny, and I take my time making a choice. Moussa's father and I narrow it down to two animals, and in the end I choose a light brown one while he recommends the white one. I make my decision based on the strength in the animal's chest. He is slightly younger than I would prefer, which is why Moussa's dad thinks I should go for the other one, but after all I went through after deferring to Kadar's opinion with the Brown, I want to trust my instincts. They tell me that the youngster will be a good animal with some training, although he is a little jumpy now.

We lead him back to the family compound. Just as I tie him up, the family shepherd comes through the gate leading Bolshy Sod and Zaina back from their sojourn in the forest.

I just gaze, slack-jawed; each of my camels have filled out like the proverbial fatted calf. They are robust and strong, and the area around their hindquarters is again plump and meaty. They have genuinely regained condition, and they eye me as if to say, *Okay then, girl, bring it on. Where are we going now?* I laugh and stroke them, cuddling their necks, and they don't pull away. Bolshy nudges me affectionately, and I sit and chatter away to them, feeding them titbits of the fruit I am eating from my hand. Moussa's family laughs, but I don't care. On this journey it's my camels who have become my only constant companions, and I love them.

Before I left for Gao the last time, I met a couple of likely guides. One in particular, a man called Ibrahim, struck me as a reliable, solid bloke. He comes to the house again this evening and we talk easily about the route. He checks all my boxes – he's well known and respected in town; he knows every step of the route, having travelled between Menaka and Tillia – and even further to Agadez. He's made the trip dozens of times with his family's herds of goats and camels, and he speaks all the languages between here and there. He doesn't make a big fuss about the price and bargaining is kept to a minimum. He can look me in the eye, and he eats from the same plate as me when dinner is served.

As a bonus, he is happily married with several children and brings his wife to meet me. She is round and cheerful, and he obviously adores her. He appears to me a very honest, hardworking man who is in desperate need of a job. I'm also impressed by the fact that, unlike most men I meet here, he has been labouring along the highway works, punching a time card for the past few months. It is tiring, backbreaking work for minimal pay, and I'm well aware that most men here, regardless of race, consider it beneath them. The fact that he is prepared to do this to feed his family is reassuring.

We make our deal and draw up a contract. I notice that Ibrahim reads it through carefully, and checks every point with me. We agree that I will pay him the price from Menaka to Tillia in advance, and Tillia to Agadez upon arrival in that town, if he chooses to continue with me. He shakes my hand in a very serious, business-like matter. Despite my somewhat cynical attitude towards guides, I find myself liking him more and more.

The morning that we leave Menaka, I am buoyed by a series of small but important triumphs.

The new camel does not want to enter the gate into the compound, and his jittery unease transmits itself to my other two camels, who previously entered without a fuss. Within seconds a little crowd gathers, all of them shouting advice and trying to harass the animals through the gate. It's the kind of scene that used to leave me feeling helpless and sidelined as other people took over the situation. But I handle it differently this time.

I walk over and calmly but decisively take Bolshy Sod's lead. I walk him away from the crowd a little distance, then fetch Zaina and tie him behind. I gesture to Moussa's dad to lead the new camel behind the other two.

I walk alongside Bolshy's neck, as I have every day for so many thousands of kilometres, and without flinching for a second he passes through the narrow doorway, Zaina following behind. I lead them straight over to the wall of the compound, turn to face them, drop the lead and gesture with my hand out, palm down. Without any other encouragement, both camels couch immediately and chew their cud.

I turn around to see the new camel still balking at the doorway, eyes rolling. The group of men behind him are brandishing sticks and shouting. I walk over, take the lead rope and lead him on exactly the same path I did Bolshy Sod, turning him at the last moment right before the gate. He walks calmly through, and again goes down behind the others without a murmur of protest.

Moussa's Dad is leaning against the wall, smiling and nodding. The other men of the crowd are gaping in astonishment. Ibrahim shoots me a grin, and I feel ten feet tall.

I go about packing the camels, and in every movement I feel the strength and confidence of all these months on the road flowing through my body. The men hang back and watch, and I quietly direct Ibrahim in the way I like things done. Every movement has a pleasure in it – this is *what* I do, and it feels wonderful to be in charge of my destiny again. With every rope I tighten and bag I carefully place, I feel the excitement of the trip welling up in me and a quiet certainty about who I am.

When the last piece is in place, I turn to face my camels and put my hand out, palm up. As one, all three of my camels rise and stand waiting, expectantly.

There is a murmur of interest from the watching men. I tie the camels into a train, each rope around the tail in front, in the elaborate knot Khabuss taught me that very rarely comes undone. Then I tie Bolshy's rope around my stick and place it up behind my shoulders as I have done every day for so many months now. His head comes up and he nudges my back. I am choked up, as if he's telling me that he is ready for this next adventure.

I walk all three camels out of the gate and hear the men mutter behind me once more. None of them baulk, even when the baggage brushes against the tin door. I walk out and down the street. When I turn to wave, the onlookers give me a round of applause and a big cheer.

I can barely wipe the smile off my face as I walk out of town, Ibrahim riding the donkey next to me. Although I've known for a long time that my camels are very well trained – not least because they have had the benefit of Khabuss and Mohammed working with them – it's the first time I have felt that these boys are really *mine,* that we have an understanding. Any residual anxiety I had about handling my animals has faded. I know how to work with them, know what they need, and I feel – rightly or not – that the hardship of the last few months has led them to trust me. Perhaps more importantly, I have faith in myself.

The first few days out of Menaka are wonderful. When I look at the map every day and check my GPS, I feel reassured in Ibrahim's decision-making. We agree on camps, route, water stops and routine. He eats everything I put in front of him without complaint, and talks cheerfully and with interest as we walk.

The terrain is similar to the stretch from Nema to Tomboctou – thankfully minus the prickles. There are undulating, sandy hills with good feed and plenty of stands of rich grasses. The camels are eating normally again, grazing all through the hot afternoon when we stop and walking easily. The contrast to their sheer exhaustion on the last leg is startling. I think back to the horrible days heading into Menaka, when I was forced to take the ropes out of their mouths and put them through the painful hole in their nose to force them to walk. I look at Bolshy walking along with his head high, his shoulder next to mine, nudging my back occasionally, and I rub his side with affection. I watch the dynamics between Bolshy, Zaina and the new guy in fascination – they're like two parents watching their unruly offspring with wry amusement.

When we stop, my two older camels snub the company of the younger. They immediately follow me to good grazing. The new one skits about and refuses to follow, then turns up and tries to harass the other two, who snap and snarl at him until he eventually wanders off in a sulk and falls down in the shade. When we are walking, he often falls to his knees if he decides he has had enough. Once, Bolshy simply refuses to stop and pretty much drags him back to his feet. Bolshy rolls his eyes at me as if to say, '*Who does this guy think he is?*'

I imagine the conversations they would have with the new one:

'*Now listen, sonny, we've walked a long way. Longer than you can even imagine. And let us tell you, there is no point dancing around and throwing a tantrum when a bit of baggage comes undone, or going down on your knees when you get a bit tired. You have to put your head down and work hard – and when you stop, you eat where you find it. None of this throwing yourself down in the shade in a sulk, now, do ya hear? We never know if we're going to find feed or not, same with water; so when it turns up, you eat and drink when you can. Now, stop your moaning and get on with it. Okay, bucko?*'

Ibrahim and I have hours of enjoyment watching their antics.

I find Ibrahim himself an interesting, wise companion. We talk a lot about Mali, the political situation and where the country is headed.

'Mali is being destroyed by NGOs,' Ibrahim tells me. 'Everyone has a proposition for a project that they are trying to get funding for. Men don't want to work because they know they can be the head of a project. Everyone registers a business and calls themselves some high-flying name. They put together a good-sounding plan and con the NGOs into giving them money to fund it. Then they sit there for years, waste the money, and the project doesn't come to fruition.

'The things that are really important are simple: roads, hospitals, schools. But NGOs don't really deal with these things, because infrastructure is the government's responsibility. Instead, NGOs fund individual projects, like wells for example. And look what happens then – people who normally camp in a region, and move when the water dries up and grazing becomes scarce, suddenly feel they can stay in one place. They build a whole settlement around the well. A school starts there. Then the grazing runs out because nobody is moving on, and poverty increases because the stock dwindles. Next thing you know, everybody in the settlement is relying on NGO handouts just to stay alive. But these organisations just insist on building more wells, as if that's the answer. It isn't. I don't know what is, but creating townships where they aren't sustainable makes no sense to me.'

The truth of his opinions hits home. I've seen evidence of exactly this scenario in every remote settlement I have walked through. Whereas the nomads of the deep desert, who remain in their tents and move every few months, have extensive herds and joyful dispositions, those in the settlements seem poor, listless and depressed.

We walk into one such settlement a few days after Menaka. Ibrahim has family here. I agree to stop as our water is low, but warn him that I don't do long family stops and would prefer to move on first thing in the morning. I have learned my lessons the hard way on this.

This time, however, it is Ibrahim who is anxious to move on, even before the day is out.

Rather than preparing a meal for us on arrival, the family immediately asks Ibrahim for supplies so they can cook for us – they say they have no food. We happily hand over the makings of dinner, in this case, pasta, onion and some of the dried meat we have left from the town. But the women turn their noses up and insist that we must have something better – or that perhaps I could pay for a goat so they can feed us fresh meat.

Both Ibrahim and I are appalled. While I've had a little more experience of this kind of attitude, particularly in Mauritania, and understand that it largely stems from me being '*Le Blanc*', Ibrahim is embarrassed in the extreme. He speaks quite harshly to the women and tells me that, although we will stay for the meal, he would prefer to leave straight afterwards.

The women sullenly prepare a plate that is not a patch on what I make every day. But most insulting of all, they tip the majority of meat onto the family plate and serve Ibrahim and me a mean dish which is oily and unsatisfying. Ibrahim is sinking deeper into embarrassment, particularly when he has to remind the women to bring water across for us to wash our hands.

I cannot help but watch the exchange with a satisfied knowing. I've been through such encounters countless times. In many ways, it's almost a rite of passage for every one of my guides to see how the rules of hospitality can be distorted when the visitor in question is white. It also helps if they go through the process early on, so that they understand *why* I don't like stopping with family. Of course there are exceptions, such as Ali's family in Tomboctou, but on the whole I rarely escape a family encounter without giving away a good amount of my stores.

As we walk out of town Ibrahim apologises profusely.

'They would *never* do this to another African,' he tells me earnestly. 'I'm so sorry. I can't believe they wanted you to buy them everything. This is what happens when they live in towns,' he says bitterly. 'They get lazy and greedy. They need to work. This life, it is no good.'

The upside of the encounter is that he becomes quite protective of me when other nomads arrive at our camp. I am grateful for his care.

The people we pass are changing as we cross another invisible border into Niger: I begin to see Peulh women emerging from low woven tents as I pass. A Sahelian African tribe, the women often wear rings through their noses and have elaborate adornments hanging from their hair that look like big, heavy earrings. They are clad in the colourful panels of African cloth and smile at me. The men are friendly and dressed similarly to the Tuareg, although their turbans are tied in a noticeably different manner – not long around the face like the Tuareg, but in more of a circular crown on top of the head. Ibrahim, though, is spare in his conversation with the Peulh men.

'They are not Tuareg. They are not my tribe, and I don't really trust them,' he tells me. It seems to me sometimes that there is no end to the racial and tribal divisions in Africa.

Through Mali I was so worried about the camels and busy dealing with the pitfalls of walking through villages and along roads, often intimidated by guards with guns, that I felt largely flustered and tired. Here I can feel the desert again and look at the world around me, noticing the fascinating changes in the facial structure of people I meet and their mode of living.

On one occasion we stop close to a lake to water the camels. We're both sleeping under a tree when I wake to find the smiling face of a Peulh woman right beside my own. I sit up to see that she has placed a bowl beside my mat. It contains a spongy, semolina-type cake, doused in a green sauce made of some kind of grass, and topped with goats' milk and oil. She sits back on her haunches and gestures at the bowl, beside which she has placed two wooden spoons. Ibrahim and I wash our hands and hook in with fervour. The food is rich and satisfying, and Ibrahim moans in satisfaction.

'My wife makes this dish,' he tells me. 'It is so good.'

I hand the woman some of my stores in return, but she declines, still smiling. I decide that if this is Niger, then I like it already.

We've walked about 400 kilometres when the weather turns.

Every day dawns the same: still with a dull sky. By midmorning the wind has picked up to a steady roar. By early afternoon visibility is all but gone, and the wind is an unrelenting force. We walk silently with our heads down. One day, I lift my head to find myself in the middle of a Peulh settlement of huts. Small children stare at me from the doors of their shelters. I was so engrossed in the strain of walking that I hadn't even seen the village.

After several days of the onslaught we agree that we should try to walk twice a day – a few hours in the morning and then in the evening. The midday wind and heat is sucking the life out of us, and it's hard work for the camels. I don't like walking twice a day but am aware enough to recognise that neither of us can continue like this.

Unfortunately, the very first day that we start our new program, I am hit again by that bloody, pernicious, angry traitor in my system – the urinary tract infection.

I'm fine all morning. We stop in a good camp for the midday wind and eat a proper meal. We both lie down to sleep a while and wait out the worst of the weather. But just as I get up to start organising the baggage for the second leg, I feel the sudden urge to urinate that I know is the beginning of these things. By the time we are packed up, I can feel the shaky heat and nagging back pain that has become so awfully, frighteningly familiar. Within an hour I am passing blood again.

I just can't believe it.

Not only have I been afflicted with another of these rotten turns, but the ferocity with which this infection has descended is truly frightening. By day's end I am literally stumbling along, holding the pannier on Bolshy's side for support, following Ibrahim's lead blindly. I normally remain on top of navigation as I go, constantly checking the compass and GPS throughout the day; now it's all I can do to put one foot in front of another.

We make camp that night well after dark, and I tumble straight into bed. At least we have agreed to eat our main meal in the middle of the day so there is no need to cook. Ibrahim asks with concern if I am okay, and I mumble something about an upset stomach. No matter how kind he is, I feel uncomfortable explaining the nature of my illness.

By torchlight I pull out every bit of medication I have. I have been taking the cranberry tablets every day, which I know can help prevent the infection. Now I pull out the heavy-strength antibiotics I got in Bamako – I bought three courses – and also take an internal antiseptic and the fizzy mix that alleviates the symptoms.

But for the first time I am really, really scared.

This doesn't feel like the other infections. My skin is tight and hot, and the pain in my lower back is intense. I feel confused and dizzy; when I stand up in the middle of the night to urinate, I almost fall over. The pain of urinating makes me cry out loud and sends spasms of pain through my lower body. The liquid itself is viscous and bloody.

I toss and turn all night, not helped by a raging sandstorm that blows up in the early hours. We hastily track and hobble the camels so they are not lost, and I huddle inside my swag. Sand piles over everything. The wind is like a heater blowing full-on, and it aggravates my skin and fever.

The morning is still and hot, and I feel utterly wretched.

I have to call a halt for the day, something I haven't done the entire walk. I can't even stand up. When I do, I vomit. I can see barely metres in front of me, and the pain in my lower back is a hellish agony, dragging my whole body down. I've never known pain like this. I'm absolutely terrified now.

I do something I never thought I would: call my mother on the satellite phone. I try to think clearly before I pick it up; I want to ask her to talk to her doctor and find out exactly what is wrong with me, as much as that's possible, and what I can do to fix it.

I can hear the panic in Mum's voice, and I try to downplay how ill I feel. I didn't call her for comfort; I just want to know how to manage this thing for long enough to get me to Tillia. From there I can get to a hospital in Niamey, the Nigerienne capital, if I need to. But I have to somehow endure the next four days to get there. There just isn't anything out here to help me.

Mum says she will phone back with information as soon as she can. Ibrahim is beside himself, and now I actually tell him what is wrong.

He shakes his head worriedly and indicates his kidneys. 'I think the sickness is here now,' he tells me. I can't bear to think about it.

'Maybe,' I reply.

Later that day, in the early afternoon, I slip out of consciousness.

One moment I'm looking up through the scant branches of the acacia tree, rocking in a foetal position, trying to look at the sky. I can't work out why my eyes hurt. The light through the tree branches flickers and irritates me, and I want it to stop. The acacia thorns look so long, thin and sharp. I want them to stop moving so the light doesn't hurt.

And then suddenly there is nothing. Just pain.

Flashes of red lightning bolts slam into my back, and I can feel the desert wind inside me, searingly hot, scouring me away. There is only pain. I see Ibrahim, once, sitting away from me, looking at me in worry. My camels are behind him. I can see a wall of flame between us, and I try to crawl towards them, but I never get any closer.

Ibrahim gave me water, he told me later. I don't remember that. I don't remember the whole night I spent under that tree. I was unconscious for nearly twenty-four hours.

I wake in the still of dawn, and Ibrahim is watching over me.

'You are very, very sick,' he says. I nod. I know.

I check my phone. My mother has tried to call, and when I didn't answer she sent a message through:

'My doctor says you are exhibiting all the symptoms of a full-blown kidney infection. She thinks you are close to renal failure. Do you understand how serious this is, Paula? You are very, very sick. I am talking to the insurance people to find out if we can get you flown out of there. You can't walk with this anymore.'

I sit up and read the words again.

No.

I don't know where the word comes from, but it is like a monolith within.

No. I am not leaving.

I pick the phone up and call Mum.

'Call off the helicopters, Mum, calm down,' I say, trying to sound upbeat. 'It's not that bad; I can make it to Tillia. When I get there, I will work out what's wrong. Please.'

'Paula, you are seriously ill,' Mum says, and I can hear the tension in her voice. 'The insurance people are going to call you in half an hour. They can get you out of there. It will cost us, but I would rather know you are safe. I'm sorry, darling, but you need to understand how serious this is.'

I will never know if I'm making a sensible decision or not. This is perhaps the exact point where someone else needs to intervene and order me home. But thankfully, for me at least, nobody can do that.

'I feel better today,' I say to Mum. 'I'll talk to the insurance guys.'

The bloke from the company phones a little later, and I have a joking conversation with him. 'You know what mothers are like,' I say to the genial Brit on the end of the line. 'Of course, if you guys want to fly me in a case of cold beer, now *then* we can talk . . .'

We laugh and he notes my GPS coordinates. I can't bring myself to make the call that will end this.

I've just come too far.

We pack the camp up that evening, and I tell Ibrahim we are going to have to go hard for Tillia. I take double doses of all my medication and have thrown at least ten litres of water down my neck. If we walk at night for the most part, I think I should make it.

Ibrahim and I have one last conversation: he wants me to ride the camels.

Of all the stupid things I do on this walk, maybe refusing to climb on the camels is the worst. All I know is that I have walked every sodding step this far, every inch from Nouadhibou. I've left a chain of unbroken prints from the Western side of this desert. And I just cannot face breaking them now. I can't bear to admit defeat right when I am in the middle of this thing. I just can't.

It's dark all around me. All that's real is Bolshy Sod, plodding steadily. I'm hanging on his panniers and I watch his feet, trying to make mine move with his. Occasionally, he turns around and nudges me.

We walk in the early morning and early evening. The days are a dark, blurry mass of red-hot pain. I lie beneath scraggy bushes and drift in and out of consciousness. I cannot eat but I make myself drink as much as I can. I take my medication and try to sleep. I can feel the illness wanting to suck me under – but I just won't let it. I will try to cure my body. I will *not* let it collapse. I send every ounce of my energy down to my kidneys, willing the infection to shrink, to leave. I walk trying to conserve every bit of energy I can. I retreat inside myself and do not talk.

The most painful part of the day is packing and unpacking the camels. Lifting the jerry cans is torture. I throw up surreptitiously after every episode, the pain flaring in my lower back. I rely so heavily on my forearms to bear the weight that I strain the muscles, like tennis elbow.

I don't want Ibrahim to see how ill I am. I know he will insist on stopping. But deep down I know there is no point in stopping. If I do, there are only two outcomes – I will either die or get flown out of here. And I don't want either option. I know if I can just get to Tillia, rest and get some more medication into me, I will be okay. I just have to keep going, I have to.

And so I walk, in a fog of pain so thick I could never have imagined it. With every fibre of my being, I make my feet plod, one after another.

One after another.

They have carried me this far, after all.

We walk into the surrounds of Tillia early in the morning on 11 May 2007.

For the last few kilometres, I can see other nomads riding their donkeys to town. There is a market on, apparently.

I notice very little. Ahead of me I can see the buildings of the town. That is my only goal. Willpower alone makes those last few footsteps possible, until finally we reach a tree on a hill. The town is spread below us, the usual desert cluster of mud-brick and dirt roads.

We couch the camels and unpack, and Ibrahim goes to find help.

I lie beneath a tree and I can feel my heart beating weakly. The rhythm is irregular, at times going too fast. There is no strength in it, it seems. I wonder just how ill I really am.

It has been days since I ate anything. I've been only vaguely aware of other, more unsettling things – smoke rising from over distant hills and nomads muttering to Ibrahim about night raids by the military. I've been cut off in my pain, but here on the outskirts of Tillia I start to feel concerned by the world around me again.

There are a lot of camps, hastily erected, around the town. I wonder if these are nomads who have come to seek shelter from whatever is happening out there. Two days ago, we passed the remains of a burnt-out camp. When Ibrahim went to inspect, he came back grey-faced. There were corpses, he said. I'm wondering what it all means.

While I'm lying beneath the tree, I find myself surrounded by the usual crowd of curious children, and some adults, who always hover further away than the kids. I'm too ill to do anything other than stare back. Normally I offer tea, smile, try to communicate – today it's all I can do to keep my eyes open.

Ibrahim comes back and tells me that he met with the chief of the village. We have been invited to his home, and the chief has called the local doctor. I'm astounded and grateful that there is even a doctor here.

We stagger down the hill and wind our way to the chief's compound. But just before we enter, a LandCruiser of military personnel pulls up alongside us.

'You will need to report to our office straightaway,' says the driver. He is tall, well dressed and wearing sunglasses. He smiles at me, but he is unequivocal.

'I am sick,' I tell him. 'I need to see a doctor, and take care of my camels. Then I will come to see you.'

'No,' he says firmly. 'My assistant will walk with you. Come to the office now. Bring all of your camels, and your guide.'

I look at Ibrahim and he shrugs. We have no choice.

In the forecourt of the run-down, crumbling concrete building, there is a makeshift shelter beneath which lounge several officials in various degrees of military dress. They eye us curiously as the LandCruiser spins into the yard with a flourish and the officers disembark. We have couched the camels, but there is no shade for them to rest beneath. I want to unpack them – they have walked a long way – but permission is denied.

I'm taken into a sparse concrete room, where I hand my passport over to the official. He begins the round of questions I have answered a million times: Where have I come from? Where did I buy the camels? Who is my guide? Where am I going?

I keep my answers short and try to maintain my calm, but I'm so dizzy I can barely see. It hurts to sit upright.

At first, he says that he sees no problem and is happy to stamp my passport even though I don't have a visa in it. I feel myself slump with relief.

But then he tells me that he must first contact his superiors in Tahoua, the next major centre to the south. He says he will hold my passport until he has spoken to the authorities there. In the meantime, I am free to go, unload my camels and see a doctor. I've been in his office for two hours.

Ibrahim and I walk down the road with the camels and into the chief's compound. The doctor is already waiting for me, and the chief welcomes us warmly. He indicates that he and his sons will unload my camels.

I go with the doctor in his car to the clinic he operates. It's a small concrete building with basic equipment.

He examines me and frowns in concern. 'I can't treat this here,' he says. 'I can give you some good medication that will reduce the symptoms, but you need to be on an intravenous antibiotic drip. This infection is in your kidneys, do you understand?' I nod. 'You can take these now, and perhaps by morning you will be well enough to travel. But you are very sick. I will tell the chief.'

He speaks English, for which I am desperately thankful. I've not been able to remember the French word for 'kidneys', and I was worried about making myself understood.

The doctor takes me back to the house and has a long conversation with the chief. I'm immediately shown in to a cool shelter, where the chief's daughter lays out a comfortable place for me to rest. I hand Ibrahim some money to go and buy a sheep for the family, and try to pass out.

Two hours later the military are back.

They file into the shelter, along with the chief and several of his henchmen. The official's face is no longer friendly.

'The authorities in Tahoua have told me that I cannot stamp your passport here. I've been told to drive you down to Tahoua straightaway, so that you can meet with the governor.'

Warning bells are going off in my head. The shelter is hot and still, and I feel horribly nauseous. I am trying to focus on the conversation, but I feel weak and close to tears. I just can't imagine having to move anywhere right now. Even to a standing position.

The chief sends for the doctor, who arrives in minutes.

'This girl is very sick,' he tells the officials in French. 'She cannot be moved right now; she needs to rest.'

The official spreads his hands in a gesture of helplessness. 'The decision is not mine. The authorities want her to come immediately.'

A long conversation ensues, and the official asks questions of the doctor, Ibrahim, and the chief. I slump in my chair in exhaustion, the conversation floating around my head. I just want it to stop. I want to lie down.

Finally, they all agree that it's too late in the day to set off now. Instead, they will check the contents of my baggage; then we will set off in the morning.

In the meantime, they will hold my passport.

I lie on the bed watching through slitted eyes as they pull every last pair of dirty knickers from my bags. They note every item on a piece of paper. I have no idea what they think they might find – drugs? I really don't care.

Sometime during the night, I can feel the fever break for the first time. The burning pain seems to settle in the cool night air into a dull ache. The drugs the doctor has given me must be strong; I can actually feel the life seep back into my body. I am still sick, but something tells me the crisis has passed. In the morning, I actually eat some of the meat the women place beside my bed and drink half a bowlful of goats' milk. It feels indescribably good to put food inside my body.

I pack the belongings I need into my old camel-leather bag. I'm only expecting to go overnight. Ibrahim has already been to the market and bought the supplies we need for the next stretch.

Just before I leave, Ibrahim calls his family. He returns in absolute shock – his sister has died suddenly in his absence. Deeply upset, he tells me he cannot continue and must go home to his family.

I grieve for him and urge him to leave immediately. But then the officials arrive. They inform Ibrahim that, in fact, his presence is also required in Tahoua.

I argue, but to no avail. I don't like the manner in which they speak to Ibrahim. There is a contempt and aggression in their tone, and I sense that they feel he is of inferior stock. The officials are Hausa, a black African tribe. Although they pretend to respect the chief, their dislike of the Tuareg is obvious beneath their polite demeanour.

Ibrahim is piled into the rear of the Toyota trayback. I pull the privileged front seat – between two other men. We set off down the bumpy, mullocky desert track.

Every jolt sends pain through my body. I am gritting my teeth in the effort not to stop and ask to pee. It's agony holding on, and the pain is beginning to flare up again.

I just need to *rest*, for Chrissake.

It takes six hours to rattle our way down to Tahoua. In the back, Ibrahim lies down with his turban wrapped around his face. Men holding machine-guns ride guard, pointing their weapons all around; I can only wonder what's with the high-level security.

We eventually pull into the compound of the authorities in the large town of Tahoua. It's a far cry from the dilapidated outpost feel of Tillia. This is a large modern building, surrounded by lush gardens tended by crisply dressed gardeners.

We wait for an hour on chairs in the shade.

A black Mercedes eventually pulls up, and a well-dressed Hausa man steps out. He does not look at me, but immediately asks the official from Tillia for my passport.

He looks through it briefly.

'Why don't you have a visa?' he asks curtly.

I begin to explain the process I went through in Mali. While I know that I did all I could to get the visa, his unforgiving gaze leaves me feeling foolish, as though my explanations are excuses. Worse, I'm suddenly aware of my ragged, dirty appearance. I have barely changed my clothes since we came in from the desert and only had a rudimentary wash. My braids are ingrained with desert dirt, my clothes stained and torn. My feet are coated with red dust. I must look a horror; the Tahoua official eyes me in barely contained disgust.

He cuts me off, minutes into my explanation, shaking his head impatiently.

'Anyway, this is not my problem,' he tells me. 'You will have to go and see the governor.'

I'm becoming more unsettled by the minute. This has gone beyond the usual chain of command and bribery. I can smell something really off about the situation. The dismissive attitude of the Tahoua official makes the guy from Tillia seem positively benign. I turn to him in confusion after the other one has rode away in his Mercedes.

'Why do I need to see the governor?' I ask him. 'Is this normal?' The official raises his eyebrows and gives his head a brief shake.

'No,' he says. 'It isn't. Normally, I would have stamped your passport in Tillia. I don't understand what all the fuss is about.'

I will later remember those words, and realise they were the most honest answer anybody gave me during the whole episode.

We're driven across town, where an imposing colonial building is set amid immaculate gardens. There is even an elaborate fountain. We are seated by the servant outside, but through the glass doors I can see rich leather furniture and glass-topped tables. I have never seen such Western-style opulence in Africa. Obviously I haven't been moving in the right circles.

The governor is fat and his manner is unpleasant. He smokes incessantly and spits after every sentence. He does not even offer us a cool drink, although he commands his servant to bring him tea.

He does not ask for my passport. The last I saw of it was when the man in the Mercedes took it away.

'This is a big problem,' he tells me portentously. 'I can't just give you a visa. We do not know why you are here. Our embassy didn't grant you a visa in Mali, so maybe there is something wrong. We need to contact your country.'

I begin to explain that I never even got to apply for a visa in Mali, but he gestures dismissively.

'This is not my problem. You are going to have to go to Niamey, the capital, and meet with the Minister for the Interior. I have spoken to him' – he puffs out his chest, as if I should be in awe of how important he is – 'and he told me that you will have to take the bus to Niamey tomorrow and meet with him. He will decide if you can have a visa or not.'

I begin to speak, but he turns his back on me and addresses Ibrahim in curt Hausa. Ibrahim answers every question courteously and calmly, but I can tell that the nature of the questioning is more of an interrogation. I'm repulsed by the governor's shifty eyes, indulged physique and the contemptuous attitude he displays towards Ibrahim.

He finishes his questioning and gestures to one of his servants.

'Tonight the Nigerienne Government will pay for you to stay in a nice hotel here – and for your dinner also. My servant will take you.' He delivers this information as if he is uncommonly generous.

'Tomorrow morning at 4 am you will catch the bus to Niamey,' he continues, pointing to me. 'He' – he points to Ibrahim – 'will return to Tillia and catch transport home to Mali.'

'How will he get back to Tillia?' I ask, even though I know we are being dismissed. Ibrahim is my responsibility, and I am angered by the governor's cavalier attitude towards him.

The governor spits dismissively. 'It is no affair of mine how the little Tuareg gets home.' His lip curls contemptuously as he speaks. Ibrahim's face is a mask of indifference.

'What about my passport?' I ask.

'You may have it back,' he says, and pulls it out of his robes. 'But only to check into the hotel. Then one of our guards will take it, and it will be delivered to the Minister for the Interior tomorrow.'

I snatch my passport out of his hands. He turns his back on us and goes inside, with no words of farewell.

As the guard drives Ibrahim and me to the hotel, I seriously contemplate doing a midnight runner. But to where?

My camels are in Tillia, along with all my electronic equipment – except for the satellite phone, which I stashed in my leather bag when the guards weren't looking. Every exit from Tahoua will have a military presence; all of these towns do. I doubt that I could possibly make it through a checkpoint – I'm sure everyone will be alert to my presence in town.

There's no way I can return to Tillia without being spotted and, even if I could, my only option would be to retreat into Mali. I wouldn't be able to enter Agadez or any other major town here.

But on top of all that, I'm still sick. The drugs and adrenalin have combined to focus my thoughts, and the pain has subsided to a manageable level. But after being scared out of my wits on the last stretch by such severe illness, I know it would be irresponsible in the extreme to think I can carry on without proper treatment. Niamey is the best place for me to get it.

In the end, I check into the hotel and meekly hand my passport back to the official.

I can't help but wonder if I am handing him the key to my own prison.

Ibrahim and I eat together in the grounds of the tourist hotel. Despite everything, I can't help but laugh. Having never eaten in a restaurant before, Ibrahim is floored by the menu, the cutlery and the entire dining experience. I order steak and fries for us both, and he watches my every move intently, totally bemused by his surroundings.

He is going to go back to Tillia with the authorities tomorrow. They will drop me at the bus in the morning, and then take him with them.

'I'm so sorry for the trouble I have caused you, Ibrahim,' I say as we eat. 'I know how worried you are about your family. Thank you for everything you've done.'

'There is something really strange about all this,' Ibrahim tells me. 'I've crossed that border a hundred times. And I've been in cars with tourists at the border. I've never heard of anything like this happening before; I don't know what's going on. Nobody is being direct with us.'

His words offer little comfort. Ever since the first post in Tillia, I have been cursing and double-cursing my own stupidity in arriving here without a visa. So what if I had wasted another week in Bamako? Even if I had to wait while I sent a copy of my passport to London, I should have got that bloody bit of paper before walking in here. I cannot forgive my own carelessness.

My satellite phone has a flat battery, and I can't charge it in the room – the socket won't work. I try to exit the hotel to use a public phone, but there is an official stationed on the door. He politely but firmly refuses to let me leave.

I sink on the bed and try to sleep. Above everything else, I need to get well. That is all I can actually do for myself right now, so I wash, turn my face to the wall and will myself to sleep.

In the dark pre-dawn, I bid Ibrahim goodbye and stand with the crowd waiting for the bus. A gun-toting official stands right beside me, and I attract more than one curious stare.

I watch in bitter impotence as the official hands my passport to the bus driver. Neither of them speaks enough French to explain what the process will be when I arrive.

I climb on yet another crowded African bus, and try to tune out the world around me as it rattles down the highway. As day breaks I look out of the window at the curious, exotic world racing past me, the rich foliage and round African huts, and feel a strange desperation. All of this country that I have still not seen is out there. There's so much that I haven't fully appreciated since I have been here – and now I can feel it slipping away from me.

I'm not ready, I think. *I'm not ready to leave here yet.*

In the late afternoon I exit the bus in a bustling terminus. I keep the driver in plain view. I wait until all of the passengers have cleared and then approach him.

'I need my passport,' I say. He smiles uncomprehendingly and shrugs his shoulders. I try to make myself understood, but get no further. In desperation, I watch as he climbs behind the wheel of the bus, ready to drive away with my passport to who knows where. My voice increases in volume as I climb the stairs to the bus and refuse to move.

A female onlooker comes over and translates for the driver.

They have a heated discussion, and the driver shakes his head.

'What's he saying?' I ask her repeatedly.

'He says that he was told to hold your passport until the officials arrive to collect you,' she tells me, frowning. 'But I've told him that he must give it back to you – he is about to go home. The officials won't find him.'

I stand on the steps and decide that no matter what, I am *not* moving without my passport. I ask the girl to translate this to the driver.

He shakes his head in resignation and hands over my passport. I could weep with relief.

I thank the girl who helped me and go out onto the road.

I am genuinely unsure what to do.

One disadvantage that people from countries like Australia have, I think, is that we are too honest. I contemplate doing any of a number of things: going to the hospital first; checking into a low-brow hotel and trying to get help; trying to find the Australian embassy or its representative here. But, in the end, I am too worried that the official trail will find me and that I will pay for my actions. I'm also trapped by the fact that my camels and belongings are in Tillia. Perhaps this is why the officials didn't send me to Niamey under armed guard the whole way; maybe they know I have too much of value to do a runner.

I settle for using a public phone to call home and let my family know what is happening.

They're still lost in worry about my health. I don't say much beyond the fact that I am in Niamey to sort out the visa stuff and will get medical help while I'm here. It all feels like an enormous mess, and I can't make sense of it myself, let alone to anyone else.

I take a taxi to the office of the Minister for the Interior and am shown into a drab waiting room, reminiscent of 1970s bad taste. In my stained travel clothes, I attract a few disdainful looks. The people here are dressed in suits and discussing NGO projects. I am dismissed as unimportant.

I'm kept waiting for several hours and am exhausted and fretful by the time I'm called in. The infection is still lurking, not helped at all by the long bus ride here. I feel feverish and dull.

I walk into a large office that smells of cigarette smoke and am introduced to the Minister for the Interior. He is a short, slim dapper man with a neat moustache, and I can tell as soon as I look at his face that this isn't going to go well.

He gestures abruptly towards a chair and we both sit down – he behind a large, forbidding desk. He doesn't offer me a drink.

'So why do you come to our country without a visa?' he asks me without preamble.

I begin to explain, again, the process I went through in Mali. Just like the governor, he waves me away.

'Your French is terrible,' he tells me. 'It is difficult to understand you.' I apologise. He is correct – the more intimidated and uncomfortable I feel, the less fluent my language is. In addition, I've been speaking French to Malian nomads of late, and my inflection and diction is a bad mélange of French, Tamashek and Arabic. He is right about it sounding bad.

I start again, speaking as slowly and clearly as possible, but without success.

'I don't care what your reasons are. Why do you think it is okay for you to walk into my country without a visa? What – you think all African countries are stupid, that we will just let you in without the proper paperwork? What would happen if I did that in *your* country? Your Prime Minister would throw me into a detention camp in the desert, no questions asked. At least here we are polite and kind to you.'

I could cringe. John Howard, it should be you sitting here answering these questions.

I smile apologetically. 'You are quite right, of course; I do not agree with my country's stance on immigration. But I wasn't trying to enter illegally. I was reliably informed, by your embassy in London and other sources, that I could be issued a visa on the border. I had no intention at all of trying to enter illegally, and I've come directly to your office to try to straighten the problem out. My only wish is to continue my walk, and I'm happy to abide by any conditions you set for me.'

Before I am one sentence in, the Minister is shaking his head.

'You silly girl. Of course you cannot continue your walk – whatever this "walk" is. Your little holiday is not my problem. I will never give you permission to walk in the north of this country, in the desert. Never! No, no my girl, your little holiday finishes right here. Now my people will take you to a hotel and you will contact your friends and find an aeroplane back to Australia. Or to anywhere. I don't care where you go. But you are finished in Niger. No more of this . . . this *walking*.' His tone, when he says these last words, is one of complete contempt. When I look at him, I can detect triumph in his expression.

I wait for my usual flash of inspiration, for the words that will change this impasse to come out of my mouth. No matter how vile the scenario, I have never been lost for words, for action. But there is just nothing. I am transfixed by the petty triumph on this little man's face.

For the first time since I put my boots on in Trafalgar Square, I feel truly defeated. Finished. And to my horror, I can feel tears welling up. If ever I have not wanted to cry, this is the time. I know my only hope right now is to maintain my calm and dignity. I breathe, swallow and nearly choke on the lump in my throat. I know he can see my struggle; I know he knows I want to cry. I stare dumbly at this horrible man and try to speak.

'Please reconsider your decision,' I say in a trembling voice. 'Please. This walk is very important to me. I have come a very, very long way. I understand that I have broken the rules of your country, and I am happy to leave – I can go back to Mali. But I need to go back to Tillia and collect my camels, my belongings. Please just allow me to do this, so I can continue my walk from Mali. Everything I own is in Tillia. I have nothing here.' I loathe myself for begging. I want to scream at this insufferable bastard that I am sick and not usually weak like this, that he has no right – *no right* – to shut my walk down.

Except, of course, he does. And he knows it.

He shakes his head and clicks his tongue in contempt of my weakness. He calls in a different official, who looks at me with concern. Without looking at me, the Minister says in French, 'Take her to a hotel. Stay with her while she organises a flight. I will hold her passport until we know she is going.' Then he looks up at me, his expression remote and disinterested.

'Rest tonight so that you can calm yourself down. Tomorrow you will go to the travel agent and book your flight. I don't want to hear anymore about your' – he rolls his eyes – 'camels, or

belongings. You are finished here. Do you understand? Finished.'
And he waves us out of his office, impatient with the stupidity of
this self-indulgent, weak tourist.

I'm so ashamed of my red face and trembling voice that all I
want to do is hide. Instead, I walk out along a long corridor, where
men in uniforms lounge, smoking. Every one of them scrutinises
my flushed face and glistening eyes. The official beside me flutters
helplessly, embarrassed by my distress. I shake his reassuring arm
off furiously, and he backs away, hands held up in a gesture of
placation.

There is something so final about that exchange. So *definite*.
I can't imagine for one second how that man can ever back down
from the stance he has taken. His imagined David-and-Goliath
victory over the powers of the West was so satisfying that I can
imagine him replaying it to every one of his cronies. Today, in one
fell swoop, he has the perfect opportunity to wipe the floor with
one of the very type he despises.

I am led to a police car and the official drives me into town,
looking for a hotel. He asks me where I would like to go. I don't
even look at him, just gesture sullenly and tell him that if his government is so clever, *they* can find me a hotel. My response is petty
and unfair, and I know it. I give him a weak smile and try to be
conciliatory, but I don't have the energy to help even if I could.

An almost comical farce ensues. We enter a number of different
hotels, and they are either full or ridiculously expensive. I'm
appalled to learn that I'm supposed to be paying for my accommodation. I have very limited funds and would never choose to stay
in the kind of hotels he is taking me to – they are for wealthy
tourists, not backpackers. I say as much and he is bemused. I am
white, after all. Surely I have money?

It takes hours until we settle on a place, which is still wildly
out of my budget. The official tells me that he will be stationed
outside the gate if I need anything. The unspoken inference, rein-
forced by his conspicuous machine-gun, is that I'll not be
permitted to leave the hotel unless in his company.

I sit in the room and stare at the wall. I'm in total shock.

I charge the satellite phone and sneak up onto the roof of the hotel. I call everyone I can think of, asking for help. But I know there really isn't much anyone can do.

I finally receive a text message with the address of the Canadian embassy, which represents Australia in Niger. On some level I still can't quite believe what has happened. A part of me still thinks that I will wake up and solve all of this, that I will somehow get my passport and jump on another bus back up to Tillia, that all of this is just another hurdle on the road to Cairo. I almost feel embarrassed about contacting the embassy. I wonder if they will dismiss me as just another stupid traveller who got herself into a jam. It hurts me to even think of asking for their help. And every time I remember the visible distress of this afternoon, I feel a hot flush of shame. I can't believe I let myself go like that. I'm lost in a mire of shame. All I can see are the mistakes I have made and the lack of true grit I have shown.

I sit like a statue all night. I can still feel the fever in my body, but it seems almost consumed by the horror I feel at losing my walk.

I never imagined it finishing like this. Of all the ways I thought it would end, all the things that could possibly go wrong, never once did I imagine that it would be taken out of my hands by some petty official with a grudge against my country. I just sit, frozen in a state of shock, staring at the wall.

I sit like that all night.

Morning brings a certain degree of resolve.

I may not be able to contest the Minister directly. But I'm not going down without a fight.

I walk out to where the official is standing by his car, gun in his hand. I guess he stayed there all night. I don't know, and I don't really care.

I hand him the address of the Canadian Embassy.

'I need to be taken here, straightaway,' I tell him firmly. He looks at me with concern and shakes his head.

'Call your boss, if you like,' I tell him. 'But I can't book a plane out of here until I contact my family for money. I have none left. I'm a journalist, and if you do not take me to the embassy now, I will make sure this story is on the front page of every newspaper in the world.' I pull out my satellite phone and show him. His eyes widen.

'I've already telephoned my employers in Australia and London. You know the BBC?' Everyone in Africa listens to the BBC world news. His eyes widen further. 'They all know you have me under house arrest and that you have my passport. They are already in contact with the Canadian Embassy.' I lean forward with a hint of menace. 'You need to take me to this address *right now.*'

I have no idea if I am convincing. I am so on the edge I don't know how else to play it; I have no idea if he will call my bluff.

I watch as he makes a few hasty phone calls. I see him gesticulating frantically and note his confused expression. I've got to him, that much I am sure of. We get into the car and I detect a degree of deference that was not there before.

'I will take you to the embassy now,' he says politely. 'Of course. It is your right.'

I nearly roll my eyes in mockery. My rights were right up there on the agenda last night, as I recall.

I watch in tense expectation as we drive. I still don't trust him to take me where I'm supposed to go. I'm not at all sure that I will not simply be driven to the edge of town and quietly knocked off.

Finally, I see concrete walls and a large building. There is a white barrier and guards at either side. On the top of the building, flies a Canadian flag.

I leap out of the car as if the hounds of hell are at my heels.

'I'm Australian,' I say in French to the African guards. 'Please, let me inside. I need to see the ambassador. Please, I'm Australian.'

'Passport?' one of them asks me. He holds out his hand.

'They took it,' I say, gesturing at the policeman behind me, who is skulking next to his car. 'I don't have it with me. They have it. Please let me in.'

I wait as the guard picks up the intercom and makes a call. He replaces the handset and smiles at me. 'You can come inside,' he says.

I scoot inside the barricade as if I'm safer just by being on the other side of it. Maybe I am. The guard follows me at a discreet distance; I don't care where he goes.

I'm buzzed inside and walk up into a quiet, well-appointed office with carpet and plants in the corners. There are posters in English on the walls. An African girl greets me in fluent French, and I begin to stumble through my story.

'Wait here,' she says.

Seconds later, a large African woman enters the room. She sits down next to me and puts a comforting hand on my shoulder. 'My name is Madame Haowa,' she says. 'Now – what is all this?'

Again, I start to blurt out my tale, still unsure if I am safe or not. I see her expression turn into a frown after the first few lines, and she gives the receptionist an order.

'Wait,' she tells me. 'Monsieur Guy will be with you in a few minutes; you must tell him your story. He is the Canadian consul.'

Seconds later, the door opens again and a solid, kind man is smiling at me.

'I am Guy Villeneuve,' he says, shaking my hand gently. 'And what has happened to you?'

I start to shake. 'The police have my passport,' I tell him. 'And I am sick. I need a doctor. My camels are in Tillia. I have no money . . .' I am suddenly aware of how I am babbling, how rattled I must sound.

I take a deep breath. 'Please help me,' I say. 'I am Australian. And I need help.'

Madame Haowa puts her arm around my shoulders. 'Of course we will help you,' she says, patting me. 'You are safe now. You are safe.'

And that is when I start to cry.

Epilogue

Guy Villeneuve, the Canadian consul, took responsibility for me. The Nigerienne Government agreed that I could stay with him and his partner, Edith, in the Canadian consulate for the two weeks that it took to negotiate the return of my passport. The process was neither straightforward nor simple, and for the eventual resolution of the diplomatic labyrinth, I am indebted to Guy and Edith.

I was shown extraordinary kindness and support by not only them but all the Australian representatives in the region. I received immediate medical care.

Unbeknownst to anyone but the highest echelon of government, the Tuareg 'rebels' in the north of the country had organised themselves into a cohesive army – the Movement for Nigerienne Justice – and begun a sustained campaign against the Niger government and military in a bid for equal access to the country's resources. Indeed, at the time I was stopped, the rebellion had only just begun. It has since escalated into an ongoing, bloody conflict.

It took Guy over a week to negotiate with the government to allow me to return to Tillia in order to collect my personal effects.

I was driven up in an embassy vehicle, with my own armed guard. It felt rather nice to face the authorities in the town accompanied by my very own man with a gun by my side.

The chief of the village kindly agreed to take responsibility for my camels until I should be able to return. I drove out to the desert and cuddled my boys goodbye. My only consolation was that the feed looked absolutely wonderful. I think the sadness in parting was entirely one-sided – Bolshy Sod almost sagged in relief when he saw me get back in the car.

My passport was held by the government almost until my leaving date. Guy eventually wrung an agreement from them that they would fully support my return at a point when the conflict is resolved. At the time, we thought that would be within months; I thought I was going back to Australia for the Saharan summer and would pick up my walk again in three months' time.

At the time of writing this, it has been nearly two years since my walk was stopped. The rebellion has become a war, and Niger is a landmine-strewn battleground. The town of Tillia is directly in the middle of the military zone. I have no way of contacting the chief, and I do not know if my camels are still alive.

I recognise that, in many ways, being forced to a halt was the best thing for me. I was indeed very ill, and it would be months back in Australia before I really recovered.

But knowing this has done little to help me accept the abrupt termination of my walk, right when I felt that I was at my most determined and capable. I had walked over half of my planned route when I was stopped – some 4200 kilometres. In total, since I set out from M'Hamid, I have walked over 7000 kilometres through the Sahara. I have only 3800 to go to reach Cairo, through some of the most fascinating areas of the whole trek. My frustration has been an extremely difficult internal mountain to negotiate. I have been wracked by feelings of failure, loss and despair. I have at times wanted to give up on the whole trek and crawl away into a hole.

I found it extremely difficult to accept that my walk had in any way been successful. For long months, all I could see is what I did wrong. Finding the joy in the journey, and feeling proud of it, took a long time. I still struggle with the fact that it is, for me, unfinished.

At odd times recollections come back to me, and I start in shock that it was really me out there doing those things. In those unexpected moments I tentatively take out the memories and examine them, and allow myself to feel a quiet pride, untarnished by the abrupt ending that hurt so much. Sometimes at speaking engagements, I find myself saying things I didn't even know I felt, and often feeling unaccountably moved by the recollections. I wonder what the trip really means to me – and for me. Gradually, I have come to appreciate that I simply needed to do it, and that the *doing* of it was, and still is, immensely satisfying and rewarding. Something wild inside myself found a stillness out there, a contentment that I had missed my whole life.

In the subsequent months, I have looked at every possible alternative route and come close to going back to either Libya or Algeria. But none of the options have proven viable.

The situation in Niger remains at an impasse, and the same Minister for the Interior who met with me retains his position and remains heavily opposed to negotiating with the Tuareg.

In the nights here at home in Australia, I look out of my window and see eucalypt trees swaying in the breeze, the stars peeping through their branches. There are times when I ache for the silent magnificence of the Big Empty, for the clear brilliance that brings me such peace. There are nights when I dream of the heat and wind, and when I wake it is with tears in my eyes for the footsteps yet untrod. My journey in the Sahara is not finished. I made a promise to myself once that it would not be over until I touched the pyramids, until my line of footsteps reached from one side of that glorious expanse to another.

Within myself, that promise still stands.

As I write this, there are rumours of a Libyan-negotiated peace treaty between the MNJ and the Nigerienne Government.

I am waiting with bated breath for the outcome.

Acknowledgements

To both of my sponsors – Dove Australia and Birkenstock Australia – I owe every thanks. This walk simply could not have continued without you. In particular, Marcel Goerke of Birkenstock, who supported me not only through sponsorship but in the aftermath of the walk. Even better, he made me a pair of sandals that walked 4200 kilometres without a blow-out. They were superb, and I am a fan for life.

To Guy Villeneuve: I am indebted to you for your hospitality, support and kindness at a time when I was at my lowest ebb.

To Brandon, the fabulous editor on this book and the last one: you did an absolutely incredible job, in no time at all. Thanks for editing out my more ridiculous overwriting and honouring my story. You are fantastic.

To Averill, my agent, who again put up with all my insecurities, and a pretty messy book to begin with, and saw it through to a great result. I am really grateful for your expertise, patience and friendship.

To my darling Graeme: you have lived with this book for over a year and my somewhat distracted mindset while I wrote it – and never once stopped believing in me or in the final outcome. Thank you for listening to me read parts of it over too much red wine, reassuring me that I don't sound too over the top, and for living with the nightmares when I remembered the tough times. At least

I have stopped mistaking you for a camel-stealing bandit, trying to knife you in the dark and rolling out of bed!

To Chloe and Taylor: thank you for being remarkably sane teenagers and for putting up with an evil stepmother writing a book you don't appreciate about an expedition you think is nuts. Yes, Chloe, I take your point that I should have just bought an extra camel to ride . . . I think you are both fantastic kids. I'm lucky to have you in my life. (Yes, yes – and I won't forget it . . .)

For Mum, the magnificent Bev: I can never thank you enough for your love, support and belief in me throughout this journey, despite your own illness and trauma. I could never have done what I have without your faith in me throughout my life. You are a wonderful mother, and I love you with all my heart.

Frankie J, my dad: your voice on the end of the phone was such a comfort to me on this walk. I felt close to you out there. I miss you every day.

To my sister, Lisa, and her family: I hope we all walk together some day. Thank you, again, for believing in me and this book. My brother, Ashley, I hope you aren't embarrassed by this one!

The Bromley Road crew – Steph, Steve, Rob and Maria: you were such a huge part of this book. More than I had room to fit in! You have all been there for me throughout the walk, the breaks between, and in spirit when I am far away. No matter what the distance is between us, I think of you all every day, and you will forever be a part of this journey. Likewise darling Jo, Stefania, Dan and Sarah. True friends are indescribably precious to me. All of you are treasured beyond words.

In Australia, Jodie, Andrea and the whole Morris clan, who have always been there for me. Jode, I will never forget the call on a sand dune when I needed it most. Lyn Fry, thanks for being a part of this journey from the start. Thanks also to you and 'Damo' for the brilliant drive down from Broome that has inspired my next adventure!

To Tommy Daniel: thanks for the spare bed and an ear when I needed one, not to mention the endless supply of red. I know you will never read this book – way too much female emotional bollocks for your analytical brain – but I hope you get to this bit.

And finally to Lockie, who is still out there cycling (Norway today, I heard by email). Mate, you are the truest inspiration I have ever met. I admire you and I love how you do what you do. May the wind be forever behind, and the road long and straight ahead. My love and blessings go with you.

I would like to leave you with a quote that has given me great comfort, both through the desert walk and in the often bewildering times since:

'Not until we are lost do we begin to understand ourselves.'

Henry David Thoreau

Thank you to everyone who has supported me throughout this adventure.

Walking in the Western Sahara.

Ali – the *zerfal* man and my guide to Tomboctou.

Follow the latest on Paula's extraordinary journey through her updated blogs, map and photos at constanttrek.com. *Everywhere is walking distance if you have the time.*

Me and my camels in the grounds of the Camping Bangu, Gao, Mali.

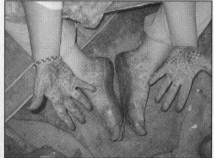

Henna hands and feet in the Western Sahara.